MW00812421

Principles Matter

ALSO BY CARLOS A. BALL

The Queering of Corporate America: How Big Business Went from LGBTQ Adversary to Ally

The First Amendment and LGBT Equality: A Contentious History

After Marriage Equality: The Future of LGBT Rights (editor)

Same-Sex Marriage and Children: A Tale of History, Social Science, and Law

The Right to Be Parents: LGBT Families and the Transformation of Parenthood

From the Closet to the Courtroom: Five LGBT Rights Lawsuits That Have Changed Our Nation

The Morality of Gay Rights: An Exploration in Political Philosophy

Cases and Materials on Sexuality, Gender Identity, and the Law (co-editor)

Principles Matter

The Constitution, Progressives, and the Trump Era

CARLOS A. BALL

OXFORD
UNIVERSITY PRESS

OXFORD
UNIVERSITY PRESS

Oxford University Press is a department of the University of Oxford. It furthers the University's objective of excellence in research, scholarship, and education by publishing worldwide. Oxford is a registered trade mark of Oxford University Press in the UK and certain other countries.

Published in the United States of America by Oxford University Press
198 Madison Avenue, New York, NY 10016, United States of America.

Library of Congress Cataloging-in-Publication Data
Names: Ball, Carlos A., author.
Title: Principles matter : the constitution, progressives, and the Trump era / Carlos A. Ball.
Description: New York, NY : Oxford University Press, [2021] |
Includes bibliographical references and index.
Identifiers: LCCN 2021000062 (print) | LCCN 2021000063 (ebook) |
ISBN 9780197584484 (hardback) | ISBN 9780197584507 (epub) |
ISBN 9780197584491 (updf) | ISBN 9780197584514 (online)
Subjects: LCSH: Constitutional law—United States. |
United States—Politics and government—2017–2021.
Classification: LCC KF4550 .B257 2021 (print) | LCC KF4550 (ebook) |
DDC 342.73009/0512—dc23
LC record available at https://lccn.loc.gov/2021000062
LC ebook record available at https://lccn.loc.gov/2021000063

DOI: 10.1093/oso/9780197584484.001.0001

1 3 5 7 9 8 6 4 2

Printed by Sheridan Books, Inc., United States of America

Note to Readers
This publication is designed to provide accurate and authoritative information in regard to the subject matter covered. It is based upon sources believed to be accurate and reliable and is intended to be current as of the time it was written. It is sold with the understanding that the publisher is not engaged in rendering legal, accounting, or other professional services. If legal advice or other expert assistance is required, the services of a competent professional person should be sought. Also, to confirm that the information has not been affected or changed by recent developments, traditional legal research techniques should be used, including checking primary sources where appropriate.

(Based on the Declaration of Principles jointly adopted by a Committee of the American Bar Association and a Committee of Publishers and Associations.)

You may order this or any other Oxford University Press publication
by visiting the Oxford University Press website at www.oup.com.

To Ray Coutu and John Lavoie, Will Hancock and Kim Mitchell, Gavin McCormick and Alex Juhasz, Donna Dennis and Nancy Louden, Jim Logatto and David Kim, Rose Marquez and Pat Dote, and Gundula Brattke—your cherished friendships helped make the four years more bearable.

Contents

Introduction   1

PART I: PRINCIPLES MATTER: FEDERALISM

1. Federalism Before Trump   15
2. Federalism During the Trump Era and Beyond   53

PART II: PRINCIPLES MATTER: SEPARATION OF POWERS

3. The Presidency Before Trump   99
4. The Presidency During the Trump Era and Beyond   147

PART III: PRINCIPLES MATTER: THE FIRST AMENDMENT

5. The First Amendment During the Trump Era and Beyond   185

Epilogue   233

Acknowledgments   239
Notes   241
Index   293

Introduction

In 2018, Democrats in New Jersey regained control of the governorship to go along with their majority in the state legislature. Three decades had passed since a Republican presidential candidate carried the state, and the last time New Jerseyans had sent a Republican to the U.S. Senate was in 1972. Democrats also outnumbered Republicans in the state by about one million registered voters. To further cement their political domination in the Garden State, Democratic state legislative leaders in 2018 proposed amending the state constitution with the aim of making Republicans a permanent minority. Specifically, the proposal sought to codify partisan gerrymandering into the constitution by requiring that future legislative districts reflect how the major political parties had performed in recent statewide elections for governor, U.S. Senate, and president. Given New Jersey's statewide voting patterns, the constitutional change would essentially guarantee Democrats a majority in about twenty-five of the state's forty legislative districts. According to a Princeton University study, the constitutional amendment would allow Democrats to control 70 percent of the state legislative districts by winning only 57 percent of the statewide vote.[1]

In the years following the 2010 census, it had been primarily Republican legislators in swing states who had gerrymandered legislative districts to give the GOP significantly higher representation in Congress and in state legislatures than was reflected in the percentage of votes the party actually received. As a result of brazen partisan gerrymandering, for example, Republicans in 2012 won a thirty-three-seat majority in the U.S. House of Representatives even though 1.4 million more Americans voted for Democratic congressional candidates that year. In 2016, a bare majority (53 percent) of North Carolina voters supported Republican congressional candidates, and yet the party captured a supermajority (ten out of thirteen, or 76 percent) of the state's seats in the House of Representatives. And in 2018, Republicans won a supermajority (64 percent) of the seats in the Wisconsin Assembly even though GOP candidates received less than half (46 percent) of the statewide votes.[2] Those who pushed for these types of egregious partisan gerrymanders seemed emboldened by the refusal of the Supreme Court's conservative majority to do anything about it.[3]

Although Democratic leaders in some states, such as Maryland, had also engaged in partisan gerrymandering, progressives across the country increasingly opposed the practice. Progressive activists, along with government

Principles Matter. Carlos A. Ball, Oxford University Press. © Carlos A. Ball 2021.
DOI: 10.1093/oso/9780197584484.003.0001

reform groups and independent voters, pushed several states in 2018, including Colorado, Michigan, and Utah, to start using independent commissions rather than self-interested state legislators to draw legislative district maps. Eric Holder, a former attorney general under Barack Obama, headed a group called the National Democratic Redistricting Committee whose mission it was to try to reverse the extreme gerrymandering that had allowed Republicans to exercise power in Congress and in several state legislatures in ways that were disproportionate to how citizens were actually voting.[4]

The push by New Jersey Democratic power brokers to enshrine partisan gerrymandering into the state constitution confronted progressives with a crucial choice. One option was to advocate on behalf of the constitutional amendment on the ground that Republican officials in other states were doing the same thing.[5] Another choice was to remain neutral by neither actively supporting nor opposing the proposal. Pursuing either of these options likely would have resulted in the amendment's approval by the legislature and perhaps eventually by voters. (Republican state legislators opposed the amendment, but they lacked the numbers to stop it.) Both of these options had some appeal to progressives because if the constitutional amendment was adopted, it would mean more Democrats in the state legislature, which, in turn, would make it easier to enact progressive reforms on issues such as racial justice, economic inequality, and the environment.

But progressives had a third option: to *oppose* the amendment on the principled ground that partisan gerrymandering is undemocratic because its purpose and effect is to maximize the power of certain voters at the expense of others. Partisan gerrymandering also prioritizes the interests of the political party whose elected officials happen to be in the majority at the time of redistricting over the public's interests.

To their credit, most progressives in New Jersey chose the third option by strongly opposing the constitutional amendment proposed by Democratic legislative leaders. A large alliance of grassroots activists, union leaders, voting rights advocates, and racial justice proponents vigorously opposed the change. More than one hundred activists and academics, representing a broad coalition of groups (including the New Jersey Working Families Alliance and the League of Women Voters), testified at legislative hearings opposing the amendment. A coalition of 130 progressive groups in the state, led by the South Jersey Progressive Women for Change, organized a letter-writing campaign urging legislators not to vote for the amendment. The ACLU and the Brennan Center for Justice, organizations that had challenged extreme partisan gerrymandering in other states, also criticized the plan. Opponents held press conferences and protests aimed at pressuring Democratic legislative leaders to drop their proposal. Governor Philip Murphy also opposed the plan, explaining that "I'm a proud

Democrat, [but] I want to win fair and square, and this is not." Confronted with essentially uniform progressive opposition to their gerrymandering scheme, Democratic legislative leaders quickly changed course and withdrew their proposed amendment.[6]

For progressives confronting the New Jersey gerrymandering proposal, principles mattered. Rather than prioritizing the short-term political and policy gains that would result from an entrenched Democratic hold on the state, progressives chose to abide by the principle that partisan gerrymandering is undemocratic and should be opposed regardless of which party benefits from it. In a similar vein, this book argues that progressives, after living through the Trump era, should strongly support and defend three constitutional principles— federalism, separation of powers, and free speech—regardless of which party controls the presidency. These principles proved crucial in resisting some of the Trump administration's most misguided, harmful, and discriminatory policies.

The Trump years presented progressives with a series of ongoing and seemingly existential challenges, leading them to spend much time and energy dissecting what went wrong in the 2016 election; how best to promote liberal social and economic reforms in the face of a belligerent and autocratic administration; and how to most effectively try to limit, whether through impeachment or other means, Trump's relentless efforts to weaken the nation's democratic institutions and traditions. The Trump years also reinforced for progressives the importance of crucial constitutional principles, including the need to provide robust equality protections for racial and other minority groups, and to safeguard reproductive freedoms and the fundamental right to vote. Rather than emphasize these important but (for progressives) obvious lessons, this book explores other crucial but less obvious constitutional lessons learned from the ways in which Trump governed. In particular, the book focuses on lessons grounded in constitutional principles that progressives generally either criticized or underemphasized *before* Trump, but that became vital for progressives *after* Trump was elected. Those lessons are that federalism matters, that separation of powers matters (in particular that the need to rein in presidential power in domestic affairs matters), and that robust free speech protections matter. Progressives should promote and defend these constitutional principles going forward regardless of whether there is an ally or an opponent in the White House.

Principles, including constitutional ones, can be defended deontologically or instrumentally. For example, the principle that torture is wrong can be defended deontologically on the ground that human beings have certain dignity and autonomy-based rights that, when enforced, prohibit the government from inflicting the degrading and dehumanizing physical and psychological injuries caused by torture. Alternatively, the principle that torture is wrong can be defended instrumentally, not on the basis of universal rights shared by all human beings but on the view that allowing the government to torture individuals leads to terrible consequences, not only for the torture victims themselves but also for the broader society. A government that tortures some of its citizens, after all, is unlikely to care about the welfare and well-being of its people.

I argue in this book that the principles of federalism, separation of powers, and free speech should matter to progressives primarily for instrumental reasons. Using dozens of examples from the ways in which Trump abused government power, I pay particular attention to how the three principles can help mitigate the harms that autocratic leaders in the Trump mold can cause both to democratic institutions and to vulnerable minorities.

When we say that an individual is principled, we usually mean that they consistently abide by certain values or beliefs. The fact that we recognize that a person of principle is a person of *integrity* suggests that there is intrinsic value in such consistency. Someone who fails to abide or live by principles they profess to value is hypocritical and perhaps even deceitful. Being principled, therefore, can be a good thing in and of itself. But I argue in this book that progressives should be principled on matters related to federalism, separation of powers, and free speech not only because being principled is good in and of itself, but also because being principled in these matters will help both advance progressive causes over the long run and reduce the threats posed by future autocratic leaders in the Trump mold to our system of self-governance, to our democratic values, and to traditionally subordinated minorities.

The three constitutional principles that I explore in this book, like many other constitutional principles, serve to *restrain* government action. It is therefore not surprising that conservatives frequently rely on those principles to try to limit the federal government's ability to pursue progressive policy objectives. As a result, the same federalism and separation-of-powers principles that made it more difficult for Trump, for example, to institute harshly anti-immigrant policies and dangerously deregulatory environmental policies will make it more difficult for future progressive presidents, for example, to implement policies promoting access to health care and economic and racial equality. I argue that conservatives' use of the constitutional principles defended in this book to challenge the policies of liberal administrations is a price that progressives should be willing to pay for being able to rely on the same principles to try to curb some of the most harmful, dangerous, and discriminatory policies of future right-wing autocratic presidents in the Trump mold.

What progressives should *not do* is try to have it both ways: that is, to ignore or undermine certain constitutional principles, such as federalism and separation of powers, when a liberal like Barack Obama or Joe Biden is in the White House, while relying on those same principles to resist federal policies when there is a conservative president, as progressives repeatedly did during Trump's years in office. To do that would be to treat constitutional principles as nothing more than means to achieve policy ends and ideological objectives, enthusiastically embracing them when they are politically useful and dismissively rejecting them when they are not. Either constitutional principles matter—in the sense that they appropriately impose meaningful limits on government authority—or they do not. To defend particular constitutional principles only when they help derail the policy objectives of our political opponents trivializes the principles' importance in maintaining the viability of our constitutional democracy regardless of which party or faction holds the reins of power at any given time.

This book encourages progressives to resist the temptations of situational constitutionalism, that is, the defending of constitutional principles only when they help attain our preferred policy objectives or defeat those of our political opponents.[7] And the book does so primarily on the ground that situational constitutionalism is less likely to promote and advance progressive causes over the long run than principled constitutionalism. If progressives want to rely on federalism and separation-of-powers principles to resist future right-wing presidents, they would be well-served by defending and fortifying those principles regardless of which party or individual controls the federal government at any given time. Indeed, if progressives ignore or underemphasize the principles when there is a liberal in the White House, those principles are less likely to be viable and helpful when there is a conservative, including a right-wing autocrat, in the Oval Office.

With the exception of the chapter on the First Amendment, this book focuses on the so-called structural Constitution. In addition to protecting individual rights, the Constitution sets forth the basic powers and organizational structure of the national government, including the horizontal division of power among the federal government's three branches and the vertical relationship between the national government and the states. One of the founders' primary objectives in adopting the Constitution was to restrain government authority by dispersing it. As a result, some progressive scholars have argued that the structural Constitution's checks and balances—what political scientists call "veto points"—have built-in biases against the attainment of progressive objectives because they make the deployment of activist government more difficult, both as a constitutional/legal matter and as a practical/political matter. Critics argue that veto points, by dissipating government authority and therefore making governance more difficult, are more compatible with a conservative and deregulatory political agenda that prioritizes the free market than with a progressive agenda that emphasizes government intervention and regulation.

Law professor Sanford Levinson, for example, is critical of the Constitution's many veto points, including the division of Congress into two chambers and the requirement that a presidential veto stand unless a supermajority in each chamber votes to override it, because he argues they protect the status quo and prevent change.[8] For her part, political scientist Lisa Miller argues that the constitutionally mandated fragmentation of government power is not a neutral principle but is instead an "*exercise* of power. Invocation of the checks-and-balances myth simply obscures the interests that are at stake, the powerful players who are exercising power, and the potential consequences for the people of the United States."[9]

I concede that veto point mechanisms that seek to enforce federalism and separation-of-powers principles can sometimes make the attainment of progressive policy objectives more difficult. In the absence of veto points, for example, liberal presidents like Bill Clinton and Barack Obama would have achieved and instituted a greater number of progressive objectives and reforms. But, on the other side of the ledger, there are three additional factors that, when combined, result in progressives gaining more than they lose from the enforcement of federalism and separation-of-powers veto points. First, as the Trump years showed, federalism and separation-of-powers mechanisms and principles can make it more difficult for conservative administrations to implement *their* preferred policies. Many of those policies are deregulatory in nature, which means that federalism and separation-of-powers mechanisms and principles *can help defend existing regulations against efforts to rescind them*. An important example of this phenomenon during the Trump era was the deployment of those mechanisms and principles by progressive states to overturn some of the administration's most misguided rollbacks of environmental regulations.[10] Another example was their deployment by progressives to resist the administration's efforts to rescind policies aimed at protecting certain categories of immigrants, including asylum seekers and Dreamers (undocumented individuals brought to the United States as children).[11]

But not all conservative objectives are pursued through deregulation. Instead, conservatives also frequently call upon activist government, including at the federal level, to achieve their objectives. The vast increase in law enforcement and correctional bureaucracies needed to administer the massive growth in the incarceration rates of Americans since the 1970s, the immense enlargement of the national security state following 9/11, and the enormous expansion of immigration enforcement mechanisms during the Trump years are just three examples of the ways in which conservatives embrace forceful and activist government intervention—including at the federal level—when they believe it helps attain their preferred policy objectives. It is a mistake, therefore, for progressives to think of structural constitutional mechanisms and principles that restrain government authority (the so-called veto points) only in the context of how they make it more difficult to institute and implement liberal government programs. Progressives should also consider those mechanisms and principles in light of the fact that when conservatives control the levers of federal power, they repeat-edly rely on activist government to pursue their preferred policies and objectives.

Veto points, then, can make it more difficult for conservatives (1) to imple-ment deregulatory objectives and (2) to attain policy goals that require the de-ployment and expansion of federal government authority. A third and vitally important benefit of federalism and separation-of-powers mechanisms and principles for progressives is that, as the Trump years showed, they can help miti-gate the harms to democratic institutions and traditionally vulnerable minorities engendered by right-wing autocratic officials in the Trump mold. I seek to de-fend this claim throughout the book.

In my estimation, the benefits of enforcing federalism and separation-of-powers principles as means for advancing liberal causes and limiting the harms that progressives believe are engendered by conservative governance outweigh the costs to progressive movements and causes that accompany conservatives' reliance on the same principles to limit liberal government. I recognize, how-ever, that reasonable people can disagree with this assessment, and I hope that this book encourages debates on this point. As a general matter, progressives have prioritized the Constitution's individual rights provisions over its structural components. This book seeks to persuade progressives to pay more attention to the benefits that the structural Constitution can offer to progressive causes and movements.

Although there can be reasonable disagreement on the question of whether progressives have more to gain than to lose from the robust enforcement of fed-eralism and separation-of-powers principles, there is less room for disagree-ment, in my view, on whether situational constitutionalism is appropriate. As I also argue throughout the book, progressives should avoid the temptation of embracing constitutional principles only when they advance their policy object-ives while dismissing or ignoring them when they serve the objectives of their political opponents. I therefore suggest that progressives, going forward, follow this rule of thumb: if a constitutional principle was worth deploying to resist Trump's harmful policies and autocratic governance, then the principle is likely worth defending in the post-Trump era even if it makes the short-term attain-ment of progressive objectives more difficult. This is because progressive causes and movements, over the *long run*, are more likely to gain than to lose from the application of that principle.

There is a tendency, perhaps a natural one, for activists across the political spectrum to pay less attention to constitutional principles when advocates are able to move the levers of government power in ways that help them achieve their preferred policy objectives. For example, if progressives can persuade govern-ment officials that universal access to health care is essential or if conservatives can convince officials that restricting immigration is vital, then the question of whether those objectives are attained through means that are consistent with certain constitutional principles does not seem to arise naturally among proponents. Instead, it is usually *opponents* of particular government policies—especially opponents who lack the political power to derail their implementation—who turn to constitutional principles as a way of blocking or challenging the policies at issue. But to value constitutional principles only in these situational circumstances is not in the best interests of progressive causes and movements in the long run. Instead, it is principled constitutionalism that makes it more likely that crucial constitutional principles will retain their strength and viability at all times, including when progressives need them most in resisting federal government efforts to attain right-wing policy objectives.

Abiding by principled constitutionalism will sometimes require progressives to *oppose* certain forms of federal government action *that advance progressive objectives in the short run.* This is because principled constitutionalism asks that progressives, in determining whether to support a statute, regulation, executive order, or similar measure look to not only whether it advances their policy objectives, but also to whether it achieves those objectives through constitutionally proper means. On the question of presidential authority, for example, my hope is that Trump's repeated and dangerous abuses of power will encourage progressives, going forward, to determine whether to support provisions of law not only depending on whether they advance liberal policy goals, but also on whether they unduly expand presidential powers.

Some may argue that asking advocates to stick with principles, even when it entails delaying the attainment of highly valued policy objectives, is politically naïve. Critics may claim, for example, that it is unrealistic to expect progressive advocates to work to limit the power of a progressive president in the name of federalism or separation of powers. I have two responses to the "naïveté" criticism. First, as the example of the strong progressive opposition to partisan gerrymandering in Democratic-controlled New Jersey showed, advocates in the real world do sometimes abide by principles even if doing so may make the attainment of desired policy objectives more difficult in the short run. Second, my argument is that progressives should consistently abide by the constitutional principles explored in this book, even when doing so may endanger the attainment of progressive goals in the short run, *because doing so will be in their best political interests over the long run.* In other words, I am not asking progressives to be consistent merely for the sake of consistency. Instead, I am asking progressives to be consistent because I believe it is in the best interests of progressive movements and causes over the long haul. My hope is that if the benefits of principled constitutionalism were not as clear to progressives as they might otherwise have been before Trump was elected, his disastrous governance—disastrous for democratic institutions and values, for traditionally subjugated minorities, and for the nation as a whole—will help to make those benefits more evident.

One of the inevitable consequences of a well-functioning democratic system of government is that the hands that control the levers of power change with some frequency. The constitutional mechanisms and principles that serve to sometimes make the attainment of progressive objectives more difficult when liberals are in charge of the federal government are the same ones that sometimes make it more difficult to implement conservative policy objectives, to say nothing of the autocratic and nationalist policies pursued by the Trump administration.

On the question of federalism, this book does not attempt to delineate precisely when and how state sovereignty concerns should limit the exercise of federal government authority. And on the question of separation of powers, the book does not seek to delineate precisely how the Constitution should best be understood to limit presidential authority. Instead, my objective is to use the Trump years to illustrate why and how constitutional mechanisms and principles that limit federal authority and presidential power can serve to advance progressive interests over the long run.

One argument I do not make in this book is that progressives should embrace principled constitutionalism in order to encourage or persuade conservatives to do the same. In my view, it would indeed be naïve to believe that the contemporary Republican Party and the conservative movement that supports it will somehow be shamed by progressives into being more principled. For example, it is highly unlikely that either the party or the movement, as currently constituted and led, would do what progressives did in New Jersey on the issue of partisan gerrymandering: put principle over short-term political advantage. There are many reasons for my abiding skepticism on this point, including (1) the GOP's fifty-year strategy of stoking white resentment and racism over the nation's increasing diversity and multiethnicity; (2) conservatives' repeated efforts to gerrymander legislative districts and to discourage racial and other minorities from voting as a means of benefiting Republican candidates; and (3) the refusal of GOP leaders and conservative activists, with the notable exception of a small number of "Never Trumpers," to oppose or object to Trump's unprecedented and egregious abuses of power.[12] All of this strongly suggests that if the GOP and the conservative movement are to embrace principled constitutionalism in the future, it will more likely be the result of electoral losses than of progressives' embrace of such constitutionalism.

The ways in which the Trump administration governed showed how a lack of principles and integrity by powerful government officials can threaten even the strongest of democratic institutions and values, while endangering the basic rights of vulnerable minorities. Few of the same conservatives who had for years decried the expansion of the federal government's power since the New

Deal and of presidential authority under liberal presidents such as Clinton and Obama raised constitutional objections to Trump's power grabs. Whether the Republican Party and the conservative movement are able to crawl out of the moral holes they created for themselves by repeatedly refusing to stand up to Trump's relentless and dangerous demagoguery and abuses of power remains to be seen. But whether that happens will not depend on whether progressives, going forward, continue to support and defend the constitutional principles that they repeatedly relied on to resist the Trump administration.

While most of this book focuses on structural constitutional issues, the final chapter explores the constitutionally protected rights to freedom of speech and of the press. Given the seemingly wide consensus in the United States regarding the fundamental importance of First Amendment protections, it may seem, at first blush, unnecessary to remind progressives, in effect, that the First Amendment matters. But I believe the Trump years powerfully demonstrated the First Amendment's vital role in protecting democratic institutions, self-governance, and the right to dissent, a role that many Americans of all political stripes, in the decades leading to Trump's election, had largely taken for granted and, therefore, become somewhat complacent about. There is nothing like a challenge to widely shared principles to encourage further thinking about and deeper appreciation for them.

Some progressives, before Trump gained power, had grown increasingly skeptical of certain expansive understandings of the First Amendment that, for example, seek to prohibit the regulation of hate speech, protect the free speech rights of corporations, and shield businesses owned by religious conservatives from laws that protect LGBTQ people from discrimination. It is important, going forward, that progressives do not allow "First Amendment skepticism," as I call it in the final chapter, to grow to the point that it undermines the amendment's ability to shield democratic processes, political dissenters, and vulnerable groups from autocratic government officials in the Trump mold. This is not to suggest, by any means, that the First Amendment worked perfectly in stopping or preventing all of Trump's abuses of power. But it is to suggest that First Amendment protections, whether explicitly enforced through the courts or not, crucially helped to curtail some of his worst autocratic policies, practices, and predilections.

In encouraging progressives to defend certain constitutional principles— regardless of who is president—this book does not contend that current constitutionally mandated structures—including those related to federalism and separation of powers—are essential to the proper functioning of our democracy. Whether a different constitution—one that, for example, eschews federalism or the presidency altogether—would better allow the American people to achieve the ideals contained in the Constitution's Preamble is a subject for another book.[13] There are good arguments to be made that some constitutional provisions are in desperate need of change, including the current requirement that states have an equal representation in the Senate (which allows as little as a third of the voting public to elect a majority of senators) and that the president be selected by an Electoral College (which allows someone to gain the office, as has happened twice in this century alone, even though an opponent received more votes).[14] But this book works within the confines of the Constitution as it exists today (and as is likely to be in place for the foreseeable future) rather than the document as it should exist.

Throughout the book, I use the term "autocratic" to describe Trump and the ways in which he governed. Recognizing that the term can be defined and understood in different ways, I want to explain how I use it in this book. One important characteristic of autocratic leaders, I believe, is that they repeatedly and purposefully deploy state power to promote their personal, political, and financial interests over the well-being of society. In addition, autocratic leaders consistently challenge the legitimacy of mechanisms, organizations, and individuals that could potentially limit their exercise of government authority. Indeed, one of the hallmarks of autocratic leaders is their equating of oversight or criticism of their leadership with disloyalty to the nation. Another hallmark characteristic of autocratic leaders is their repeated claims that only they are capable of protecting the nation from a seemingly endless list of both internal and external threats and enemies. Autocratic leaders also refuse to abide by the concept of *independent* law enforcement; instead, they use their control of law enforcement agencies to target political opponents and critics while blocking or undermining investigations of their friends and allies. For complicated reasons that are also beyond the book's scope, at the same time Trump served as president, there were other autocratic leaders, many of them elected (at least initially), firmly in control of countries all over the world. Those leaders included Vladimir Putin in Russia, Narendra Modi in India, Viktor Orban in Hungary, Nicolás Maduro in Venezuela, Recep Tayyip Erdoğan in Turkey, and Rodrigo Duterte in the Philippines.[15]

I also want to provide a definition of the term "progressive" because I use it throughout the book. The term is intended to describe individuals who are on the left side of the American political spectrum. I use the term capaciously enough to include, for example, democratic socialists, who are more to the left, and liberals, who are closer to the political center. I recognize that there is always a danger of overgeneralizing when using an umbrella term such as "progressive" to describe a multiplicity of individuals with varying ideological viewpoints and policy objectives. I want to make it clear, therefore, that nothing in this book is intended to suggest that progressives hold monolithic views on the federalism, separation-of-powers, and free speech issues that I explore. Although, in different parts of the book, I describe *general trends* in progressive constitutional thought, political views, and policy preferences, there have always been, and will always continue to be, progressives who take positions contrary to those trends.

Although the book pays particular attention to events that took place and disputes that arose during the Trump years, its outlook is intended to be as much forward-looking as it is backward-looking. It is undoubtedly true that for many progressives, the Trump years felt like a devastating and demoralizing defeat for their principles, values, and objectives. But one of the main reasons why I wrote this book is because I firmly believe it is important for progressives to turn the hand-wringing, the worrying, the fretting—and, quite frankly, the despair— engendered by Trump's multiple autocratic threats to the nation's democratic values and to the rights of its vulnerable minorities into a *positive* agenda. That agenda should include the defense of certain constitutional principles that, when consistently applied, can help the country move forward in constructive and beneficial directions. It is my hope that the constitutional principles explored in this book—some of which have not been generally emphasized by progressives in recent decades—will be of value to progressives and to the country long after the difficult, painful, and disturbing Trump years have receded into memory.

Finally, there is much truth to the saying that "to a hammer, everything looks like a nail." Since I am a scholar and teacher of constitutional law, this book focuses on the workings of certain constitutional mechanisms and the implications of particular constitutional principles. But it is important to recognize upfront that there is only so much that can be accomplished through the deployment of con- stitutional arguments and understandings. Ultimately, the creation of a fairer, more just, and more equal society, in which the hopes and aspirations of all of its members are respected and encouraged, depends much more on the diffi- cult work of political and policy advocacy that are part of electoral choices and legislative debates than on the domains of constitutional law and the courts. At the end of the day, what helped the most in reducing the harms engendered by Trump's autocratic and disastrous governance was not the application of consti- tutional doctrine as understood by judges, law professors, and lawyers, but was instead the voters' wise decision in 2020 to deny him a second term.

PART I
PRINCIPLES MATTER: FEDERALISM

1

Federalism Before Trump

In the approximately 150 years that elapsed between the Civil War and the election of Donald Trump, progressives had many reasons to be skeptical of federalism as a constitutional principle. During that century and a half, conservatives repeatedly turned to the idea of states' rights to try to limit the federal government's ability, for example, to protect civil rights and regulate businesses. It is therefore not surprising that many progressives generally have been distrustful of arguments grounded in the notion that state sovereignty considerations appropriately limit the federal government's authority. Time and time again, when progressives turned to the federal government to try to achieve liberal objectives—everything from promoting civil rights to reducing economic inequality to expanding health-care access to implementing environmental and consumer protections—they confronted conservative claims that their efforts were unconstitutional because they violated states' sovereignty.

Of course, progressives have never believed in wholly unrestrained federal government authority. But those on the left generally assert that the restraints emanate from constitutional protections for basic individual rights rather than from so-called states' rights. As a general matter, progressives have not viewed federalist mechanisms and principles as a legitimate and appropriate source of limitation on the federal government's power. This perspective is reflected in the notion, traditionally embraced by liberal Supreme Court justices, that the Bill of Rights' Tenth Amendment—the provision that reserves to the states and the people those government powers that the Constitution does not grant to the federal government—is a mere truism. According to this view, the amendment stands for nothing more than the basic proposition that the federal government cannot exercise powers that the Constitution fails to grant it. As a result, it is argued, the Tenth Amendment does not serve as an independent source of limitation on the federal government's authority.[1]

But there is a difference between (1) defending federalism as a crucial constitutional principle and (2) using government structures and mechanisms at the state and local levels to advance progressive policy objectives and to oppose conservative ones.[2] While progressives have rarely done the former, they have, at different times in American history, most recently during the Trump years, repeatedly done the latter. The overarching purpose of this and the next chapter is to persuade progressives to not only do number 2, but also number 1. My claim

Principles Matter. Carlos A. Ball, Oxford University Press. © Carlos A. Ball 2021.
DOI: 10.1093/oso/9780197584484.003.0002

is that doing so is in the best interests of progressive movements and causes over the long run.

Despite the refusal by many on the left to embrace federalism as a constitutional principle, the nation's history offers important examples of how the exercise of government authority at the state level, sometimes constitutionally protected from federal interference, can advance progressive objectives.[3] One of those examples was the way in which northern states, in the decades leading up to the Civil War, relied on their constitutionally protected sovereignty, first, to abolish slavery within their borders and, later, to try to limit its expansion outside of the South. In addition, during the last decades of the twentieth century and into this century, progressives relied on the American system of dispersed government authority to pursue policy objectives, such as marriage equality and marijuana legalization, which were not, as an initial matter, attainable at the national level. And, between 2017 and 2020, many progressives supported the repeated efforts by liberal states to exercise their authority as sovereigns to resist and undermine what they considered to be some of the Trump administration's most dangerous, misguided, and harmful policies.

There are three reasons that are usually given to support the constitutional protection for state sovereignty and the corresponding limits on federal authority. First, that protecting state sovereignty promotes individual liberty by reducing the likelihood of federal tyranny. Second, that states are closer to the people than the federal government and are therefore more responsive to their needs and concerns. And third, that states, as Justice Louis Brandeis famously put it, can serve as helpful laboratories for policy experimentation; rather than seeking a uniform and national solution to social and economic problems, federalism allows for the testing of multiple ideas and proposals in an effort to determine which policies are most effective in advancing the public's interests.[4]

These arguments in favor of federalism as a constitutional principle have some validity as far as they go. For example, it is true that protecting state sovereignty *sometimes* reduces the harms associated with tyrannical and autocratic federal rule. As explored in the next chapter, this is a point that should resonate with progressives who lived through the difficult Trump years. Similarly, federalism *sometimes* encourages local experimentation that leads to the adoption of beneficial policies and reforms—progressives can point to marriage equality and marijuana decriminalization as examples—which would not initially have been implemented at the national level.

At the same time, history provides multiple reasons for being skeptical of the notion that there is an *inherent* relationship between limiting federal authority (cause) and protecting liberty (effect). Those who defend that intrinsic relationship frequently contend, as the Supreme Court put it in 1991, that federalism "was adopted by the framers to ensure protection of our fundamental liberties."[5] Unfortunately, there have been countless instances in American history—including, most prominently, those that occurred during the post-Reconstruction period, the progressive era of the early twentieth century, and the civil rights era of the 1950s and 1960s—in which *restraining* federal power to accommodate state interests have *undermined rather than promoted liberty*—and, just as importantly, *equality*—interests. This is especially true of the liberty and equality interests of working-class people, the poor, and traditionally subjugated minorities.

Similarly, the states' greater "responsiveness" to the people and their ability to engage in policy "experimentation" under our constitutional regime should not be valued for their own sake because states' responsiveness and experimentation have frequently been used to protect economic and social privileges and to institutionalize and strengthen racism and other forms of systemic prejudices. Here too, unfortunately, American history is replete with highly problematic examples, including the apartheid Jim Crow regimes of southern states and the forced sterilization by state officials of cognitively disabled individuals during the first decades of the twentieth century.[6]

If we use history rather than theory as our guide, as I seek to do in this book, the most (or best) that can be said about federalism is that it is a substantively neutral principle that—in requiring, in some circumstances, that state-level decision-making be protected from federal interference—has *sometimes been used for good and sometimes for ill*. Federalism, as law professor Nancy Knauer puts it, "is a decision-making process and not an ideology."[7] Federalism, in other words, is about which level of government (federal or state or both) should make which types of policy decisions rather than about the policies' substantive content. As such, federalism—the dividing of government power between federal and state authorities—is a neutral principle of governance that can and should be separated from its deployment to pursue particular policy objectives.

The fact that federalism is a substantively neutral principle that can limit the national government's authority for purposes both good and ill means that it is a mistake to think of federalism as somehow essential to democratic rule and individual liberty. Without knowing the content of the substantive decisions that result from the application of federalist principles, it is impossible to know whether those principles are being used to promote or threaten, for example, democratic values, individual liberty, and racial equality.

Federalism, then, can be *useful* in resisting harmful federal policies and promoting beneficial policies at the state level. Therein lies the value of federalism for progressives—federalism should matter to progressives because resistance to the federal government and protection of state sovereignty can sometimes help defend democratic institutions, promote the public good, and protect traditionally vulnerable minorities. In other words, federalism can sometimes help advance progressive objectives while limiting ill-advised, harmful, and discriminatory federal policies.

The purpose of this and the next chapter is not to defend federalism as an unalloyed good, or as essential to liberty and representative democracy, or because state experimentation in policy matters is always something to be promoted or cherished. The chapters' purpose is also not to try to delineate precisely when and how state sovereignty concerns should limit the exercise of federal government authority. Instead, their purpose is to persuade progressives that federalist mechanisms and principles should matter to them even though conservatives have repeatedly deployed them in the past, and will undoubtedly do so again in the future, to try to limit the ability of the federal government to pursue progressive policies. It is true that the federalist mechanisms and principles that emanate from our constitutional structure can be used to undermine progressive causes and promote conservative ones. But they can also be deployed to promote progressive policies at the state level and, as the Trump years made clear, to resist misguided, harmful, and discriminatory federal policies. My claim is that the benefits of federalism for progressive causes and movements outweigh its costs.

The Roots of Federalism in Our Constitutional System

It all started with how Britain governed its American colonies. One of the ways Britain kept a firm grip on those colonies—a tight control that eventually led to the revolutionary uprising in the name of freedom for some—was by making sure that the colonies remained independent from and not aligned with *each other*. Britain established different American colonies at different times to be partially governed locally by different leaders under different governing charters and laws, resulting in a lack of formal and legal relationships between them. As law professor Akhil Reed Amar puts it, "mid-eighteenth-century British North America . . . formed a partial wheel, with imperial spokes radiating from London to each colony but precious little legal rim binding the colonies directly to one another."[8] When the colonies rebelled and declared independence, they did so as separate and sovereign states that did not, up until that point, have formal connections to each other.

Following the signing of the Declaration of Independence, the former colonies used the Articles of Confederation to establish an alliance. That legal document, however, was not a constitution that created one indivisible nation; instead, it was effectively a treaty agreed to by sovereign nation states that allowed them to pursue common interests, but one that did not bind them into one country or even required them to remain in the Confederation (or what we today might call a "league of nations" and what the Articles called "a firm league of friendship") without their ongoing individual consent.[9]

In the eyes of many American leaders at the time, including most prominently James Madison and Alexander Hamilton, the governing structure set up by the Articles quickly proved to be ineffective and inefficient. In hindsight, the governance problems engendered by the Articles were hardly surprising given that the document did not allow the Confederation, for example, to directly tax individuals, regulate commerce, or even enforce its own laws. As law professor George Van Cleve puts it, "since a government's ability to enforce its laws is one of the essential attributes of sovereignty, the Confederation was not an actual sovereign."[10] Indeed, the states retained for themselves most of the attributes of government and no new power could be granted to the Confederation without the unanimous consent of all the (nation) states. It was precisely because of the need to create, in the words of the Constitution's Preamble, "a more perfect union" that delegates gathered in Philadelphia in 1787 to draft a new legal compact that would form one nation (a *United* States) out of heretofore independent sovereign states.

In joining the new union, states gave up some important attributes of sovereignty. For example, states were no longer permitted to engage in foreign relations or coin money. The states also granted to the federal government independent powers to tax, provide for the national defense, and regulate commerce. In addition, the new document's Supremacy Clause made clear that the Constitution and federal statutes both trumped state laws and were binding on state courts. At the same time, the Constitution permitted states to *retain* vital aspects of their sovereignty. In fact, it is generally agreed that if the Constitution had not allowed states to retain crucial aspects of their sovereignty, the document would not have enjoyed the support of a majority of the delegates who gathered in Philadelphia in 1787 to draft it or of those who later approved it as part of state ratification conventions.[11]

The Constitution, in other words, was the subject of a grand bargain: the national government's powers were significantly increased while, at the same time, some of the independent interests of the states, as distinct sovereign entities, were protected. The document accomplished the latter objective in several different ways, starting with the creation of a national government with *limited* powers. The Constitution did not grant Congress the type of broad and general regulatory authority to promote and protect the public's health, safety, morals, and general welfare—usually referred to as a government's "police power"— enjoyed by the states both before and after the document became legally binding through ratification. Instead, the Constitution granted Congress a list of particular powers, such as the authority to regulate interstate commerce and to enact bankruptcy laws. Furthermore, the protections of individual rights contained in the Bill of Rights amendments, adopted in 1791, originally applied only to the federal government and were not intended to limit the states' authority.[12] In addition, the last of those amendments explicitly stated that "the powers not delegated to the United States by the Constitution, nor prohibited by it to the States, are reserved to the States respectively, or to the people."[13]

The Constitution also contained several structural components that protected the interests of states as distinct sovereign entities. For example, the document granted each state equal representation in the Senate regardless of population. The Constitution also prohibited its own amendment without the approval of three-fourths of the states.

While the Constitution granted to the federal government its sovereign powers, it did not do the same for the states. The states' sovereignty powers were instead derived from their respective state constitutions. While the federal Constitution limited state sovereignty to the extent the founders believed was necessary in order to create a "more perfect union," that sovereignty both pre-existed and survived (in more limited form) the creation of the new republic. There were those who wanted to go further in empowering the national government at the states' expense. Madison was firmly in that group—he proposed, for example, that the Constitution grant Congress the authority to veto state legislation. But most of the delegates who drafted the document, and later ratified it, were opposed to such expansive formulations of centralized government power. It was not until the twentieth century that Congress began to legislate in areas that the Constitution granted it significant powers (such as in interstate commerce) in ways that, under the Supremacy Clause, sometimes preempted or limited the exercise of state sovereignty in important policy matters related, for example, to labor relations, workplace safety, and consumer protection.

Slavery, *Prigg v. Pennsylvania*, and Personal Liberty Laws

There is no uglier example in American history of the ways in which federalist mechanisms and principles can threaten human dignity and liberty than the manner in which they were used, during the decades leading up to the Civil War, to defend, strengthen, and expand the institution of slavery. But there is another side to the intersection of federalism and slavery that is less well-understood and that progressives should keep in mind when assessing the value of federalism as a constitutional principle: the ways in which northern states, during the antebellum period, *relied on federalist mechanisms and principles to resist slavery*.

Furthermore, the fact that the federal government eventually fought a war to preserve the union, and in the process to abolish slavery, does not mean that it resisted the expansion of slavery before the war. Indeed, what happened was just the opposite: in the years leading up to the war, it was *white southerners who repeatedly and successfully turned to the federal government to protect and expand slavery.* White southerners were able to do this in large part because the Constitution gave them greater political power than their numbers justified by counting enslaved people as three-fifths of individuals for purposes of apportionment in the House of Representatives. This racist mechanism—which counted enslaved people for purposes of apportionment, despite the fact that they were simultaneously denied all basic human rights and dignity—gave the South disproportionate political power in Congress. It also gave white southerners outsized influence in choosing the president through the Electoral College.

In the years before the Civil War, southern states successfully marshaled their significant federal political power to *nationalize* the institution of slavery; they did so by deploying the federal government's authority to help return fugitive enslaved people to bondage and to expand slavery into new states and territories. In contrast, it was northern states that *repeatedly turned to considerations of federalism to resist southern efforts to nationalize slavery* in the years before the Civil War. In this section, I explore the northern states' resistance to slavery in some detail because I believe it supports my claim that federalism is a normatively neutral principle that serves to limit the national government's authority in the name of state sovereignty, sometimes for good and sometimes for great ill.

When the Constitution was adopted in 1787, there were about seven hundred thousand enslaved people in the United States (a number that would balloon to approximately four million by the start of the Civil War). At the time of the nation's founding, "it was almost universally agreed that the Constitution left slavery beyond the reach of the national government."[14] It was for the states to decide whether to allow slavery and, if so, how to regulate it. The fact that the Constitution permitted states to exercise unfettered discretion to maintain and even expand the institution of slavery was, by far, its deepest moral and legal flaw because, despite the founders' claimed commitments to liberty and freedom, it allowed southern states, first, to use their authority to protect the genocidal institution within their borders and, later, to seek to expand it beyond those boundaries.

At the same time, however, the Constitution allowed northern states to exercise *their* sovereignty in ways that first curtailed and later ended slavery in their territories. In 1780, Pennsylvania enacted a law prohibiting the further importation of enslaved people into the commonwealth, something that the colonial governments of Connecticut and Rhode Island had done two years before the Declaration of Independence was signed. The Pennsylvania statute also required that children born to enslaved mothers be emancipated when they reached the age of twenty-eight, making it the first gradual abolition law in history. Connecticut and Rhode Island soon enacted similar laws. Slavery in

Massachusetts ended as a result of judicial rulings based in part on a state constitutional provision holding that "all men are born free and equal"—an egalitarian principle found in the Declaration of Independence, but conspicuously and embarrassingly absent from both the original Constitution and the Bill of Rights. By the time Vermont joined the union in 1791, it had already abolished slavery. New York and New Jersey began taking gradual steps to abolish slavery in 1799 and 1804, respectively. By 1827, when New York finally got around to emancipating all of its enslaved residents, all northern states had outlawed slavery within their borders.[15]

While northern states were moving to first limit and later abolish slavery, southern states, as their economies and wealth became increasingly dependent on free human labor, exercised their sovereignty by further protecting and promoting slavery within their territories. Had these inconsistent exercises of state sovereignty involved mundane issues of economic or social regulation, they could have coexisted within a federal union without creating significant tension or conflict. But as the nineteenth century progressed, an increasing number of northerners came to view the continued existence of slavery anywhere in the country as morally unacceptable. This was true even of some of the many white northerners who believed in the supremacy of white people and the need to keep the races segregated, but who also increasingly felt compelled to criticize slavery for the inhumane and barbaric institution that it was.

The expansion of the South's plantation agricultural system, and therefore of slavery, was driven by the growing demand for cotton by northern states and European countries. Technological changes in the crop's harvesting and processing, when coupled with the availability of free enslaved labor, made it possible for plantation owners to meet the mounting demand. The cotton market's explosive growth made many plantation owners phenomenally wealthy. "By the eve of the Civil War, the Mississippi Valley was home to more millionaires per capita than anywhere else in the United States. . . .The combined value of enslaved people exceeded that of all the railroads and factories in the nation."[16]

The rising tension between the North's growing objections to slavery and the South's increasing economic dependence on it manifested itself primarily in two ways. First, as the nation grew westward, there were repeated disagreements over whether slavery should be permitted in the new states and territories. Southerners desperately wanted to expand the geographic reach of slavery in order to maintain the viability of their economic system, one that was entirely dependent on enslaved labor.[17] While northerners, through their manufacturing plants and shipping companies, also greatly benefited economically from cotton grown by enslaved human beings, they became increasingly resentful of how the expansion of slavery served to enlarge the political power of southerners at their expense.

Second, the widening gap in how the North and the South viewed and treated slavery created obvious incentives for enslaved people to try to escape to the North, leading to disputes based on vigorous assertions of state sovereignty *by both sides*. Although the number of fugitive slaves was never very large relative to the total number of enslaved individuals on American soil, plantation owners feared that even if only a small number of fugitive enslaved people were allowed to live in freedom in the North, it might imperil the institution of slavery and, with it, the allocation of wealth and power both in the South and nationally. Many "owners" of enslaved people, therefore, did everything they could to prevent their subjects from escaping, including physically torturing those caught or suspected of trying to escape. As for the enslaved individuals who made it across the Mason-Dixon line, they had to contend with the vicious bounty hunters whom enslavers sent to the North to kidnap and return them to slavery using whatever means necessary.[18] For their part, southern elected officials demanded federal assistance in the return of enslaved people to their "owners," relying on property rights arguments and the Constitution's Fugitive Slave Clause. That provision required—without explaining precisely how—that enslaved individuals be returned to their owners when they were "found in another state."

In the decades leading to the Civil War, northern states exercised their sovereign authority to regulate individuals within their borders by enacting an increasingly expansive series of laws—collectively known as Personal Liberty Laws—aimed at making it more difficult for the "owners" of enslaved individuals and their agents to cross state lines in order to hunt down and kidnap Black people. The enactment of Personal Liberty Laws by northern states constituted a crucial progressive exercise of state sovereignty under our federal system that sought to resist the nationalization of slavery.

Pennsylvania in 1826 became one of the first states to enact a Personal Liberty Law. Conflicts arising from efforts to kidnap alleged fugitive enslaved people to return them to bondage were particularly frequent in Pennsylvania given its large border with the slave states of Maryland, Virginia, and Delaware. One of the incidents that led the Pennsylvania legislature to enact the law was the kidnapping by bounty hunters of a group of African American boys who spent their time in the Philadelphia docks; the kidnappers, much to the outrage of many Pennsylvanians, whisked the children onto a ship that took them south, after which they were sold as slaves in Georgia and Mississippi.[19]

The new statute did not criminalize the kidnapping of fugitive enslaved people as such. Instead, the law prohibited the kidnapping of *free* Black residents of Pennsylvania. Before the statute's enactment, bounty hunters were essentially free to determine who was a fugitive enslaved person and therefore whom to remove from the state through the use of force. The new Personal Liberty Law required that that determination be made by state courts and explicitly rejected the notion that someone with Black skin should be presumed to be an enslaved person. The objective was to make sure that free African American individuals residing in Pennsylvania—many of whom were non-fugitive former slaves—were not ripped from their homes and communities by violent and ruthless bounty hunters. At the same time, by requiring southerners to support their claims of "ownership" of human beings with evidence in court proceedings, the law made it more difficult for them to retrieve "their" runaways. Among its provisions, the law required that two witnesses, neither of whom could be the person claiming ownership rights, provide evidence of that ownership to a Pennsylvania court.[20]

Maine, New Jersey, and New York also enacted Personal Liberty Laws in the 1820s. In doing so, these states asserted their sovereign authority to determine how to regulate the use of force within their territories, while deciding which actions by private individuals should be criminalized. The laws were an important exercise of sovereignty by northern states aimed at protecting the interests of African Americans. As the legal historian Paul Finkelman explains, "states' rights in antebellum America often meant the right of northern states to free visiting slaves, to protect free blacks from kidnapping, to prevent the extradition to the South of whites or blacks who helped slaves escape, and even the right of northerners to interfere in the rendition of fugitive slaves, if it could be done under the color of state law."[21]

The kidnapping of a wife and mother by the name of Margaret Morgan in Pennsylvania in 1837 made the state's Personal Liberty Law a subject of national debate and eventual Supreme Court review. Margaret's parents were enslaved individuals "owned" by a Maryland farmer by the name of John Ashmore. Ashmore allowed Margaret's parents to live in relative freedom on his estate in their old age; although Ashmore never formally manumitted the couple, he seems to have informally released them from their human bondage. Furthermore, he never claimed Margaret as his enslaved property. When Ashmore died without a will in 1824, all of his property passed through operation of law to his wife. The inventory of his estate included two enslaved children, both of them boys.[22]

Following John Ashmore's death, Margaret married Jerry Morgan, a free Black man from Pennsylvania living in Maryland, and had two children with him. In 1832, after Margaret's parents died, the Morgan family, with the apparent knowledge of Mrs. Ashmore, moved to York County, Pennsylvania, across the border from Maryland. The couple lived there undisturbed for five years and had another child.

For reasons we do not know, Mrs. Ashmore in 1837 decided to lay claim to Margaret and her children as her property. She made arrangements for four Maryland men, including a lawyer by the name of Edward Prigg, to travel to Pennsylvania as her agents to bring Margaret and her children back to Maryland. The four men had no trouble finding Margaret living openly in York County, suggesting that she did not consider herself to be a fugitive enslaved person. As required by the Pennsylvania Personal Liberty Law, the men secured an arrest warrant from a local justice of the peace. But when the bounty hunters brought Margaret and her three children before the same magistrate, he refused to grant them a certificate of removal from the state as also required by the Personal Liberty Law. Although we do not know why the magistrate refused to do so, it is possible that he concluded, entirely reasonably, that Margaret and her children, one of whom had been born in Pennsylvania, were free residents of the state.[23]

Although Prigg and his associates assured the magistrate that they would return Margaret and the children to their family home, they instead took their captives across the border to Maryland without a court order. Shortly thereafter, Jerry Morgan, on his way back to York County after meeting with the governor in Harrisburg to beg for help in the return of his family, lost his jacket holding the papers that proved he was a free man. After bounty hunters during that same trip attempted to seize him on the suspicion of being a fugitive enslaved person, Morgan tried to escape their capture and fell to his death in the Susquehanna River.[24] As for his wife and children, they were "sold to trade slavers, disappearing from the historical record."[25]

A Pennsylvania grand jury eventually indicted all four of Mrs. Ashmore's bounty hunters under the Personal Liberty Law for kidnapping Margaret and her children, but only Prigg was returned to York County for trial as part of a negotiated arrangement between Maryland and Pennsylvania to seek a final legal resolution from the U.S. Supreme Court.[26] After a Pennsylvania jury convicted Prigg, he challenged the constitutionality of the Personal Liberty Law. The Supreme Court in *Prigg v. Pennsylvania* struck down the Pennsylvania statute in 1842, constituting the first time that the Court used its power of judicial review to entirely void a state law.[27]

On its face, the Supreme Court's ruling in *Prigg* was a clear defeat for the concept of state sovereignty. The Court accepted the defendant's argument that Pennsylvania's Personal Liberty Law was unconstitutional under the Supremacy Clause because it was inconsistent with the Fugitive Slave Act of 1793. That federal statute allowed someone who claimed to be the owner of an enslaved person (or an owner's agent), after filing an affidavit with a local justice of the peace, to obtain a certificate of removal from a federal or state judge authorizing the taking of the person out of the state and back to slavery in the South. The federal law gave enslavers the right to sue any person who interfered with the removal process; that person could be subject to a $500 criminal penalty and liable for civil damages as a result of any economic injuries to owners caused by the interference. At the same time, the federal statute did not call for legal procedures allowing the person subject to the removal order to challenge it on the basis of mistaken identity. It was primarily for that reason that northern states enacted

Personal Liberty Laws: to protect free African Americans from being kidnapped and forced into slavery in the South. But the Supreme Court in *Prigg* held that Congress, under the Constitution's Fugitive Slave Clause, had the *exclusive* authority to legislate in matters related to fugitive slaves, leaving no room for state regulations. With one stroke of the pen, the Court deemed all Personal Liberty Laws unconstitutional.

The Court's opinion in *Prigg* was written by Joseph Story, a justice who was committed to strengthening the federal government's powers and had little patience for states' rights claims. He was also a critic of slavery. In having to choose between, on the one hand, protecting Congress's prerogative to preempt or displace state laws in those areas over which the Constitution granted it legislative authority and, on the other, his opposition to slavery, the nationalist and anti-states' rights Story chose the former.[28]

According to Story, the Constitution's Fugitive Slave Clause, despite its textual silence on the subject, not only authorized Congress to enact the Fugitive Slave Act of 1793, but also rendered exclusive its authority to regulate in matters related to fugitive slaves. In justifying one of the Court's first rulings applying Congress's constitutional authority under the Supremacy Clause to preempt state legislation, Story explained that the Fugitive Slave Clause created a "new and positive right" to "seize and retake fugitive slaves." This right was "confined to no territorial limits, and bounded by no state institutions or policy. The natural inference deductible from this consideration certainly is . . . that it belongs to the legislative department of the national government, to which it owes its origin and establishment."[29] According to Story, *uniformity* of policy was constitutionally mandated because the recovery of fugitive slaves would be impossible if different states imposed different procedural and other legal requirements before such recovery could take place. Only by placing the authority to regulate the return of fugitive slaves "exclusive[ly] in Congress" would "every evil and every danger" purportedly associated with a multiplicity of different state requirements be effectively addressed.[30]

In defending the federal government's broad authority to preempt state legislation impacting fugitive slaves, Story's ruling in *Prigg* nationalized the institution of slavery, which up until then had been understood to be entirely a creature of state law. By preempting all state laws that might burden an enslaver's so-called right of recapture, *Prigg* applied to the entire nation the presumption codified in the laws of southern states that Blackness equaled enslaved status. In addition, under *Prigg*, federal law immunized slaveholders and their agents from the application of state anti-kidnapping laws. As Finkelman explains, *Prigg* meant that "all free blacks were subject to being seized as slaves, and no northern law could protect them. Under Story's ruling, the Constitution fundamentally altered the principle that slavery was a creature of local . . . regulation. It was now a national institution." Unfortunately, Story used "*Prigg* to further strengthen the federal government [at] the cost [of] the freedom of some blacks—such as Margaret Morgan and her children. It was a cost Story was willing to make African-Americans pay—as long as he could rationalize it as essential to expanding federal power."[31] In the end, Story disagreed with the states' sovereignty arguments that served as the foundations for the Personal Liberty Laws' constitutionality more than he disapproved of slavery, viewing such laws as a greater threat to the union than slavery.

But even a committed nationalist like Story had to accept that the *Constitution's recognition of state sovereignty placed some limits on the federal government's authority* to regulate fugitive slaves. In particular, and crucially, the Constitution prohibited the national government from using state officials to enforce a federal law (in this case, the Fugitive Slave Act of 1793) over the objections of their states. As Story explained in *Prigg*, "the states cannot . . . be compelled to enforce [federal law]; and it might well be deemed an unconstitutional exercise of the power of interpretation, to insist, that the states are bound to provide means to carry into effect the duties of the national government, nowhere delegated or intrusted to them by the constitution."[32] This meant that the part of the Fugitive Slave Act that required state magistrates to issue certificates of removal could not be constitutionally enforced in the face of northern states' objections to having their judges and other officials participate in the return of African Americans to slavery.

Story made clear in *Prigg* that states were free to enact legislation prohibiting their officials from assisting with the return of fugitive slaves. While northern states could not institute procedural requirements making it more difficult for enslavers to recapture their human property, states were *constitutionally empowered* to prevent their officials from being commandeered by the federal government to assist in detaining African Americans simply on the basis that they were alleged to be runaway slaves.

Given that the Court in *Prigg* struck down Personal Liberty Laws while deeming federal authority to regulate in the area of fugitive slaves to be so extensive that it preempted or precluded the exercise of state sovereignty, it may seem that the Court's additional holding that the federal government could not commandeer state officials to participate in returning fugitive enslaved people to their "owners" was a minor victory for state sovereignty. But it turned out that the federalist principle, recognized in *Prigg*, that states are constitutionally entitled to control how their officials and resources are used to achieve national objectives was of immense *practical* importance because, as late as the 1840s, there were almost no federal mechanisms or personnel available to enforce the federal Fugitive Slave Act of 1793. At the time Prigg and the other men kidnapped Margaret Morgan, for example, there were only two federal judges in the entire state of Pennsylvania, neither of whom heard cases close to where she lived.[33] It would have been considerably more expensive and time consuming for the kidnappers to take Margaret before a federal judge than to a local state magistrate. This type of practical, as opposed to legal, roadblock meant that Story's recognition that states had the constitutional authority to refuse to make their officials and resources available to assist the federal government in the pursuit of its policy objectives (in this case, to return runaway enslaved people to their "owners"), made the return of fugitive slaves, ironically enough, significantly more difficult after *Prigg* than before it. The reality was that the federalist component of Story's otherwise nationalist ruling allowed northern states, in effect, to nullify the Fugitive Slave Act.[34]

The nullification first became apparent in Massachusetts a few months after *Prigg* when a Boston police constable, enforcing a warrant issued by a state court on behalf of a Virginia plantation owner, arrested a Black man by the name of George Latimer. Justice Lemuel Shaw of the Massachusetts Supreme Judicial Court refused to order Latimer's release from a city jail pending a hearing in federal court, explaining that *Prigg* had granted the enslaver the right to keep the prisoner detained until the federal courts could determine his fate. But, as the American studies scholar Andrew Delbanco explains, "the Latimer case drove Boston into a fury. . . . Petitions with over sixty-five thousand signatures and weighing more than 150 pounds were delivered in a barrel to the Massachusetts State Senate demanding a new law prohibiting cooperation by state authorities" with the forced removal of Black people from the commonwealth.[35] The state legislature obliged by enacting what became known as the Latimer Law, prohibiting Massachusetts officials from detaining anyone under the federal Fugitive Slave Act of 1793 and from using state facilities for that purpose.

Connecticut, New Hampshire, Pennsylvania, and Vermont soon enacted their own new Personal Liberty Laws, "closing their jails and courtrooms to slave catchers and prohibiting state officials from helping to recover runaway slaves."[36] These new statutes were more abolitionist in spirit and intent than the earlier Personal Liberty Laws enacted in the 1820s. The objective now became more explicitly to protect fugitive enslaved people and not just free northern African Americans living in fear of being indiscriminately kidnapped by bounty hunters. Also in the 1840s, northern states such as Pennsylvania and New York, which previously had accommodated southerners by permitting them to visit with their "human property" for a few months, lifted those accommodations in order to free all enslaved people who were brought into their territories by enslavers.[37] At around the same time, the governors of New York and Maine relied on states' rights arguments to refuse to hand over free African Americans who were wanted in the South for helping enslaved individuals escape.[38]

The Supreme Court, in its infamous ruling in *Dred Scott v. Sandford*, eventually held that enslavers had constitutionally protected property rights in Black human beings, which meant that neither the federal government nor northern states had the constitutional authority to render enslaved people free regardless of their physical presence outside of the South. In addition to holding that neither enslaved people nor their descendants were citizens protected by the Constitution, *Dred Scott* further *nationalized* the slavery issue by holding that enslavers had protected rights over their human property under the federal Constitution.[39] This led pro-South President James Buchanan in 1859 to boast that *Dred Scott* granted enslavers a "vested right under the Federal Constitution, [which] neither Congress nor a Territorial legislature nor any human power has any authority to annul or impair."[40]

The lack of a federal workforce available to assist in the forced return of fugitive enslaved people, when coupled with the northern states' unwillingness to make their officials available to help with that despicable task, meant that in the years following *Prigg* it became increasingly more difficult for enslavers to recover their human property who had escaped to the North. This led white southerners to continue to press for a *national* solution to the fugitive slave issue. What southerners truly wanted was a new federal statute that would (1) invalidate the northern states' new Personal Liberty Laws codifying *Prigg's* anti-commandeering principle and (2) require those states to assist in the capture of runaway slaves. But slavery supporters had to accept that *Prigg's* anti-commandeering principle prevented Congress from enacting legislation requiring northern states to fulfill what southerners believed were their constitutional obligations.[41]

While *Prigg* did not allow southerners to use federal law to force northern states to assist in the rendition of enslaved people, it did encourage other forms of federal involvement in protecting the interests of enslavers. After much internal debate and conflict, Congress in 1850 enacted a new Fugitive Slave Act. That statute authorized a claimant to bring the alleged fugitive before *federal officials*, including ones commissioned under the statute in every county in the nation. The new law prohibited captured individuals from testifying on their own behalf and called for the imposition of a steep fine or imprisonment of up to six months for anyone who obstructed enforcement, including by harboring or concealing fugitives. Finkelman notes that, "if literally enforced, a northerner could be fined, sued, or jailed [under the new federal law] for merely giving a black person walking down the road a piece of bread or a cup of water, or allowing the black traveler to sleep in his barn."[42] At the same time, the statute did not impose penalties on those who kidnapped free African Americans, which was precisely what the northern states' Personal Liberty Laws struck down in *Prigg* had attempted to do. Among other things, the federal 1850 law aimed to dismantle the procedural protections for Black people, deemed to be fugitive enslaved individuals, implemented by the northern states' Personal Liberty Laws.[43]

In the end, neither side was satisfied with the new federal fugitive slave statute. Despite their success in enacting a law that turned the federal government into an aider and abettor of slavery, southerners remained resentful of and agitated by the constitutional impediment that prevented them from going even further by using federal law to force northern states to assist with rendition efforts. In the 1850s, several additional northern states enacted new Personal Liberty Laws prohibiting their officials from assisting in the capture of African Americans on behalf of their purported southern owners and granting individuals accused of being fugitive enslaved people further procedural rights, including the provision of free legal representation.[44] These latest laws "were greeted in the South with something between exasperation and outrage."[45]

For their part, northerners were angered by the new Fugitive Slave Act's nationalization of slavery. The inability of northern states to prevent the increased incursion into their jurisdictions of federal authority seeking to protect the interests of enslavers further flamed abolitionist sentiments. In 1854, a rowdy crowd in Milwaukee freed a fugitive enslaved person by the name of Joshua Glover after he was captured by a federal marshal, allowing him to escape to freedom in Canada. Federal officials then arrested Sherman Booth, the editor of a Milwaukee abolitionist newspaper, for violating the Fugitive Slave Act, accusing him of aiding and abetting a fugitive enslaved person. Reflecting the extent to which many in the North resisted federal involvement on the question of fugitive enslaved people, the Wisconsin Supreme Court issued a writ of habeas corpus ordering Booth released and then refused to submit to federal jurisdiction by withholding the official record in the case from the U.S. Supreme Court. In 1858, that court reversed the state court's issuance of the writ anyway in a ruling that upheld the Fugitive Slave Act's constitutionality.[46]

A similar dispute arose in Oberlin, Ohio, after abolitionists rescued a fugitive enslaved person by the name of John Price. The federal government successfully prosecuted two local abolitionists for liberating Price; the two men had hidden Price in the home of Oberlin College's president and then arranged to have him taken to freedom in Canada. The abolitionists took their case before the Ohio Supreme Court. Unlike Wisconsin's high court, the Ohio court denied a writ of habeas corpus, but it did so over the dissent of two justices.[47] As the historian H. Robert Baker explains, the Wisconsin and Ohio judges "who defied the Fugitive Slave Act grounded their resistance not just in abstract notions of natural law, but in the power of the state to defend real liberty against public or private encroachment. Their claim boiled down to this: alleged fugitives deserved the same protections of their liberty as any other resident of the state."[48]

Southerners in the late 1850s had no real grounds for complaining about federal intrusion into the internal affairs of their states or about an insufficient federal commitment to slavery. In fact, during the years leading up to the Civil War, the federal government repeatedly came to the assistance of enslavers. As Finkelman explains, "by the end of the [1850s], slavery was legal in all the federal territories, the federal government was vigorously enforcing a draconian fugitive slave law that had enabled hundreds of masters to recover their runaways, and the Supreme Court had expanded the right of masters to travel in the free states with their slaves."[49] Although southerners, following the example of South Carolina senator John Calhoun, repeatedly raised states' rights arguments when they found it politically convenient to do so, *they also frequently complained that the federal government was not doing more to force* recalcitrant northern states to assist with the rendition of enslaved African Americans. As Finkelman notes, "because the Constitution of 1787 was deeply protective of slavery, and the Supreme Court enhanced this protection, there was a direct tie [between] nationalism and slavery. This meant that, before 1861, the slave states did not need to have a states' rights ideology to protect their most important social and economic institutions. A nationalist position did that for them."[50]

It was southerners, before the presidential election of 1860, who pushed for a *national* solution to the slavery question. And it was northerners who, time and again, relied on *states' rights* arguments to try to undermine slavery. This historical record starkly illustrates how the mere push for uniform national policies, or, alternatively, the push for state-based ones, by itself tells us nothing about the rightness or appropriateness of those policies.

Historians disagree on the question of whether Story foresaw the practical consequences of his *Prigg* ruling. They disagree, in other words, on whether Story *purposefully* undermined slavery by upholding Congress's exclusive authority to legislate in matters related to fugitive enslaved people while at the same time effectively rendering the Fugitive Slave Act of 1793 toothless because of the unavailability of viable federal enforcement mechanisms, in the absence of cooperation by northern states, for returning African Americans to the horrors of slavery.[51] But regardless of what Story intended, there can be little doubt of the importance of the anti-commandeering principle his ruling announced. That principle stands for the crucial federalist proposition that even when the national government is exercising its otherwise constitutional authority to regulate, it cannot mandate that state and local officials help implement federal policy over the objections of state governments.

The Supreme Court returned to enforcing the anti-commandeering principle at the end of the twentieth century, including in a 1997 case called *Printz v. United States*.[52] At issue in *Printz* was a provision of the Brady Handgun Violence Prevention Act of 1993 that required the U.S. Attorney General to establish a national background check program that would, by 1998, vet individuals who wanted to purchase firearms from gun dealers. The new statute also required state and local law enforcement officials, during the five years needed to establish the federal background check system, to conduct the checks before issuing handgun permits. A handful of Arizona law enforcement officials challenged the federal statute's constitutionality by arguing that forcing state and local officials to pursue federal policy objectives violated the Tenth Amendment's anti-commandeering principle.

As tends to happen with controversial issues of policy such as those involving gun safety regulations, the federalism dispute in *Printz* was viewed by many people through predictable ideological lenses. On one side, conservative supporters of gun rights argued that the Brady Act entailed an unconstitutional overreach by the federal government that violated state sovereignty. On the other side, liberal supporters of gun safety laws saw the measure as a reasonable way for Congress to address the national epidemic of gun violence, one that did not impermissibly infringe on state prerogatives. The Supreme Court's ruling in *Printz* mirrored this predictable ideological divide. In an opinion written by Justice Antonin Scalia, the Court's five conservative justices struck down the Brady Act provision at issue on the ground that it violated the Tenth Amendment because it mandated that state and local officials help the federal government implement federal policy. Four liberal justices vigorously dissented, largely rejecting the anti-commandeering principle by concluding that "when Congress exercises the powers delegated to it by the Constitution, it may impose affirmative obligations on executive and judicial officers of state and local governments as well as ordinary citizens."[53]

I am not interested here in addressing whether particular Supreme Court opinions, such as *Prigg* and *Printz*, were correctly decided as a matter of constitutional law. Instead, my objective is to explore the federalist principles behind those rulings and their relevance to progressives. The juxtaposition of *Prigg* and *Printz* shows that there is no intrinsic link between the deployment of federalist principles, on the one hand, and either particular ideological perspectives or specific policy objectives, on the other. In *Prigg*, it was liberals who benefited from the implementation of the federalist anti-commandeering principle because it allowed state and local officials in northern states to refuse to help the national government enforce its fugitive slave law. In *Printz*, it was the opposite: the application of federalist principles allowed conservative opponents of gun safety regulations to delay the implementation and enforcement of a national gun background check program until the federal government had the capability to carry it out by itself.

It is true, of course, that the issue in *Prigg* of whether and how to return fugitive enslaved human beings to the genocidal southern plantations raised very different moral and policy questions than those at stake under the gun safety measure in *Printz*. But those undoubtedly crucial differences are *external* to the federalist principle upheld in both rulings. In other words, *the question of whether the federal government has the constitutional authority to require state and local officials to implement federal regulations can and should be answered independently of whether particular federal policies are defensible on policy or moral grounds.* The federalist principle of limiting federal authority in order to protect state sovereignty is itself programmatically and morally neutral and, as such, can be deployed either for good or for ill.

It is understandable, given the unconscionable number of deaths and injuries caused by the easy availability of firearms in the United States, a human carnage that has only grown worse in the decades since *Printz*, that many progressives criticize the use of federalist principles, as the Court did in *Printz*, to undermine the federal government's ability to implement policies that respond effectively to national problems such as the gun violence epidemic. But, as I argue throughout this book, some constitutional principles are worth defending regardless of whether their application make the attainment of our short-term policy objectives in any particular context more difficult. If it is hard for progressives to accept the value of federalism in the context of *Printz*, they should be able to immediately recognize it in the context of *Prigg* given that northern states repeatedly relied on federalist mechanisms and principles to try to undermine slavery.

The value of federalism for progressives was also evident in the efforts by state and local officials to resist the Trump administration's implementation of deeply misguided and harmful immigration and environmental policies, among others. The value should also be evident from the ways in which some states have responded to the lack of an effective federal response to the bloodshed caused by gun violence by enacting sensible gun regulations of their own (more on all of this in the next chapter).

The bottom line is this: sometimes the federal government uses its power for good (as, in my opinion, in the case of the Brady Handgun Violence Prevention Act of 1993) and sometimes for ill (as, we can all agree, in the case of the Fugitive Slave Act of 1793). It is precisely because the latter is a possibility that progressives should accept and even embrace some constitutional limits on federal government power that result from protecting state sovereignty. Sometimes protecting the sovereignty interests of states will make it more difficult for the federal government to implement important and worthwhile progressive policies; at other times, such protection will make it more difficult for the national government to carry out policies that progressives believe are misguided, harmful, or discriminatory. As explored in the next chapter, the Trump years showed why the costs for progressives arising from the application of federalist mechanisms and principles in the former context is a price that progressives should be willing to pay to enjoy the benefits and protections engendered by the application of the same mechanisms and principles in the latter situation.

Federalism and States' Rights between the Civil War and Trump's Election

One of the reasons many contemporary progressives are skeptical of federalist principles and accompanying states' rights arguments is that they associate them with right-wing, reactionary, and racist claims. As a historical matter, that association is an entirely understandable one. After all, the practical impact of northern states' reliance on federalism to defend their Personal Liberty Laws paled in comparison to that of southerners' reliance on state sovereignty claims to justify both the enslavement of African Americans and the secession of southern states from the union over the slavery issue.

Abraham Lincoln's quest for the presidency was a game changer for southerners because they correctly surmised that if the former Illinois congressman became president, they could no longer count on the federal government to help expand slavery into new territories and states. It was at that point that southerners began to more forcefully supplement their states' rights defense of slavery with the ultimate states' rights claim: that states enjoyed an intrinsic and inviolable sovereignty that allowed them to unilaterally secede from the union, eviscerating the nation as it then existed. But one of the southerners' principal complaints, up to that point, had been grounded in the northern states' unwillingness to cooperate with what slavery defenders considered to be the constitutional obligations of *all* states to protect the property rights of enslavers. As South Carolina's secession declaration of 1860 put it, "we assert that fourteen of the states have deliberately refused for years past to fulfill their constitutional obligations, and we refer to their own statutes [the Personal Liberty Laws] for the proof."[54]

There can be no more dangerous and pernicious understanding of federalism claims than one that rationalizes and justifies both the enslavement of human beings and the power of states to leave the union and take arms up against it for the purpose of defending slavery. To contend that the Constitution allowed states to leave the union was to defend a deeply flawed misunderstanding of the document's meaning. The transition from a league of independent nation states under the Articles of Confederation to the formation of a unified republic under the Constitution required states, once they chose to join the new nation, to waive their power to unilaterally exit.[55] Although the constitutional issue should have been clear, arguments and claims based on constitutional meanings and obligations were, of course, incapable of keeping southern states in the fold once they rejected the legitimacy of federal government authority following Lincoln's election. After the Confederacy took up arms against the U.S. government and the northern states in order to defend the institution of slavery, the future of the union was decided not in the halls of Congress or by the Supreme Court, but on countless battlefields on both sides of the Mason-Dixon line at the tragic cost of hundreds of thousands of lives.

Southern whites might have been eventually defeated in those battlefields, but that defeat only served to strengthen their commitment to state sovereignty as a means of maintaining as much of the economic, legal, and social privileges they had enjoyed before the war, privileges that depended on the continued subordination and exploitation of Black people and their labor. States' rights became the rallying cry around which southern whites first opposed Reconstruction and then instituted the apartheid Jim Crow regime that followed.

The federal government sought to promote the civil and political equality of formerly enslaved people during the Reconstruction years in several different ways. One way was through the Freedmen's Bureau, a federal agency tasked with assisting formerly enslaved people with their transition into civil society. The Bureau helped to make possible a limited redistribution of abandoned or confiscated property to former slaves. It also established some schools and hospitals for formerly enslaved people, oversaw the introduction of a system of free labor for African Americans in the South, and prodded southern courts to adjudicate disputes in race neutral ways.[56]

The year after the Thirteenth Amendment abolished slavery in 1865, Congress enacted the nation's first federal civil rights law, prohibiting discrimination on the basis of race "under color of law" in the enforcement of contracts and the enjoyment of property rights. In 1868, Congress proposed and the states approved the Fourteenth Amendment which, among other things, granted citizenship status to almost everyone born in the United States while guaranteeing to all persons the equal protection of the law. In 1870, the Constitution was amended again to prohibit the federal and state governments from denying voting rights on the basis of race. Crucially, the three post-Civil War amendments granted Congress the authority to enact legislation to enforce them, constituting the first time that the Constitution was amended to *expand* the federal government's power. All of this meant that, as the historian Eric Foner explains, "the Civil War crystalized in the minds of northerners the idea of a powerful national state protecting the rights of citizens." This period constituted, in effect, the nation's second founding, one that "not only put abolition, equal rights, and black male suffrage into the Constitution, but in its provisions for national enforcement made the federal government for the first time what [the abolitionist Massachusetts senator Charles] Sumner called 'the custodian of freedom.'"[57]

White southern resistance to federal efforts to guarantee a minimum of economic, civil, and political equality for African Americans was immediate, fierce, and relentless. Within months of the Civil War's end, almost all of the former Confederate states had enacted laws, known as Black Codes, which required African Americans, among other things, to sign annual employment contracts in order to work and expanded vagrancy statutes to harass and intimidate formerly enslaved people. The Mississippi code prohibited African Americans from renting land in urban areas while the South Carolina version prohibited Blacks from working in any capacity other than as farmers or servants unless they paid a financially ruinous tax. After the enactment of the federal Civil Rights Act of 1866, southern states responded by making the Black Codes racially neutral on their face, but enforcement remained deeply racist and biased. President Andrew Johnson had vetoed the civil rights bill—a veto overridden by the Republican-controlled Congress—on the ground that federal protection of African Americans' civil rights reflected such a broad understanding of the national government's power that it violated "all our experience as a people" and constituted a "stride toward centralization, and the concentration of all legislative powers in the national government."[58] As Frederick Douglass noted around this time, no "political idea" was "more deeply rooted in the minds of men of all sections of the country [than] the right of each State to control its own local affairs."[59]

The white supremacy cause in the South was aided by the reactionary terror and hatred spread by the Ku Klux Klan between 1868 and 1871. During that period, the Klan was responsible for thousands of acts of violence targeting the lives and property of Blacks and white Republicans in the South.[60] The human pain and suffering caused by the terrorism reached such disturbing levels that Congress responded in 1871 by enacting the Ku Klux Klan Act, which deemed efforts to deny citizens the right to vote, serve on juries, and enjoy the equal protection of the law on the basis of race to be a criminal offense to be prosecuted by federal attorneys. The statute, which led to the successful federal indictments of hundreds of Klansmen, was criticized by almost all Democrats and even some Republicans on the ground that it was an unwarranted intrusion into states' prerogatives. As one opponent put it, the states "remained 'the depositories of the rights of the individual'—if Congress could enact a 'general criminal code' and punish offenses like assault and murder, 'what is the need of the state governments?'"[61]

Congress's Reconstruction Act of 1867 called for temporary federal military rule over the former Confederate states (with the exception of Tennessee, which by then already had rejoined the Union). It also required those states to adopt new constitutions guaranteeing the right of men to vote regardless of race and to ratify the Fourteenth Amendment. The federal guarantees of political and voting rights for African American men resulted in the election of new southern legislatures that included Blacks, many of them former slaves, among their members. These legislatures enacted some reforms—states such as Louisiana, Mississippi, and South Carolina swept away their Black Codes while adopting new laws prohibiting discrimination on the basis of race by transportation and other licensed businesses. But the reality was that conservative whites remained firmly in control of almost all aspects of political, social, and economic life in the South. Soon, the limited civil rights progress of the early Reconstruction years ended as Republicans in Congress began to lose their enthusiasm for further federal involvement in the South and as the Democratic Party regained its influence in southern state governments and in Congress through racist and states' rights appeals to the millions of southern white supremacists—rich and poor alike—who mourned the loss of the Confederacy.

Reconstruction's last gasp was Congress's long-delayed enactment in 1875 of a federal civil rights statute, championed for years by Massachusetts senator Charles Sumner, which prohibited some businesses, such as inns, theaters, and railroads, from discriminating among their customers on the basis of race. The only reason the bill passed was because its supporters, following Sumner's death, dropped a highly controversial provision that would have required the racial integration of public schools.[62] Shortly after a lame duck Congress enacted the 1875 civil rights law, a large Democratic majority took over both houses of Congress determined to end Reconstruction. Following the contested 1876 presidential election, the Republicans agreed to end federal involvement in southern affairs as a means of guaranteeing the basic civil rights of African Americans in return for the Democrats allowing Republican Rutherford Hayes to become president.[63]

In 1883, the Supreme Court struck down the Civil Rights Act of 1875 as an unconstitutional exercise of federal authority that purportedly interfered with state sovereignty. According to the Court in *The Civil Rights Cases*, the Fourteenth Amendment only authorized Congress to address discrimination by the states, not the type of discrimination by private parties prohibited by the federal statute. As the Court put it, the amendment "does not invest Congress with power to legislate upon subjects which are within the domain of State legislation." It was for the states, and not Congress, to regulate and protect the rights of private individuals vis-à-vis one another. According to the Court, allowing Congress to regulate the private provision of goods and services to customers would be "repugnant to the Tenth Amendment" because it would "supersede[] and displace[] State legislation on the same subject . . . and assumes that the matter is one that belongs to the domain of national regulation."[64] The Court's decision in *The Civil Rights Cases* followed another ruling in which the justices, in *The Slaughterhouse Cases*, had interpreted the post–Civil War constitutional amendments extremely narrowly, including by holding that federalist concerns prevented the Fourteenth Amendment's Privileges or Immunities Clause from altering the balance between the federal and state governments by making the Bill of Rights protections applicable to the states.[65]

In the years that followed, the states of the former Confederacy exercised their power "within the domain of State legislation" by enacting dozens of laws mandating racial segregation in almost every aspect of public, economic, and social life. As the historian C. Vann Woodward explained in his classic account of the Jim Crow era, "the phase that began in 1877 was inaugurated by the withdrawal of federal troops from the South, the abandonment of the Negro as a ward of the nation, the giving up of the attempt to give the freedman his civil and political equality, and the acquiescence of the rest of the country in the South's demand that the whole problem be left to the disposition of the dominant Southern white people."[66]

When the segregation statutes that constituted Jim Crow's legal backbone were challenged in court as violating the Fourteenth Amendment, southern states argued that the Constitution did not limit their regulatory authority to keep the races apart. To its great shame, the Supreme Court agreed—it upheld the constitutionality of Jim Crow laws by claiming that requiring racially "separate but equal" facilities, services, and opportunities did not violate the Equal Protection Clause.[67]

In addition to enacting laws that segregated the races in almost all aspects of public, economic, and social life, southern states at the end of the century moved to aggressively limit the ability of African American men to vote, thereby nullifying the Fifteenth Amendment's prohibition on racial discrimination in voting. Between 1885 and 1908, all eleven of the former Confederacy states instituted literacy tests, property requirements, and poll taxes, with accompanying "grandfather clause" exemptions for whites, rendering the federal guarantee against racial discrimination in voting a sham. As a result, turnout by African American male voters "in the South fell to 2 percent in 1912 from 61 percent in 1880."[68] In Louisiana, for example, there were 130,334 African American men registered to vote in 1895; eight years later, that number was down to a paltry 1,342.[69] Voting restrictions intended to disenfranchise African Americans remained firmly in place until Congress enacted the Voting Rights Act of 1965. That statute's ability to guarantee racial minorities equal access to the ballot box, as we will see, was gutted in 2013 when the Supreme Court, in the name of federalism, struck down one of its key provisions.[70]

The fact that the federal government in 1877 ended its efforts to promote the basic civil rights of formerly enslaved individuals did not mean, in the years that followed, that it was reluctant to intervene, sometimes with force, in local affairs. But that intervention was now done not on behalf of racial equality, but to protect the interests of economic elites. Within months of Reconstruction's end and the removal of federal troops from the South, the Hayes administration began deploying those same troops to help break railroad and industrial strikes called for by an increasingly assertive labor movement. Former President Ulysses Grant noted the irony that while the entire Democratic Party and many Republicans had thought it "horrible" to use federal troops during his administration "to protect the lives of negroes[,] now . . . there is no hesitation about exhausting the whole power of the [federal] government to suppress a strike on the slightest intimation that danger threatens."[71]

The same conservative forces that had decried federal involvement in trying to provide formerly enslaved individuals with a modicum of civil equality, now demanded federal intervention to protect the property rights and wealth of the nation's capitalist class. Similarly, the same people who bristled at the notion that federal courts, in enforcing the Constitution, had the authority to strike down racist state laws, now pleaded for federal judicial intervention to strike down laws that regulated the operation of the free market. Unfortunately, the federal courts, led by the Supreme Court, were only too willing to oblige.

The insidious uses of federalist principles in American history have often been motivated by racism, given that they have been intended to keep the federal government from interfering with the ability of states and local governments to maintain racially subordinating policies and practices firmly in place. But the problematic deployment of federalist arguments has not been limited to issues of race; such claims have also been used to protect the property interests of America's economic elites. An ideologically driven Supreme Court was a leading contributor to this use of federalism during the early decades of the twentieth century when it repeatedly struck down reasonable, and, in hindsight, clearly constitutional economic regulations that sought to temper some of the most harmful effects of unrestrained capitalism.

This particular group of Supreme Court justices was brazenly inconsistent in its legal approach. On the one hand, the justices claimed that the Constitution protected the right to contract as a fundamental liberty under the Due Process Clause. The Court during this era struck down a slew of *state* laws—regulating everything from minimum wages to maximum work hours to consumer safety—on the ground that they violated the constitutionally protected economic liberties of businesses and employers.[72] In doing so, the justices greatly *expanded* the power of the federal judiciary to *limit* state sovereignty. But, on the other hand, the conservative justices embraced states' rights claims to strike down similar *federal* legislation.[73] In short, a majority of the justices during the first decades of the twentieth century prioritized the protection of laissez-faire capitalism over all other considerations, leading them to repeatedly strike down democratically enacted laws at both the federal and state levels. The justices conveniently ignored federalism concerns in striking down state laws that regulated the marketplace, while relying on those concerns to strike down federal laws that did the same.

The pernicious use of federalism to advance a rigid capitalist ideology was evident in the Court's response to a constitutional challenge to the Keating-Owen Act, a 1916 federal statute prohibiting the movement in interstate commerce of goods manufactured by children under the age of fourteen or at factories where children between the ages of fourteen and sixteen worked for more than eight hours a day. Congress, through this law, did not attempt to categorically ban child labor across the country. Instead, it sought to use its constitutional authority to regulate interstate commerce by banning such commerce in goods made by child labor.

But the Supreme Court in the 1918 case of *Hammer v. Dagenhart* ruled that the Tenth Amendment required that regulations related to the production of commercial goods be enacted *exclusively* by the states. As the Court saw it, state sovereignty, in effect, blocked Congress's power to regulate the production of goods under its interstate commerce authority. According to the Court's expansive understanding of exclusive state sovereignty, the Constitution entrusted the power to regulate the labor used to produce commercial products, whether of children or adults, "purely [to] state authority."[74]

In reaching this perplexing conclusion, the Court ignored the fact that the goods in question were being moved through interstate commerce, thus seeming to fall directly under Congress's constitutionally delegated authority to regulate such commerce. The Court also refused to account for practical economic considerations—states that wanted to ban child labor would pay a steep economic price for doing so as long as other states refused to follow suit given that manufacturers in the latter group of states would be able to produce goods more cheaply by using children and, in doing so, reap significant economic benefits. The issue of perverse economic incentives associated with child labor justified a national solution to a pressing human problem. All of this means, as law professor Erwin Chemerinsky explains, that the child labor ruling "cannot be understood as anything other than a reflection of the ideology of the justices at the time and their hostility to regulation of business, even when it was a law to protect children."[75]

The Court's reliance on states' rights claims to strike down economic federal legislation continued well into the 1930s. As the Roosevelt administration and Congress tried desperately to cope with the financial and social devastation wrought by the Great Depression, their regulatory efforts were relentlessly undermined by Supreme Court justices who relied on federalism considerations, among others, to repeatedly strike down legislation.

In 1936, for example, the Court in *Carter v. Carter Coal Company* struck down a federal statute that allowed local coal boards, following collective bargaining between coal companies and unions, to set the wages and hours of employees. According to the justices, wages and working conditions were matters related to the production of goods and, as a result, fell under the states' exclusive control. The Court explained that the legislation in question presented a "danger" because it was the "first step" in the direction of "the federal government . . . taking over the power of the states." If not stopped, "the end of the journey may find the states so despoiled of their powers . . . as to reduce them to little more than geographic subdivisions of the national domain."[76]

The Court, around this time, struck down several other federal economic regulations, including ones providing a pension system for railroad workers, stabilizing the prices of agricultural products, and ensuring the quality of poultry shipped in interstate commerce.[77] The Court's judicial activism in the face of a severe nationwide economic crisis led to mounting political pressure to abandon its broad understanding of state sovereignty as a limitation on federal authority, as well as its expansive claims regarding economic liberties as fundamental rights. After a newly re-elected and emboldened President Roosevelt tried to dilute the power of conservative justices by controversially proposing that Congress expand the number of Supreme Court justices, the Court in 1937 abruptly changed course and began upholding Congress's authority to regulate the conditions of economic production and exchange, including those related to labor and safety issues, in all sorts of ways.[78] Almost sixty years went by before the Supreme Court would again strike down a federal statute as an unconstitutional exercise of Congress's authority to regulate interstate commerce.[79]

The federal government's budget grew larger as a result of the continued economic problems and dislocations caused by the Great Depression and of the nation's entry into World War II. In fact, 1940 was a notable year "because it was the last time state and local government revenues and outlays were roughly on a par with those of the federal government."[80] At the same time, the number of federal government employees did not keep pace with its spending, requiring the national government to rely on state officials to manage and administer federally funded programs. This combination of national funding and state administration, which is still very much with us today, allowed states to manage a slew of new federal programs—everything from subsidized health care and homeownership to the G.I. Bill—in ways that effectively excluded Black people.[81] In addition, the federal government routinely crafted New Deal programs in ways that appeased the racist concerns of many white southerners, a crucial component of Roosevelt's voting bloc. For example, "it was largely at the behest of Southern Democrats that farm and domestic workers—more than half of the nation's Black work force at the time—were excluded from New Deal policies, including the Social Security and Wagner Acts of 1935 (the Wagner Act ensured the right of workers to collective bargaining), and the Fair Labor Standards Act of 1938, which set a minimum wage and established the eight-hour workday."[82]

States' rights arguments were also the rhetorical weapon of choice embraced by southerners who opposed the Supreme Court's 1954 ruling in *Brown v. Board of Education*.[83] Many white southerners resentfully viewed *Brown*'s call for the racial desegregation of public schools as yet another pernicious form of federal interference with states' prerogatives. Senator Harry Byrd of Virginia, for example, contended that the decision was "the most serious blow that has yet been struck against the rights of the states in a matter vitally affecting their autonomy and welfare."[84] The federal government, this time represented by the Supreme Court, was once again viewed by white southerners as improperly and unconstitutionally meddling in their affairs.

Southern states responded to *Brown* with a panoply of laws meant to resist federal incursion into how they operated their public schools. Louisiana in 1954 made clear its disdain for *Brown* by adding a provision to its constitution bluntly stating that "all public elementary and secondary schools . . . shall be operated separately for white and colored children."[85] For their part, Arkansas voters approved a state constitutional amendment in 1956 requiring the legislature to interpose state sovereignty by doing everything within its power to nullify *Brown*.[86]

Alabama also amended its constitution in 1956 by making it clear that (1) there was no right to a public education and (2) the legislature had the authority to enact laws allowing parents to have their children "attend schools provided for their own race."[87] The first provision aimed to permit school districts to close down altogether rather than to integrate, an option pursued by some localities in the South until the Supreme Court put an end to the racist practice in 1964.[88] The second provision was a constitutional codification of a policy pursued by all southern states after *Brown* through what became known as "freedom to choose" laws. These measures, which the Supreme Court did not strike down until 1968, gave parents, rather than government officials, the ability to determine which schools their children attended.[89] The laws, in other words, sought to replace a system of de jure segregation with one of de facto segregation. The laws' supporters knew that the vast majority of white parents would choose to keep their children in white schools, while a significant number of African American parents would choose to try to protect their children from racist intimidation and violence by keeping them in Black schools.

In addition to closing down schools and implementing freedom to choose laws, southern states responded to *Brown* by enacting pupil placement laws and adopting so-called grade-a-year desegregation plans. The purpose of the former was to use seemingly neutral criteria, such as aptitude, psychological fitness, and health, to make school assignment decisions in ways that left racial segregation firmly in place.[90] The purpose of the latter was to make sure that no school system was fully desegregated in fewer than twelve years.[91] The Supreme Court, sensitive to southern opposition to *Brown*, refused to strike down either set of laws in the 1950s.[92]

The other branches of the federal government responded in similarly meek ways to the southern states' resistance to racial integration. President Dwight Eisenhower refused to support *Brown* in public and was quite critical of the ruling in private.[93] Congress enacted a civil rights statute in 1957, the first since the Reconstruction era, but its scope was limited and had no impact on the pace of school desegregation in the South. With the exception of Eisenhower's decision to send federal troops to restore order in Little Rock in 1957 after that city descended into violent chaos when school officials made a modest effort to desegregate one high school, the federal government in the 1950s remained a bystander observing from the sidelines. In fact, the most vocal federal officials on the issue of school integration were southern senators and congressmen. About one hundred of them issued a proclamation in 1956, dubbed the Southern Manifesto, which criticized *Brown* for constituting a "clear abuse of judicial power" and called on "all lawful means to bring about a reversal of this decision which is contrary to the Constitution." The signatories pledged their support for southern states in their resistance to federal authority and commended "the motives of those states which have declared the intention to resist forced integration by any lawful means."[94]

It was not until the 1960s that the Supreme Court began to strike down southern states' efforts to defy its order to racially integrate public schools. The federal government's feeble response to southern resistance to judicially-mandated school desegregation meant that in 1964, a full decade after *Brown*, *only 1 percent* of African American students in the eleven states that made up the old Confederacy attended schools with white children.[95]

By the early 1960s, the focus of racist resistance to federal civil rights protections expanded to include not just objections to school integration, but also fierce opposition to a comprehensive federal statute, eventually enacted as the Civil Rights Act of 1964, aimed at prohibiting racial discrimination by private employers, places of public accommodation, and recipients of federal funds. Opponents raised two principal arguments against the proposed statute. First, that it would impermissibly limit the liberty rights of business owners and employers to decide with whom to associate.[96] Second, that the bill constituted an effort to establish a form of oppressive federal control over the states' internal affairs. As Senator Norris Cotton put it in 1964, "the Founding Fathers learned from . . . history that civil rights enforced by a central government all too soon became oppressive tyrannies."[97] For their part, two southern congressmen complained that "this is not a proper field for Federal legislation. A matter such as discrimination in employment or in labor-union membership is best handled at the State or local level, or through the force of public opinion."[98] Opponents also claimed that "the destruction of individual liberty and freedom of choice resulting from the almost limitless extension of Federal Government control over individuals and businesses, rather than being in support of the Bill of Rights, is directly contrary to the spirit and intent thereof."[99]

The opponents' objections proved to be insufficient in the face of growing national disapproval of the ways in which southern racists, including state and local officials, responded violently to peaceful civil rights protests in states like Alabama and Mississippi. It now seemed that a majority of white Americans, for the first time in the nation's history, was ready to accept meaningful federal mandates promoting racial equality. After overcoming the longest filibuster in the Senate's history, spearheaded by southern Democrats and lasting 534 hours, 1 minute, and 51 seconds, the civil rights bill passed the Senate by a vote of 73 to 27. The House followed with its approval shortly thereafter.

The relationship between states' rights rhetoric and the defense of racist policies had become so tightly linked by the early 1960s that political scientist William Riker encapsulated the view of many progressives when he argued that federalism had nothing to do with protecting liberty and everything to do with promoting racism. As Riker explained in 1964, "the most persistent exponents of 'states' rights'—a doctrine that makes much of the freedom encouraging features of federalism—have been those who use the doctrine as a veiled defense first of slavery, then of civil tyranny. Here it seems that federalism may have more to do with destroying freedom than with encouraging it." Riker did not mince words when he added that if "one approves of Southern white racists, then one should approve of American federalism. If, on the other hand, . . . one disapproves of racism, one should disapprove of federalism."[100] This type of deep skepticism of federalism by progressives remained firmly in place for decades to come, as reflected, for example, in the claim by two liberal law professors in 1994 that federalism was nothing more than an "American neurosis" that lacked "any normative principle . . . worthy of protection."[101]

States' rights objections to the enactment and enforcement of federal civil rights laws gained less traction after 1964, but they by no means ceased. One area of continued southern resentment of federal oversight was that of voting regulations. The Voting Rights Act of 1965 required, among other things, that certain jurisdictions with a long history of racial discrimination in voting, most located in the South, seek pre-approval from either the Department of Justice or the federal courts before implementing new voting restrictions. After 1965, Congress reauthorized the federal pre-approval requirement four times by overwhelming majorities. The last time it did so, in 2006, the measure passed the House of Representatives by a vote of 393 to 33, and the Senate by a vote of 98 to 0.

Having lost overwhelmingly in Congress, states' rights critics of the Voting Rights Act turned to the federal courts claiming that the pre-approval requirement violated state sovereignty in derogation of the Constitution. After their claim failed in the lower courts, the challengers found a receptive audience among five conservative Supreme Court justices. In 2013, a 5-4 majority in *Shelby County, Alabama v. Holder* struck down the federal pre-approval requirement, ruling for the first time in the nation's history that the federal government violated the Constitution when it treated some states differently than others.[102] The ruling has opened the floodgates of voting restriction measures, as Republican-dominated states have enacted a slew of new laws and regulations that are either intended or have the effect of making it more difficult for racial minorities and poor people to vote.[103] These measures, ostensibly aimed at *unproven* voter fraud, include new voter ID requirements, stringent voter registration rules, and broad voter purge statutes. *Shelby County* was only the latest iteration, going back to the Civil War, of the deployment of federalist arguments in ways that have helped maintain systemic racial inequality and injustice in the United States firmly in place.

As a result of the post-Civil War constitutional amendments and the enactment of comprehensive federal civil rights laws during the 1960s, progressives have viewed the federal government as a crucial source of protection for racial minorities and other vulnerable groups. At the same time, many progressives have understandably been highly skeptical of the use of federalist arguments to limit the national government's ability to combat racism and inequality. But as the issue of fugitive enslaved people showed in the nineteenth century, and as the Trump administration made clear in the early twenty-first century, the fact that particular policies are pursued by the federal government does not, by itself, tell us whether those policies are intended to protect the interests of vulnerable and disadvantaged populations.[104] It is sometimes the case, to put it simply, that the federal government, from a progressive perspective, is the problem. As a result, progressives should recognize that federalism considerations have a role to play in limiting the ability of the federal government to pursue misguided, harmful, and discriminatory policies.

The next chapter will explain why the Trump years proved this to be the case. But before we explore how progressives used federalism "on defense" to resist many of Trump's policies, it is worth discussing briefly how progressives in recent decades have also used federalism "on offense." This process entails the affirmative exercise of state sovereignty to attain progressive policy objectives, such as marriage equality and marijuana decriminalization, that were not, at least as an initial matter, achievable at the federal level.

Marriage and Marijuana Federalism

The successful quest for nationwide marriage equality began with one lawsuit brought under the constitution of one state. After three same-sex couples in 1991 sued Hawaii challenging its same-sex marriage ban, the state supreme court ruled that the ban might violate the state constitution's equal protection guarantee.[105] Conservative opponents of marriage equality responded by mobilizing and securing a state constitutional amendment granting Hawaii's legislature the authority to keep the marriage ban in place. Social conservatives also began advocating, often successfully, for new statutory and constitutional provisions in other states aimed at maintaining the gender of prospective spouses as an essential element of the definition of marriage.

But marriage equality opponents were not satisfied with state-level measures. Instead, social conservatives moved to *nationalize* the issue by pressuring Congress to enact the Defense of Marriage Act of 1996 (DOMA). That statute, among other things, defined marriage at the federal level as the union of one man and one woman.

Until Congress enacted DOMA, federal law had generally looked to state law to determine whether a couple was legally married and therefore entitled to the hundreds of rights and benefits that the federal government makes available to married couples. One of DOMA's effects was to *displace state sovereignty* on the question of marriage equality—while federal law had permitted states before DOMA to determine who was married for federal purposes, the statute, on the question of spousal gender, took that authority away from the states and gave it to the federal government. This nationalizing of the definition of marriage meant that even after some states started recognizing same-sex marriages, the federal government refused to deem those unions valid under federal law.

The LGBTQ rights movement did not have enough nationwide political clout to stop DOMA, as shown by the dispiriting fact that two-thirds of congressional Democrats voted for the measure and that Bill Clinton signed it. But the movement did have the ability to continue to push for marriage equality at the *state level*. At first, the progress in promoting that equality was largely the result of successful lawsuits brought under state constitutions in states like California, Connecticut, Iowa, and Massachusetts.[106] But after a few years, the attention that the lawsuits brought to the issue of marriage inequality helped secure legislative victories as some states, like New York and New Hampshire, enacted marriage equality statutes without being required to do so by the courts. And, in 2012, voters in four states (Maine, Maryland, Minnesota, and Washington) approved the legal recognition of same-sex marriages via the ballot box.[107]

Marriage equality advocates in the years following the Hawaii lawsuit recognized that there was little chance of success in seeking a national solution to marriage discrimination against LGBTQ people, either through Congress or the federal courts. That is why advocates pursued a state-based strategy that sought to gradually challenge same-sex marriage bans on a state-by-state basis.[108] It was only after the state-based strategy had succeeded in providing tens of thousands of same-sex couples with the opportunity to marry in a growing number of progressive states that marriage equality advocates shifted their attention to the federal courts and nationwide marriage equality. By the time advocates challenged the validity of both DOMA and the remaining same-sex marriage state bans under the U.S. Constitution, large numbers of heterosexual Americans in progressive states had been sharing workplaces, schools, and neighborhoods with married LGBTQ couples. This permitted countless straight people to experience and understand firsthand just how wrong opponents of marriage equality were when they claimed that the recognition of same-sex marriages would somehow harm children and undermine the family.[109] The "experimentation" by some states with marriage equality helped many heterosexuals living in those states, and eventually many heterosexuals in other states, to fully comprehend the fundamental unfairness of denying same-sex couples the opportunity to marry, and therefore denying them—and their children, if they had them—the many rights and benefits that came with marriage.[110]

This process of gradual but steady persuasion eventually helped pave the way for the Supreme Court's striking down of DOMA in 2013 and, two years later, of the remaining same-sex marriage bans.[111] On the question of marriage equality, the earlier progress at the state level made the later progress at the national level possible. As law professor Heather Gerken puts it in discussing the marriage equality movement's nationwide accomplishments, "national movements rarely begin as national movements. They start small and grow. . . . Local [organizing] platforms don't just facilitate early mobilization, but also help connect nascent movements to the large and powerful policymaking networks that fuel national politics. National policy, after all, is a giant gear to move. As with a clock, you need movement from lots of small, interlocking gears to move a bigger one. And that's precisely what we saw in the marriage-equality debate—small movements leading to bigger ones."[112]

Progressive headway in gaining employment anti-discrimination protection for LGBTQ people followed a similar pattern: gradual liberal advances at the state level preceded liberal accomplishments at the national level.[113] While progressive legislators introduced bills prohibiting employment discrimination on the basis of sexual orientation in every Congress for more than forty years beginning in 1974, none of those measures became federal law. In contrast, LGBTQ advocates working at the state level, starting in Wisconsin in 1982, succeeded in persuading a growing number of state legislatures to enact laws, first, prohibiting sexual orientation discrimination and, later, gender identity discrimination as well. By the time the Supreme Court in 2020 finally got around to answering, in the affirmative, the question of whether the federal Civil Rights Act of 1964 prohibited employment discrimination against LGBTQ people, that protection was already available to a little more than half of LGBTQ employees across the country as a result of the exercise of state sovereignty through the enactment of state laws that explicitly prohibited employment discrimination on the basis of sexual orientation and gender identity.[114] Once again, progress on LGBTQ rights at the state level paved the way for progress at the federal level. Although from an LGBTQ rights perspective, it undoubtedly would have been better to have national employment discrimination protection earlier, the crucial point is that such protection did not become politically feasible at the federal level until a significant number of state (and local) governments had first made that protection available through their laws.[115]

The federal system also helped to undermine the efforts by social conservatives, during the 2010s, to push for laws allowing religious business owners, employers, and landlords to discriminate against LGBTQ people and for regulations prohibiting transgender people from using the public bathrooms of their choice. Large corporations, working alongside progressive advocates, strongly opposed these measures. The companies' threats to move their workers and investments to states committed to LGBTQ equality helped to overturn or defeat most of the anti-LGBTQ measures.[116]

Federalism has also proven extremely helpful to progressives in other areas of law and policy, including that of marijuana legalization. Although many progressives remain generally skeptical of federalism, especially when defended in terms of "states' rights," most people on the left support *both* the decriminalization of marijuana and the ability of states to legalize the drug despite federal law's continued criminalization of its possession and use.[117]

Until 1913, marijuana was legal in all states. California that year criminalized the drug, and Utah followed suit in 1914. By 1930, thirty states had criminalized marijuana. The federal government regulated marijuana for the first time in 1937 when Congress enacted the Marijuana Tax Act, a law that essentially prohibited the drug's use by imposing a prohibitive tax on it. The federal government criminalized marijuana for the first time in 1952, requiring a minimum prison term of two years for marijuana possession. In 1970, Congress repealed the mandatory minimum, while simultaneously classifying marijuana as a "Schedule I" drug under the Controlled Substances Act (CSA), a federal classification that was still in place at the end of the Trump era. According to the statute, there is "no currently accepted medical use" for the drug. In addition, Congress has concluded that there is "a high potential for abuse" and a significant likelihood of "severe psychological or physical dependence" by those who smoke marijuana. Under the CSA, possession of marijuana for any purpose is a misdemeanor, while its cultivation and distribution constitute felonies.[118]

At around the same time that the federal government was doubling down on the criminalization of marijuana, some states began moving in the opposite direction by partially decriminalizing it. In the 1970s, eleven states, including California, Mississippi, Ohio, and Oregon, decriminalized the possession or use of small amounts (usually less than an ounce) of marijuana. A second wave of decriminalization took place in the 1990s as evidence grew that marijuana could have medicinal and palliative benefits for some individuals with, for example, cancer or AIDS. Between 1996 and 2000, eight states, including Alaska, California, Hawaii, and Maine, legalized the cultivation, distribution, possession, and use of marijuana for medicinal purposes. In 2012, Colorado and Washington became the first two states to decriminalize the recreational use of marijuana. The push to decriminalize the drug grew more successful in the years that followed—by the end of Trump's term, three dozen states had decriminalized medical marijuana and another fifteen had legalized recreational use. In a matter of only a few years, the number of states that, like the federal government, still criminalized all uses of marijuana became a distinct minority.[119]

The steady state-level decriminalization of marijuana, while federal law continued to prohibit all of the drug's uses, was aided in crucial ways by practical, political, and constitutional considerations grounded in federalism. First, as a practical matter, the federal government lacks the personnel to enforce its marijuana prohibitions. The fact that state and local police officials outnumber federal officers by about ten to one—and that, for example, the number of state and local police officials in just two states, Colorado and Washington, is more than four times the number employed by the federal Drug Enforcement Agency—means that the viability of the federal marijuana ban depends on the willingness of state and local officials to help in its enforcement.[120] For understandable and predictable reasons, law enforcement officials in states that have decriminalized marijuana have shown little interest in using their resources and personnel to discourage the use of the drug in circumstances that do not violate state law. This means that, as law professor Jonathan Adler puts it, "the federal government must wage its war on drugs without many foot soldiers."[121]

Second, the gradual but steady move toward legalization at the *state level* affected the *national* political dynamics around the decriminalization question. It was now the federal government that increasingly seemed to be out of step with a majority of the country on the question of marijuana criminalization. This new political reality led the Obama Department of Justice to issue memoranda explaining that the federal government did not consider marijuana prosecutions to be an enforcement priority. Although the department under Trump rescinded the memoranda, the Republican administration took few practical steps to enforce the federal prohibition, especially in states that had moved to decriminalize marijuana. For its part, Congress starting in 2014 began including riders in appropriation bills prohibiting federal law enforcement agencies from interfering with the ability of states to implement their medical marijuana laws.[122]

Finally, the constitutionally-based anti-commandeering principle prohibits the federal government from attempting to overcome the practical and political obstacles to the enforcement of federal marijuana law by requiring state and local officials to assist in that enforcement. As we explored in the context of fugitive enslaved people, and as we will see again in that of the Trump administration's harsh anti-immigration policies, the Constitution prohibits the federal government from using state employees and resources to attain federal policy goals over the objection of state officials. The fact that it is, as a constitutional matter, for the states, and not for the federal government, to decide how their law enforcement personnel and resources are used means that the federal government cannot conscript state officials to fight a "war against marijuana" even if it wants to.

Unlike the issue of marriage equality, which was ultimately settled by the Supreme Court as a matter of federal constitutional law, it was not clear, at the end of the Trump era, how the tension between the federal criminalization of marijuana and the gradual but steady legalization by many states would ultimately be resolved. In 2017, Elizabeth Warren, the liberal senator from Massachusetts, introduced legislation, called the Strengthening the Tenth Amendment by Entrusting States (STATES), seeking to allow states to opt out of the CSA's ban on marijuana. By the time Warren ran for president in 2020, she had joined a growing number of progressives in calling for the outright federal legalization of marijuana. After the 2020 election, the House of Representatives passed a bipartisan measure, by a 228 to 164 vote, to legalize marijuana at the federal level.[123]

If marijuana is eventually decriminalized nationally, it will be because the country's federalist government structure allowed legalization advocates to "start small" on a state-by-state basis, seeking first to decriminalize small amounts of marijuana, then to legalize medical marijuana, and finally to decriminalize the cultivation, distribution, and use of recreational marijuana. It is entirely possible that, as happened with marriage equality, state-based marijuana reforms—permitted and encouraged by the nation's federalist structure—will lead to a fundamental change of policy at the national level favored by most progressives. A mere generation ago, in the midst of an intense and federally led "War on Drugs," few people believed that the nationwide legalization of marijuana was possible. If that happens, it will be because federalist mechanisms and principles allowed and encouraged it.

There have been several other policy changes favored by progressives that have been aided by federalist mechanisms and principles. One example is the growing move by states to adopt minimum wage requirements that exceed, as of 2020, the woefully low federal minimum wage of $7.25. Although polls consistently showed a large majority of Americans (more than 70 percent) supporting a higher federal minimum wage, Congress did not raise the national minimum between 2009 and the end of the Trump presidency. As a result, the push for higher minimum wages during that period came primarily at the state and local level.[124] By 2020, twenty-nine states had a minimum wage requirement that was higher than the federal minimum wage, with thirteen of them requiring employers to pay workers at least $10.50 an hour.[125] Also by 2020, seven states were phasing in a $15 per-hour requirement. While such a high minimum wage was once dismissed as a fringe idea, its adoption by a growing number of states and localities significantly increased its chances of being adopted at the federal level.[126]

Similarly, after the Supreme Court in 1997 ruled that the Constitution does not grant terminally ill individuals a fundamental right to choose to receive medical assistance in ending their lives, eight states and the District of Columbia enacted laws permitting physician-assisted dying (also known as dignity-in-dying laws) on humanitarian grounds in some circumstances.[127] In 2001, the George W. Bush administration claimed that the CSA allowed the U.S. Attorney General to prohibit doctors from prescribing medications to be used for physician-assisted dying even in states that allowed such prescriptions. But the Supreme Court, relying on federalism principles, deemed that effort unconstitutional. As the Court explained, "the background principles of our federal system . . . belie the notion that Congress would use such an obscure grant of authority to regulate areas traditionally supervised by the states' police power."[128]

While progressives generally celebrated all of these liberal gains made possible by the nation's federalist mechanisms and principles, many of them were dismayed when the Supreme Court in 2012, after generally upholding the constitutionality of the Affordable Care Act (ACA), struck down the part of the ACA that would have denied a state all federal Medicaid funds if it refused to expand the program to certain categories of individuals whose income placed them above the poverty line. The Court struck down that section of the ACA on federalism grounds, ruling that conditioning *all* federal Medicaid monies on a state's willingness to expand the program was unconstitutional because it entailed federal coercion of states in pursuit of national policy. Although the application of federalist principles to the Medicaid expansion issue impeded the attainment of the important progressive objective of expanding government-subsidized health care, it is important to remember that Congress adopted the ACA only after some states had exercised their sovereignty by experimenting with policies aimed at expanding access to health care.[129] In fact, the ACA was largely modeled on comprehensive health-care reforms implemented by Massachusetts several years earlier.[130] It is also important to remember that the same federalist principle prohibiting federal coercion of states that rendered a part of the ACA unconstitutional was extremely helpful, as we will see in the next chapter, in protecting the ability of sanctuary jurisdictions to resist the Trump administration's draconian and inhumane immigration policies.

In short, progressive causes and movements have gained much from state-level experimentation, an experimentation that sometimes has been reflected in later national policies. Even before Trump became president, progressives had repeatedly relied on federalist mechanisms and principles "on offense" to attain and advance liberal objectives. It may be that some progressives, even after the Trump era, will continue to resist embracing federalism, in part because of its historic uses to promote racism and anti-regulatory policies and in part on the ground that the greatest challenges facing the United States are national and global in nature rather than state and local. But it is important to be cognizant of and clear-eyed about the costs to progressive causes and objectives—as illustrated by the examples of marriage equality and marijuana decriminalization, among others—that would accompany a weakening of the country's federalist structures and traditions.

Of course, federalism has also allowed conservatives to implement *their* preferred policies in states controlled by Republicans. These policies have included the implementation of welfare work requirements and the protection of gun rights. It could be argued, therefore, that federalism has undermined progressive goals as frequently as it has promoted them. But even if we assume, for argument sake, that this is the case, what in my view breaks the tie, so to speak, is the many ways in which progressives successfully used federalist mechanisms and principles during the Trump years to limit the impact of some of the administration's most misguided, harmful, and discriminatory policies. To put it simply, the Trump years painfully proved to progressives that the federal government is not always on the side of the angels. As a consequence, there can be significant benefits—to progressives and to the democratic system itself—to using federalist principles and mechanisms as a means of restraining a federal government led by an autocratic and dangerous leader such as Trump.

2

Federalism During the Trump Era and Beyond

During Trump's years in office, liberal states, with the enthusiastic support of progressives across the country, repeatedly exercised their authority as sovereigns to oppose and challenge some of the administration's policies that were, from a left-of-center perspective, misguided, harmful, or discriminatory. State-based resistance to the Trump administration was particularly robust in matters related to immigration and environmental regulations. State-based policies during the Trump years were also crucial in filling the voids left by the administration's failures to provide effective national leadership on issues that desperately demanded it, including the stemming of gun violence and controlling the spread of the coronavirus pandemic, with its devastating toll in deaths, illnesses, and jobs.

Issues as varied as environmental degradation, gun violence, and the deadly coronavirus illustrate how many of the nation's most important social, economic, and health challenges are not circumscribed by state boundaries. It is often the case, therefore, that national problems deserve and require national solutions; nothing in this book is intended to suggest otherwise. In addition, as we saw in the last chapter, federalist mechanisms and principles historically have been used to attain *both* progressive and racist/reactionary objectives. As a result, left-of-center thinkers, commentators, and activists face a difficult question going forward: Do progressive movements and causes have more to gain than to lose by embracing and supporting constitutional mechanisms and principles aimed at limiting federal government authority? Although I argue in this chapter that the Trump era shows why progressives have more to gain than to lose by doing so, I recognize that reasonable people can disagree on that "costs vs. benefits" assessment.

At the same time, it is worth noting that few, if any, progressives sided with the Trump administration in its multiple battles with liberal states on the ground that, for example, the Tenth Amendment is nothing but a truism and that state sovereignty should not be understood to constitute an independent limitation on the federal government's power. Whether as a matter of principle or simply of political convenience, progressives showed few qualms with embracing

Principles Matter. Carlos A. Ball, Oxford University Press. © Carlos A. Ball 2021.
DOI: 10.1093/oso/9780197584484.003.0003

federalist mechanisms and principles as a source of resistance to the Trump administration.

If progressives going forward embrace federalism only situationally—defending it when there is a conservative in the White House, but dismissing its relevance or appropriateness when there is a liberal in that position—then it is less likely that the principle will remain a viable and effective tool in resisting the misguided, harmful, or discriminatory policies of a future right-wing administration in the Trumpian mold. In contrast, if progressives after the Trump era defend federalism as a matter of principle regardless of who is in office, then it is more likely that the concept will retain its constitutional and political legitimacy, making it available to progressives in future years when confronting another right-wing and potentially autocratic federal administration.

Sanctuary Federalism

There was no policy area in which progressive resistance to the Trump administration was more committed and intense than in that of immigration. Trump's racist, harsh, and harmful immigration policies and rhetoric fundamentally challenged a progressive vision of the United States as a welcoming, pluralistic, and multicultural society. Starting on the day he announced his candidacy for president, Trump made clear that the targeting and demonizing of immigrants, and in particular immigrants of color, would be a cornerstone of his government. In announcing his candidacy, Trump accused Mexican immigrants of being criminals and rapists.[1] He also as a candidate claimed that Islam represented a threat to the United States, called for prohibiting immigration by Muslims, and insinuated that those of Islamic faith—the hundreds of millions of them around the world—had little respect for human life.[2] Several days into his presidency, Trump ordered that immigrants from several Muslim countries immediately be denied entry into the United States.[3] And in the months and years that followed, he repeatedly claimed that immigrants crossing the Mexico-U.S. border constituted an existential threat to the nation. Administration officials translated Trump's racist anti-immigrant vision into draconian, ruthless, and harmful policies, including forcing tens of thousands of asylum applicants to wait for the adjudication of their claims in unsanitary, overcrowded, and unsafe camps near the border and separating immigrant children from their parents. Progressives fought the Trump administration's immigration policies every step of the way, including through activism, protests, and lawsuits. As this section explains, federalist mechanisms and principles constituted a crucially effective component of that resistance.

For most of the nation's history, "immigration enforcement efforts were focused at the border and carried out almost exclusively by federal officials."[4] In
addition, for most of that history, immigration enforcement was almost entirely
a matter of civil regulation, having little overlap with the criminal law, which is
enforced primarily by state and local officials.

The distinction between the enforcement of federal immigration laws and
criminal laws began to blur with the adoption of so-called war on drugs policies. Those policies—first implemented nationally by President Richard Nixon
in the early 1970s, later raised to an even higher level of enforcement intensity by
President Ronald Reagan in the 1980s, and still generally in place today—have
had a series of devastatingly harmful effects. One such effect has been the vast
increase in the number of incarcerated people, an increase that has been particularly devastating to African American communities.[5] Another exceedingly
harmful effect has been the extent to which the "war on drugs" has led to the
rhetorically explosive but factually inaccurate association of illegal immigration
with criminality.[6] As one group of immigration law professors puts it, "in the
1980s the Reagan administration's 'war on drugs' provided politicians with an
opportunity to promote a myth of immigrant criminality that would ultimately
lead to an unprecedented entanglement of immigration enforcement with criminal justice goals. . . . The narrative of immigrants-as-criminals made it appear
more natural for local law enforcement to become involved in immigration
enforcement."[7]

The ramped-up enforcement of immigration laws in the 1980s gave rise to
a sanctuary movement. It began when a handful of churches, in cities such as
Tucson and Chicago, started offering organized assistance to the thousands of
people who had come to the United States seeking refuge from Central America's
civil wars. At around the same time, cities such as Los Angeles, New York, and San
Francisco began adopting policies prohibiting their employees from assisting in
the enforcement of federal immigration laws, usually with the exception of cases
involving immigrants accused of serious crimes.[8]

In 1996, Congress authorized voluntary partnerships between the federal
government and local law enforcement agencies in immigration matters. The
program is sometimes called the "287(g) program" for the provision of the
Immigration and Naturalization Act under which it arises.[9] Under the program,
federal officials deputized local government employees to perform some immigration enforcement functions under their supervision. A few months after
the September 11, 2001, attacks, the Department of Justice issued an opinion
reversing its long-standing view, which corresponded with that of most experts
in the field, that local officials lacked the legal authority to enforce federal immigration laws, including by making civil immigration arrests.[10]

States and local communities across the country responded to these policy changes at the federal level in various ways. Some jurisdictions eagerly made their resources and employees available to assist in the regulation of immigration. But other jurisdictions, especially those with large immigrant communities, objected to the blurring of the lines between the public services they provided their residents, including police protection, and the enforcement of federal immigration law.

A growing number of these jurisdictions—which included states, counties, cities, and towns—began to embrace the "sanctuary" label; while that term does not have a legal meaning or effect, it does reflect a policy choice to restrict the deployment of state and local resources and employees in enforcing immigration laws. There are different reasons why dozens of jurisdictions across the country have chosen to self-identify as sanctuary jurisdictions. One important reason is the view that it is for state and local officials, and not the federal government, to set criminal justice priorities and to determine how best to allocate state and local funds and deploy government employees to achieve them. Other reasons for adopting so-called sanctuary policies are to avoid unlawful arrests and detentions of both citizens and immigrants; to maintain effective policing by creating and maintaining trust between law enforcement agencies and minority communities; and to express disagreement with aggressive federal immigration enforcement policies.

Soon after Barack Obama became president, his administration ramped up immigration enforcement, with a special focus on increasing the number of deportations. During Obama's eight years in office, the federal government deported a total of 2.7 million individuals, with most of the removals occurring during the administration's first term.[11] In order to attain its deportation objectives, the administration early on increased pressure on local communities to turn over their undocumented residents for deportation. One way it did so was by pushing to increase the number of joint enforcement partnerships under the 287(g) program.

But it soon became clear that the growing use of local law enforcement personnel to help enforce federal immigration law under 287(g) was resulting in both the increased use of racial profiling and a mounting distrust between local communities with large immigrant populations and their police forces.[12] In the face of criticism, the Obama administration in 2012 stopped renewing 287(g) enforcement agreements; around the same time, a growing number of jurisdictions pledged not to enter into them to begin with. The Trump administration later moved in the exact opposite direction by expanding the number of new immigration enforcement agreements between the federal and local governments.[13]

Local governments also became entangled with federal immigration enforcement through the so-called Secure Communities program first implemented by the George W. Bush administration in 2008. Secure Communities created an information-sharing system that permitted the Department of Homeland Security (DHS) to enforce immigration regulations by using biometric data collected by local police and sheriffs. Once the program was in place, the fingerprints of every person booked by law enforcement agencies in participating communities were forwarded automatically to DHS so that they could be cross-checked with its immigration databases.[14]

The Secure Communities program had many detractors. "The program [was] criticized for promoting racial profiling, errors in DHS databases, and making communities less safe by causing immigrants to fear local law enforcement there for their protection."[15] In the face of growing criticism, the Obama administration ended the Secure Communities program in 2014, only to be re-initiated by Trump officials three years later.[16]

The implementation of Secure Communities was accompanied by the increased use by federal immigration officials of "detainer orders." Such orders ask state and local law enforcement agencies to keep detained individuals incarcerated beyond their scheduled release dates to help federal officials take them into custody for alleged immigration violations. The federal government took the position that state and local governments were required by federal law to comply with detainer orders. Some jurisdictions complied with all such orders, sometimes leading to the illegal detention of individuals misidentified as undocumented immigrants. In 2014, a federal appellate court in *Galarza v. Szalczyk* found a Pennsylvania county liable for detaining a U.S. citizen who had been erroneously targeted by the federal government pursuant to an immigration detainer order.[17]

It is important to emphasize that immigration detainer orders are not grounded in criminal law violations. As the U.S. Supreme Court notes, "as a general rule, it is not a crime for a removable alien to remain present in the United States."[18] And as the Massachusetts Supreme Judicial Court explains, the detainers "do not charge anyone with a crime, indicate that anyone has been charged with a crime, or ask that anyone be detained in order that he or she can be prosecuted for a crime. Detainers . . . are [instead] used to detain individuals because the Federal authorities believe that they are civilly removable from the country."[19]

Some jurisdictions declined to participate in the Secure Communities program and refused to comply with detainer orders, unless the individuals in question were charged with serious crimes or had been convicted of such crimes in the past. The *Galarza* court held that federal authorities could not require state and local governments to comply with immigration detainers over their objections. To do so would entail the commandeering of state and local officials to implement federal policies in violation of the Constitution as interpreted by the Supreme Court in *Printz v. United States*.[20] As explored in Chapter 1, *Printz* involved the federal government's unconstitutional mandate that state and local law enforcement officials conduct firearm background checks on its behalf.[21] Although the *Galarza* court did not cite the case, the anti-commandeering principle, as we have seen, can be traced all the way back to *Prigg v. Pennsylvania* (1842) and the issue of fugitive enslaved people in antebellum America.[22] Indeed, it is worth emphasizing that the commandeering considerations are the same in both instances—the constitutional question is whether the federal government can *require* state and local governments to use their officials and resources to help the federal government accomplish its policy goals over the states' objections. The answer in the context of immigration, as it was in that of the rendition of fugitive enslaved people, is a clear *no*.

By the end of the Obama years, dozens of jurisdictions across the country had declared themselves to be sanctuary jurisdictions by exercising their authority under our constitutional system to adopt policies with objectives that are different from those of the federal government. In order, among other reasons, to foster and maintain the trust necessary to effectively provide police and other services to their communities, these jurisdictions adopted one or more of the following policies: barring their law enforcement officials from investigating civil or criminal immigration violations; limiting compliance with immigration detainer orders; refusing to allow Immigration and Customs Enforcement (ICE) agents access to their jails; limiting the disclosure of sensitive information about their residents (such as their release dates if they were being detained or whether they were recipients of public assistance); and precluding their employees from joining federal officials in immigration enforcement actions such as raids and arrests.[23]

Although the sanctuary jurisdiction movement grew during the Obama years, it reached new heights after Trump became president. One study found that jurisdictions across the country adopted more sanctuary regulations during Trump's first year in office than were instituted during the previous *twelve years combined*.[24]

As a presidential candidate, Trump made clear that he viewed immigration in general, and immigration by certain groups in particular, most prominently Muslims and Central Americans, as a threat to the nation's well-being and security. On the day he formally announced his presidential candidacy in 2015, he accused Mexican immigrants of being drug dealers and rapists ("They're bringing drugs. They're bringing crime. They're rapists."). He also during the campaign issued a statement "calling for a total and complete shutdown of Muslims entering the United States." He later defended his proposal to ban Muslim immigrants by pointing to the precedent of the internment of Japanese Americans during World War II. And on the day he accepted his party's nomination in 2016, Trump falsely claimed that there were at least two million undocumented individuals who had committed crimes in the United States (he called them "criminal aliens") and vowed to show them "zero tolerance."[25]

During the acceptance speech, as he had done on the campaign trail, Trump raised the murder in 2015 of a San Francisco woman by the name of Kathryn Steinle to foster the impression that immigrants, as a class, represented a public safety threat. The person arrested for that killing was an immigrant who was in the United States without legal permission. In his speech, Trump mentioned Steinle and others purportedly killed by undocumented immigrants, asking "where was sanctuary for Kate Steinle" and for "all the other Americans who have been so brutally murdered, and who have suffered so horribly?"[26] Ten months into Trump's presidency, a California jury acquitted the immigrant charged with Steinle's murder. Trump called the verdict disgraceful, while his Attorney General Jeff Sessions blamed Steinle's death on the fact that San Francisco was a sanctuary city.[27] In 2017, President Trump gave a speech on Long Island in which he called immigrant gang members "animals" who have turned American cities into "bloodstained killing fields."[28] In his 2019 State of the Union address, Trump claimed that "year-after-year countless Americans are murdered by criminal illegal aliens."[29] And in his 2020 address, he blamed New York City's sanctuary laws for the rape and murder of a ninety-two-year-old woman.[30]

During the 2016 presidential campaign, Trump had bragged that he would "end sanctuary cities" and promised that his administration would punish them by cutting off their federal funding if they did not cooperate with his immigration enforcement program.[31] Just five days into his presidency, Trump signed an executive order targeting sanctuary jurisdictions, accusing them of "willfully violat[ing] Federal law in an attempt to shield aliens from removal from the United States." The order called on the Attorney General and the Secretary of DHS to make sure that sanctuary jurisdictions "are not eligible to receive federal grants, except as deemed necessary for law enforcement purposes by the Attorney General or the Secretary." The order also required the Attorney General to "take appropriate enforcement action against any entity that violates 8 U.S.C. §1373, or which has in effect a statute, policy, or practice that prevents or hinders the enforcement of federal law."[32] Section 1373, which will be explored, is a federal statute, enacted in 1996, which seeks to make it a violation of federal law for state and local governments to prohibit their employees from sending or receiving information about the citizenship or immigration status of any individual.

Trump's executive order revealed a breathtakingly expansive understanding of the power of the federal government's executive branch. The order claimed, in effect, that the administration had the authority (1) to cut off *all* federal funding, regardless of its purpose, including monies for Medicare, Medicaid, transportation, child welfare services, and emergency preparedness (2) to *any* jurisdiction (whether state or local) that (3) in *any way* hindered "the enforcement of federal law," with only one exception: federal funding earmarked for law enforcement that two cabinet members, at their sole discretion, chose to allow to continue flowing.

Two California jurisdictions, San Francisco and Santa Clara county, quickly sued the administration in federal court, arguing that the executive order violated the Tenth Amendment's anti-commandeering prohibition and separation-of-powers principles. Santa Clara county had several sanctuary policies in place. One such policy prohibited its employees from sharing information with ICE about its residents collected by the county while providing services or benefits to them. Another policy prohibited "using county resources to pursue an individual solely because of an actual or suspected violation of immigration law." In addition, county policy prohibited its employees from responding to or complying with ICE civil detainer orders. The policy exempted orders pertaining to individuals who had been convicted of serious felonies, but only if the federal government reimbursed the county for the costs of detaining such individuals, something the federal government refused to do.[33] San Francisco had similar sanctuary policies in place. The stated purpose of these policies was "to foster respect and trust between law enforcement and residents, to protect limited local resources, to encourage cooperation between residents and City officials, including especially law enforcement and public health officers and employees, and to ensure community security, and due process for all."[34]

Trump's executive order targeting sanctuary jurisdictions across the country for punishment placed billions of federal dollars at risk. Santa Clara county alone received about $1.7 billion in federal funds annually, accounting for more than a third of its budget. The executive order placed essential services at risk, including those provided by the county's only public safety-net hospital, which received more than 70 percent of its funding from the federal government, and by its Social Services Agency, which received about 40 percent of its budget from federal funds to provide "various services to vulnerable residents, including child welfare and protection, aid to needy families, and support for disabled children, adults and the elderly."[35] For its part, San Francisco received approximately $1.2 billion in annual federal funds. Federal money made up "100 percent of Medicare for San Francisco residents; 30 percent of the budget for San Francisco's Department of Emergency Management; 33 percent of the budget for San Francisco's Human Services Agency; and 40 percent of the budget for San Francisco's Department of Public Health."[36]

A federal appellate court eventually held that Trump's executive order seeking to punish sanctuary jurisdictions was unconstitutional because it violated separation-of-powers principles given that only Congress can authorize the placing of conditions on the receipt of federal funds.[37] Two other appellate courts also ruled, on the same ground, that a subsequent and narrower effort by the administration to target sanctuary jurisdictions by withholding federal money earmarked for state and local law enforcement efforts was unconstitutional.[38] These rulings show the extent to which *separation-of-powers* principles can be used both to mitigate the dangers of an imperial domestic presidency and to protect vulnerable populations from federal executive policies that harm them by either intent or effect. I will explore those principles in the next two chapters. For now, I want to highlight the extent to which Trump's policies targeting sanctuary jurisdictions also violated constitutional federalism principles.

A good place to begin is with a federal statute, section 1373, which while enacted before Trump became president, was a central tool in his targeting of sanctuary jurisdictions. As already noted, that provision seeks to make it a violation of federal law for state and local governments to prohibit their employees from sending or receiving information about the citizenship or immigration status of any individual.

An analogy to the fugitive slave issue illustrates why section 1373 is unconstitutional. Under the federalist component of the *Prigg v. Pennsylvania* ruling from 1842, states had the constitutional authority to prohibit their employees from assisting in the rendition of fugitive enslaved people as mandated by federal law. That ruling was partly grounded in the anti-commandeering principle that prohibits the federal government from demanding that state and local officials assist it in attaining national policy objectives. In short, states—and by extension local governments, given that their sovereignty derives from the states—have the constitutional authority to choose to prohibit their employees from assisting in the enforcement of federal laws, including immigration regulations.

It therefore stands to reason that a federal statute, such as section 1373, which seeks to *prevent* state and local governments from prohibiting their employees from assisting in the enforcement of immigration law is unconstitutional. Furthermore, it is unconstitutional for the federal government to withhold funds from state and local governments as a way of punishing them, as the Trump administration attempted to do, for failing to abide by a federal statute that is itself unconstitutional.

A further analogy to *Printz v. United States* also helps illustrate the unconstitutionality of section 1373. Imagine that Congress, as part of its effort to require state and local officials to conduct background checks before issuing gun permits under the Brady Handgun Violence Act, had prohibited state and local governments from preventing their employees from refusing to help implement federal gun safety policies. It seems clear that the Court would have struck that measure down because it would have allowed Congress to do precisely what *Printz* held it could not do: force state and local law enforcement officials to assist in the enforcement and implementation of federal policies over their objection.

At the end of the day, there is no constitutional difference between, on the one hand, the federal government's commandeering of state and local officials to achieve its policy objectives and, on the other, its mandating that state and local governments not prohibit their employees from assisting in the attainment of federal goals. Both efforts are unconstitutional because they both violate basic federalism principles.[39]

It was not just local governments that resisted Trump's immigration regulations; some states did as well. California led progressive states in opposing the Trump administration's immigration policies.[40] Ten months into the Trump presidency, California enacted a series of laws with the goal "of protecting immigrants from an expected increase in federal immigration enforcement actions."[41] One law prohibits state and local law enforcement agencies from providing the federal government with a detained person's release date or other personal information unless the individual in question has been convicted of a serious crime. The statute also prohibits state and local authorities from transferring a detainee to federal custody unless a judge issues a warrant (an ICE detainer order is not enough).[42] A second law requires the California Attorney General to review the conditions at all federal, state, and local facilities in the state used to detain non-citizens to make sure they comply with requisite standards of care. The statute also calls on the attorney general to review the circumstances of the detainees' apprehension and transfer to those facilities.[43] A third California statute enacted in 2017 prohibits private employers from permitting federal immigration officials to enter the non-public areas of their workplaces unless such entering is required by federal law or done pursuant to a judicial warrant. In the case of legally authorized inspections, the California law requires private employers to provide their employees with at least 72 hours' notice of them.[44]

In an effort to block these exercises of state sovereignty, the Trump administration sued California in federal court contending that the provisions were unconstitutional under the Supremacy Clause because they conflicted with federal immigration laws. At the same time, and not surprisingly, the Trump administration did not challenge efforts by some states, such as Texas, to *prohibit* local governments from adopting sanctuary policies.[45] According to the administration, it was apparently permissible for states to legislate in matters related to sanctuary jurisdictions as long as the objective was to prohibit rather than allow local officials to decide for themselves how best to deploy their employees and resources.

In a strong victory for federalist principles, a federal appellate court in 2019 rejected the administration's claims that the California statutes impermissibly burdened or conflicted with federal law.[46] The fact that California's sanctuary laws might make it more difficult for the federal government to enforce its immigration laws did not render them unconstitutional in the absence of a clear congressional statement to that effect. The judges noted that the federal government was asking the court to conclude that its interest in enforcing immigration laws *implicitly* limited a state's authority to legislate. But the court was unwilling to find such an implicit limitation in a "state's historic police power" in matters traditionally subject to state regulation, such as the deployment of state and local law enforcement resources and the regulation of detention facilities within the state's borders. The court made clear that the Constitution generally presumes that a state properly exercises its police powers under the Tenth Amendment; in contrast, it does not presume that federal law preempts state law under the Supremacy Clause.[47]

The court also held that California had the constitutional authority to withhold assistance to federal immigration authorities by refusing (1) to disclose information about particular residents and (2) to enforce ICE detainer orders. Specifically, the court ruled that the Tenth Amendment requires that such cooperation be voluntary and not mandatory. California had the constitutional authority to refuse to assist in the attainment of federal objectives, an authority that could not be overridden through a congressional statute (such as section 1373). To contend that California's sanctuary laws were preempted by federal law "would, in effect, dictate what a state legislature may and may not do because it would imply that a state's otherwise lawful decision *not* to assist federal authorities is made unlawful when it is codified as state law."[48] In so ruling, the court recognized that the California statute prohibiting its state and local officials from assisting in immigration enforcement efforts might very well frustrate those endeavors.

> However, whatever the wisdom of the underlying policy adopted by California, that frustration is permissible, because California has the right, pursuant to the anticommandeering rule, to refrain from assisting with federal efforts. The United States stresses that, in crafting the Immigration and Naturalization Act, Congress expected cooperation between states and federal immigration authorities. That is likely the case. But when questions of federalism are involved, we must distinguish between expectations and requirements. In this context, the federal government was free to *expect* as much as it wanted, but it could not *require* California's cooperation without running afoul of the Tenth Amendment.[49]

California was not the only state targeted by the Trump administration. In 2020, the federal government sought to punish New York state for refusing to grant federal immigration officials access to its motor vehicle and driving license records. It did this by denying *all* New York residents the ability to participate in the federal Trusted Traveler program, which allows for expedited transit through airports and border checkpoints. In response, the New York Attorney General sued the administration, contending that the exclusion of state residents from the federal program was, among other things, unconstitutional under the Tenth Amendment because it was a federal effort to coerce the state into changing its regulations denying immigration officials access to state records. The Trump administration eventually allowed New Yorkers to once again participate in the Trusted Traveler program after federal government lawyers admitted that DHS officials had misled the federal judge hearing the case when trying to hide the obvious fact that the administration was using the exclusion of New Yorkers from the program as a way of *punishing* the state for its resistance to federal immigration policies.[50]

All of these cases illustrate how the Trump administration, thanks largely to our constitutional system's protections for state sovereignty, was unable, despite its repeated efforts, to significantly limit the ability of state and local governments to enact and enforce sanctuary policies in defiance of federal government priorities.

States also challenged the Trump administration's immigration policies in matters that went beyond sanctuary laws and policies. For example, twenty-one states and the District of Columbia sued the administration after it announced it would institute a new "public charge" rule aimed at denying permanent residency to legal immigrants who used—or the government believed would in the future use—government benefits such as Medicaid, housing assistance, and food stamps. The new rule was consistent with the administration's objective of reducing the number of poor immigrants. The rule had a disproportionate impact on immigrants from Africa and Latin America while favoring "those who are educated and wealthy, more likely to hail from Europe than from the developing world."[51] In their lawsuit, the states and the District of Columbia argued that the rule "discriminate[d] against low-income people from developing countries and undermine[d] the well-being of children whose families might avoid using nutritional, health and other programs."[52] In granting an injunction prohibiting the enforcement of the rule, a federal judge noted that it would also harm the states because they would need to reallocate resources to mitigate the harms to children, including American children of immigrant parents, that would result from a decision not to apply for government benefits, under programs such as Medicaid and food stamps, in order to remain eligible for permanent residency.[53] Another federal judge, in enjoining the rule's enforcement, complained that it "is simply a new agency policy of exclusion in search of a justification," a view affirmed by a federal appellate court when it noted that the federal government had "failed to provide a reasoned explanation for its" new restrictive immigration policy.[54] Unfortunately, the Supreme Court allowed the Trump administration to enforce the rule while the litigation proceeded, a decision that placed tens of thousands of poor immigrant parents in the excruciatingly difficult position of choosing between preserving the possibility of attaining legal immigrant status in the future and properly feeding their children.[55]

A group of nineteen states also sued the administration contending that its reallocation of military funds to build a wall along the Mexico-U.S. border, following Congress's refusal to fund such a project, was unconstitutional.[56] (We will explore the separation-of-powers issues raised by the wall's funding in Chapter 4.) In addition, states led the way in challenging the constitutionality of what Trump called an immigration "Muslim ban."[57] In Chapter 4, we will see how the Supreme Court's refusal to strike down the ban, despite the clear anti-Muslim animus behind it, is a glaring and disturbing example of the Court's repeated refusal to restrict presidential powers. For now, it is enough to note that two days after Trump signed an executive order—one week into his presidency—immediately prohibiting immigration from seven Muslim-majority countries and indefinitely suspending refugee admissions from Syria, the attorneys general of fifteen states and the District of Columbia issued a statement condemning the order as "unconstitutional, un-American, and unlawful."[58] Within twenty-four hours, the states of Washington and Minnesota sued the Trump administration over the Muslim ban. Two days later, a federal court granted a temporary restraining order prohibiting the executive order's enforcement on the ground that it adversely affected the states' residents in their employment, education, business, family relations, and freedom to travel, as well as the states' "public universities and other institutions of higher learning, [while causing] injury to the states' operations, tax bases, and public funds."[59]

In the days and months that followed, several states, including California, Hawaii, Massachusetts, and New York, filed additional lawsuits against the administration challenging what Trump called the "Muslim ban." The lawsuits kept coming even after the administration, desperate to keep the federal courts from striking down the policy, began tweaking it by, for example, adding immigration restrictions for certain categories of individuals from non-Muslim countries such as North Korea and Venezuela. The Supreme Court ultimately upheld the final version of the immigration policy in a lawsuit brought by Hawaii. In doing so, the Court refused to grapple with the central question in the case—whether the policy reflected impermissible animus on the basis of religion in violation of the First Amendment's Establishment Clause—because there were ostensible non-discriminatory reasons for implementing the policy.[60] Although the lawsuits against the immigration ban were ultimately unsuccessful, *it was states that led the 18-month effort to challenge the Trump administration's anti-Muslim policy* in ways that forced it to defend its views in court. Among other things, the suits served as vehicles for states to explain repeatedly to the public why the president's actions were "unconstitutional, un-American, and unlawful."[61]

In addition, Massachusetts, New York, and Washington state sued ICE to prevent federal officials from arresting individuals for civil immigration violations in or near state courthouses. Prior administrations generally had limited so-called courthouse immigration arrests, recognizing that they interfered with the ability of states to administer their laws and dispense justice through their courts. But ICE officials under Trump, intent on implementing his desired crackdown on undocumented immigrants, showed no qualms about courthouse arrests, especially in sanctuary jurisdictions. The targeted jurisdictions vehemently complained that the change in federal policy "significantly chilled participation" in their independent court systems, "deterring victims from reporting crimes, plaintiffs from bringing lawsuits and witnesses from helping law enforcement out of fear they would be detained."[62]

Several federal courts ordered the Trump administration to cease making courthouse arrests. As one of the courts explained, state courts should not "have to grapple with disruptions and intimidations artificially imposed by an agency of the federal government in violation of longstanding privileges and fundamental principles of federalism and separation of powers."[63]

For decades, progressives have correctly believed that the federal government can and should play an essential role in protecting the interests of racial minorities and other disadvantaged and vulnerable groups, in part by prohibiting and policing discrimination by the states. But as the Trump administration painfully proved to progressives, the federal government can also be a source of misguided, harmful, and discriminatory policies. In the immigration context, those policies included imposing draconian asylum restrictions, separating children from their parents at the Mexican border to discourage additional immigration, imprisoning detainees near the border in inhumane and demeaning conditions to achieve the same objective, and targeting Latinx and Muslim immigrants. These policies illustrate how the federal government, and not just the states, can institute policies that harm vulnerable groups. Fortunately, our federalist system allowed states to respond to Trump's disturbing and punitive immigration policies both by adopting measures aimed at mitigating their harms and by legally challenging them in the courts. Furthermore, our constitutional system's protections for state sovereignty blocked the Trump administration's repeated efforts to punish state and local jurisdictions for refusing to participate in the implementation and enforcement of those policies.

Of course, there are limits to what states can accomplish when opposing a federal administration committed to instituting policies targeting marginalized groups. In the particular context of immigration, the federal government's authority under the Constitution is extensive enough to preclude states from directly regulating immigration.[64] Furthermore, under our constitutional system, states cannot interfere with federal immigration enforcement, much less *require* that the federal government regulate immigration in certain ways. It is only Congress, exercising its legislative functions and its power of the purse, which can tell the executive branch how to regulate immigration.

But states can exercise their police power sovereignty by regulating in ways that make it more difficult for the federal government to enforce ill-advised, harmful, and discriminatory immigration policies. This is because our constitutional system allows states and localities to control how *their* employees and resources are used. That control, from a progressive perspective, can have beneficial practical consequences because it can help protect the interests of individuals who are left unprotected by federal law. The exercise of state sovereignty also has political implications because it can be used both to criticize federal policies and to help organize and mobilize resistance to them.

It is true, of course, that state objections to federal policies can go the other way: the objections can be based on conservative opposition to the federal government's pursuit of progressive policies. The Obama administration learned this the hard way when red states repeatedly challenged its most important programs and regulations, including those related to the environment, Obamacare, and the Dreamers immigration policy that largely ended the deportation of undocumented immigrants brought to the country as children. As Greg Abbott, the conservative attorney general (and later governor) of Texas who sued the Obama administration twenty-seven times in its first five years in office, put it in explaining how he did his job, "I go into the office in the morning. I sue Barack Obama, and then I go home."[65] But, as the states' resistance to the Trump immigration policies showed, the use of federalist mechanisms and principles to resist federal policies is neither intrinsically conservative nor problematic. Instead, those mechanisms and principles sometimes can be deployed in ways that advance progressive objectives by helping to mitigate the harms engendered by misguided and discriminatory federal policies. As a result, progressives should consider defending federalist mechanisms and principles, even if their application sometimes may make it more difficult for future progressive federal administrations to pursue their policy objectives.

Environmental Federalism

Between the end of the nineteenth century and 1937, the Supreme Court generally understood the division of power between the federal government and the states to be one of "dual sovereignty federalism," with each side enjoying separate and independent spheres of authority.[66] The New Deal's expansion of federal government authority, one that continued largely unabated for decades after the Great Depression ended, challenged the notion of dual sovereignty federalism.

Once Congress began to repeatedly legislate in matters related, for example, to labor relations, workplace safety, consumer safety, the provision of health care, and environmental protection, it became less tenable to contend that such important areas of regulation should be left *exclusively* to the states. At the same time, the federal government lacked the resources and personnel to implement many of its national policies on its own. This made the attainment of federal domestic objectives dependent on the assistance of state and local governments. This dependency gave rise to the concept of "cooperative federalism," which emphasized the overlapping and intersecting spheres of federal *and* state regulation rather than the notion of distinct and independent spheres of sovereignty. The Supreme Court in recent decades has made clear that while states cannot be forced or coerced into helping the federal government achieve its objectives, they can voluntarily choose to help craft and implement policies jointly with the federal government to achieve common objectives. At the same time, the Constitution allows the federal government to offer financial inducements to procure state cooperation. All of this means that, as legal scholar Adam Babich puts it, "cooperative federalism holds the promise of allowing the states continued primacy and flexibility in their traditional realms of protecting public health and welfare, while ensuring that protections for all citizens meet minimum federal standards."[67]

During the second half of the twentieth century, Congress repeatedly legislated in ways that embraced the principle of cooperative federalism. One prominent example was Congress's creation of Medicaid in 1965, a program that relies on states to disburse federal funds, along with their own monies, to pay for health care for the poor. The Clean Air Act and the Clean Water Act also promote cooperative federalism. Under the statutes, the federal government, through the Environmental Protection Agency (EPA), sets minimum pollution control standards and then primarily relies on states to implement and enforce them. The statutes also permit states in some circumstances to set higher environmental standards than required by federal law. It is significant that the statutes allow for the attainment of more progressive environmental protection objectives, in states that seek to pursue them, than are otherwise called for by federal standards.[68]

One of the most important ways in which federalist mechanisms have been used to *expand* environmental protections relates to the regulation of vehicle emissions by California. It was Californian scientists who, as early as the 1950s, identified automobile exhaust as the main culprit in creating Los Angeles's infamous and harmful smog.[69] California was a pioneer in combating pollution by establishing the nation's first tail pipe emission standard in 1966 and by creating the California Air Resources Board (CARB) to oversee an ambitious regulatory effort to aggressively reduce air pollution across the state. When Congress amended the Clean Air Act in 1970 to regulate emissions standards for new automobiles, it carved out an exception that allowed California to set its own car emissions regulations.[70] The statutory waiver recognized that California both had a unique problem with air pollution and already had in place innovative regulations to address the problem. The statutory waiver allowed California to continue to develop its expertise in addressing and reducing air pollution while maintaining its authority to enact regulations despite federal regulatory involvement. In short, the waiver was intended to permit California to continue to be a leader in the area of automobile emissions regulations.

The Clean Air Act requires the EPA to maintain the waiver in place unless the agency concludes that the state's emissions standards are "arbitrary and capricious" or that "the state does not need such state standards to meet compelling and extraordinary conditions."[71] Congress in 1977 amended the Clean Air Act to allow other states to adopt California's car emissions standards without having to apply for separate waivers or demonstrate a compelling need for more stringent standards.[72]

Prior to 2007, fuel economy standards were not under the EPA's purview but were instead regulated by the National Highway Traffic Safety Administration (NHTSA). Under the authority of the Energy Policy and Conservation Act of 1975, the NHTSA developed the Corporate Average Fuel Economy (CAFE) standards in 1978 requiring car manufactures to meet a specific target for the "average mileage traveled by a vehicle per gallon of gasoline."[73]

By regulating the amount of vehicles' fuel consumption, the CAFE standards indirectly limited the amount of greenhouse gases released by them. But at the time the first standards were established, little attention was paid to the gases' harmful effects. As scientific evidence mounted showing the environmental damage caused by greenhouse gases, including their dangerous contribution to global warming, the EPA came under growing pressure to begin regulating them as pollutants. Nineteen environmental organizations petitioned the EPA to do so in 1999, a petition that the agency under President George W. Bush denied four years later. A group of twelve states, along with a handful of local governments and environmental groups, challenged that denial in federal court.

When the case, *Massachusetts v. EPA*, reached the Supreme Court in 2007, the justices grappled with the question of whether the plaintiffs could show sufficiently imminent and concrete injuries caused by global warming that would grant them legal standing, that is, the ability to sue in federal court. The Court held that states in particular could make out the necessary showing of injury. In doing so, the justices explained that states' sovereign interests grant them "special solicitude in [the] standing analysis." The Court added that states are in a special position when seeking federal court jurisdiction to protect themselves from harms created by the federal government's acts or omissions because, in ratifying the Constitution, they had delegated, as we saw in Chapter 1, significant portions of their sovereignty to the national government. After concluding that Massachusetts had standing to sue the EPA, the Court held that greenhouse gases fit within the Clean Air Act's definition of an "air pollutant," requiring the EPA to determine whether the emission of such gases by new vehicles contributed to air pollution or explain why it was unable to make that finding.[74]

After studying the issue, the Obama EPA in 2009 concluded that greenhouse gases "endanger both public health and welfare, and that [their] emissions from new motor vehicles contribute to that endangerment."[75] Since carbon dioxide from fuel combustion is a major source of greenhouse gases, President Obama directed the EPA to work with the NHSTA to align the greenhouse gas standards with the CAFE standards.

It is worth noting that several years *before* the federal government finally began to consider regulating greenhouse gases, California had already moved to do so. In 2002, the California legislature enacted a law calling for the setting of greenhouse gas emission standards for passenger vehicles. The standards were established in 2004 and were intended to apply to new automobiles and small trucks beginning in 2009. California then applied for a waiver from the EPA that would allow it to set its own standards under the Clean Air Act. Notably, these were the first proposed regulations to limit greenhouse gases in the United States—the regulations came not from the federal government, but from a state.

The Bush administration in 2008 denied California's waiver request claiming that it did not meet the Clean Air Act's "compelling and extraordinary conditions" standard. But that decision was overturned by the Obama administration in 2009. In doing so, the Obama EPA noted that the Clean Air Act required a presumption in favor of the waiver's approval. It also relied on Congress's objective, as explained in a 1977 congressional report, to "provide the broadest possible discretion [to California] in selecting the best means to protect the health of its citizens and the public welfare."[76] Thirteen states and the District of Columbia, representing about one-third of the national automobile market, chose to align their greenhouse gas emission standards with those of California, as they were authorized to do by the Clean Air Act. For his part, President Obama directed the EPA and NHTSA to align the federal fuel economy and greenhouse gas emission standards with those developed by California. The administration issued regulations in 2012 requiring "automakers to nearly double the average fuel economy of new cars and trucks to 54.5 miles per gallon by 2025, curbing carbon dioxide pollution [a major contributor to global warming] by about six billion tons over the lifetime of all cars affected by the regulations, about the same amount the United States produces in a year."[77]

The day after Trump announced in 2015 that he was running for president, he went on Fox News to claim that the idea that humans were contributing to global warming was "madness" and a "hoax," a contention he repeated frequently during the presidential campaign. While electioneering in West Virginia in 2016, Trump boasted that he loved coal and that he would bring back coal jobs by repealing Obama's "ridiculous rules and regulations." After elected president, Trump chose Scott Pruitt, a former attorney general of Oklahoma who had repeatedly sued the Obama EPA and was an outspoken climate change denier, to lead the EPA. Following a cold spell in the East in 2017, Trump took to Twitter to suggest that "perhaps we could use a little bit of that good old Global Warming that our Country, but not other countries, was going to pay TRILLIONS OF DOLLARS to protect against. Bundle Up!"[78]

It was hardly surprising, therefore, when the Trump EPA in 2018 announced it was going to revise the federal fuel economy standards by requiring that automobile manufacturers build vehicles that averaged 37 miles per gallon rather than the more than 54 miles required by the Obama rule.[79] The Trump EPA also announced that it was re-evaluating the emissions waiver granted by the Obama administration to California under the Clean Air Act. Director Pruitt criticized the waiver, complaining that "cooperative federalism doesn't mean that one state can dictate standards for the rest of the country."[80] This statement was perplexing given that California did not claim the authority *to require* other states to adopt its higher vehicle emissions standards. What California could do, under the cooperative federalist regulatory mechanism created by Congress, was to set standards that were higher than those of the federal government. As Congress also provided for in the Clean Air Act, other states could *voluntarily choose* to adopt California's stricter standards. But obviously no state has the authority to demand that other states adopt its preferred regulations, something that California has never attempted to do.

California and sixteen other states responded to the Trump EPA's proposed changes by suing in federal court arguing that the administration was acting arbitrarily and capriciously in seeking to roll back the Obama fuel economy standards, a step that would "increase greenhouse gas emissions in the United States by more than the amount many midsize countries put out."[81] One study concluded that cars and trucks in the United States would emit into the atmosphere an additional 321 million to 935 million metric tons of carbon dioxide between 2018 and 2035 if the Trump rule replaced the Obama rule. In addition, the study found that the Trump rule would raise oil consumption by 1.8 billion barrels by 2035 and cost drivers an additional $231 billion.[82]

California also made clear that it would legally challenge any effort by the Trump administration to rescind the waiver that allowed it and thirteen other states to set their own automobile emissions standard regardless of what the administration did at the federal level. As California Attorney General Xavier Becerra explained, "enough is enough. We're not looking to pick a fight with the

Trump administration, but when the stakes are this high for our families' health and our economic prosperity, we have a responsibility to do what is necessary to defend them."[83]

Although automobile manufacturers at first supported a limited rollback of the Obama emission standards, they soon grew alarmed both by the extent to which the Trump EPA might lower those standards and the likelihood that the companies would be subject to two different sets of regulatory regimes: the higher standards established by California, and followed by thirteen other states, and the lower standards set by the federal government that would apply in the rest of the country.[84] Automakers urged both sides to compromise by agreeing to one national standard that lay somewhere in the middle. Although discussions between the federal government and California ensued, the talks eventually stalled, leading the EPA to walk away from the negotiations.[85] Several months later, four automakers—Ford, BMW, Honda, and Volkswagen—signed a deal with the CARB to produce cars that would meet an emission standard of 50 miles per gallon by 2026, a benchmark only slightly less demanding than that established by the Obama administration.[86] The *New York Times* reported that California's deal with the automakers had "enraged" President Trump and had left his plans to roll back the automobile pollution rules in "disarray." The newspaper explained that "the administration's efforts to weaken the Obama-era pollution rules could be rendered irrelevant if too many automakers join California before the Trump plan can be put into effect."[87]

A few weeks later, the media reported that the Department of Justice, in an obvious effort to intimidate the automakers that had displeased Trump by negotiating with California, had opened an antitrust investigation of the four companies. This led California Governor Gavin Newsom to respond angrily that "the Trump administration has been attempting and failing to bully car companies for months now. California stands up to bullies and will keep fighting for stronger clean car protections."[88] The Department of Justice's intimidation effort—described in a *New York Times* editorial as "an act of bullying, plain and simple: a nakedly political abuse of authority"—quickly bore fruit as the German government warned Mercedes Benz not to join the California agreement in order not to anger Trump.[89]

It is worth noting that the federal government's antitrust investigation of the automobile companies that had dared to negotiate separately with California stood in stark contrast to the Trump administration's blessing of T-Mobile's acquisition of Sprint, which left the cell service market essentially in the hands of only three corporations. At the same time, the government's investigation of the car companies that angered Trump was reminiscent of the administration's antitrust challenge to the merger of AT&T and Time Warner, the owner of CNN.[90] The latter was one of the media outlets that, as we will see in Chapter 5, Trump deemed to be "enemies of the people" and purveyors of "fake news" because they included stories that were critical of him and his administration's policies.[91] Not surprisingly, given that the automobile antitrust investigation was politically motivated and lacked any basis in law, the federal government eventually dropped it without fanfare.[92]

Ten days after the Department of Justice began investigating the recalcitrant automobile companies, the Trump administration moved to formally revoke California's authority to set higher vehicle emissions standards than those required by the federal government. No administration had ever before revoked the statutorily granted authority of a state to set its own air quality standards. Andrew Wheeler, the then new head of the EPA, in announcing the revocation, claimed that "we embrace federalism and the role of the states." But, like his predecessor Scott Pruitt, Wheeler proceeded to nonsensically argue that "federalism does not mean that one state can dictate standards for the nation."[93] Again, no one claimed that California had the legal authority *to force* other states to follow its lead in setting higher car emission standards than required by the federal government. But Congress had granted California the ability to set its own standards, which other states could *voluntarily* follow if they so chose.

Twenty-four states quickly sued the Trump administration claiming that the waiver's revocation constituted an impermissible exercise of federal executive authority in the face of clear statutory language requiring that the waiver be granted.[94] As with the issue of the Trump administration's imposition of funding conditions not authorized by Congress as a way of punishing sanctuary jurisdictions, the attempt to revoke California's waiver illustrated the administration's relentless expansion of presidential and executive branch powers in ways that threatened fundamental separation-of-powers principles. We will return to this subject in Chapter 4.

The rollback of automobile emissions standards was only one of more than one hundred environmental regulations that the Trump administration attempted to eliminate or weaken.[95] Among the most ill-advised and dangerous of those rollbacks were those that contributed to the planet's further warming. For example, the Trump EPA overturned an Obama-era regulation that required oil and gas companies to detect and fix leaks of methane gas from wells, pipelines, and storage facilities. Methane is a greenhouse gas that has eighty times the heat-trapping power of carbon dioxide during the twenty years that it remains in the atmosphere. In an indication of just how extreme the Trump administration's evisceration of environmental regulations was, most large oil and gas companies, including ExxonMobil and Shell, opposed the methane regulation rollback.[96] The Trump administration also withdrew the United States from the Paris Climate Agreement entered into by the Obama administration; promoted drilling for oil and gas on public lands that had been protected by presidents

Clinton and Obama, including the Alaska National Wildlife Refuge and the Outer Continental Shelf; and boosted the ability of fossil fuel companies to drill and mine by weakening regulations enacted under the Endangered Species Act.[97]

Progressive states, along with environmental organizations and some cities, led efforts to oppose and resist the Trump administration's dangerous deregulatory policies that increased rather than reduced the multiplicity of environmental, economic, and social harms engendered by the warming atmosphere.[98] One of the most important of those challenges related to electricity plants' production of greenhouse gases. The Supreme Court's 2007 decision in *Massachusetts v. EPA*, which concluded that the EPA could deem carbon dioxide and other greenhouse gases to be air pollutants under the Clean Air Act, not only allowed the agency to regulate motor vehicle emissions but also carbon dioxide emitted from large, stationary sources such as steel mills and power plants. The Obama administration had adopted regulations, known as the Clean Power Plan (CPP), requiring that new and existing power plants reduce, by 2030, their emissions of carbon dioxide by 30 percent.[99] The regulations aimed to diminish the number of old and heavily polluting electricity-generating plants fueled by coal and encourage the building of new power plants run on cleaner natural gas or renewable energy. As the Clean Air Act provides, and as is typical of the cooperative federalism framework that undergirds most federal environmental law, the CPP called on the states to develop and implement plans to meet the emissions reduction targets.[100]

After the Obama administration adopted the CPP in 2015, several utility companies and two-dozen Republican-led states immediately challenged it in court.[101] In the same way that progressive states during the Trump years claimed that the EPA went beyond its statutory authority in *rolling back* environmental regulations, the states that challenged the CPP argued that Congress had not provided the agency with the power to *expand* its regulatory authority by requiring power plants to significantly reduce their greenhouse gas emissions.

In February, 2016, four days before conservative Justice Antonin Scalia died, the Supreme Court, in a 5-4 ruling, delayed the implementation of the CPP pending a decision by the U.S. Court of Appeals for the District of Columbia. That court heard oral arguments in the case later in 2016, but did not issue a final ruling before Trump took office in 2017.

Two months after Trump became president, he signed an executive order directing the EPA to consider rescinding the CPP on the ground that it would harm the coal industry.[102] Later in 2017, the EPA proposed retracting the CPP, claiming that it was premised on "a novel and expansive view of agency authority."[103] The agency formally replaced the CPP in 2018 with watered-down rules under what it called an "Affordable Clean Energy" plan. Trump's EPA administrator proudly announced the deregulatory move at an event that, according to the *New York Times*, was "attended by coal-industry leaders, utility lobbyists, and prominent deniers of climate change science." The new Trump plan, unlike the CPP, did "not cap greenhouse gas emissions. Instead it [left] it up to states to decide whether, or if, to scale back emissions and pick from a menu of technologies to improve power-plant efficiency at the facility level" in ways that did not encourage the replacement of coal with cleaner fuels and would only marginally reduce greenhouse emissions.[104]

Less than a month after the Trump administration announced its deregulatory scheme, a coalition of twenty-nine states and cities, led by the New York Attorney General, filed a lawsuit arguing that it violated the Clean Air Act because it did not curtail greenhouse gas emissions by energy plants. The lawsuit pointed out "that the new rule would actually extend the life of dirty and aging coal-burning plants, promoting an increase in pollution instead of curbing it." On the last day of the Trump presidency, a federal appellate court struck down the administration's attempt to weaken regulations restricting emissions of greenhouse gases by power plants because it was inconsistent with the Clean Air Act. The court also concluded that the Trump EPA's effort "to slow the process for reductions of emissions is arbitrary and capricious."[105]

Progressive states challenged the Trump administration in many other areas of environmental law and policy. One of those involved the protection of the nation's waterways. The Trump EPA stripped back the definition of "navigable waters" protected by the Clean Water Act that had been adopted by the Obama administration. Under rules issued in 2019, waters that ran only in response to rainfalls were no longer subject to Clean Water Act requirements. Additionally, bodies of water without a permanent surface connection to navigable waters were no longer included in the definition of "navigable waters." The U.S. Geological Survey estimated that the Trump deregulatory move "would erase federal protections for the more than 51 percent of wetlands and 18 percent of streams without relatively permanent surface water connections to nearby waterways."[106] According to the *New York Times*, "an immediate effect of the clean water repeal is that polluters will no longer need a permit to discharge potentially harmful substances into many streams and wetlands."[107]

A coalition of fourteen states sued the Trump administration seeking to block the repeal of the Obama clean water regulation.[108] Twenty states also sued the Trump EPA after it limited the ability of states to block infrastructure projects under the Clean Water Act.[109] In addition, a group of ten eastern states, some led by Republican governors (Massachusetts, Maryland, and South Carolina), joined a lawsuit brought by environmental groups against the Trump administration for allowing oil and gas companies to drill off shore utilizing methods that are harmful to the environment and that the states alleged violated the National Environmental Policy Act, the Endangered Species Act, and the Marine

Mammal Protection Act.[110] And following a lawsuit by New York state, a federal court of appeals held that the Trump EPA had impermissibly allowed upwind states to continue emitting air pollution that had detrimental effects on the air quality of downwind states.[111]

It is clear, then, that states during the Trump years sought, time and time again, to make it more difficult for the administration to roll back regulations in ways that were harmful to the environment and, quite frankly, to the future of humankind on the planet. Although progressive states were by no means the only parties that challenged the Trump administration's deregulatory environmental efforts (local governments and progressive groups, for example, did as well), states sometimes incur distinctive injuries caused by federal government actions and omissions. Those injuries can both help give states legal standing to sue and provide support for judicial intervention.[112] In addition, states, and especially *coalitions* of states, can frequently bring more resources to bear in challenging the federal government than advocacy organizations. All of this meant that, during the Trump years, our federalist constitutional structure was an ally to those who care about climate change, clean air, and clean water.

State-based challenges to Trump administration policies were not limited to the areas of immigration and the environment; instead, those challenges covered a wide range of issues and disputes. For example, following Trump's abrupt declaration via Twitter in 2017 that transgender individuals would be banned from the military, several states, including California, Nevada, and New Mexico, announced that their national guards welcomed such individuals among their ranks.[113]

In addition, some states sought to prevent the administration from cutting back on health-care insurance subsidies and guarantees under Obamacare. Several states, including some governed by Republicans (such as Missouri and Utah) expanded Medicaid during the Trump era, making health care more accessible and affordable for their low-income residents, despite the Trump administration's opposition to such expansion. After the administration pushed Congress to eliminate Obamacare's individual mandate that penalized individuals who could afford health insurance but chose not to purchase it, states like New Jersey and Vermont established their own individual mandates.[114] As the New Jersey health care policy director explained, "our position is [that] we're really not going to let Trump decide the fate of health care in our state."[115]

Several states also resisted the Trump administration's efforts to push individuals into skimpy health insurance plans that attracted healthier customers, depleting the pool of healthy individuals available to participate in Obamacare, leading to a rise in premiums. Several states outright banned these plans, while others significantly limited their use.[116] As a spokesperson for a health-care advocacy group explained, "nothing is going to happen at the federal level [under the Trump administration] in a significant way to advance policies to make health care more affordable or more accessible to the American people. States are taking it on themselves to make changes and get around this gridlock."[117]

In addition, a group of nineteen states, joined by the District of Columbia and the City of Chicago, succeeded in petitioning a federal district court to vacate a Department of Health and Human Services rule allowing health-care providers to refuse to treat patients based on religious and moral objections.[118] And in a lawsuit brought by eleven states, a federal district court concluded that a rule issued by Trump's Department of Labor was illegal because it was designed to circumvent Obamacare's statutory requirements and exceeded the agency's authority under the Employee Retirement Income Security Act (ERISA).[119]

In short, progressive federalism was an essential source of resistance to the Trump administration's policies. According to one study issued one month into Trump's fourth year in office, the number "of multistate lawsuits against Trump in his first term [was] over four times higher than what President Barack Obama faced in his first term." As the report explained, "lawsuits pushed by Democrats have had an 80 percent success rate against Trump, 20 percent higher than Republican-led lawsuits against the Obama administration."[120]

The blue-state resistance, of course, did not succeed in derailing all of the Trump administration's many harmful policies. Such an outcome would have been impossible given both the federal government's immense powers and the ever-growing authority accumulated by the presidency over the last few decades (more on that topic in the next chapter). But the period between 2017 and 2020 repeatedly showed how the exercise and assertion of state sovereignty and interests helped mitigate some of the harms engendered by the misguided, dangerous, and discriminatory policies of a far-right president such as Donald Trump.

Finally, when we juxtapose the environmental federalism that took place during the Trump years with the sanctuary federalism (explored in the previous section) of that same period, it further illustrates the substantive neutrality of federalism. Sometimes federalist principles and mechanisms can be deployed to *prevent* the adoption of new regulations, as was true in the context of immigration policy during the Trump era. At other times, the principles and mechanisms can be used to *protect* existing regulations from efforts to rescind them, as was the case in the context of environmental policy during the Trump years. The fact that federalism can be used for both pro-regulatory and anti-regulatory purposes further illustrates how there is nothing intrinsically good or bad, or progressive or conservative, about dividing authority between the federal and state governments.

Blue-State Federalism in Filling Federal Voids: Gun Regulations and Coronavirus Response

In exploring how liberal states exercised their sovereignty during the Trump years, I have focused on how they responded to the administration's *actions*. But blue states also helpfully exercised their sovereignty in response to the federal government's misguided and harmful *omissions*. Here I am thinking in particular of instances in which the Trump administration failed to provide effective national leadership on issues that desperately required it, such as gun violence and the coronavirus.

When focusing on the salutary effects of limiting federal authority as a means of protecting state sovereignty, it is tempting to underestimate or underemphasize the need for federal leadership and policies. But the reality is that *federal involvement is essential in addressing problems that transcend state boundaries.* For example, the fact that the harmful consequences of air and water pollution frequently cross state lines calls for robust forms of federal environmental regulation that, among other things, impose minimum standards of protection for the health and safety of all of the nation's residents regardless of which state they reside in. Also, the fact that it is impossible for states, regardless of how strictly they regulate the possession and use of guns, to keep firearms from being brought in from neighboring states, counsels in favor of a strong federal response to the horrifying problem of gun violence in the United States. Similarly, the fact that many public health threats—such as, most notably, that presented by the coronavirus—cannot be contained within particular states, calls for focused efforts at the national level to help fund, manage, and coordinate effective responses to those threats. In short, it is important that the federal government take the lead in addressing problems that have national causes, implications, or effects and nothing in this book is intended to suggest otherwise.

On the question of firearms, it was unfortunately the case that the frightening increase in mass shootings and other forms of gun violence continued unabated during the Trump era. Before Trump ran for office, he supported gun safety measures. In 2012, for example, he praised President Obama for calling for tighter federal regulations of guns following the school massacre in Newtown, Connecticut, which left twenty-six children and teachers dead. But by the time he ran for president, Trump had rebranded himself as a defender of Second Amendment rights. At a presidential primary debate in 2015, he boasted that he carried handguns "a lot" and claimed that the number of victims in mass shootings would be reduced if more citizens were armed. The National Rifle Association (NRA) endorsed Trump in 2016 and spent $30 million to help him get elected.[121]

As president, Trump repeatedly assured his supporters that he would protect their Second Amendment rights against liberals whom he claimed wanted to take their guns away.[122] After some of the worst gun tragedies during his tenure, such as the shooting in 2018 at a high school in Parkland, Florida, which left seventeen students and staff members dead and the same-day mass shootings in 2019—in El Paso, Texas (twenty-two people killed at a shopping mall) and Dayton, Ohio (nine individuals murdered near downtown)—Trump made vague comments about needing to solve the gun violence problem in America.[123] But when it came time to actually supporting meaningful federal legislation that would, for example, expand background checks to private gun sales or help states implement so-called red flag regulations, aimed at keeping weapons away from individuals likely to harm themselves or others, Trump ultimately refused to do so, usually following phone conversations with NRA leaders.[124]

Many states, during the Trump years, tried to fill the large regulatory holes left by the woefully inadequate federal response to gun violence. In 2018, more than half the states enacted at least one gun safety measure for a total of sixty-nine such regulations, a threefold increase from 2017; eighteen of those measures were approved by Republican-controlled legislatures.[125]

For example, California raised the minimum age for buying shotguns and handguns from 18 to 21, while setting tougher standards for concealed weapon permits. In addition, Florida raised the minimum purchase age to 21, imposed a three-day waiting period for gun purchases, and adopted a red flag law. Maryland and Rhode Island also enacted such a law. New Jersey and Vermont required background checks for almost all private gun sales and banned the sale of bump stocks, an attachment that allows semi-automatic weapons to fire bullets faster. In addition, Delaware, Hawaii, Maryland, and Washington state prohibited the sale of bump stocks in 2018. Also in that year, state legislators rejected 90 percent of bills endorsed by the NRA.[126]

States also attempted to make up for the federal government's refusal to fund research on the causes and effects of gun violence. In 1993, researchers published a study funded by the Centers for Disease Control and Prevention (CDC) which concluded that having a gun at home puts household members at greater risk of being victims of homicides, factual findings that undermined the NRA's political agenda.[127] As a result, the gun rights organization pushed Congress to enact a statute (known as the Dickey amendment) making it illegal for federal agencies "to advocate or promote gun control."[128] The statute practically ended federal funding for the study of gun violence in the United States. In the twenty-two years that followed the passage of the Dickey amendment, more than 600,000 people in the country were killed or injured by firearms.[129]

After Trump was elected, some progressive states tried to make up for the lack of federal involvement by funding gun violence research, leading the *New York*

Times in 2019 to conclude that "gun research is suddenly hot." California led the way by investing $5 million to create the Violence Prevention Research Program at the University of California, Davis, the first state-funded gun violence research center in the country. Similarly, New Jersey invested $2 million to help create the New Jersey Center on Gun Violence Research at Rutgers University. Washington state gave $1 million to the Harborview Injury and Prevention Research Center, an organization that studies the impact of gun violence and looks for ways to prevent deaths by firearms.[130]

The nationwide public health crisis engendered by the coronavirus, which killed approximately 350,000 Americans in 2020, also illustrated the importance of marshaling state authority, resources, and expertise *to try to fill the voids* created by ineffective and incompetent federal governance. Historians and public health scholars, among others, will undoubtedly spend years dissecting the Trump administration's woefully inadequate and ineffectual response to the epidemic. To put it simply and bluntly, the lives of tens of thousands of people could have been saved had the federal government effectively and rationally exercised its considerable legal, organizational, and financial powers to put in place the necessary mechanisms and policies to better protect the American public from the coronavirus threat. According to a Columbia University report published seven months into the epidemic, at least 130,000 American deaths would have been avoided had it not been for the Trump administration's "abject failures."[131]

The crisis, for example, urgently called for federal intervention and coordination to make sure that, early in the epidemic, the necessary medical equipment and protective gear were available in sufficient quantities in the parts of the country where they were needed most, areas that changed from one section of the United States to another as the epidemic progressed and spread. Instead of providing desperately needed federal leadership and coordination, the Trump administration, in the spring of 2020, left states to fend for themselves in their frantic search for lifesaving equipment and gear. Astonishingly, this resulted in states being forced to compete with each other, with the federal government, and with foreign countries in the open marketplace for essential medical necessities and protective gear. The result was entirely predictable: a massive increase in demand for the essential materials, in the absence of greater supply, resulted in exorbitant increases in prices. As New York Governor Andrew Cuomo explained, "we are literally bidding up the prices ourselves" after the cost for a ventilator increased from $25,000 to $40,000 in a matter of days during the epidemic's first month.[132]

When desperate governors turned to the federal government for help, they were told that fighting the virus was their responsibility and that the federal government's role, as Trump put it in a letter to Senator Charles Schumer of New York, "is merely a back-up for state governments." The federal government's passivity in the face of a deadly and spreading pandemic was the equivalent, as one angry governor put it, of Franklin D. Roosevelt saying after Pearl Harbor: "We'll be right behind you, Connecticut. Good luck building those battleships."[133]

The lack of federal coordination and support meant that, as thousands of Americans were dying of COVID-19, the medical equipment and protective gear that were available in the marketplace were not necessarily going to where they were most indispensable; instead it was the buyers that had the connections and financial resources to locate and purchase the materials that succeeded in procuring them. This was, to put it simply, an absolutely insane way of distributing desperately needed medical equipment during a pandemic. In the meantime, Trump and his administration officials kept falsely claiming that there were no shortages of any of the desperately needed medical supplies.[134]

To make matters even worse, the same president who, as we will see in Chapter 4, was quick to claim that he had expansive legal authority to deal with national emergencies that did not exist—to justify, for example, the circumvention of congressional appropriations to finance a border wall with Mexico that Congress refused to fund—initially declined to exercise his authority under the Defense Production Act to deal with the true national emergency created by the coronavirus pandemic. That statute, which was enacted by Congress during the Korean War, authorizes the president to require the private sector to produce equipment and materials necessary to protect the nation's security and defense. And when Trump did finally exercise his authority under the act, he did so hesitatingly and ineffectively.[135]

At the end of February 2020, Trump claimed that the total number of coronavirus cases nationwide would soon be zero and that the virus would disappear causing few if any deaths.[136] This is likely the most consequentially misleading (or, at least, deeply misinformed) prediction that any president has publicly made in the nation's history: six months later, approximately six million Americans had tested positive for the virus, and more than 180,000 had died of the disease. Trump also repeatedly lied when he claimed that everyone in the United States who wanted to receive a coronavirus test could do so and that the country was doing more testing per capita than any other nation in the world.[137] Rather than using the federal government's powers to make sure there was sufficient testing capacity in the parts of the country that needed it most, the administration repeatedly left it to states to compete with each other in finding essential testing supplies and laboratory equipment. As a *New York Times* editorial explained in April 2020, at a time when the daily COVID-19 deaths in the United States exceeded 2,000 individuals a day, "labs across the country report that they could conduct more tests but for shortages of critical supplies—swabs to gather nasal samples, containers to transport samples, chemicals to test samples. Moreover, a lack of coordination has forced labs to compete for available supplies, creating huge inefficiencies: Some places have plenty of swabs but not enough containers, or containers but not chemicals. . . . The director of Maine's Center for Disease Control and Prevention said he would not disclose what kind of testing equipment the state was buying for fear others would hoard necessary supplies." The editorial went on to complain that "the Trump administration's insistence that states fend for themselves means the [federal] government is not trying to identify the best approaches, or to encourage production on a national scale."[138]

In defending his policy of allowing states to compete with and outbid each other when it came to desperately needed medical, preventive, and testing equipment and supplies, Trump claimed that it was not for the federal government to take the lead in fighting the virus.[139] At the same time, in a naked attempt to gain political credit for reopening the economy, Trump asserted that he as president, and not state governors, had the ultimate authority to lift "shut down" and "stay at home" orders that governors had instituted earlier. As he put it, "when somebody's the president of the United States, the authority is total." Trump further claimed that the governors "can't do anything without the approval of the president of the United States."[140] But as constitutional law commentators across the ideological spectrum pointed out, a president's power over the nation and its governors is obviously not "total." Although the federal government appropriately has significant power to address a nationwide epidemic, it was simply not the case that governors had to ask for presidential permission to leave in place preventive measures they had instituted to protect their residents' health.[141]

Rather than embracing a cooperative form of federalism that sought to combine the federal government's public health expertise and financial resources with state governments' greater knowledge of local conditions and needs, Trump embraced what one newspaper commentator called "a toxic doctrine of laissez-faire federalism" in which he disastrously paired a claim to total authority with a complete abdication of responsibility.[142] Law professor Nancy Knauer made a similar point when she noted that the epidemic "upended the concept of cooperative federalism that is at the heart of disaster policy and pandemic planning. . . . Instead, it has been replaced by something much more confrontational and combative" which "is antithetical to the type of cooperation necessary to mount an effective response to the COVID-19 pandemic."[143]

The country, particularly during the pandemic's early months, was in desperate need of "nationwide standards or guideposts based on scientific evidence for reopening the various geographical sectors of the United States."[144] But the Trump administration repeatedly failed to provide clear and consistent scientifically based guidance on when and how to reopen the economy. While some career government scientists, most prominently Anthony Fauci, the director of the National Institute of Allergy and Infectious Diseases, did their best to provide such guidance, Trump and his political appointees repeatedly confused and misled the public by minimizing the impact of the virus, questioning the need to take precautionary steps such as wearing masks in public, and underestimating the health risks of too quickly reopening the economy in May and June of 2020 when the contagion rates first began to decrease after spiking in March and April.[145]

As part of his campaign to sow misinformation and mistrust, Trump went so far as to encourage armed protestors to swarm state capitols, in states with Democratic governors, to demand the lifting of business lockdowns and mask-wearing rules.[146] Trump also encouraged people to take an anti-malaria medication despite the lack of any scientific evidence of efficacy in fighting COVID-19.[147] The president at one point even suggested that Americans might want to inject household bleach as a remedy for the disease.[148]

Some governors did their best to respond to this appalling failure of federal leadership by organizing regionally.[149] In addition, New York state in the summer of 2020 found it necessary to pay for a nationwide public service television campaign aimed at urging Americans to socially distance and use masks in public. State officials explained that after managing to control the outbreak, which devastatingly had killed more than 30,000 New Yorkers by the early summer, they were now using the national advertising campaign to try "to prevent the virus from seeping back into the state."[150] The fact that it was a state and not the federal government that paid for a *nationwide* public service health campaign illustrated the extent to which the federal government failed to lead by clearly and effectively informing and educating Americans about how best to protect themselves from the virus.

Although Trump, seemingly more concerned with his re-election chances than with how to develop and implement national policies to slow down the spread of a pandemic that was killing tens of thousands of Americans every few weeks, pushed to have the country reopen in April and May, 2020, he was unable to force resisting governors in states like California, Connecticut, Illinois, Maryland, Massachusetts, New York, and Washington to lift quarantining orders. Officials in those states, led by governors such as Democrats Andrew Cuomo of New York and Jay Inslee of Washington, and Republicans Larry Hogan of Maryland and Charlie Baker of Massachusetts, had a better understanding of the health emergencies and challenges that their communities and residents were experiencing than did the president and his cadre of incompetent advisers in Washington, D.C.[151] Sadly, it was primarily residents in states, such as Florida, South Carolina, and Texas, whose governors buckled under Trump's relentless pressure to quickly reopen their economies, in the face of almost universal opposition by epidemiologists and other public health experts, who suffered the greatest increases in coronavirus positive tests and numbers of COVID-19 deaths during the harrowing summer of 2020.[152] And due to a lack of federal leadership, when the long-expected second wave of the pandemic hit at the end of 2020, pervasive shortages of protective gear across the country once again forced governors to compete with one another to procure lifesaving materials.[153]

In many ways, the coronavirus exposed what two commentators, writing in the *New England Journal of Medicine*, dubbed the "dark side of federalism" by encouraging "a patchwork response to epidemics." The dispersal of government power among federal, state, and local public agencies made it more difficult to effectively grapple with a health epidemic caused by a virus that "is highly transmissible, crosses borders efficiently, and threatens our national infrastructure and economy."[154] At the same time, there can be little doubt that the Trump administration, even while working within a federalist structure that purposefully disperses government authority and responsibility, could have prevented many deaths and much suffering if it had provided clear and scientifically driven guidance on the best public health practices for slowing down the disease; if it had coordinated a unified response by states that recognized that effectively controlling transmission in one state would not stop the epidemic if neighboring states were not doing the same; and if it had replaced competition by states for scarce medical resources with sensible allocation mechanisms driven by shifting needs, including geographically based ones.

None of this is to suggest, of course, that state-led responses to the virus were always effective or appropriate. For example, New York officials, in the early weeks of the epidemic, made the fateful decision to send nursing home residents who had been hospitalized due to the virus back to nursing homes, leading to scores of further infections and deaths in those institutions.[155] In addition, I am not arguing that states are intrinsically better able than the federal government to address public health emergencies. Indeed, as I have noted, the federal government, when properly and intelligently operated, is particularly well-suited to take the lead in responding to national public health emergencies such as the coronavirus one. My point instead is that a federalist system such as ours at least allows states to attempt to fill the voids left by a federal government operated in incompetent and ineffectual ways. In the face of a frighteningly inept and negligent federal response to the COVID-19 epidemic, the residents of at least some states, such as New York, Maryland, Massachusetts, and Washington, benefited from policies instituted at the state level aimed at reducing the transmission of the disease, reallocating medical personnel and equipment within state boundaries in response to shifting needs, and engaging in policy coordination with other states in their regions.[156] The nation as a whole would have benefited immensely, and lives would have been saved, if there had been similar coordinated and helpful responses by the federal government to COVID-19. But if the federal government under Trump's control was unable and unwilling to take the necessary steps, the country at least benefited from the fact that, under our federal system, states had the authority to try to fill the voids left by the dangerous and devastating absence of effective and competent federal leadership.[157]

Progressives and the Future of Federalism

One of the defining features of progressive politics in the United States is the belief that government interventions and subsidies can help to address many of the nation's social and economic ills. Progressives generally believe that the government, for example, should regulate the marketplace and economic actors in ways that protect workers, consumers, and the environment. Progressives also support vigorous enforcement of civil rights laws, generous public subsidies that make education through college affordable for everyone, and universal access to health care. It is important to ask, therefore, whether the types of federalist claims that progressives repeatedly relied on to try to resist some of the Trump administration's most ill-advised and harmful policies might be used by conservatives to make it more difficult for future progressive administrations to institute the kinds of activist government policies required to attain progressive objectives.

The honest answer to that question is "yes." In the past, conservatives have repeatedly relied on states' rights claims to try to block liberal activist government at the federal level, and there is no reason to believe that they will cease doing so in the future. Conservatives' use of federalist mechanisms and principles to try to undermine progressive policies at the national level was reflected in the multiple court challenges filed by conservative states to try to derail many of the Obama administration's most far-ranging and impactful liberal policies related to health care, immigration, and the environment, among other matters.[158] In one of the most important conservative victories, the Supreme Court in 2012 held that Obamacare's attempted expansion of Medicaid rolls was unconstitutional. Congress, in enacting the Affordable Care Act in 2010, had authorized the withholding of *all* federal Medicaid funds from states that refused to expand Medicaid coverage to a significantly greater number of individuals. In striking down that part of Obamacare, the Court concluded that the federal government was unconstitutionally trying to *coerce* states into pursuing a policy objective— in this case, the expansion of government-subsidized health insurance—in ways that violated state sovereignty.[159] It can be expected, as this book goes to press, that the same type of states-based challenges will repeatedly be brought against some of the Biden administration's progressive policies.

Given that the same federalist mechanisms and principles that progressive states used to resist the Trump administration can be deployed to challenge the future policies of liberal administrations, progressives are confronted with a crucial choice between two alternatives. One option is to support and defend the proposition, as progressive states consistently did throughout the Trump years, that federalist mechanisms and principles sometimes appropriately limit the ability of the federal government to pursue national policies in ways that infringe on state sovereignty. The second option is to reject the idea that federalist mechanisms and principles should serve as independent sources of restrictions on federal authority. Instead, progressives can defend the proposition that federal authority is, as a constitutional matter, sufficiently limited by (1) the federal government's lack of general police power enjoyed by the states and (2) the Bill of Rights' protections for individual rights, such as those related to free speech, equality, and privacy.

A clear benefit of the second alternative, from a progressive perspective, is that it would enhance the ability of the federal government to confront some of the country's biggest problems through centralized and cohesive policies at the national level. Many of the country's most significant challenges—everything from reducing and mitigating the harms of climate change to increasing access to health care to fighting pandemics like COVID-19—cannot be sufficiently or effectively addressed through fifty different sets of regulations and policies that end at the borders of each state. In a highly mobile and interconnected society such as ours, individual states cannot, on their own, address problems whose causes and effects are not contained within their borders. To put it simply, neither Rhode Island nor Ohio, for example, can reduce nationwide emissions of gases that are warming the planet or provide adequate access to health insurance for Americans as they move from one state to another or prevent the nationwide spread of highly contagious and deadly organisms such as the coronavirus.

Law professor Erwin Chemerinsky, one of the nation's leading liberal constitutional scholars, urges progressives to embrace the second option. According to Chemerinsky, the Constitution does not protect state sovereignty in ways that independently restrict federal authority. He argues that the crucial federalism question is whether the federal law or program that is subject to challenge under federalist principles is needed for "effective governance." As Chemerinsky sees it, a "progressive vision of federalism" should focus on "empower[ing] government at all levels to deal with social problems." The value of federalism, from this perspective, is in its "redundancy"—if one level of government cannot solve the social problem at issue, then another level might.[160] Chemerinsky argues that "federalism should not be seen as a basis for limiting the powers of either Congress or the federal courts. Rather it should be seen as an empowerment; it is desirable to have multiple levels of government all with the capability of dealing with the countless social problems that face the United States."[161]

One upside to Chemerinsky's understanding of federalism, from a progressive perspective, is that it encourages activist government interventions at the federal, state, and local levels as means for solving the country's most pressing problems. Another upside, from that same perspective, is that it does not bolster or strengthen the federalist mechanisms and principles that conservatives, through the decades, have repeatedly relied on to try to weaken and undermine the federal government's ability to pursue liberal policies.

But the downsides of such an understanding of federalism for progressives are also significant, especially when considering the fact that, obviously, liberals do not always control the federal government. Although that government under the Constitution is theoretically a government of limited powers, the reality is that the Supreme Court since 1937, with a few exceptions, has provided expansive understandings of its powers, especially as they relate to its regulation of interstate commerce and its ability to pursue police power objectives indirectly through its taxing and spending authority.[162] Those expansive understandings, when coupled with the fact that the federal government, under the Supremacy Clause, can preempt or displace state regulations when acting pursuant to its delegated powers, mean that a federal government controlled by right-wingers can, from a progressive perspective, lead to the adoption of highly problematic policies. Federalism mechanisms and principles can help mitigate the harms caused by those policies.

As we have seen, constitutionally based principles of state sovereignty were at the center of state resistance to the Trump administration's most misguided, injurious, or discriminatory policies in crucial areas such as immigration and the environment. The ability of progressive states to challenge, in some cases successfully, the Trump administration's exercise of federal authority served as a crucial bulwark against a long list of highly problematic policies that promoted discrimination (like racist immigration policies) and endangered the public's well-being (like rollbacks of environmental regulations). The repeated reliance by progressive states on federalist mechanisms and principles to try to curb some of the Trump administration's more misbegotten and harmful—and, in some cases, illegal or unconstitutional—actions illustrates how federalism, from a progressive perspective, can play a helpful and valuable role in limiting the federal government's power.

The Trump years proved to progressives that a federalist government structure can sometimes promote the country's welfare and protect the interests of vulnerable and disadvantaged populations from a federal administration's dangerous and discriminatory policies. Progressives should therefore recognize that, under our constitutional system of governance that seeks, among other things, to disperse government authority, there is an appropriate role for states, as independent sovereigns, to serve as counterweights to the exercise of federal authority. Conservatives' use of that same principle to challenge the policies of liberal administrations is a political price that progressives should consider paying for being able to rely on it to try to curb some of the worst and most harmful policies of future right-wing and nationalist presidents in the Trump mold.

In addition, as we saw in Chapter 1, our federalist system of governance has allowed progressives to attain policy objectives at the state level, on issues as varied as marriage equality and marijuana decriminalization, that were not attainable initially at the national level. Those state-level reforms have been important not only for the changes they have brought to state laws and regulations, but also for their ability to influence national debates and policies.

Furthermore, federalism can play a helpful role in reducing the dangers associated with and harms resulting from autocratic federal rule. In Chapter 4, we will explore the multiple ways in which Trump asserted presidential authority in autocratic ways, including using the office of the presidency and the Department of Justice to gain personal and political benefits, to protect his friends and allies, and to target his political opponents. Trump also asserted presidential power to try to obstruct special counsel Robert Mueller's investigation of links between his 2016 presidential campaign and Russian operatives, to impede Congress's impeachment and other investigatory powers, and to fire inspectors general who were investigating possible wrongdoing by administration officials.

Trump's abuses of presidential power would have been considerably more pernicious and damaging had he also been able to control state governments' levers of power, including by using state prosecutors and other law enforcement officials to protect his personal and political interests and by commandeering state officials and resources to pursue his relentless anti-immigrant and anti-minority agendas. The fact that the nation's federalist mechanisms and principles insulate state and local officials and resources from presidential control helped keep Trump's autocratic governance from being even worse than it was.[163] Federalism helped prevent the type of consolidation of executive authority at the federal level that Trump ruthlessly sought; such a further concentration of presidential power could have served as a potential fatal blow to our democratic institutions while leaving traditionally subjugated minorities vulnerable to even greater amounts of state-sanctioned harassment and discrimination.

Before Trump was elected to office, much of the focus of federalism disputes pitted Congress's authority to legislate under Article I of the Constitution against state sovereignty as protected by the Tenth Amendment. Indeed, almost all of the important Supreme Court cases raising federalism questions have pitted congressional authority against state sovereignty.[164] But the Trump years showed how states can serve to limit and counterbalance not only the exercise of congressional authority, but that of federal executive authority as well.

Federalism worked alongside separation-of-powers principles to limit some of Trump's abusive exercises and dangerous claims of presidential authority. For example, many of the state-led challenges (federalism) to the Trump administration's immigration and environmental policies were grounded in the claim that the executive branch was implementing federal laws inconsistently with congressional mandates (separation of powers). In other words, in challenging some of the Trump administration's most problematic policies, progressive states not only sought to exercise and protect their sovereignty, but also to maintain at least a modicum of balance between congressional authority and presidential power.[165] In this way, federalism and separation-of-powers principles functioned as a double helix of constraint on the exercise of autocratic presidential authority.[166]

Federalism helped mitigate Trumpian autocracy in other ways. For example, the state of Oregon and its city Portland challenged and resisted Trump's sending of federal law enforcement agents, including officials from Customs and Border Protection and from ICE, to patrol the area around the federal courthouse in Portland in response to Black Lives Matter demonstrations in the summer of 2020. The federal agents sent by Trump, who did not wear identifying markers or names on their military-style uniforms, attacked protestors violently by beating them with batons, shooting projectiles at demonstrators, detonating tear gas containers, and abruptly pulling people into unmarked vans without identifying themselves or explaining their actions.[167]

Trump's militarized crackdown of protestors in Portland shocked millions of people across the country, many of whom questioned the federal government's authority to police areas beyond federal property. Although federalism issues can sometimes seem theoretical and conceptual, there was nothing abstract about heavily militarized federal police forces running amok on the streets of a major American city. There was a wide consensus, shared by some conservatives, that this was an illegal and dangerous exercise of federal power that, in completely ignoring the interests and preferences of state and local officials, threatened the basic liberties and rights of protestors and residents.[168] After wide-ranging and withering criticism of its use of militarized police forces in Portland, the Trump administration abruptly changed course by turning over the responsibility for maintaining peace and order near the federal courthouse where it should have remained all along: with state and local officials.[169]

The constitutionally mandated dispersal of authority to the states also made it more difficult for Trump to successfully implement his deceitful and brazenly authoritarian and anti-democratic efforts to challenge the results of the 2020 presidential election. For understandable reasons, many progressives for years have been calling for greater federal oversight of elections as a way of helping to enforce the fundamental right to vote. Such calls continued in the tense days

following the 2020 election as the nation anxiously waited for the piecemeal reporting of votes cast in fifty states and hundreds of counties across the country.
A new federal agency with robust authority to oversee federal elections, some
argued, could help both to expand franchise rights and make the reporting of
election results more efficient and uniform.[170] But there can be little doubt that
if such a federal agency had existed in 2020, Trump would have abused the immense powers of the presidency in efforts to direct and pressure the agency
both to restrict franchise rights and to deploy its authority, as an arbiter of electoral fairness and appropriate electoral processes, to support his false claims
of electoral fraud. It was a very good thing for American democracy that such
a federal agency did not exist in 2020 during the waning days of the Trump
administration.

Rather than assisting Trump's deeply anti-democratic quest to overturn the
results of the presidential election, our federalist system helped insulate state
officials charged with protecting the election's integrity from the president's outrageous efforts to pressure and intimidate them into doing his political dirty
work. For example, three weeks before Trump left office, he telephoned Georgia's
secretary of state and threatened him with a "criminal offense" if the Republican
state official continued to refuse "to find [the] 11,780 votes" that the president
needed to be awarded the state's Electoral College votes. Although, as we will
explore in the next chapter, presidents have accumulated an immense amount
of power over the last century, they continue to lack the constitutional authority
to force state officials to help them politically. Trump's intimidating phone call
was widely criticized, even by some Republican officials. It was also included
in the article of impeachment, approved by the House of Representatives, following Trump's efforts to instigate his supporters' violent takeover of the Capitol
on January 6, 2021, which resulted in the deaths of five people and threatened
the lives of hundreds of elected officials. According to the impeachment document, the phone call was evidence of Trump's insidious attempts to undermine
the legitimacy of the presidential election.[171] The fact that federalism protections
prevented Trump from ordering state officials to do his dirty work helped guarantee that the will of a majority of Americans, expressed via the ballot box, was
respected.

In short, progressive movements and causes have enjoyed significant benefits
from using federalist mechanisms and principles (1) to advance liberal policies
at the state level, often with progressive national repercussions (using federalism
"on offense"); (2) to serve as braking mechanisms for the implementation of
right-wing policies when the federal government is controlled by conservatives
(using federalism "on defense"); and (3) to limit the exercise of autocratic federal authority (also using federalism "on defense"). In my view, these benefits
outweigh the costs to progressives engendered by conservatives' use of the same

federalist mechanisms and principles to advance right-wing policy objectives at the state level and derail liberal ones at the federal level.

I recognize that reasonable people can disagree on the ultimate question of whether progressive movements and causes, and more importantly, Americans as a whole, have benefited more from a constitutionally-mandated federalist government structure than they have been harmed by such a structure. I understand, and fully expect, that there will be some, perhaps many, progressives who will remain skeptical of federalism even after experiencing or observing the harms engendered by the federal government under Trump's control.

But what I hope most progressives will recognize is the problematic nature of *situational* federalism. What progressives should not do going forward is try to have it both ways: that is, to reject or ignore federalism concerns when a liberal such as Joe Biden is in the White House while repeatedly relying on those same concerns to resist federal policies, as blue states did to the delight of millions of progressives across the country during the Trump years, when there is a conservative president. To do that would be to treat constitutional principles as nothing more than means to achieve policy ends and ideological objectives, enthusiastically embracing them when they are politically helpful and dismissively rejecting or ignoring them when they are not. Either constitutionally-based federalist principles matter—in the sense that they sometimes appropriately place meaningful limits on federal government authority—or they do not. To defend particular constitutional principles only when they help us defeat our political opponents trivializes their importance in maintaining the viability of our constitutional democracy regardless of which party or faction holds the reins of federal power at any given time.

Situational constitutionalism is less likely to promote and advance progressive causes over the long run than principled constitutionalism. If progressives want to rely on federalism (and separation-of-powers) principles to resist future right-wing presidents, they would be well-served by defending and fortifying those principles regardless of which party or individual controls the federal government at any given time. Indeed, if progressives ignore or underemphasize federalist principles when there is a liberal in the White House, those principles are less likely to be viable and helpful when there is a conservative, including a right-wing autocrat, in the Oval Office.

There are some skeptics of federalism who argue that it is an empty concept more accurately described as a rhetorical tool than a normative principle. I believe much of this skepticism is the result of repeated unprincipled uses of federalism that have sought to limit the federal government's power only when it advances particular political or policy agendas. The fact that federalism, as a system of government, as I have explained, is substantively neutral also contributes to the belief that it is a normatively empty concept. But in my view, it is precisely federalism's substantive neutrality that makes it appealing as a principle of government restraint, a restraint that is achieved through the dispersion of sovereign authority among different levels of government. It is the very fact that federalism can be used, for example, to prohibit the national government from requiring that states assist it in enforcing federal laws, whether it be liberal gun safety laws or conservative immigration regulations, that makes it a valuable principle of constitutional law under our current system.

This book does not argue that there is intrinsic value to federalism; there may be other and better ways to restrain government authority than dividing it between the federal and state levels. But even if that is the case, the federal system, as currently constitutionally mandated, can offer significant benefits to those interested in attaining progressive objectives.

It is also important to keep in mind that many questions regarding the role of state sovereignty in our constitutional democracy do not require "either/or" answers. This is because the issue usually is not whether federal sovereignty completely preempts or displaces state sovereignty or vice versa. Instead, the crucial question frequently is how the exercise of federal authority *interacts and is shaped by* state authority and vice versa. Although, as a constitutional matter, the federal government has the power, under the Supremacy Clause, to preempt state authority in regulatory matters that the Constitution delegates to it, the federal government, *as a practical matter*, lacks the personnel and resources to pursue all of the federal policies that it is otherwise constitutionally authorized to enact and implement. (We saw an example of this phenomenon in Chapter 1 when exploring the enforcement of federal laws that criminalize the cultivation, possession, and distribution of marijuana.) As a result, the federal government *needs* state and local officials and resources to attain many of its most important domestic policy objectives. In addition, the anti-commandeering doctrine's requirement that the federal government not mandate that state and local officials serve as its enforcement agents encourages the national government to seek *the voluntary cooperation* of those officials in implementing regulations in fields as varied as health care, the environment, and education.

All of this means that federalism does not always or even primarily require the formation and protection of separate and distinct jurisdictional spheres. That this is the case is clear from our currently existing federalist system in which federal and state powers and responsibilities frequently overlap and interact with each other. Under this framework, the federal government's dependence on state governments for the attainment of national objectives allows and encourages states to help determine what those objectives should be and how they should be pursued. As law professor Heather Gerken explains, "states are not separate and autonomous enclaves that facilitate a retreat from national norms but are at the center of the fight over what our national norms should be."[172]

The type of cooperative federalism that the federal government must frequently rely on to attain its objectives gives states the opportunity to influence the setting of national priorities by allowing them to *withhold* their cooperation. This form of "uncooperative federalism" proved to be crucial to blue states and progressives in resisting some of the Trump administration's most misguided, harmful, or discriminatory policies.[173]

There are some progressives who argue that federalism exacerbates social and economic inequalities. The political scientist Donald Kettl, for example, contends that federalism allows and encourages state differences in how federal policies are enforced, making it more difficult to fight inequality. Kettl argues that the wide variation in state-level policies aimed at promoting education, health, and economic opportunities results in ever-greater inequality not only within states, but *among* states as well.[174] It is fair to ask, however, whether the problem is fundamentally one of federalism or, instead, of an insufficient political commitment by a sufficiently large number of Americans to address inequality. Furthermore, although centralizing decision-making in a progressive federal government can reduce social and economic inequalities through the enforcement of robust redistributive and anti-discrimination national policies, the Trump years showed how centralizing decision-making can be a decidedly double-edged sword for progressives. Unless progressives are confident that they will never again need federalist principles to resist an autocratic and right-wing leader, such as Trump, who had precisely zero interest in addressing or reducing social and economic inequalities, they may want to think twice before dispensing with or undermining those principles.

Some progressives have also criticized federalist (and separation-of-powers) mechanisms and principles for expanding so-called veto points that, in dispersing government authority and creating friction, make the attainment of progressive objectives through activist government interventions more difficult, both as a constitutional/legal matter and as a practical/political matter. Critics argue that veto points, in making governance more difficult, are more compatible with a conservative political agenda that is deregulatory in nature and that prioritizes the free market over government intervention and regulation.[175]

I have two responses to this claim. First, the Trump years showed the ways in which progressives used federalist—and, as we will see in more detail in Chapter 4, separation-of-powers—mechanisms and principles to challenge, sometimes successfully, the committed efforts by a right-wing administration to deregulate. The salutary and helpful phenomenon, from a progressive perspective, of deploying veto points to prevent deregulation was perhaps clearest in the context of environmental law in which states relied on federalist and separation-of-powers principles to defend existing regulations from the Trump administration's repeated efforts to void or weaken them. In short, although federalist mechanisms and principles can sometimes be deployed to challenge government regulations, they can at other times be used to *defend* regulations that are already in place.

Second, it is simply not true that conservatives always seek to deregulate and therefore to reduce the size of government. Instead, conservatives frequently call upon activist government authority, including that of the federal government, to achieve their objectives. The vast increase in law enforcement and correctional bureaucracies to administer the massive growth in the incarceration rates of Americans since the 1970s, the immense enlargement of the national security state following 9/11, and the enormous expansion of immigration enforcement during the Trump years are just three examples of the ways in which conservatives embrace forceful and activist government regulation and intervention—including at the federal level—when they believe it helps attain their preferred policy objectives. Fortunately, progressive states during the Trump years had some success in deploying federalist and separation-of-powers claims to resist harsh, vindictive, and harmful uses of activist federal government authority, including in the field of immigration.

It is a mistake, therefore, for progressives to think of structural constitutional mechanisms and principles that restrain federal government authority only in the context of how they make it more difficult to institute and implement New Deal and Great Society-type government programs. Progressives also need to consider those mechanisms and principles in light of the fact that, when conservatives control the federal government, they repeatedly rely on activist government to pursue right-wing policies and objectives.

It is also crucial to emphasize that the same Constitution that makes it possible for states to refuse to cooperate with the pursuit of federal objectives with which they disagree also, when properly enforced by the courts, protects basic individual civil liberties and rights. This means that states and localities, in resisting the federal government's pursuit of certain national objectives, cannot do so in ways that violate, for example, constitutional protections for free speech, equality, and privacy. Indeed, while the Tenth Amendment language that receives the most attention relates to the states' *reservation* of powers that the Constitution does not delegate to the federal government, the amendment's text also makes clear that the states' reserved powers do not include those that the Constitution *denies* to them.[176] And the Constitution's most important limitations on state powers are those that derive from the protection of individual rights and liberties through the enforcement of the Bill of Rights against the states through the Fourteenth Amendment's Due Process Clause. To put it simply, constitutionally protected individual rights trump otherwise constitutionally reserved exercises of state authority.

When courts are willing to enforce the Constitution's protections of individual rights, it prevents states and localities from relying on federalist mechanisms and principles to resist federal policies in ways that violate basic civil rights and liberties. In this manner, the Bill of Rights, acting together with the post-Civil War constitutional amendments, serve as vital backstops that, when properly enforced by the courts, can prevent a return to the shameful days in American history when federalism was used to justify the adoption and implementation of racist and discriminatory laws and policies.

At the same time, it is undoubtedly the case that in those instances in which constitutional provisions protecting individual rights do not limit the ability of the states to rely on federalist mechanisms and principles to resist federal policies, states dominated by political conservatives will continue to seek to undermine liberal national policies in ways that are comparable to how progressive states sought to resist the Trump administration. But the costs associated with such conservative resistance is the price that progressives should consider paying for the ability to rely on federalist mechanisms and principles to mitigate the worst excesses of dangerous right-wing federal administrations. Since it is unlikely that the Trump government will be the last such administration, it behooves progressives to recognize and even embrace the idea that federalist mechanisms and principles have an important role to play in our democracy by constraining the authority of the national government.

PART II
PRINCIPLES MATTER: SEPARATION OF POWERS

3

The Presidency Before Trump

Two days before Trump's fateful 2019 phone conversation with the president of Ukraine that led to his first impeachment, in which he asked for the "favor" of investigating his political opponent Joe Biden in return for the release of congressionally approved military aid, he spoke at a gathering for young people in Washington, D.C. During his remarks, Trump claimed that under "Article II [of the Constitution], . . . I have the right to do whatever I want as president." The following year, during the coronavirus epidemic, he contended that "when somebody is the president of the United States, the authority is total." At other times, Trump claimed both that "the president cannot have a conflict of interest" and that "I have the absolute right to do what I want with the Department of Justice." These assertions of unlimited presidential power were reminiscent of Richard Nixon's infamous assertion "that when the president does it, that means that it is not illegal."[1]

Trump's and Nixon's statements reflect a breathtaking level of presidential arrogance—both men claimed that presidents are above (or outside) the law because they are, in effect, the sources of their own power. In reflecting an understanding of the presidency that is monarchical rather than democratic and republican, the statements also depart in fundamental ways from what the founders intended when they drafted the Constitution. Such claims of absolute presidential power are entirely inconsistent with the Constitution's separation-of-powers framework, one that purposefully limits the authority of each branch of the federal government.

But the statements also reflect the extent to which Congress, the courts, and we the people have permitted presidents for the last ninety years to accumulate an immense amount of power with few meaningful and effective restraints. During that period, presidents have exercised unilateral and expansive authority in multiple ways, including by sending hundreds of thousands of American troops to fight in wars without congressional declarations of war, ordering national security and law enforcement agencies to surveil and conduct searches of Americans without judicial warrants, directing that administrative agencies regulate or deregulate in particular ways with little or any congressional guidance and usually without meaningful judicial oversight, and prohibiting the spending of congressionally authorized funds (as Nixon did) or mandating the spending of funds that Congress explicitly failed to authorize (as Trump did).

Principles Matter. Carlos A. Ball, Oxford University Press. © Carlos A. Ball 2021.
DOI: 10.1093/oso/9780197584484.003.0004

Ever since the Vietnam War, progressives have worked, to their credit, to limit presidential authority in matters related to armed conflicts abroad and national security at home. It was liberals in the 1970s, for example, who pushed for the War Powers Resolution and for statutory limits in the ability of intelligence agencies to conduct surveillance inside the country. Progressives also repeatedly criticized and challenged George W. Bush's expansive understandings of presidential powers following 9/11, under which he claimed, among other things, to have the constitutional authority to formulate and implement whichever policies and restrictions he believed, in his sole discretion, were necessary to protect the American people from terrorism.

But progressives before the Trump era did not generally emphasize the need to rein in presidential powers in *domestic* policy matters. My objective in this and the next chapter is to try to persuade progressives of the importance of limiting presidential powers across the board, not just in foreign affairs and national security but in purely domestic matters as well. In doing so, I will aim to show how Trump's abuses of presidential authority were not only the actions of a reckless and autocratic leader, but were also the outgrowth of the steady accumulation of presidential powers that has taken place since the 1930s under both Republican and Democratic administrations.

It is time to end the constant expansion of presidential authority that has received, at different times, explicit or implicit support from across the political spectrum. In particular, it is time for progressives to take into account the extent to which proposed laws, regulations, and executive orders expand presidential domestic powers when determining whether such measures merit their political support. This means that there may be times when progressives should refuse to support measures because they unduly expand presidential authority *even when they help advance progressive policy goals*. To illustrate this point, I argue at the end of this chapter that progressives should have been more cognizant of the extent to which President Obama's humanitarian but unilateral decision to cease deporting Dreamers—the large number of undocumented immigrants brought to the United States as children—expanded presidential powers. Although Obama's implementation of the Deferred Action for Childhood Arrivals (DACA) program was, in my view, the correct policy choice, its adoption through unilateral presidential action raised important separation-of-powers questions; rather than pressuring Obama to adopt DACA, progressives may have been better served by continuing to demand that Congress statutorily grant Dreamers the ability to remain in the country, a step that would have prevented a future president from taking their legal status away. That this approach may have better served progressive interests is reflected in the fact that Trump also relied on the exercise of unilateral presidential authority to institute a series of harsh and punitive anti-immigrant measures, including the rescission of DACA, the

enforcement of what Trump called an immigration "Muslim ban," and the imposition of a slew of new draconian restrictions that essentially made it impossible
to seek asylum along the Mexico-U.S. border. Trump showed how the exercise of
unilateral presidential authority can be used to harm and maltreat as much as to
help and protect immigrant populations in the United States.

In exploring separation-of-powers issues, as with my earlier discussion
of federalism, I do not try to delineate precisely how the Constitution should
be understood to limit presidential powers. The contours and specifics of
separation-of-powers principles as they apply to the office of the presidency are
multifaceted and complex, making it challenging to capture fully in one book,
much less in two chapters. My objective in this chapter and the next is instead to
show just how bloated and dangerous presidential powers have become in the
hope that progressives will make the reining in of presidential domestic power
a political priority in the years and decades following Trump's presidency. In
thinking about this issue, progressives should keep in mind that the relentless
expansion of presidential powers, and their associated and inevitable abuses,
by no means started with Trump and, unless presidential authority is effectively
constrained going forward, it did not end when Trump left office.

Indeed, it would be a grave mistake for progressives to view Trump's misuses
of power solely as the actions of an unprincipled and rogue president. Instead, as
I hope to make clear in this chapter, those misuses also reflect the ways in which
presidential power had grown exponentially and dangerously *before* Trump was
elected.

The Roots of Separation of Powers in Our Constitutional System

The Americans who declared their independence from Britain did so in the
name of freedom (for some) and self-rule (by some) in response to tyrannical
rule by the king of England and his largely aristocratic minions in the British
Parliament. For Americans during the revolutionary period, tyranny was primarily a function of the *misallocation* of power in too few hands. For the founders,
sovereignty did not, as an initial matter, rest in a king or in an aristocracy; instead, power initially resided in the people (which for the founders generally
meant white men who owned a modicum of property). It is for this reason that
the Constitution's Preamble states that "*We the People* of the United States . . . do
ordain and establish this Constitution for the United States of America."

In their fraught dealings with their British rulers, the American colonists had
learned the dangers that came with *concentrated* political authority. In calling for
a government that would be republican rather than monarchical or aristocratic,

the founders crafted a constitutional system that sought to disperse rather than concentrate power with the intent of both promoting self-rule by the people and avoiding the dangers of autocratic rule. Part of that dispersal of authority was reflected in the federalist system that accommodated both federal sovereignty at the national level and state sovereignty at the local level. The dispersal of authority was also reflected in the ways in which each of the Constitution's first three Articles created a separate branch of government—the legislative, executive, and judicial—with distinct functions and responsibilities, some of which included the checking and balancing of the other two branches' powers.

In crafting a constitutional government that prioritized separation of powers, the founders were responding not only to their travails under the thumb of autocratic British rule, but also to their experiences following the Declaration of Independence. Although some states, most prominently Massachusetts in 1780, adopted constitutions that separated powers among three different branches of government, other states initially concentrated almost all authority in their legislatures. This was consistent with the last few decades of the colonial experience, during which colonial assemblies were generally successful in increasing their power at the expense of that of royal governors.[2] This concentration of power in legislative hands continued after independence. As the legal historian Michael Klarman puts it, "in response to perceived abuses of executive power by the king and his royal governors, state constitutions of the Revolutionary era generally provided for eviscerated executive branches, which were made largely subordinate to state legislatures."[3]

Most early state governors were selected by legislators, served only one-year terms, lacked the authority to appoint members of the executive branch and to veto legislation, and had to act in concert with advisory councils chosen by legislatures.[4] State legislatures also sometimes sought to influence judicial decisions by intervening in individual lawsuits and even by reducing the salaries of judges who issued disfavored rulings. This concentration and abuse of legislative power led the Constitution's drafters to prioritize the creation of independent executive and judicial branches as antidotes to tyrannical legislative rule. As James Madison noted in *The Federalist Papers*, "the legislative department is everywhere extending the sphere of its activity and drawing all powers into its impetuous vortex."[5] The "accumulation of all powers, legislative, executive, and judiciary, in the same hands, whether of one, a few or many, and whether hereditary, self-appointed, or elected," Madison warned, "may justly be pronounced the very definition of tyranny."[6] It was the dangers engendered by this concentration of government authority that made it essential, in Madison's view, for the Constitution to delineate, separate, and check the powers of the federal government's three branches: "The great security against a gradual concentration of the several powers in the same department consists in giving to [each branch] the necessary constitutional means and personal motives to resist encroachment [by] the others."[7]

The Articles of Confederation had also concentrated executive, legislative, and judicial powers in the Congress. The Articles' drafters sought to prevent federal tyranny not through separation of powers, but by strictly limiting the substantive areas in which Congress could regulate. In stark contrast, the new Constitution granted Congress significant legislative authority, including the power to regulate and tax individuals directly without having to go through the states.

But the new and robust congressional authority required constitutional mechanisms to prevent Congress from legislating in despotic and arbitrary ways. Some of those mechanisms dispersed power *within* the legislative branch. These measures included dividing Congress into two chambers, each with different lengths of terms (two years for the House and six years for the Senate) and different electoral mechanisms (direct vote by qualified voters for the House and selection by state legislatures for the Senate). The bicameralism requirement that all bills be approved by both chambers before they become law was another crucial way of dispersing legislative authority.[8]

But the Constitution, of course, also sought to disperse power by distributing it *among* the three different branches. It was Congress that would enact laws, the executive that would apply and enforce them, and the judiciary that would interpret them. In addition, the Constitution put into place a system of checks and balances intended to use the constitutionally granted authority of one branch to oversee or limit the exercise of power by another branch. In Madison's famous language, protection against tyranny "must be supplied, by so contriving the interior structure of the government as that its several constituent parts may, by their mutual relations, be the means of keeping each other in their proper places."[9]

The Constitution is chock-full of these "check and balance" mechanisms. They include the president's authority to both propose legislation and to veto bills approved by Congress; Congress's authority, under a supermajority requirement, to overrule a presidential veto; the president's power to nominate federal judges and the Senate's power, in effect, to veto those nominations (as well as nominations for important executive branch positions); the requirement that the Senate approve, by a two-thirds majority, treaties that presidents sign with other nations; Congress's power to impeach members of the executive and judicial branches; although not explicitly stated in the Constitution, the judiciary's power to strike down legislative and executive actions as unconstitutional through the exercise of judicial review; and Congress's authority to generally determine the federal courts' jurisdiction. All of these constitutional mechanisms were intended to disperse government authority in order to reduce the chances of despotic and arbitrary exercises of that authority.

The Presidency in the Constitution

The men who drafted the Constitution in Philadelphia in 1787 had several important decisions to make regarding the executive branch. One of those was whether it would be headed by a committee or by one person. There were some delegates, led by Virginia governor Edmund Randolph, who feared that concentrating executive power in the hands of only one person would encourage a despotism analogous to that of King George III. For these founders, it was important to disperse power not only between the different branches of government, but also *within* the executive branch (as it would be dispersed within the legislature through, for example, bicameralism). As George Mason explained, "if strong and extensive powers are vested in the Executive, and that Executive consists only of one person; the Government will of course degenerate . . . into a Monarchy." Rather than concentrating executive power in a single individual—what Randolph called "the foetus of monarchy"—such power should be vested in a council consisting of, for example, three or six individuals.[10]

However, a majority of the delegates eventually accepted Pennsylvania's James Wilson's proposal that the executive be led by only one person: a president. Two principal reasons accounted for this choice. First, there was a consensus among delegates that the governing structure created by the Articles of Confederation had failed in part because it included weak mechanisms for the administration and enforcement of the laws. Under the Articles, there was no separate executive branch; executive powers were instead exercised, most ineffectively, by congressional committees. Second, while the experience with monarchical rule during the colonial period highlighted the tyrannical dangers of an executive that was too powerful, the experience during the 1780s highlighted the tyrannical dangers posed by state legislatures whose authority was unrestrained by generally powerless and ineffective state executives. Many of the founders, who were men of considerable privilege and property, viewed with particular alarm the populist policies adopted by some state legislatures, including the issuing of paper money at inflated rates and allowing debts to be satisfied without full payments. In the end, a majority of delegates at the Constitutional Convention believed that the benefits of (1) effective executive administration and (2) assertive executive power as a counterbalance to legislative authority outweighed the risks of tyrannical executive rule that came with the creation of the presidency.

But even after a majority of the delegates accepted the need to create the office of the president, crucial questions remained, including how the president would be selected, whether he would be permitted to serve for more than one term, and what his powers would be.

There were some delegates, such as James Wilson and Gouverneur Morris, who argued that the president should be elected directly by voters. But other framers were mistrustful of direct voting by the (male and white) public, at least when it came to the Senate and the presidency, because of the dangers they believed accompanied majoritarian rule by an electorate that had little formal education and limited access to means of communication. Madison's original Virginia Plan for the Constitution had called on the legislature to choose the head of the executive branch, as was the practice in most states at the time. But a significant number of delegates worried that such a scheme would make the president beholden to Congress and therefore undermine his ability to meaningfully check the exercise of legislative authority. Gouverneur Morris, a committed opponent of congressional selection of the president, claimed that it would lead to "the work of intrigue, of cabal, and of faction" analogous to the election of the pope or of the Polish king by the Diet.[11]

After much back and forth, an alternative emerged: having the states choose a slate of electors who would then choose the president (and vice president). Under the proposed Electoral College, each state would be given the number of electors that equaled its number of senators plus its number of apportioned representatives in the House. The former number was set at two for each state, a representational parity that increased the influence of smaller states. But the latter number depended on the state's population, which benefited the more populous states. In the end, a majority of delegates supported the Electoral College, in large part because it was viewed as a compromise "between those who wanted direct election and [those who supported] legislative selection (since state legislatures could pick electors directly if so desired)."[12] It was also a compromise "between those who wanted proportional representation and [those who backed] equal states' rights."[13] For their part, southern supporters of slavery approved of the Electoral College because its composition was linked to the counting of enslaved people—as three-fifths of persons—for purposes of apportioning seats in the House of Representatives.[14] The three-fifths rule not only gave the South disproportionate representation in the House, it also gave it an outsized influence in selecting the president. Indeed, of the first seven presidents, serving between 1789 and 1837, five were southern "owners" of enslaved people (George Washington, Thomas Jefferson, James Madison, James Monroe, and Andrew Jackson). The same was true of John Tyler, James Polk, and Zachary Taylor who served as presidents between 1841 and 1850.

Although an early draft of the Constitution allowed the president to serve only one term of seven years without the possibility of re-election, that was eventually changed to four-year terms without term limits. In the end, a majority of delegates thought it best to shorten the length of presidential terms while allowing elections to determine whether the president deserved to remain in office for longer. Although not included as a limitation in the original Constitution, it was generally expected that presidents would not seek a third term, an example set by George Washington when he retired after his second term. Presidents abided by that norm for 150 years until Franklin D. Roosevelt shattered it by seeking re-election *three* times, leading to the adoption of the Twenty-Second Amendment in 1951 prohibiting presidents from running for re-election more than one time.

As for the scope of the president's powers, Article II is relatively brief, especially when compared to Article I's grants of legislative authority to Congress. Among other things, Article I contains seventeen different provisions listing the many areas in which Congress is empowered to legislate, such as regulating foreign and interstate commerce, as well as taxing and spending to promote the general welfare. An additional provision allows Congress to enact any law that is "necessary and proper" to exercise its constitutionally delegated legislative authority. Importantly, many of Congress's powers (such as to coin money, regulate trade, establish courts, naturalize citizens, and raise armies) were royal (or executive) powers in England. But rather than assign those powers to the president, the founders chose to place them with the legislative branch instead.

In contrast to the relative expansiveness of Article I, Article II is significantly shorter. About half of it addresses issues such as who is eligible to be president, how the president is to be selected, and what happens if the president is removed from office, dies, or resigns. The remainder of Article II sets forth a relatively short list of assignations of authority, the most important of which are the power to be commander-in-chief of the military, to issue pardons (except in cases of impeachment), to make treaties (with the Senate's approval), and to appoint Supreme Court justices and leading executive branch officials (also with the Senate's approval). In addition, Article II imposes two explicit obligations on the president: to provide information on "the state of the union" and "to take care that the laws be faithfully executed."

Although the Constitution granted the president only a limited number of explicit powers, even that was too much for many who opposed the document during the ratification process. Much of that opposition was grounded in the criticism of an executive controlled by only one individual. As Virginia's Patrick Henry complained, "Your President may easily become king. . . . If your American chief be a man of ambition, and abilities, how easy is it for him to render himself absolute?"[15] New York's Cato mocked the Constitution's supporters' apparent belief that no American president could ever turn himself into a tyrant: "[Y]our posterity will find [the president's] great power connected with ambition, luxury, and flattery. . . . [It] will . . . readily produce a Caesar, Caligula, Nero, and Domitian in America."[16]

But the Constitution's defenders emphasized crucial differences between an autocratic monarch à la George III and a president under the Constitution. Unlike the former, the latter would be elected to a fixed term that could be renewed only through another election; he could be impeached; his vetoes could be overridden by Congress; he did not have the authority to dismiss the legislature; Congress could reject his treaties, appointments, and proposed legislation; and while the Constitution designated him as the military's commander-in-chief, he could not, in theory at least, plunge the nation into war without congressional approval.

The Constitution's proponents were also helped by the fact that it was generally expected that George Washington would serve as the first president. There was wide agreement that Washington was likely to govern with restraint and without abusing the powers of the office. There was a wide consensus, in other words, that the man who had led the War of Independence could be trusted not to govern like George III.

The arguments of the Constitution's supporters, including those regarding presidential powers, carried the day when delegates at the Virginia and New York ratification conventions narrowly approved the document in the summer of 1788, bringing the total number of ratifying states to eleven as required by the document's Article VII.

It bears emphasizing that the extensive powers accrued by contemporary presidents are only loosely based, if at all, on the actual text of the Constitution. As already noted, Article II is strikingly brief and provides the president with only a handful of explicit powers. As Edward Corwin, a leading presidential scholar of the twentieth century, put it: "Article II is the most loosely drawn chapter of the Constitution. To those who think that a Constitution ought to settle everything beforehand it should be a nightmare; by the same token, to those who think that constitution makers ought to leave considerable leeway for the future play of political forces, it should be a vision realized."[17] To the extent, then, that the presidency's accumulation of extensive powers in recent decades is constitutional, it is the result of evolving and changing understandings of the authority presidents need to lead the country in addressing national and international problems, challenges, and emergencies, rather than of powers explicitly granted by the Constitution. In other words, the history of the presidency and of the country tell us much more about the current scope of presidential authority than does the Constitution's text.

The Presidency in American History Before Trump

The fruitful partnership between James Madison and Alexander Hamilton, who co-wrote (along with John Jay) the highly influential *The Federalist Papers*, broke down in part as a result of disagreements over presidential powers. (The two men would also disagree strongly over whether Congress had the authority to create the Bank of the United States, the first federally chartered bank.) As the threat of war between France and England grew in 1793, President Washington refused to take sides between the two European powers and instead issued a Neutrality Proclamation. For Hamilton, such a proclamation was entirely consistent with the president's foreign policy authority. While Congress had the power to declare war, it was the executive branch that both negotiated treaties and had the duty "to preserve Peace until war is declared; . . . it becomes both its province and its duty to enforce the laws incident to that state of the Nation." But as Madison saw it, the neutrality declaration was a change in policy that required congressional approval. According to Madison, presidents, unlike monarchs, lacked prerogative powers, that is, powers not explicitly authorized by either the Constitution or Congress.[18]

John Locke, in his *Second Treatise of Government*, had defined the executive's prerogative as "the power to act according to discretion, for the public good, without the prescription of law, and sometimes even against it."[19] Locke defended executive prerogative authority on practical grounds: Legislatures are deliberative bodies that depend on the time-consuming process of forging a majoritarian consensus before they can act; to limit the executive to only those actions that have been pre-approved by the legislature was to leave a nation unprepared to address new challenges and emergencies that required the type of quick and effective response that only the executive branch, led by only one person, could provide.

Although Locke argued that the executive's prerogative power was limited by the obligation to seek eventual (and retroactive) legislative approval, Hamilton disagreed. In doing so, he made a textualist argument that has been repeated many times by defenders of extensive presidential powers in the more than two centuries since: in contrast to Article I, which delegates to Congress "all legislative powers *herein* granted," Article II, it is contended, vests *the entirety* of executive authority in the president ("The executive Power shall be vested in a President of the United States of America."). According to Hamilton and his presidentialist descendants, this language allows presidents to exercise the full spectrum of executive authority regardless of whether such exercise is approved by Congress, either before or after they act.

Madison disagreed with the notion that the president enjoys inherent powers not explicitly granted by either the Constitution or Congress. For him, such an expansive understanding of presidential authority threatened the basic separation-of-powers principle that it is for Congress to set policy, and for the president to implement it.

Historians disagree over which vision of presidential powers is more consistent with the preferences of those who participated in the Constitutional Convention of 1787. But most presidents, not surprisingly, have embraced the Hamiltonian rather than the Madisonian understanding of presidential powers.

That is what Thomas Jefferson did in 1803 when he ordered the purchase of the Louisiana territory without congressional approval. And it is what Abraham Lincoln did when, at the start of the Civil War, he expanded the army's size, spent $2 million in unappropriated funds to purchase military supplies, ordered blockades of southern ports, censored the mail, imposed restrictions on foreign travel, suspended the writ of habeas corpus (while ignoring a federal court ruling holding that he lacked the constitutional power to do so), and instituted military tribunals, all without prior congressional authorization. For Lincoln, the Civil War's exigency justified presidential actions that otherwise would have been unconstitutional. As he put it later during the war, "by general law life and limb must be protected; yet often a limb must be amputated to save a life; but a life is never wisely given to save a limb. I felt that measures, otherwise unconstitutional, might become lawful, by becoming indispensable to the preservation of the constitution, through the preservation of the nation."[20]

Congress later approved many of Lincoln's unilateral decisions, including those related to budgeting and the blockade. But the Supreme Court, albeit after the Civil War ended, held that Lincoln had lacked the constitutional authority to bypass civilian courts by instituting non-jury, military tribunals in Union territory.[21]

In addition to claiming inherent powers under the Constitution, presidents became more assertive, as the nineteenth century progressed, in exercising explicitly delegated powers, including their veto authority. The first six presidents issued a combined total of six vetoes. Andrew Jackson, the seventh president, doubled that number on his own. Andrew Johnson, Lincoln's successor and committed opponent of Reconstruction, vetoed twenty-one bills. At the end of the century, Grover Cleveland vetoed more than three hundred bills in his eight years in office.

The second half of the nineteenth century also saw disputes over whether the president had the exclusive authority to remove executive officials whose appointment had been approved by the Senate, a question that the Constitution does not explicitly address. In 1867, as tension between President Johnson and congressional Republicans grew over Johnson's feeble implementation of Reconstruction measures, Congress enacted the Tenure in Office Act to prevent Johnson from dispensing with cabinet members chosen by Lincoln. Johnson's subsequent firing of Secretary of War Edwin Stanton led the House of Representatives to impeach him, the first presidential impeachment in American history. Johnson's presidency was saved only after the Senate failed to convict him by just one vote.[22]

In 1926, the Supreme Court held that presidents have an implied right under the Constitution to remove executive branch officials and struck down the Tenure in Office Act as a violation of separation of powers.[23] The Court later in the twentieth century held that Congress can under some circumstances limit the president's removal power by requiring that the firing of certain officials, such as co-heads of independent federal agencies and special counsels charged with investigating executive branch employees, be done only "for cause."[24]

The federal government's growth also contributed to the expansion of presidential power. In 1830, the federal government had eleven thousand civilian employees. A century later, that number reached six hundred thousand.[25] A major reason for the growth was Congress's creation of new federal agencies and departments. The birth of the administrative state in the United States is generally traced to Congress's creation of the Interstate Commerce Commission (ICC) in 1887, the first independent federal agency that was unattached to any department. Congress charged the ICC with the responsibility of overseeing interstate railroads—and later, other forms of interstate transportation—by granting the new agency the authority to issue legally binding regulations. In the decades that followed, Congress created many other administrative agencies, endowing them with similar authority. These agencies included the Food and Drug Administration (first created, under a different name, in 1906), the Federal Trade Commission (1914), the Federal Communications Commission (1934), the Securities and Exchange Commission (1934), the National Labor Relations Board (1935), and the Environmental Protection Agency (1970). Congress also created new executive departments, including the Department of Commerce (1903), the Department of Labor (1913), and the Department of Health, Education, and Welfare (formed in 1953, and divided in 1979 into the Department of Education and the Department of Health and Human Services). Today, the executive branch has grown to over four million civilian and military employees, across fifteen cabinet-level departments and more than one hundred other agencies, managing a budget of close to five trillion dollars.

The growth of the administrative state greatly contributed to the expansion of presidential authority. As political scientist Andrew Rudalevige explains, "growth in government made power over appointments and removals more critical; it also forced Congress to delegate more powers to the president through statutes. Each time an executive agency was created with the power to promulgate regulations, presidential powers expanded. While Congress could not constitutionally delegate its legislative powers, the delegation of regulatory authority sometimes amounted to something close, especially when Congress passed vague statutory standards or neglected to conduct adequate oversight of administrative behavior."[26]

The Supreme Court in 1935 twice struck down federal statutes on the ground that they improperly delegated legislative authority to the executive branch in violation of separation-of-powers principles.[27] By failing to give the executive branch sufficient guidance regarding which policies to pursue, Congress was essentially allowing it to legislate. But the Court since 1935 has repeatedly refused to strike down *any* statute granting regulatory authority to the executive branch, no matter how vaguely or broadly written, on improper delegation grounds. All the Constitution requires, the Court has held, is that Congress provide the executive with "an intelligible principle" to guide its lawmaking authority through the issuance of regulations.[28] This judicial standard is so deferential (read: meaningless) that it is satisfied even when Congress does nothing more than require that an administrative agency regulate in the "public interest" or to "protect the public health."[29]

Congress's preference for enacting statutes granting administrative agencies extensive regulatory authority while providing only the broadest and vaguest policy guidance, combined with the Supreme Court's refusal to give any meaningful force to the nondelegation doctrine, has served to significantly expand presidential power in domestic policy matters over the last century. Presidents from both parties have taken full advantage of the discretion provided to them by vague statutes to adopt and implement a broad range of policies never explicitly approved by Congress. These policies, in turn, are generally immune to judicial review due both to the demise of the nondelegation doctrine and to the general deference that courts have given the executive branch in setting policies in the face of ambiguous guidance by Congress.[30]

Of course, if a president exercises congressionally delegated authority in a way that Congress disapproves, it can always enact new legislation reversing the president's actions. But that legislation is subject to a presidential veto, which, if exercised, requires a supermajority to override. And modern presidents can usually rely on a cadre of diehard supporters in Congress to block almost all efforts to override vetoes. This means that the veto mechanism, originally intended to limit the power of Congress, has in practice served to problematically expand presidential power. As Neal Katyal, a former Solicitor General under President Barack Obama, puts it, "the combination of [judicial] deference and the veto is especially insidious—it means that a president can interpret a vague statute to give himself additional powers, receive deference in that interpretation from courts, and then lock that decision into place by brandishing the veto. This ratchet-and-lock scheme makes it almost impossible to rein in executive power."[31]

Presidents' repeated deployment of troops abroad in order to protect what they, in their sole discretion, take to be American interests has also served to greatly expand presidential authority. Relying on their constitutional status as commanders-in-chief, presidents from both parties repeatedly have deployed the American military all over the world to achieve a broad set of strategic and economic objectives, often with little or no input from Congress. Sometimes the objective was to expand American territory, as when President James Polk sent troops to the border between Texas and Mexico in 1845 with the apparent aim of provoking an armed conflict that would allow the United States to annex a substantial portion of Mexican territory. At other times, presidents deployed troops to protect the economic interests of the United States and those of its political allies abroad. This happened repeatedly in the early twentieth century as William McKinley, Theodore Roosevelt, William Taft, Woodrow Wilson, and Calvin Coolidge sent American troops to help rule Cuba, Nicaragua, Haiti, and the Dominican Republic, among other countries in Latin America. At yet other times, presidents relied not on military troops, but on undercover and other government operatives, along with financial support for local allies, to help bring down democratically elected governments that the presidents believed, again in their sole discretion, were not sufficiently committed to protecting American political and economic interests. This happened, for example, in Guatemala and Iran in the 1950s under the direction of Dwight Eisenhower and in Chile in 1973 under that of Richard Nixon.[32]

One of the ways in which presidents justified their unilateral decisions to send military troops into armed conflicts was to claim that the missions constituted "police actions" that fell short of outright wars, and therefore supposedly did not trigger Article I's requirement that Congress declare war before troops are deployed. But whatever meaningful distinction might have existed between "police actions" and "wars" before the mid-twentieth century, the distinction lost all possible meaning when President Harry Truman ordered tens of thousands of troops to fight in what was clearly a war—about thirty-seven thousand Americans died—against communist North Korea without first seeking congressional approval. Congress likely would have granted the approval had Truman requested it, but the president was loath to set a precedent of congressional authorization for the many military engagements that were likely to take place during the Cold War with the Russians in the upcoming years.

Similarly, presidents John F. Kennedy, Lyndon Johnson, and Richard Nixon sent tens of thousands of troops to fight and die in Vietnam without formally asking that Congress first declare war. Almost sixty thousand Americans, along with hundreds of thousands of Vietnamese on both sides of the border, died during the Vietnam War. When Congress in 1971, on behalf of a nation increasingly exhausted, infuriated, and saddened by the war's brutality and futility, included a provision in a defense appropriation bill calling for an end to the armed conflict, President Nixon claimed, in signing it, that it had no binding effect on him and "will not change the policies I have pursued and that I shall continue to pursue."[33] Two years earlier, Nixon had expanded the war by ordering the bombing of Cambodia, a military campaign that was so secret that not even Nixon's Secretary of State, Secretary of the Air Force, or Air Force chief of staff knew about it, much less Congress or the public.[34]

The Supreme Court, as already noted, aided and abetted the expansion of presidential powers in domestic matters by failing to enforce the nondelegation doctrine. Similarly, the Court aided and abetted the expansion of presidential powers in foreign affairs by claiming in a 1936 ruling that the president has "plenary and exclusive power . . . as the sole organ of the federal government in the field of international relations." According to the Court, this power "does not require as a basis for its exercise an act of Congress over issues related to international affairs," a conclusion that leaves presidential authority in this area essentially unrestrained.[35] In so ruling, the Court conveniently ignored the long list of Article I provisions that grant Congress powers in matters related to foreign affairs, the military, and armed conflicts. Not only does Article I grant Congress the exclusive authority to declare war, but it also grants it the power (1) to "define and punish offenses . . . against the law of nations"; (2) regulate commerce with foreign nations; (3) raise, support, and maintain armies and a Navy; and (4) regulate the military. Clearly, the Constitution's text has not stood in the way of the Court's insistence that presidential powers in international affairs are effectively unbounded by congressional authority.

It is problematic enough that the Supreme Court has expanded executive branch power, time and time again, in matters related to foreign affairs and national security at the expense of Congress. But the Court has made the situation worse by repeatedly relying on a broad swath of judge-made legal doctrines— such as standing rules and the state secrets privilege—to insulate executive actions in these matters from judicial review. As law professor David Rudenstine argues in his book *The Age of Deference*, this has led the Court not only to deny relief to individuals and to shield the executive from judicial scrutiny, but also to "effectively elevate[] the executive in national security cases above the law, and thus it has contributed not only to the emergence but also the continued strengthening of the presidency and the departments and agencies that comprise the National Security State."[36] With almost no role for Congress or the judiciary, presidents have enjoyed unfettered and unconstrained authority for decades in matters related to foreign affairs, the use of the military, and national security.

The most infamous exercise of unilateral presidential authority in the twentieth century inside the United States was Franklin D. Roosevelt's use of executive orders to exclude more than one hundred thousand Japanese Americans from their West Coast homes and to intern them in detention camps on the specious ground that their national origin made them potential enemies of the nation. To its great shame, the Supreme Court upheld the constitutionality of the executive orders in *Korematsu v. United States*. Although the Court held that treating individuals differently because of their race or national origin merited strict judicial scrutiny under the Equal Protection Clause, a majority of the justices also concluded that the president had the authority, given the national emergency presented by the war, to take national origin into account in prohibiting Japanese Americans from returning to their homes on the ground that they constituted, as a group, a threat to the nation's security.[37] The Court did not get around to overturning *Korematsu* until 2018. Ironically, it did so in a ruling that once again upheld the assertion of essentially unlimited presidential powers in matters related to the nation's relationships with other countries by rejecting a constitutional challenge to President Trump's self-described immigration "Muslim ban."[38]

It was also during the Roosevelt years that a new governing phenomenon made its appearance: presidents setting much of Congress's legislative agenda. On the day after taking office, Roosevelt issued an executive order temporarily closing all of the nation's banks, an order of questionable constitutionality given that he claimed it was authorized by a World War I-era statute that prohibited commercial trading with enemy nations.[39] Four days later, Roosevelt sent Congress an emergency banking bill, which the legislature approved without bothering to formally print it or to debate it for more than two hours. Roosevelt's actions set a new pattern whereby Congress and the public expected presidents to propose significant amounts of new legislation during an administration's first one hundred days and to essentially set the legislative agenda throughout its term. During his first year in office, President Eisenhower refused to send Congress "a legislative program, and was pilloried for it in the press."[40] Presidents between 1949 and 1965 "sent between fifty and ninety messages to Congress each year, containing anywhere from sixty-five to more than four hundred separate proposals for legislative consideration."[41]

Another way in which presidents enlarged their power was through the expansion of White House staff. It was not until 1939 "that President Roosevelt won the right to name six presidential assistants to serve on his staff."[42] Before then, presidents governed exclusively through their cabinets. Since then, multiple layers of presidentially controlled bureaucracies have been added, with thousands of federal employees working directly for the White House. Presidents in recent decades have also delegated policymaking authority to so-called "czars"—officials appointed, usually without Senate confirmation, to wield authority over policy areas (such as drugs, AIDS, automobile-industry bailouts, and cybersecurity) in ways that are analogous to the power exercised by cabinet secretaries.[43]

Part of the growth in White House staffing resulted from Congress's creation of new executive agencies run directly from the White House. In 1946, Congress established the Council of Economic Advisers to gather information for the president so that he could set national economic policy. A year later, Congress created the National Security Council (NSC). By the 1950s, the NSC had assumed the responsibility of providing the president with most of the information needed to make national security decisions, often based on reams of classified, and sometimes conflicting, information gathered by the State Department, the Department of Defense, and the CIA.

In 1952, the Executive Office of the President had fourteen hundred employees; twenty years later under Nixon, that number had grown to fifty-six hundred.[44] Nixon also expanded the NSC's responsibilities. Under the leadership of Henry Kissinger, the NSC (rather than the Department of State) became the primary vehicle through which Nixon pursued crucial foreign policy endeavors, from negotiating an end to the war with North Vietnam to the opening to China.[45] Nixon also formed the Office of Policy Development to serve as the domestic version of the NSC, as well as the Office of Management and Budget, through which he and all subsequent presidents and their staff have kept a tight rein on executive agencies.

With the growth of White House staffers and counselors came ever-expanding claims that their advice to presidents, as well as other forms of internal communications, were strictly confidential. William Rogers, Eisenhower's Attorney General, came up with the phrase "executive privilege" to justify keeping Congress and the judiciary uninformed about the conversations, communications, and documents that the administration, in its sole discretion, deemed improper to reveal.[46] Most presidents since Eisenhower—the two exceptions were Gerald Ford and Jimmy Carter in the post-Watergate 1970s—have repeatedly relied on the privilege to deny Congress and the courts access to information created or shared inside the White House. The privilege, it bears noting, appears nowhere in the Constitution.

Before Trump, Richard Nixon was the president who made the broadest claim to executive privilege. Nixon contended that the privilege applied both to former and current presidential staff and to information requests by Congress, special prosecutors, and grand juries. In addition, even before the Watergate scandal, Nixon claimed that the privilege applied to "all documents, produced or received by the President or any member of the White House staff in connection with his official duties."[47] He also maintained that the privilege was absolute; once the president invoked it, there could be no countervailing claim asserted by Congress or the courts. In 1974, the Supreme Court, in deciding whether Nixon had to comply with a subpoena ordering him to turn over White House recordings of conversations he had had with aides about Watergate matters, unanimously disagreed and held that the executive privilege, whatever its scope, was not absolute and that it did not justify the executive branch's withholding of information that was relevant to criminal prosecutions.[48]

During the middle decades of the twentieth century, when the country faced severe challenges engendered by the Great Depression, fascism in Europe, and the later Soviet push to spread communism around the world, there was a general political and academic consensus in the United States on the need for powerful presidents.[49] That consensus held that of the three branches of government, only the executive, led by just one individual, could respond with the speed, effectiveness, and forcefulness required to help the country navigate a seemingly endless list of new crises and challenges.[50]

This presidentialist consensus began to break down as a result, first, of the Vietnam War debacle, and, second, of the Watergate scandals and associated abuses of presidential power. Arthur Schlesinger—the historian and former adviser to President Kennedy who had earlier in his career lionized strong presidents in books such as *The Age of Jackson* (winner of the Pulitzer prize in 1946) and *The Age of Roosevelt* (three volumes published between 1957 and 1960)—issued a clarion-call warning about the dangers of excessive presidential powers in his highly influential 1973 book titled *The Imperial Presidency*. Suddenly, the office of the presidency, which many Americans for decades had viewed as reflecting the best of the country's democracy and as essential to protecting the nation's security and well-being, was now increasingly viewed as having grown so powerful and unmoored from any meaningful checks and balances that *it* threatened the country's safety and welfare, as well as its democratic system and values. As Schlesinger explained, the conception of presidential power by the 1970s had grown to such an extent that it worked "a radical transformation of the traditional polity" so "that presidential primacy, so indispensable to the political order, has turned into presidential supremacy." Furthermore, he warned, "the constitutional Presidency . . . has become the imperial Presidency and threatens to be the revolutionary [or all-powerful] Presidency."[51]

The Vietnam War's devastating policy, military, and moral failures reflected the systemic problems created by unrestrained presidential power. Three different presidents had overseen a disastrous military conflict that resulted in the deaths of hundreds of thousands of people, both Vietnamese and American, for seemingly little purpose or need. In conducting the war, all three presidents had made misguided and erroneous policy judgments; to make matters worse, two of them (Johnson and Nixon) repeatedly lied to the American people about the progress of U.S. troops on the ground and the need for continued fighting.

America's foreign policy disaster in Vietnam raised questions among a growing number of elected officials, academics, and ordinary Americans about the wisdom of vesting increasing amounts of power on the presidency. Such doubts only grew stronger after revelations of Richard Nixon's abuses of power, ones that eventually led to Congress's impeachment investigation and his resignation. Those abuses included using CIA, FBI, and IRS agents to investigate left-wing groups and other Nixon opponents as part of a "Political Enemies Project."[52] The fifty or so CIA staffers who conducted that agency's domestic surveillance program—in place from 1969 until 1974—alone "compiled dossiers on some seventy-two hundred American citizens, conducted their own break-ins (or contracted them out), opened mail (some 380,000 letters, between the CIA's and FBI's combined efforts), and tapped phones," all without judicial authorization.[53]

Richard Nixon was not the first president to rely on extensive wiretapping to keep tabs on those he deemed untrustworthy. Franklin D. Roosevelt had ordered the wiretapping of "a diverse cast of targets including columnist Drew Pearson, Roosevelt cabinet secretary Harold Ickes, and nuclear scientist J. Robert Oppenheimer (as well as his lawyer)."[54] FBI Director J. Edgar Hoover provided the president with "reams of political intelligence while Roosevelt brought his domestic critics to Hoover's attention."[55] After the Supreme Court held that a statute prohibited the FBI and other federal agencies from conducting wiretapping without judicial authorization, Roosevelt ordered his Attorney General to *ignore the ruling* as it applied to "the conversations or other communications of persons suspected of subversive activities against the Government of the United States, including suspected spies."[56]

The troubling phenomenon of an administration blatantly ignoring a Supreme Court ruling on the legality of surveillance practices repeated itself in the 1950s. In 1954, the Court held that government agents violate the Fourth Amendment when they break into a home or office, without judicial authorization, to plant a listening device.[57] At the request of FBI Director Hoover, Eisenhower's Attorney General "authorized" the agency to ignore the Court's ruling in order to record the private conversations of "espionage agents, possible saboteurs, and subversive persons."[58] In 1956, the FBI created "its own counter-intelligence program COINTELPRO, which included surveillance, forgery, and even the use of infiltrated agents to incite violence, especially by communist groups."[59] Fifteen years later, a group of leftist activists broke into an FBI office in Media, Pennsylvania, stole COINTELPRO documents, and distributed them to the press. The documents detailed warrantless wiretapping, burglaries, mail interceptions, "attempts to provoke street violence between members of targeted groups, and covert actions designed to topple [leftist] movement leaders by, among other things, tagging them as 'snitch jackets' [and using] forged documents containing trumped-up evidence of cooperation with the FBI and police."[60]

Much of the federal government's warrantless wiretapping was approved at the highest levels. This is what Attorney General Robert Kennedy did in approving wiretaps in investigating the Mafia and in keeping tabs on the private life of Martin Luther King Jr. on the patently absurd ground that he was a communist. Kennedy also ordered wiretaps of congressmen and of *New York Times* and *Newsweek* reporters.[61] In all, during Robert Kennedy's "years as attorney general, the FBI conducted 842 wiretaps and installed 378 bugs, most of which involved break-ins."[62] Despite these clear abuses of power, "not a single person in the federal government was ever held criminally liable for decades of illegal surveillance through the 1960s that affected many thousands of U.S. citizens."[63]

Although the Nixon administration was not, by any means, the first to order illegal wiretapping, its other abuses of power seemed to be of a different magnitude than those of its predecessors. John Ehrlichman, Nixon's chief domestic affairs adviser, using money from the Committee to Reelect the President (CREEP), formed the infamous and illegal "Plumbers" clandestine group and assigned it the task of stopping government leaks. Members of the group burglarized the office of Daniel Ellsberg's psychiatrist hoping to find dirt on the former Department of Defense analyst who had leaked the *Pentagon Papers* to the press. They also attempted to set up listening devices at the Democratic National Committee headquarters at the Watergate Hotel, only to be foiled by Washington, D.C., police officers responding to a report of a break-in. When the press started asking questions about the Watergate break-in, top presidential advisers such as Ehrlichman, Attorney General John Mitchell, and Chief of Staff H.R. Halderman conspired, first, to try to get the CIA to stop the FBI from investigating the Plumbers and, later, to lie to investigators and to use CREEP funds to bribe the Plumbers into silence. Eventually the White House tapes ordered released by the Supreme Court revealed that the president, despite his multiple denials (read: lies), had known early on about the Watergate break-in and had ordered that CIA agents be used to try to stop the investigation on the fabricated ground that national security interests had made the break-in necessary. Ehrlichman, Mitchell, and Halderman all went to prison for their Watergate-related crimes.

Many of the president's men offered exceedingly expansive understandings of presidential power during the Nixon years. Attorney General Richard Kleindienst, Elliot Richardson's predecessor, claimed that the president had "uncontrolled discretion" to keep information from Congress and that Congress had no power to compel *any* federal employee to provide testimony over the president's objection.[64] Congress's only mechanism for restraining the president, the Attorney General claimed, was either to cut off appropriations or to impeach him. For his part, Ehrlichman blithely asserted that the burglarizing of Ellsberg's psychiatrist's office was "well within the president's inherent power" to protect national security. When Ehrlichman was asked whether the president's power went so far as to call for someone's murder, he replied that he would not want to say where the line of the president's power should be drawn and refused to disclaim that the president had any such power.[65] Forty-five years later, as we will see in the next chapter, Trump and his abettors would assert claims of presidential prerogatives that, incredibly, went beyond even Ehrlichman's outrageous contentions.

In order to fully understand the extent of the dangerous expansion of presidential authority under Richard Nixon, it is necessary to look beyond the Watergate scandal and its associated abuses of power. As Schlesinger explained in *The Imperial Presidency*, "Watergate's importance was not simply in itself. Its importance was in the way it brought to the surface, symbolized and made politically accessible the great question posed by the Nixon administration in every sector—the question of presidential power. The unwarranted and unprecedented expansion of presidential power, because it ran through the whole Nixon system, was bound, if repressed at one point, to break out at another. This, not Watergate, was the central issue."[66]

One of Schlesinger's crucial observations was that after the presidency first became imperial in foreign policy matters, it then proceeded to dominate domestic affairs as well. A series of doctrines and beliefs—the permanent crises engendered by the Cold War, the fear of communism, and the view that the United States was legally and morally entitled to defend its interests anywhere in the world through military intervention—conspired to assign to the president alone decisions over war and peace. "With this came an unprecedented exclusion of the rest of the executive branch, of Congress, of the press and of public opinion in general from these decisions. . . . So the imperial presidency grew at the expense of the constitutional order. Like the cowbird, it hatched its own eggs and pushed the others out of the nest. And, as it overwhelmed the traditional separation of powers in foreign affairs, it began to aspire toward an equivalent centralization of power in the domestic polity."[67]

In many ways, Watergate was a scandal waiting to happen, or to put it differently, Watergate was a scandal waiting for the ascension to the presidency of a deceitful and power-hungry leader who was willing and able to abuse the vast amounts of power that presidents had accumulated in the previous decades. The problem was not only that Nixon was a scheming and dishonest human being. The problem was also that the federal government's executive branch was led by an office, the presidency, that had gradually but consistently amassed huge amounts of power over the period of several decades. This toxic combination of a conniving and mendacious individual at the helm of a bloated and unbounded presidency would replicate itself, even more dangerously and perniciously, decades later during the Trump era.

One of the many ways in which Nixon expanded presidential power was by impounding (refusing to spend) federal funds allocated by Congress. In a typical manifestation of presidential arrogance, Nixon claimed that the "constitutional right for the president to impound funds—and . . . not to spend [congressionally appropriated money], when the spending of money would mean either increasing prices or increasing taxes for all the people—that right is absolutely clear."[68] This statement was patently incorrect because that type of impoundment violated fundamental separation-of-powers principles.

It had been generally understood since the republic's early days that "presidents were not required to spend every dollar that Congress appropriated."[69] It was generally accepted, for example, that the executive branch could postpone the spending of appropriated money to first create mechanisms and procedures for the efficient disbursement of federal funds. But it was one thing for a president to promote reasonable savings in government; it was quite another to claim, as Nixon did, that he had the constitutional power to refuse to spend congressionally appropriated funds *because he disagreed with Congress's policy choices.*

Nixon claimed constitutional authority to impound funds for congressionally approved programs that he believed, in his sole discretion, would not promote the general welfare. As the political scientist James Sundquist put it in 1981, "Nixon brought the impoundment issue to a climax by asserting that his power to withhold appropriated funds, derived from whatever constitutional and statutory sources, was without limits—and by acting accordingly."[70] And as Schlesinger explained, "Nixon's distinctive contribution was . . . 'policy impoundment': that is, impoundment employed precisely as FDR had said it should not be employed—to set aside or nullify the expressed will of Congress."[71] While earlier presidents who impounded funds had claimed that Congress had granted them the discretion to withhold the monies, Nixon and his aides contended that the president was *constitutionally entitled* to refuse to disburse funds in order "to set aside or nullify the expressed will of Congress."[72]

The Nixon administration took the legal position that the Constitution's Take Care Clause, which requires the president to make sure "that the laws be faithfully executed," authorized him to refuse to spend appropriations that he had either failed to veto or for which Congress had overridden his veto. The administration also claimed that while Congress had the power to *appropriate*, it was for the executive to decide what money should actually be *expended*. As Nixon's deputy budget director Caspar Weinberger put it, "a law appropriating funds is permissive and not mandatory in nature."[73] But this reasoning made no sense: if Congress had the authority to appropriate, but it was for the president to decide whether the money should be spent, then Congress's appropriation power was entirely dependent, as a practical matter, on the president's discretion. Such an absolutist view of executive power was deeply inconsistent with the understanding, expressed by James Madison in *The Federalist Papers*, that Congress's power of the purse under Article I constitutes "the most complete and effectual weapon with which any constitution can arm the immediate representatives of the people."[74]

It is no exaggeration to say that the Nixon administration went impoundment crazy, especially after the president's landslide re-election in 1972. Two months after the election, Nixon announced he was placing a cap on federal expenditures "with or without the cooperation of Congress."[75] By that time, the administration had already impounded an astonishing $15 billion in congressionally appropriated funds, representing about 20 percent of total discretionary federal spending.[76] In some instances, the administration withheld significant amounts of congressionally appropriated funds for certain programs. But even more brazenly, it also began eliminating *entire* congressionally approved programs altogether by refusing to disburse *any* appropriated funds to pay for them. Programs that Nixon sought to unilaterally abolish included a rural environmental assistance program in place since 1936, a wetland preservation program, and a loan program run by the Rural Electrification Administration. Nixon also ordered the closing of the Office of Economic Opportunity (OEO)—a cornerstone of President Johnson's War on Poverty—even though Congress was still funding the agency. All of this led Senator Sam Ervin (D-NC) to complain that the executive was dangerously seizing power with little congressional response.[77]

The impoundments were challenged in court through about eighty lawsuits, almost all of which the administration lost on separation-of-powers grounds.[78] To their credit, the courts consistently rejected the administration's outlandish claims that it was constitutionally entitled to refuse to fund programs at the levels mandated by Congress. As a federal court explained in a challenge to the OEO impoundment, "if the power sought here were found valid, no barrier would remain to the executive ignoring any and all Congressional authorizations if he deemed them . . . to be contrary to the needs of the nation. . . . The Constitution cannot support such a gloss and still remain a viable instrument."[79]

In 1972, Congress amended the Federal Water Pollution Control Act to provide funds to municipalities, through the Environmental Protection Agency (EPA), to help pay for sewer infrastructure and sewage treatment. Nixon vetoed the bill, but Congress overturned the veto and the legislation became law. Having lost on a policy question using the constitutional mechanism available to him as president (the veto), Nixon then chose to go outside the Constitution by attempting to prohibit the spending of more than half of the $11 billion that Congress had authorized for the program over a two-year period. A unanimous Supreme Court concluded that Congress had not granted the executive branch the authority to reduce the payments and ordered the EPA to allot the monies appropriated by Congress. In doing so, the Court made clear that it is for Congress, and not the executive branch, to determine the amount of federal funds that should be expended for particular purposes.[80]

Nixon's audacious claim that he could use his executive authority to essentially void Congress's policy judgments, as reflected in its appropriations, outside of his veto power led Congress to enact the Impoundment Control Act (ICA) of 1974. The law passed unanimously in the Senate and with only six votes in opposition in the House. By the time the bill reached Nixon's desk, four weeks before he resigned, he was so battered and weakened by the Watergate scandal that he had no choice but to sign it without complaint. The statute required that all impoundments involving refusals to spend appropriated monies (outside of short-term delays) be sent to Congress for its evaluation. The legislation made clear that unless Congress approved the impoundment, it was to have no effect. President Ford continued to press the point by seeking to withhold certain appropriations that were higher than he had requested. But Congress repeatedly "overturned his decisions (just 12 percent of Ford's $3.3 billion in rescission requests were approved), and the administration eventually gave up."[81] The ICA settled, once and for all, the question of whether a president has the authority to refuse to spend congressionally appropriated funds because of policy disagreements with Congress. "As both branches accepted their respective roles, the hostility and tension of the Nixon years over the impoundment question dissolved."[82]

The ICA was not the only statute that Congress enacted in response to Nixon's abuses of presidential powers. In 1976, Congress adopted the National Emergencies Act (NEA) with the purpose of terminating the more than five hundred discretionary powers that Congress had granted presidents since 1933 to deal with so-called emergencies. Congress had granted presidents, and never rescinded, a wide array of powers that allowed them, after declaring an emergency, to "seize property, limit travel or communications, declare martial law, and nationalize various industries."[83] Presidents could also use their emergency powers to do everything from ordering the internment of a large group of American citizens (as Roosevelt did during World War II) to suspending publication of their own orders in the Federal Registry (as Nixon did during his secret bombing of Cambodia).[84]

The NEA terminated all standing states of emergency as of 1978. The statute also prevented presidents from accessing emergency powers by mere proclamation, and instead required them to specifically declare a national emergency as outlined in the Act, identify the statutory basis for each emergency power they intended to use, and periodically report to Congress on the government's emergency-related expenditures.[85] Additionally, each state of emergency would automatically end after one year unless the president published a notice of renewal and notified Congress. The Act also allowed Congress to end a state of emergency six months after a president declared it or every six months thereafter.[86] As discussed in Chapter 4, Congress in 2019 twice invoked the NEA to terminate Trump's so-called emergency funding of a wall along the Mexico-U.S. border after Congress explicitly refused to provide such funding. Trump vetoed the revocations, but there were not enough congressional votes to overturn the vetoes.

To also limit presidential power, Congress in 1974 added an amendment (the Hughes-Ryan Amendment) to a foreign aid bill requiring (1) the president to make a written finding of the need for the CIA to take covert actions abroad that went beyond the gathering of intelligence and (2) the administration to brief specific congressional committees on the actions' objectives; otherwise, the amendment prohibited the expending of funds on covert actions. A year later, a special Senate committee chaired by Senator Frank Church (D-ID) exposed government surveillance abuses going back five decades, including illegal wiretaps, break-ins, mail openings, subversion campaigns, and the monitoring of the political activities of U.S. citizens.[87]

Partly as a result of Church Committee recommendations, Congress in 1978 enacted the Foreign Intelligence Surveillance Act (FISA) with the goal of limiting the executive's ability to use its sole discretion to determine when surveillance inside the United States should be used to protect national security. In order to prevent a repeat of Nixon's spurious use of national security claims to justify the surveillance of his domestic political opponents, the FISA defined "foreign intelligence information" to include only information involving the clandestine intelligence activities, sabotage, terrorism, or other hostile acts taken by foreign governments. The statute also required that the surveillance's purpose be to limit foreign intelligence rather than to bring domestic criminal prosecutions.[88]

In addition, the new law created the Foreign Intelligence Surveillance Court (FISC) to review surveillance applications. That court has been appropriately criticized by many because its proceedings are not open to the public and are almost never adversarial, consisting of nothing more than the government presenting its allegations to judges in secret. A study of the more than thirty-three thousand surveillance applications filed by the government with FISC between 1979 and 2013 found that the court had denied an infinitesimal percentage of petitions (twelve, or .0003 percent).[89] Nonetheless, under the FISA, the government must provide evidence to judges that the subject of the proposed surveillance is suspected of working for a foreign government and not simply advocating policy positions in ways that are protected by the First Amendment. This requirement makes it more difficult for officials to engage in the type of brazenly unconstitutional surveillance of domestic political opponents ordered by the Nixon administration.[90]

Congress in 1978 also enacted the Ethics in Government Act (EGA) to try to prevent a repeat of some of the worst executive branch abuses associated with Watergate. The statute requires senior administration officials (as well as members of Congress) to file public financial disclosure forms and to divulge gifts over a certain value. Furthermore, the statute prohibits federal employees from lobbying their former agencies for two years after leaving their positions and created the Office on Government Ethics to monitor executive branch compliance with the law's requirements.

In addition, the EGA created a mechanism for appointing independent prosecutors to investigate possible wrongdoing by government officials. The law's objective was to avoid a repeat of the 1973 "Saturday Night Massacre," in which Solicitor General Robert Bork, acting pursuant to Nixon's direct order, fired special Watergate prosecutor Archibald Cox following the refusals to do so by, and the resignations of, Attorney General Elliot Richardson and Deputy Attorney General William Ruckelshaus. Under the EGA, a specially designated court appointed an independent prosecutor after the Attorney General determined that allegations of wrongdoing merited such an appointment. The new law made clear that the independent prosecutors could not be removed at the whim of the president or the Attorney General; instead, they could be removed only if there was a "just cause" for the dismissal.

In 1988, the Supreme Court upheld the constitutionality of the independent counsel law in the face of a challenge claiming that it violated the president's constitutional authority to appoint and remove executive branch officials.[91] The Court concluded that there was no separation-of-powers violation because the EGA called on the Attorney General, and not Congress or the courts, to trigger the appointment mechanism and because the statute limited but did not eliminate the president's power to remove independent counsels given that they could still be fired for cause. In 1999, after the prolonged, expensive, and, in the view of some, partisan investigation of President Bill Clinton by independent counsel Kenneth Starr, Congress allowed the independent counsel law to expire.

Congress also in the 1970s created a slew of new inspectors general (IG) positions that required Senate confirmation. Congress placed IGs inside most executive departments and agencies, and tasked them with the responsibility of investigating possible waste, fraud, and corruption. The Inspectors General Act of 1978 requires that IGs be appointed "without regard to political affiliation and solely on the basis of integrity and demonstrated ability." It also prohibits the heads of executive agencies from interfering with IG investigations; demands that IG reports be sent not only to agency heads but to Congress as well; and requires the president to provide Congress with written reasons, thirty days in advance, for removing an IG.[92]

In short, Congress in the 1970s responded to Watergate and other executive branch abuses by enacting a series of laws meant to place some limits on the ever-increasing power of presidents. Although the statutes, when viewed collectively, constituted the most important steps ever taken by Congress to use its constitutional powers to limit the authority of the presidency, they failed to slow the expansion of presidential powers. One reason for that failure was that Congress, once the Watergate crisis and abuses receded in time, returned to its past practice of enthusiastically and robustly enlarging presidential powers.

An example of this troubling phenomenon was Congress's enactment of the Line-Item Veto Act (LIVA) of 1996. That statute sought to allow the president, after signing appropriation bills into law, to rescind some of the individual appropriations contained in the measures. Under the LIVA, the rescission would take effect unless Congress passed a new bill that reinstated the spending. That reinstating bill, of course, would have to be signed by the president (an unlikely occurrence given that it would follow the president's exercise of their "line-item veto" authority). If the president vetoed the new bill, then Congress would have to overturn it via a two-thirds majority vote for it to become law.

The LIVA was a misguided attempt to address Congress's apparent failure to bring greater financial discipline to its appropriations decisions by flagrantly attempting to increase the president's power. Through the LIVA, Congress essentially delegated to the president the authority to determine what constituted "wasteful spending." As explained by Republican senator Ted Stevens of Alaska, a strong supporter of the legislation, the LIVA constituted "the most significant delegation of authority by the Congress to the President since the Constitution was ratified."[93]

This expansion of presidential authority was so extreme that even the Supreme Court, which has generally shown little concern with the growing powers of the presidency, balked. As the Court saw it, the LIVA created an end run around the constitutional requirement that the president either sign a bill into law or veto it. The statute allowed presidents to have it both ways by signing an appropriation bill into law and then essentially unilaterally voiding the parts of the law that they disagreed with. While the Constitution grants presidents the authority to veto a bill *before* it becomes law, it does not grant them the power to void parts of a bill *after* it becomes law.[94] The LIVA fiasco was a glaring example of the extent to which Congress was willing to grant presidents even more authority than they had already accumulated on their own over the previous decades.

A second reason why the post-Watergate statutes failed to meaningfully restrain presidential authority is that Ronald Reagan came into office in 1981 determined to reassert presidential power and prerogatives following two administrations (those of Ford and Carter) that had been more modest in their assertions of presidential powers. Many of Reagan's Department of Justice appointees, including Attorney General Edwin Meese, were ideologically committed to expansive presidential powers and a "unitary" understanding of the executive branch, one that gives the president complete and unfettered control of the government's executive functions. In addition, the conservative political movement that brought Reagan to power now embraced and defended expansive presidentialism. As journalist Charlie Savage notes, many conservatives, prior to Reagan, had opposed the presidentialism of Franklin D. Roosevelt, Harry Truman, and Lyndon Johnson based on their "distrust of concentrated government power. But the new generation of conservative activists, who had no first-hand memory of those fights, began to associate unchecked presidential authority with their desire for lower taxes, a more aggressive stance against communism, and domestic policies that advanced traditional social values."[95] Gene

Healy makes a similar point when he notes that "the post-World War II Right, led by William F. Buckley's *National Review*, had previously appreciated the dangers of concentrated power better than any other political movement of its time." But by the time Reagan came to office reflecting the "emerging Republican majority in the Electoral College, the Right had largely abandoned its distaste for presidential activism and begun to look upon executive power as a key weapon in the battle against creeping liberalism."[96]

One way in which Reagan expanded presidential authority was by issuing an executive order requiring that all executive agencies conduct cost-benefits analyses of proposed regulations and that the results be submitted to the White House's Office of Management and Budget for approval.[97] The legal authority for the order was vague, but its implications were immense. As law professor Peter Shane explains, "in issuing this order, Reagan revolutionized the rule making process by routinizing White House oversight of proposed agency rules and specifying a general regulatory philosophy that agency heads would be required to follow, to the extent permitted by law."[98] Although there can be reasonable disagreements over whether it is a good idea, as a policy matter, to strictly weigh the benefits of regulations against their costs—it is usually easier to put a dollar amount on the latter (for example, the cost of pollution controls) than on the former (for example, the benefits associated with longer lives that result from cleaner air and water)—it was clear that Reagan's order expanded presidential authority by increasing White House oversight of executive agencies.

Of course, presidents had always asserted control of executive departments through their appointment of top agency officials. And the number of presidential appointments grew alongside presidential power. In 1980, the president was statutorily authorized to appoint about 800 executive branch officials. Only fifteen years later, that number had grown threefold to about 2,400.[99] In addition, federal civil servants had always understood that their careers would benefit if they promoted presidential priorities and those of the growing cadre of presidential appointees. But before the 1980s, it was rare for presidents to order agencies, as Reagan did, to take certain factors into account in issuing regulations.

And because the exercise of presidential power, with few exceptions, moves in only one direction (toward expansion), it was just a matter of time before presidents began to regularly direct agencies not only to take certain factors into account in adopting regulations, but also to issue specific regulations in order to achieve particular policy objectives. Proving that the imperial domestic presidency appeals to presidents of both political parties, President Clinton frequently urged executive agencies to take regulatory action covering a wide range of issues from parental paid leave to enhanced rules on water pollution to the safety of imported foods.[100] In fact, while presidents Reagan and George H.W. Bush issued a combined 13 directives to executive branch agencies, Clinton issued 107 such directives, many of which instructed "agencies to take regulatory action to deal with particular problems."[101] As law professor Bruce Ackerman notes, "these directives did not leave it up to the agency to design its own regulatory program after undertaking an in-depth study of one issue or another."[102] Instead, the directives told the agencies which regulatory objectives the president wanted to reach and essentially required them to conduct studies and deploy their regulatory expertise in ways that fulfilled those objectives.

There was almost no criticism of President Clinton's expansion of presidential power. Members of Congress neither actively criticized nor explicitly authorized "this latest power grab."[103] Conservatives, who were otherwise extremely critical of Clinton's policies, remained largely silent because the power grab was consistent with the type of expansive presidential powers they had embraced since the Reagan years.[104] And progressives, now that there was a Democrat in the White House, seemed more interested in justifying than in criticizing such an expansion.

One of the progressives who did so was Elena Kagan, an influential member of the Clinton White House staff and future Supreme Court justice. Kagan published an article in the *Harvard Law Review* during the year that Clinton left office in which she celebrated presidential control of the regulatory work of administrative agencies because, she argued, that control rendered the federal bureaucracy more accountable and effective. Unlike conservatives, who contended that presidential control of the administrative state was constitutional because it was based on (what they took to be) the plenary powers of presidents to direct the executive branch as a unified whole, the liberal Kagan argued that the control was constitutional due to congressionally delegated authority. When Congress delegates policy-setting authority to an executive agency official, Kagan argued, it allows the president to direct how that authority is to be exercised.[105] But however justified, presidents of both parties expanded the power of their office by demanding that federal agencies regulate in ways that advanced their policy priorities rather than those of Congress.

Peter Shane points out that this type of "steady accretion of presidential authority over domestic regulatory activity threaten[s] a radical transformation of our constitutional lawmaking process." This is particularly true given that administrative agencies issue a significantly greater number of binding rules than does Congress.[106] To posit that presidents have complete and unilateral control over the discretionary actions of administrative agencies

> suggests a transformation of the president not only from overseer to decider, but from chief executive to chief lawmaker. Becoming the sole decider with regard to the vast output of legally binding administrative regulations would potentially give the president a single-handed role dwarfing the role of Congress in

prescribing rules that Americans are compelled to obey. Such rules, whether focused on environmental protection or worker safety, involve policy judgments and economic trade-offs no less profound than those entailed in most congressional statutes. Centralizing presidential control over this lawmaking activity is arguably presidentialism at its most audacious but, for most Americans, its least visible manifestation.[107]

The slow but steady accretion of presidential power has gone largely unchallenged. In fact, the accumulation has many defenders, in particular among conservative proponents of the unitary understanding of the presidency, one which holds that *any* congressional effort to circumscribe the president's executive authority is unconstitutional. This expansive understanding of presidential power leads some to conclude, for instance, that congressional attempts to disperse executive branch policymaking power at levels below the president is unconstitutional.[108] A particularly contentious issue has been whether Congress can limit the president's authority to remove certain officials, such as the commissioners of so-called independent federal agencies like the Securities and Exchange Commission and the Federal Communications Commission, as well as independent counsels investigating members of the executive branch. Although the Supreme Court has upheld restrictions on the president's removal power in some contexts, defenders of the unitary theory of the presidency are strongly critical of such rulings.[109]

Those who defend expansive understandings of presidential power also claim that a president cannot be charged with a criminal violation while in office.[110] In addition, presidentialists insist that the concept of executive privilege fully shields the communications of the president's closest advisers from congressional efforts to investigate wrongdoing by the executive branch. As we will see in Chapter 4, Trump and his defenders repeatedly relied on these claims during his controversial presidency.

In seeking to direct the work of the administrative state, presidents have routinely turned to unilateral directives such as executive orders, proclamations, and memoranda. Some of the most famous and infamous presidential actions in American history have relied on these types of unilateral directives as purported sources of law. These measures include Lincoln's Emancipation Proclamation, Roosevelt's internment of Japanese Americans during World War II, Truman's desegregation of the armed forces, Truman and Eisenhower's loyalty and security programs of the 1940s and 1950s, Nixon's imposition of price and wage freezes, and George W. Bush's authorization of domestic spying and the suspension of habeas corpus rights for terrorism suspects.[111] But there have been many other important and controversial unilateral directives along the way, including a memorandum signed by Ronald Reagan on the day he became president, freezing federal hiring that angered liberals; Bill Clinton's proclamation (based on a 1906 statute—called the Antiquities Act—"long forgotten by Congress but not by presidents") declaring two million acres of land in Utah a national monument that angered conservatives; and George W. Bush's executive order creating faith-based social services initiatives that angered liberals.[112] Like Clinton, Obama relied on an executive order to designate areas in the West as new national monuments, a move that Trump rescinded through his own order.[113]

In the last few decades, presidents repeatedly have issued executive orders in the wake of Congress's inability or unwillingness to legislate in ways that they wanted. As Clinton's top domestic policy aide Rahm Emmanuel put it, "sometimes we use [an executive order] in reaction to legislative delay or setbacks. Obviously, you'd rather pass legislation that can do X, but you're willing to make whatever progress you can on an agenda matter." Or, as Paul Begala, another Clinton aide, put it more succinctly: "Stroke of the pen. Law of the land. Kind of cool."[114]

Most American law students are asked to read a case called *Youngstown Sheet & Tube Co. v. Sawyer* in their constitutional law classes.[115] The Supreme Court in that case struck down a 1952 Truman directive ordering the Secretary of Commerce to seize and operate the nation's steel mills. Truman claimed that the seizures were necessary to make sure the country's production of steel was not impacted by labor unrest at a time when the country was fighting a (congressionally unapproved) war in Korea. A deeply divided Court essentially held that the directive was unconstitutional because Congress had considered but ultimately rejected giving the president the power to seize manufacturing plants that might experience labor unrest. As a result, Truman had acted beyond his powers when he ordered the government to seize the steel mills. Read in isolation, *Youngstown* makes it seem as if the courts are jealous protectors of congressional prerogatives in the face of undue presidential encroachment. But what law students do not always fully appreciate is the extent to which *Youngstown* is the exception to the rule—courts almost never strike down executive orders as unconstitutional. One study found that of the approximately four thousand executive orders issued by presidents between 1942 and 1996, a paltry eighty-six were challenged in court. And challengers won only twelve of those cases, meaning that the courts, in a fifty-four-year period before and after *Youngstown*, struck down a miniscule 0.3 percent of executive orders.[116]

Presidential rhetoric has also contributed to the expansion of presidential power. As already noted, since Truman's "police action" in Korea, presidents have repeatedly led the country into military conflicts without first seeking congressional approval, arguing that whatever threat the country purportedly faced at the time required a military response. Presidents from both parties have also sought repeatedly to use the *idea of war* as a rhetorical metaphor to claim the need for forceful national responses to problems that purportedly can only be addressed effectively by the federal executive branch under strict presidential control. We therefore have had Johnson's War on Poverty; Nixon's, Reagan's, Clinton's, and both Bushes' Wars on Drugs and Wars on Crime; and the more recent War on Terror. As Bruce Ackerman notes, "this incessant [rhetorical] drumbeat keeps alive the president's special mystique as commander in chief, with its claims to unilateral authority when things get tough."[117] This drumbeat, which seeks to legitimize "government by emergency," helps to expand presidential powers and, because the emergencies are never truly resolved (there still are and will always be poverty, drugs, crime, and terrorism), those powers are never rolled back.[118]

Much of the expansion of executive branch power in the last few decades has come in pursuit of foreign policy objectives, sometimes in violation of congressional mandates. One of the most infamous examples of this abuse of executive authority led to the Iran-Contra scandal of the 1980s. After the Iranian government was complicit in the holding of American hostages at the former U.S. embassy in Tehran starting in 1979, the State Department instituted a policy prohibiting the sale of American weaponry to Iran, a prohibition that some argued was statutorily required by the Arms Export Control Act. But neither law nor policy prevented rogue NSC officials, working out of the Reagan White House, from selling anti-aircraft missiles to Iran in order to facilitate the release of American hostages held by terrorist groups in the Middle East after the Tehran hostages were freed. To make matters (much) worse, NSC and CIA employees then funneled $18 million of the funds received from the illegal weapons sales (along with money raised from private sources) to right-wing rebels who were waging a civil war to dislodge the left-wing Sandinista government in Nicaragua. The covert funneling of funds was done in brazen violation of (1) the constitutional command that money spent by the government be appropriated by Congress, (2) a specific congressional prohibition against government funding of the Nicaraguan rebels, and (3) the statutory requirement that Congress be informed of the government's covert actions abroad. As Peter Shane notes, "in a stunning three-pronged attack on Congress's authority in this area, the executive sought to raise money for the Contras independently of Congress (in evasion of Congress's fiscal powers), facilitate that fund-raising through arms sales that flouted applicable federal law (in evasion of Congress's legislative powers), and to lie about it, even under oath (in evasion of Congress's investigative powers)."[119]

An investigation of the Iran-Contra scandal by an independent counsel appointed under the EGA of 1978 resulted in the filing of criminal charges against more than a dozen government officials, some of whom pled guilty. Juries found John Poindexter, Reagan's National Security Adviser, and Oliver North, an NSC staffer, guilty of conspiracy, obstruction of justice, and theft of government property. Appellate courts eventually vacated the convictions on the ground that some of the evidence used against the defendants had been derived from testimony they had provided to Congress following their being granted immunity. The trials of five other officials, including Caspar Weinberger, Reagan's Secretary of Defense, were preempted when George H.W. Bush, three weeks before leaving office after losing his re-election bid in 1992, issued them presidential pardons.[120]

One of the ways in which Congress had tried, in the wake of the Vietnam War, to rein in the imperial presidency in foreign affairs and national security matters was by passing, over Nixon's veto, the War Powers Resolution (WPR) in 1973. Supporters of the WPR hoped that it would constrain a president's ability to use American military forces in combat without congressional authorization. Unfortunately, the WPR has failed to accomplish that crucial objective. One of the reasons for that failure is that the resolution requires the president to "consult" with Congress (it does not explain what "consult" means) before service members are sent into combat only when such consultation is "possible." Not surprisingly, presidents almost always conclude that such pre-deployment consultation is not possible. In addition, the WPR *assumes* that the president has the *unilateral authority* to send American troops into combat by permitting such deployments for up to ninety days without congressional approval. The WPR consultation process has been formally invoked by a president only once (by Ford in 1975 following the seizure by Khmer Rouge guerillas of a ship off the coast of Cambodia). In contrast, presidents of both parties have repeatedly ordered military interventions all over the world while ignoring the WPR, including by Reagan in Lebanon and Grenada, George H.W. Bush in Panama and Somalia, Clinton in Haiti and the former Yugoslavia, and Obama in Libya.[121] Although the elder Bush sought congressional authorization to use military force for the Gulf War of 1991, and the younger Bush did the same in 2002 before sending troops to invade Iraq, neither president conceded that he was legally required to seek the authorizations under the WPR. Furthermore, during the two decades that followed the 9/11 attacks, the younger Bush, Obama, and Trump repeatedly relied on the 2001 congressional authorization to use military force against the terrorist perpetrators of those attacks to justify the use of military personnel in many countries in North Africa and the Middle East, most in circumstances and against groups that had no direct or indirect connection to Al Qaeda.[122]

The 9/11 terrorist attacks served to expand presidential powers in other ways. Indeed, the attacks led to the most extensive push for increased presidential powers between the Nixon and Trump administrations. Following 9/11, the Bush administration contended that the president had the constitutional authority to formulate and implement whatever policies and restrictions he believed, in his sole discretion, were necessary to protect the American people from terrorism. According to the administration, "only the commander in chief could decide how the executive branch should go about defending America," leaving no room for congressional input or judicial restraints.[123] Presaging the even more outrageous claims made by Trump a few years later about presidential prerogatives, Bush at one point explained that "I'm the commander—see, I don't need to explain—I do not need to explain why I say things. That's the interesting thing about being the president. Maybe somebody needs to explain to me why they say something, but I don't feel like I owe anybody an explanation."[124]

Bush's unilateral measures included suspending the Geneva Conventions in order (1) to detain hundreds of individuals in prisons outside the United States (in places like Guantanamo, Cuba, and Abu Ghraib, Iraq) and (2) to authorize, with the blessing of Department of Justice lawyers, interrogation techniques that led to the torture and abuse of some of those detainees.[125] Bush also ordered the National Security Agency to conduct electronic surveillance of Americans' international telephone and e-mail communications without warrants as required by the Fourth Amendment and the FISA of 1978. Whistleblower Edward Snowden later revealed that the government, without congressional authorization and in apparent violation of the Fourth Amendment, was compiling a massive database of millions of phone calls that Americans placed with the three largest telecommunications companies.[126]

In addition, Bush in November 2001, without congressional authorization, issued an order creating a system of military tribunals for "enemy combatants" that denied individuals so designated by the administration, whether American citizens or not, access to the federal courts. The Department of Defense, following Bush's order, later adopted rules for the military tribunals authorizing the introduction of "secret" evidence that could be kept from defendants and of evidence obtained through coercive interrogations.[127] Government officials also relied on Bush's order to arrest an American citizen (José Padilla) on American soil in 2002, label him an "enemy combatant," and keep him detained in military facilities without charging him with a crime for more than three years. Further flexing presidential muscle, Bush's order suspended the writ of habeas corpus for "enemy combatants." The Constitution authorizes Congress to suspend the writ in instances of rebellion or invasion, but does not explicitly grant the president a similar authority. Yet that constitutional omission did not prevent Bush from asserting he had the unilateral power to deny terrorism suspects habeas corpus rights solely at his own discretion.

Going even further, Bush claimed the power to deny enemy combatants protections under the Geneva Conventions. Those conventions were adopted after World War II and later ratified by the Senate following North Korea's mistreatment of American prisoners during the Korean War. The conventions were intended to guarantee basic human rights for captured members of enemy forces by prohibiting torture as well as cruel, humiliating, and degrading treatment.[128]

Johnson and Nixon had provided protections under the conventions to captured Vietcong guerilla fighters. And in 1996, Congress enacted the War Crimes Act, making it a felony for any U.S. official to commit a "grave breach" of the Geneva Conventions, whether inside or outside of the nation's borders.[129] But Bush, based on then-secret legal assessments made by political appointee lawyers in the Department of Justice's Office of Legal Counsel (OLC), claimed that he had the exclusive constitutional authority, as part of the fight against terrorism, to determine whether the conventions applied to any particular individual imprisoned by the U.S. government, regardless of whether the individual was being detained abroad or on American soil.[130]

Lawyers at the OLC also claimed that the president had the authority to hand over detainees to foreign governments whose interrogators were known to torture prisoners despite the fact that the Senate in 1994 had ratified the Convention against Torture Treaty, signed by Reagan six years earlier, which banned such renditions.[131] Under the ostensible cover provided by the OLC's secret legal assessments, the administration instituted "a policy of transferring terrorist suspects to the custody of security forces for such countries as Egypt and Syria—whom the State Department's own reports accused of regularly torturing prisoners—for further questioning."[132]

The administration lawyers' breathtaking claims of presidential power contended that Congress lacked all authority to restrict the president's discretion as commander-in-chief of the armed services in any way. As a result, OLC lawyers claimed, *the president could ignore treaties and statutes* as long as he was exercising that discretion. "In the administration's view . . . *any* law that gets in the way of *any* tactic the president wants to pursue" as commander-in-chief is unconstitutional—"whether that tactic is torture or wiretapping or locking up American citizens without charges."[133] Unlike Nixon before him and Trump after him, Bush did not use the presidency to put himself above the law in order to procure investigations of and gain advantages over his political opponents. But he did claim the unilateral authority to limit the scope of binding treaties and laws such as the Geneva Conventions and the FISA.[134]

Rather than standing up for its constitutional prerogatives by placing some limits on presidential authority in national security matters, Congress was complicit in its expansion by retroactively approving Bush's unilateral measures. For example, Congress in 2005 enacted the Detainee Treatment Act (DTA) that, while prohibiting U.S. personnel from engaging in torture anywhere in the world, stripped federal courts of the ability to hear habeas corpus petitions brought by Guantanamo detainees.[135] A year later, the Supreme Court struck down the Bush administration's system of military tribunals tasked with hearing Guantanamo detainee cases because it was not authorized by Congress. The justices also held that the DTA stripped federal courts of habeas corpus in future Guantanamo cases, but not in pending ones.[136] Congress quickly responded to the Court's limitation on presidential authority by enacting the Military Commissions Act (MCA). The MCA (1) authorized the use of military tribunals to adjudicate the cases of Guantanamo detainees; (2) made clear that federal courts could hear neither pending nor future habeas corpus petitions by non-citizens whom the administration deemed to be enemy combatants; and (3) permitted the president to unilaterally decide what constituted torture under Common Article 3 of the Geneva Conventions.[137] And in 2007, Congress amended the FISA to allow the administration to collect Americans' phone records in bulk without seeking warrants beforehand.[138] In short, throughout the Bush years, Congress cared a great deal about giving the president the vast powers he demanded and little about either limiting presidential authority or exercising its legislative authority to assist in setting antiterrorism policies.[139]

Bush also greatly expanded the use of so-called signing statements to express his opposition to or disagreement with congressional bills *he signed into law*. Many of those statements complained that the statutes in question limited presidential authority in unconstitutional ways. The Constitution, of course, grants presidents the power to veto bills they disapprove of, including those they deem unconstitutional. But the Constitution does not authorize presidents to have it both ways, that is, to sign bills into law while lodging their objections in ways that seek to give them legal force.

The constitutional infirmity of signing statements—in 2007, the American Bar Association issued a report condemning the statements as unconstitutional—has not prevented modern era presidents from regularly issuing them.[140] By one count, presidents between 1817 and 1980 used signing statements to object to the constitutionality of 101 provisions that they signed into law. In his eight years as president, Ronald Reagan objected to 71 provisions; and presidents George H.W. Bush and Bill Clinton followed with 146 (in four years) and 105 (in eight years) objections, respectively.[141] This meant that by the time George W. Bush came to office, presidents had used signing statements to object to approximately 425 laws. Bush single-handedly *almost tripled* the number of such statements by *all previous presidents combined* by objecting to 1,168 provisions that he signed into law.[142] Such an abnormal, by historical standards, use of signing statements reflected Bush's expansive understanding of presidential power and the ferocity with which his administration defended what it understood to be presidential prerogatives from congressional interference.

At the same time, Bush used his constitutional authority to veto legislation sparingly, vetoing only twelve pieces of legislation compared to Clinton's thirty-six, Bush senior's twenty-nine (in four years), and Reagan's thirty-nine. Rather than veto legislation, Bush relied on constitutionally suspect signing statements to instruct the federal government to deem selected legal provisions null and void. When presidents veto bills, they (1) invite further discussion with Congress and the public over the issues in question and (2) provide Congress with the opportunity to override the vetoes (something which admittedly rarely happens).[143] But when presidents deem sections of a bill that they sign into law unenforceable through a signing statement, there is no opportunity for further discussion or dialogue, much less for congressional override. Bush was repeatedly drawn to the absolute and unilateral power that his administration's lawyers claimed he had to render parts of legal provisions unenforceable with the stroke of his pen. As journalist Charlie Savage wrote in 2006, "Bush has quietly claimed the authority to disobey more than 750 laws [the number would be more than 1,100 by the end of his second term] enacted since he took office, asserting that he has the power to set aside any statute passed by Congress when it conflicts with his interpretation of the Constitution."[144]

The history of presidential power summarized in this section has two crucial characteristics. First, while presidential authority frequently expands, it seldom retreats. This has been not only because presidents since Franklin D. Roosevelt have pushed hard for its enlargement but also because Congress has been generally willing to support that expansion and loath to place restrictions on it. As a result, the political scientist Andrew Rudalevige is correct when he argues that "the presidency is contingently, not inherently, imperial."[145] Congress, through its oversight, budgetary, and lawmaking authorities has the constitutional power to place effective limits on the imperial presidency. Its failure to do so has been the result not of a lack of constitutional power, but an absence of political will and courage.

Second, Democratic presidents generally have sought to expand presidential authority with a similar forcefulness as Republican ones, sometimes with the enthusiastic approval of Democratic-controlled congresses. The expansion of presidential power, unfortunately, has been a decidedly bipartisan endeavor.

It is time to end the constant expansion of presidential authority that has received, at different times, explicit or implicit support from across the political spectrum. In particular, it is time for progressives to take into account the extent to which statutes, regulations, executive orders, and similar changes in law expand domestic presidential powers when determining whether such measures merit their political support. This means that there may be times when progressives should refuse to support measures that unduly expand presidential authority *even in instances in which the exercise of that authority advances progressive goals.* As much as it pains me to write this, I believe that progressives should have raised separation-of-powers concerns about President Obama's expansive claims of presidential authority in protecting Dreamers from deportation. Although the deportation suspension was the right thing to do as a matter of policy, its implementation through unilateral presidential action was problematic and should have been examined by progressives on that ground.

Obama and the Dreamers

In the same way that I argued in the previous chapter that progressives should not rely on federalism mechanisms and principles, as a means of restraining federal government authority, only when there is a conservative president, they should not seek to rein in presidential power in domestic affairs only when there is a right-winger in the White House. The history summarized in the previous section shows how the expansion of presidential power builds on itself; when liberal presidents expand presidential authority to attain progressive objectives, they make it easier for right-wing and autocratic presidents like Trump both to achieve highly problematic policy objectives and to abuse their authority.

It undoubtedly takes a considerable amount of political fortitude to defend constitutional principles such as federalism and separation of powers when doing so makes the short-term attainment of otherwise valuable and important policy objectives more difficult. But it is sometimes necessary to postpone or even sacrifice the attainment of policy objectives in order to defend vital constitutional principles. Over the long run, our democracy will be stronger and function better if presidential power ceases to continuously expand as it has in recent decades. For that reason, instead of pressuring Obama to act unilaterally to protect Dreamers, progressives may have better served if they had continued to vigorously seek those same protections from Congress.

I should emphasize that my argument is not that DACA was illegal. I leave it for others to determine whether Obama had the constitutional authority to implement the program under the discretion granted to presidents by the Immigration and Naturalization Act.[146] Instead, my point is that, at the very least, Obama's implementation of DACA stretched the boundaries of presidential power to such an extent that progressives should have been more cautious in their support for the unilateral implementation of the program in the absence of congressional approval. In my view, in determining whether to support changes to federal law, progressives should keep in mind not only the policy objectives brought by those changes, but also the extent to which they may dangerously expand presidential authority. To put it simply, the strong policy arguments in favor of DACA needed to be weighed against the expansion of presidential power required to implement it. Very few progressives engaged in that weighing. I count myself as one of the progressives who failed in that endeavor. The fact that even a law professor such as myself failed, at the time, to fully consider the degree to which DACA could be used as a precedent for dangerously expanded presidential powers illustrates the extent to which it is possible to be seduced by the appeal of attaining important policy objectives in ways that blind us to the perils of the relentless and never-ending expansion of those powers.

In the early years of his presidency, Obama supported comprehensive immigration reform, such as that proposed in 2010 by senators Charles Schumer (D-NY) and Lindsay Graham (R-SC), which would have added significant resources to making the Mexico-U.S. border more "secure" (i.e., more difficult to cross illegally) while implementing a "tough but fair path to legalization" for undocumented individuals already in the country.[147] In public statements about immigration, Obama in 2010 repeatedly noted that it was important to fix the "broken immigration system" by (1) penalizing employers who hired undocumented workers, (2) strengthening border security, and (3) offering the estimated eleven million undocumented individuals living in the United States opportunities to remain in the country. On the latter point, Obama rejected calls by some in the immigration rights community to halt all deportations. In fact, in an apparent effort to show Republicans that he was serious about enforcing immigration laws, the administration removed about 775,000 undocumented individuals during its first two years in office.[148] At the same time, Obama called for the creation of legal mechanisms making it possible for those in the country without legal permission to gain citizenship after paying penalties and taxes, demonstrating English proficiency, and passing criminal background checks.[149]

As had happened several times in the previous decade, the type of comprehensive immigration reform sought by Obama (and earlier by George W. Bush) stalled in Congress. The prospects for such reform became even bleaker after Republicans regained control of the House of Representatives following the 2010 midterm elections by winning sixty-three seats previously held by Democrats. After losing the election, the lame duck Democratic-controlled House passed the DREAM Act, a measure—first introduced in 2001—that would provide Dreamers a pathway to legal immigration status. But the bill failed to win Senate approval, receiving only fifty-five votes, five short of the number required to overcome a filibuster. In 2011, Harry Reid (D-NV), the Senate majority leader, reintroduced the DREAM Act, but this time around, the measure received even fewer votes because several Republican senators who had earlier supported the measure, such as Graham and John McCain (R-AZ), now withheld support unless it was accompanied by more funding for border security and enforcement.

Following the failed vote in the Senate in 2011, a reporter asked President Obama whether he would suspend deporting Dreamers while he waited for Congress to act. Obama responded by explaining that while he supported providing Dreamers with the legal opportunity to remain in the United States, his hands as president were tied until Congress enacted new protective legislation. As he put it, "with regard to the notion that I can just suspend deportations through executive order, that's just not the case, because there are laws on the books that Congress has passed." Obama added that "we've got three branches of government. Congress passes the law. The executive branch's job is to enforce and implement these laws. And then the judiciary has to interpret the laws." On another occasion, in an unusual (if not extraordinary) moment for a modern president, Obama explicitly recognized that there were limits to what he could do as president: "There are enough laws on the books by Congress that are very clear in terms of how we have to enforce our immigration system that for me to simply through executive order ignore those congressional mandates would not conform to my appropriate role as president."[150]

Similarly, while giving a commencement speech at Miami Dade College, Obama explained that "like all of this country's movements towards justice, [immigration reform] will take time. I know some here wish that I could just bypass Congress and change the law myself. But that's not how democracy works. See, democracy is hard. But it's right."[151] Obama urged activists to continue pushing Congress to adopt comprehensive immigration reform that included both deportation protections and citizenship paths for Dreamers. In doing so, Obama explained that "I am president, I am not king. I can't do these things just by myself. . . . There's a limit to the discretion that I can show because I am obliged to execute the law. . . . I can't just make the laws up by myself." And in response to a question about why he was not doing more to protect families from deportation, Obama replied that "this is something that I've struggled with throughout my presidency. The problem is that, you know, I'm the president of the United States. I'm not the emperor of the United States. My job is to execute laws that are passed, and Congress right now has not changed what I consider to be a broken immigration system."[152]

Obama's statements about the limits of presidential authority were striking exceptions to the ways in which presidents since the 1930s, as we have seen, have relentlessly defended expansive understandings of presidential power, while rarely conceding publicly that those powers are subject to limitations. In making such statements, Obama was taking a principled position, grounded in the concept of separation of powers, that was independent of the underlying policy and moral questions raised by the presence of approximately one million hard-working and deserving Dreamers in the United States. The question was not whether Dreamers should be offered both protections from deportation and paths to citizenship; in Obama's view, from a policy and moral perspective, the federal government clearly should have afforded them with both years earlier. Instead, the question was whether a president could *unilaterally* provide Dreamers the same legal protections and benefits that Congress, however misguidedly and irresponsibly, was refusing to provide.

Fortunately for Dreamers, but unfortunately for the principle of limited presidential authority, Obama eventually changed his mind. As the 2012 presidential election approached, Latinx and immigrants' rights groups intensified the political pressure on the administration to protect Dreamers, leading the president to begin publicly asserting that his patience with Congress was running out. For example, only a year after his commencement speech in Miami, in which he had asserted that he lacked the constitutional authority to act unilaterally, Obama now claimed that he could protect Dreamers on his own: "We're still waiting for Congress to act. But we can't afford to just wait for Congress. . . . So where Congress won't act, I will."[153]

Four months before the election, the administration, through a legal memorandum issued by the Secretary of Homeland Security acting under the president's orders, announced that it would no longer deport qualifying undocumented individuals who had been brought to the United States as minors. Under the administration's new DACA policy, individuals who met certain criteria were entitled to renewable two-year terms of deferred immigration enforcement that would allow them to work legally. In order to qualify, the individuals had to be under the age of thirty-one in 2012; have been brought to the United States under the age of sixteen and lived in the country continuously since 2007; be current students, high school graduates, or honorably discharged veterans; and not have been convicted of a felony or significant misdemeanor.[154]

As a policy and moral matter, the arguments in favor of DACA were compelling. The program's beneficiaries had not chosen to enter the country without legal permission; instead, that decision had been made by others, usually their parents. Many of the Dreamers had spent most of their lives in the United States and had few memories of or connections to their nations of origin. They had all been educated in the United States; many were pursuing or had received college degrees. The vast majority were productive members of the American society. To forcibly remove them in order to return them to their countries of birth, where they had only lived as children (some only as toddlers or babies), was cruel, disruptive, wasteful, and unnecessary.

Nonetheless, Obama's original response to the Dreamers issue, one that recognized that Congress should be the entity that exempts a class of around one million individuals from the enforcement of otherwise applicable immigration laws, was the response that recognized the importance of separation-of-powers principles and of limited presidential authority. After Obama changed his mind by claiming the unilateral power to act based on *Congress's failure to legislate*, the administration contended that the executive branch's prosecutorial discretion justified the adoption of DACA. It is undoubtedly true that prosecutorial discretion grants the executive branch significant leeway in determining whether the law should be enforced against particular individuals. But DACA, at the very least, implicated the very outer boundaries of that discretion because the policy was not fundamentally about *how* to enforce the law in particular cases, but about *whether* to enforce it at all against a large class of individuals.

It bears noting that DACA was not the first time that an administration had deferred deportation of a class of individuals. As a federal court of appeals noted in 2019, President Eisenhower in 1956 "extended immigration parole to over thirty thousand Hungarian refugees who were otherwise unable to immigrate to the United States because of restrictive quotas then in existence."[155] And the Reagan and Bush senior administrations deferred the deportation of minor children of non-citizens who attained legal immigration status under the Immigration Reform and Control Act of 1986. However, the fact that DACA would defer deportation for about a million individuals meant that its scale and impact was much greater than earlier deferment programs.

Two years after adopting DACA, the administration announced a new moratorium on deportations of another large class—approximately four million—of undocumented individuals: those who were parents of U.S. citizens or legal residents and who met certain criteria, such as having been in the country for more than five years and passing a criminal background check. In addition to halting deportations, the administration's Deferred Action for Parents of Americans and Lawful Permanent Residents (DAPA) program rendered qualifying individuals eligible for some federal benefits such as Medicare and Social Security.[156]

When Obama was asked whether he was now impermissibly exercising presidential authority by providing deportation protection to millions of undocumented individuals, he responded by saying that his actions were lawful because they were "the kinds of act[s] taken by every single Republican President and every single Democratic President for the past half century." To members of Congress who criticized his suspensions of deportations for qualifying individuals through DACA and DAPA, Obama responded by saying "I have one answer: pass a bill."[157]

Obama was correct that previous presidents, on other policy issues, had acted unilaterally in the face of congressional inaction. But that did not mean either that earlier presidents had acted constitutionally or that Obama, from a separation-of-powers perspective, had acted appropriately by unilaterally staying the deportation of almost half of the foreign nationals who were living in the country without legal permission.

In 2015, a federal court of appeals, in a lawsuit brought by twenty-six states, upheld a preliminary injunction issued against DAPA by a trial court on the ground that the administration had not complied with the Administrative Procedure Act's (APA) requirement that regulations adopting new substantive rules be subject to notice and comment procedures. The administration claimed that DAPA was a mere policy statement or guidance, and thus was not subject to the APA's notice and comment requirements. The court disagreed on the ground that DAPA not only called for the non-enforcement of immigration laws against the individuals in question, but also conferred on them temporary legal status that, while revocable, was sufficient to render them eligible for federal benefits such as Medicare and Social Security. The appellate court issued a nationwide injunction against DAPA's enforcement, one that the Supreme Court affirmed.[158]

Progressives should defend the principle of limited presidential powers regardless of whether its application, in any particular context, advances or undermines progressive policy objectives. After all, in adopting DACA and DAPA, Obama embraced a similar expansive understanding of presidential power—one which holds that presidents have the constitutional power to engage in unilateral lawmaking authority in response to congressional inaction—that conservative presidents such as Nixon, Bush, and Trump used to pursue conservative policy goals over the objection of progressives. Presidents of both parties have consistently taken the position that important policy ends justify the means of never-ending expansions of presidential authority. But progressives should abide by a principled constitutionalism that cares about *both* means and ends. Otherwise, in opposing broad exercises of authority by Republican presidents, they would be left with defending the type of problematic situational constitutionalism which holds that separation of powers and limited presidential authority are principles worth supporting only when there is a conservative in the White House. In the long run, left-of-center causes might have been better served if progressives had continued to pressure Congress to adopt the DREAM Act rather than insist that Obama embrace the type of expansive understandings of presidential power that encouraged him to unilaterally implement a policy that Congress had considered but, unfortunately and unwisely, rejected.

Of course, if progressives had kept their focus firmly on Congress rather than on the presidency in seeking protections for Dreamers, there would have been no guarantee that it would have enacted the DREAM Act before Obama left office. And, in the meantime, Dreamers would have been denied the crucial protections against deportation afforded by DACA. But, as it turned out, those protections were short-lived anyway because the Trump administration rescinded DACA (and DAPA) in 2017. And it did so using *precisely the same mechanism*—a legal memorandum from the Secretary of Homeland Security acting under a presidential mandate—that the Obama administration had used to adopt the policy.[159] In announcing DACA's termination, Attorney General Jeff Sessions referred to Dreamers as "illegal aliens" and claimed that ending DACA was necessary to protect the national interest.[160] As a result of the rescission, progressives lost twice: first, by losing the DACA protections at the stroke-of-the-pen whim of a new fiercely anti-immigrant administration; and second, by contributing to the never-ending expansion of presidential power that Trump, throughout his years in office, was only too happy to exploit and abuse. Unfortunately, when right-wing presidents, from now on, take unilateral actions to implement policies that stretch the boundaries of presidential power, their conservative supporters can point to the DACA precedent and argue that "Obama did the same thing."

I recognize that many progressives will be troubled by my suggestion that those on the left should have questioned whether it was prudent for Obama to assert expansive presidential powers in adopting DACA. I understand and respect the view that the moral need to protect Dreamers from deportation outweighed apparent niceties regarding separation-of-powers principles. But my hope is that progressives, whether they agree with me on DACA or not, will give more consideration to the problematic long-term consequences of continuously and relentlessly expanding presidential powers, including when future liberal presidents have to choose between attaining crucial policy objectives and recognizing that there must be limits to presidential authority.

Progressives in 2020 understandably cheered when the Supreme Court left DACA in place after striking down the Trump administration's effort to rescind the policy for failing to abide by the APA's requirements in implementing that termination.[161] But the administration quickly pivoted to take the necessary procedural steps to rescind the policy under the APA, proving once again that the most effective and secure way of crafting a comprehensive policy aimed at protecting Dreamers is through legislative action rather than by presidential fiat.[162] As political scientist Corey Brettschneider explains, "whether you support the program or not, DACA is a good example of why legislation cannot be replaced by executive action. Important protections for immigrants should not be subject to disappearance at the stroke of the pen; laws, not executive orders, are what best protect people's rights."[163]

Like Obama when it came to DACA, Trump embraced the notion of expansive presidential powers in immigration matters. Unlike Obama, who relied on that notion to protect Dreamers, Trump used it to restrict immigration generally and to target Muslim and Central American immigrants in particular. He relied on claims of far-reaching presidential authority to call for the immediate implementation of what he called an immigration "Muslim ban" just a few days after he became president. And Trump in 2018 invoked national security powers to issue a presidential proclamation that prohibited all who crossed the border with Mexico to apply for asylum unless they entered the country through an official port of entry. On that same day, the Departments of Homeland Security and Justice issued an interim rule implementing the new asylum policy, rendering all individuals in the United States who crossed the Mexican border without legal permission ineligible for asylum.[164]

A group of social and legal organizations immediately challenged the new rule in federal court claiming, among other things, that the president exceeded the scope of his authority under the Immigration and Naturalization Act (INA).[165] A federal district court blocked the new asylum rule from taking effect. In doing so, it noted that Congress had explicitly allowed a non-citizen who was "*physically present in the United States* or who arrives in the United States (whether or not at a designated port of arrival. . . .), *irrespective of such alien's status*," to apply for asylum. The court held that "whatever the scope of the president's authority, he may not rewrite the immigration laws to impose a condition that Congress has expressly forbidden."[166] A federal appellate court denied the administration's request for a stay of the lower court's restraining order, rejecting the government's claim that the INA's granting to the president the authority to keep certain non-citizens from entering the country via a proclamation gave him the power to penalize non-citizens *already present* in the United States through an across-the-board denial of asylum eligibility. As the appellate court put it, Trump's proclamation violated separation-of-powers principles because it attempted "to amend the INA. Just as we may not, as we are often reminded, 'legislate from the bench,' neither may the Executive legislate from the Oval Office."[167]

Undeterred, the Trump administration quickly pivoted by issuing two new rules placing heavy burdens on asylum seekers from Central America. In doing so, it claimed it had the power to restrict asylum petitions in ways not explicitly authorized by Congress. One rule required most individuals who filed for asylum at the Mexico-U.S. border to await the processing of their applications in Mexico. The enforcement of this rule led to the setting up of crowded and unsanitary camps in several Mexican municipalities for the tens of thousands— about fifty-five thousand by the end of 2019—of individuals awaiting the adjudication of their asylum applications.[168] Some of these individuals were victimized by drug cartels and other criminal organizations in what the *New York Times* described as "lawless Mexican border towns."[169] In 2020, a federal appellate court upheld an injunction against the enforcement of the administration's rule on the separation-of-powers ground that it had not been authorized by Congress.[170] Of the tens of thousands of asylum applicants whom the administration expelled to Mexico by the end of 2019, the government had granted asylum to eleven individuals, representing an infinitesimal approval rate of 0.1 percent.[171] In short, the administration, for all intents and purposes, *unilaterally* ended the statutorily granted right to asylum as it applied to individuals along the Mexico-U.S. border.

The second rule required asylum applicants who had traveled through other countries to reach the United States to first unsuccessfully apply for asylum in one of those nations before being allowed to do the same with American officials at the border. The rule required, for example, someone traveling from El Salvador or Honduras to unsuccessfully apply for asylum in Guatemala or Mexico before

seeking asylum from the United States. The rule was clearly designed to discourage as many asylum applications as possible from the three countries—
Honduras, El Salvador, and Guatemala—whose nationals file, by far, the largest
number of asylum petitions.[172] A federal court of appeals in 2020 affirmed a
lower court's granting of an injunction against the enforcement of the new rule
on the ground that the administration had gone beyond its statutorily delegated
authority and that the rule was arbitrary and capricious.[173]

The Trump administration in 2020 used the coronavirus pandemic as a justification to further impose a series of draconian immigration restrictions that had
no meaningful connection to public health efforts aimed at halting the virus's
spread. For example, the administration used the pandemic to close the southern
border to asylum applicants completely, preventing more than forty thousand
migrants from seeking asylum at all. It also suspended the issuance of green cards
to many applicants located outside the country. In addition, it proposed new
rules for after the epidemic that "would raise the standard of proof for migrants
hoping to obtain asylum and allow immigration judges to deny applications for
protection without giving migrants an opportunity to testify in court."[174]

In short, Trump relied on far-reaching understandings of presidential authority *to unilaterally, severely, and ruthlessly restrict immigration in ways that
Congress had not envisioned or authorized* in the asylum context. The Trump
administration's actions counsel in favor of progressives opposing, on principle,
expansive exercises of presidential authority as an alternative to or replacement for congressional action even when the exercise of that authority helps to
attain progressive objectives. As the Trump administration's draconian immigration policies clearly showed, the exercise of seemingly unlimited presidential authority in implementing policies not approved by Congress is very much a
double-edged sword for progressives.

In making this argument, I am not contending that there was a moral or
legal equivalence between what Obama did in implementing DACA and what
Trump did, for example, in unilaterally blocking, for all intents and purposes,
all asylum applications along the Mexico-U.S. border. As a moral matter, there
is a vast difference between protecting young people from the harms caused
by being forcibly returned to countries they barely know, on the one hand, and
refusing to lend aid to asylum applicants who have been persecuted (or are at risk
of being persecuted) in their home countries because of their membership in
minority groups or political beliefs, on the other. There are also legal differences
between the two scenarios: DACA is defensible as an exercise of prosecutorial
discretion, while many of the Trump administration's asylum restrictions, as the
courts found, violated statutory mandates. Despite these important differences,
the presidentially-created DACA program was an example of the ever-growing
expansion of presidential authority in the face of congressional inaction,

an expansion that, as we saw in the Trump years, can have gravely negative consequences for progressive values and causes.

The Obama administration flexed its regulatory muscles in policy areas beyond immigration, including most prominently on environmental issues. For example, after a so-called cap-and-trade bill that he supported passed the House of Representatives but died at the hands of a Senate filibuster in 2009, Obama pushed for more aggressive environmental regulations. This push included an ambitious Climate Action Plan announced in 2013 that directed the EPA to issue regulations to combat greenhouse gas emissions. The agency responded with its Clear Power Plan, which, as we saw in Chapter 2, was later rescinded by the Trump administration.[175]

Nonetheless, Obama was significantly more circumspect in his use of unilateral presidential authority than was Trump. Shortly after he was re-elected in 2012, Obama explained at a political fundraiser in California that he wanted Congress to act in a series of important policy areas. After an audience member yelled out "executive order!" several times, a seemingly annoyed Obama departed from his prepared remarks by stating that there was a misconception that he could simply sign executive orders "to pretty much do anything and basically nullify Congress." That was not how our constitutional system worked: "We got this Constitution. We got this whole thing about separation of powers and branches." There was no "shortcut to politics and no shortcut to democracy." Under our system, Obama explained, the president is required "to win on the merits of the argument with the American people."[176]

Compared to Trump, Obama was a model of presidential restraint. Unlike Trump, Obama never claimed that the president was, in effect, above the law in that he could not be investigated for violating the law, including for obstructing justice. Unlike Trump, Obama never claimed he had the authority to prevent *all* executive branch members from cooperating with *all* congressional investigations of his administration, including those conducted pursuant to Congress's impeachment powers. Unlike Trump, Obama did not use his presidential powers to ask a foreign nation to investigate a political opponent in return for the release of congressionally approved military aid. Unlike Trump, Obama never pressured the Department of Justice to investigate his political opponents and to ignore federal crimes committed by his political allies. Unlike Trump, Obama never ordered his administration, without congressional authorization, to cut off federal funding of local jurisdictions that were pursuing policies with which he disagreed. And, unlike Trump, Obama never ordered the spending of federal funds for a project that Congress explicitly had refused to appropriate monies for (as happened with Trump's border wall). Nonetheless, Obama may have gone too far in implementing DACA without congressional authorization. Going forward, progressives should not be attuned to the perils of unrestrained and unilateral presidential authority only when it is exercised by a conservative president like Trump—instead of embracing this type of situational constitutionalism, progressives should value, defend, and abide by separation-of-powers principles even when it might limit the exercise of presidential authority deployed in the pursuit of progressive objectives. Although this type of principled constitutionalism will make the attainment of some progressive policy goals more difficult in the short term, it will help reduce the grave threats to progressive causes, democratic values, and traditionally subordinated minorities engendered by the governance and priorities of right-wing and autocratic presidents like Trump.

4

The Presidency During the Trump Era and Beyond

The relentless expansion of presidential power, which began in the 1930s, reached its most dangerous apotheosis with the election of Donald Trump. From the moment he became president in 2017, Trump challenged any and all constraints on his authority. There were multiple ways in which Trump claimed that he, as president, was free from all checks and balances, or to put it differently, that he was a law onto himself. When it came to separation-of-powers principles and constraints, Trump's presidency was a veritable Madisonian nightmare.

In the same way that I argued earlier that progressives should not rely on federalist mechanisms and principles, as a means of restraining federal government authority, only when there is a conservative president, they should not seek to rein in presidential power only when there is a right-winger in the White House. Instead, separation-of-powers principles, including those that limit presidential authority, are worth defending and promoting regardless of the politics, objectives, and morals of any particular president.

We are likely to see Trump's misuses of power repeat themselves in the absence of reforms that seek to oversee and constrain the exercise of presidential authority. For this reason, progressives should prioritize reining in presidential power in domestic affairs as a political issue, adding that objective to traditional liberal concerns such as economic justice, anti-discrimination protections, and reproductive freedoms. Progressives should assess whether particular candidates for elected federal offices, including for the presidency, merit support in part depending on whether the candidates believe that presidential powers need to be restrained. In addition, progressives going forward should determine whether to support particular statutes, regulations, executive orders, and similar measures depending not only on their substantive policy goals, but also on whether they unduly expand domestic presidential powers. Finally, progressives in the post-Trump years should support reforms that reasonably seek to limit presidential powers. At the end of this chapter, I make some specific suggestions on how Congress and the courts can constitutionally limit the powers of the presidency in domestic affairs in ways that can help deter the types of repeated and dangerous presidential abuses of power that the nation experienced during the Trump era.

Principles Matter. Carlos A. Ball, Oxford University Press. © Carlos A. Ball 2021.
DOI: 10.1093/oso/9780197584484.003.0005

The Trump Madisonian Nightmare

One of the many ways in which the Trump presidency constituted a Madisonian nightmare resulted from Trump's relentless attempts to obstruct any and all efforts—including by the press, by Congress, and by a special counsel—to investigate links between members of his 2016 presidential campaign and Russian government operatives. Three weeks into the presidency, the *New York Times* reported that, according to four former and then-current U.S. government officials, "phone records and intercepted calls show that members of Donald J. Trump's 2016 presidential campaign and other Trump associates had repeated contacts with senior Russian intelligence officials in the year before the election."[1] As a presidential candidate, Trump had stated that he hoped Russian intelligence services would hack into his opponent Hillary Clinton's e-mails and make them public.[2]

In the months leading up to the 2016 election, Republican senator Jeff Sessions of Alabama, one of candidate Trump's top foreign policy advisers, met twice with the Russian ambassador, meetings that he failed to disclose while the Senate considered his nomination to be Trump's first Attorney General.[3] After the Senate approved the nomination, Sessions recused himself from any matters related to Russia's interference with the election. Trump, who repeatedly claimed that any contacts between his campaign and the Russian government were "fake news" and "a total hoax," erupted with fury when told of Sessions's recusal, "saying he needed his attorney general to protect him."[4]

Trump did not care one whit that the "recusal was in line with the counsel of career government attorneys and was required under Department of Justice conflict regulations."[5] For the next two years, the president repeatedly lambasted Sessions in public for the recusal (by, among other things, calling Sessions "very weak" and "disgraceful"), showing the extent to which Trump believed that top administration officials, including the nation's chief law enforcement officer, were obligated, first and foremost, to protect him legally and politically.[6] For Trump, the Department of Justice was not an independent law enforcement agency; instead, as he saw it, the department had the *obligation* to protect and advance his personal and political interests. It was for this reason that Trump went so far as to "publicly badger[] Mr. Sessions to open investigations into his defeated rival, Hillary Clinton."[7] He also demanded that the Department of Justice investigate the former chairwoman of the Democratic National Committee and asked "Why aren't Dem crimes under investigation? Ask Jeff Sessions." Several weeks before the 2020 election, Trump called on the Department of Justice to criminally investigate his Democratic rival Joe Biden, as well as former president Obama, for supposedly fueling false charges that his 2016 campaign had links to Russia.[8]

During his first months in office, Trump asked FBI director James Comey to drop the agency's investigation of his former National Security Adviser Michael Flynn, who had resigned after only three weeks on the job because he had lied to investigators about his contacts with Russian operatives during the Obama administration's waning days.[9] (Although Flynn eventually pled guilty to two perjury counts, the Department of Justice in 2020, as we will see, caved to Trump's repeated haranguing by taking the unprecedented step of dropping the charges even though Flynn had admitted to lying to the FBI.) Trump also demanded Comey's loyalty and pressured the FBI director to announce that he (Trump) was not under investigation. After Comey refused either (1) to drop the Flynn investigation or (2) to make a public announcement exonerating Trump, the president fired him, eventually admitting he did so because he wanted the FBI's Russian investigation to end.[10]

There are no legal constraints on a president's ability to fire FBI directors for any reason (other than on unconstitutional bases such as race, gender, or religion). But even if it was legal, there was something deeply problematic about a president firing the FBI director for investigating his close associates. A president with any sense of self-restraint—a trait clearly lacking in Trump—would have recognized the massive conflict of interest that inhered in attempting to stop an investigation of his friends and associates by firing the director of the federal law enforcement agency that was conducting it.

A week after Trump fired Comey, Rod Rosenstein, the deputy U.S. attorney general, appointed Robert Mueller, a former prosecutor and FBI director, as special counsel to investigate the ties between the Trump campaign and Russian operatives. Trump responded angrily to Mueller's appointment and demanded that Sessions resign. Sessions submitted his resignation, but the president ultimately did not accept it.[11] A month later, in a scene that replicated Nixon's Saturday Night Massacre more than forty years earlier, Trump ordered White House Counsel Donald McGhan to ask the Department of Justice to fire Mueller. Unlike Solicitor General Robert Bork, who followed Nixon's order to fire the Watergate special prosecutor (after Nixon's attorney general and deputy attorney general refused to do so and resigned instead), McGhan told the president that he would not ask the Department of Justice to dismiss Mueller and offered to resign instead.[12]

Trump's attempt to pressure the White House Counsel to fire the special prosecutor was one of many instances detailed by Mueller, in his eventual report to the Department of Justice, in which the president tried to obstruct the criminal investigation. Mueller's team concluded that Trump, in addition to demanding "loyalty" from his FBI director in matters related to the Russian investigation and urging Comey to stop looking into Flynn's contacts with the Russians, also (1) asked his former campaign manager to deliver a message to Sessions ordering him to withdraw his recusal and to limit Mueller's investigation to future foreign interference with U.S. elections (the aide did not deliver the message); (2) called Sessions at home to urge him to withdraw his recusal (Sessions did not do so); (3) asked White House aides to tell McGhan, after the press reported Trump's order to McGhan to tell the Department of Justice to fire Mueller, to lie by "disput[ing] the story and creat[ing] a record stating he had not been ordered [by Trump] to have the Special Counsel removed" (McGhan refused to do so); and (4) publicly called his former personal attorney Michael Cohen, after he started cooperating with investigators, "a 'rat,' and suggested that his family members had committed crimes."[13]

In the end, Mueller did not recommend that Trump be criminally charged with obstruction of justice because it is Department of Justice policy not to prosecute a sitting president. Although the courts have never weighed in on the matter, the Office of Legal Counsel issued an opinion, at the tail end of the Clinton administration, contending that "the indictment or criminal prosecution of a sitting President would impermissibly undermine the capacity of the executive branch to perform its constitutionally assigned functions" in violation of "the constitutional separation of powers."[14] Mueller claimed that the Department of Justice's policy prevented him from making the ultimate assessment of whether Trump's actions violated the federal statute that criminalizes obstruction of justice. At the same time, Mueller explained in his report that the facts did not permit him to exonerate Trump. As the report stated, "if we had confidence after a thorough investigation of the facts that the President clearly did not commit obstruction of justice, we would so state. Based on the facts and the applicable legal standards, however, we are unable to reach that judgment. The evidence we obtained about the President's actions and intent presents difficult issues that prevent us from conclusively determining that no criminal conduct occurred. Accordingly, while this report does not conclude that the President committed a crime, *it also does not exonerate him.*"[15]

In 2017, Mueller indicted Paul Manafort, the former chairman of Trump's presidential campaign, for money laundering, tax fraud, and making false statements to federal investigators. Shortly thereafter, Trump's personal attorney broached the idea of pardoning Manafort and Flynn with the two men's attorneys.[16] This was one of several instances in which Trump signaled that he had no qualms with using the presidency's pardon power as bargaining chips in return for his former aides' continued loyalty and silence.[17] As we will see, Trump in 2020 used the president's clemency power under the Constitution, first, to commute the prison sentence of Roger Stone, his long-time friend and campaign adviser, and later to pardon him. A federal judge had sentenced Stone to more than three years in federal prison for lying to Congress and obstructing its investigation of the contacts between the Trump 2016 campaign and Russian operatives.

As we will also see, after he lost his re-election bid, Trump pardoned Flynn and Manafort.

Trump and his lawyers also took the uncompromising presidentialist position that it was, as a matter of law, impossible for a president to "obstruct justice because he is the chief law enforcement officer under Article II [of the Constitution]."[18] As accusations of wrongdoing against Trump multiplied in the months to come, his lawyers expanded that argument to contend that not only could a president not obstruct justice as a matter of law, but he could not even be investigated for having committed *any* crime before or after assuming office.[19] It is difficult to imagine a more breathtaking assertion of presidential power, one that literally places the president above the law or, to put it differently, outside of its regulation.

In the summer of 2018, the Manhattan District Attorney's Office, headed by Cyrus Vance, opened an investigation into criminal wrongdoing by Trump and business organizations affiliated with him in the years before he became president. A year later, Vance's office served a subpoena on Mazars USA, Trump's personal accounting firm, asking for copies of financial records relating to Trump and his business organizations. Consistent with his position that a president was entirely beyond the reach of the criminal law, Trump sued Vance in federal court contending that the Constitution's Supremacy Clause granted a sitting president absolute immunity from state criminal investigations.

Also in 2019, three different House of Representatives committees issued subpoenas to Mazars USA and two banks seeking financial records related to Trump and his businesses on the ground that Congress needed the records to investigate and legislate in matters related to corruption, money laundering, foreign interference with U.S. elections, and possible criminal conduct by the president while in office. Trump once again sued, challenging the subpoenas on the ground that they lacked "a legitimate legislative purpose and violated the separation of powers."[20]

Both subpoena cases—the one involving the Manhattan District Attorney's Office and the other involving the House committees—reached the Supreme Court. Several months before the 2020 election, the Court issued two rulings—both written by Chief Justice John Roberts—rejecting Trump's absolutist positions aimed at blocking the release of all information related to a sitting president's personal affairs. In the New York case, *Trump v. Vance*, the Court reaffirmed its holding from several decades earlier in *United States v. Nixon* that a president is not immune from criminal subpoenas.[21] The Court also refused to require that prosecutors show "a heightened standard of need" to subpoena the personal papers of a sitting president. The ruling was an important confirmation of a basic principle that was evident before *Trump v. Vance* and was now crystal clear: the president is not above the law.

Similarly, the Court in *Trump v. Mazars USA* refused to quash the congressional subpoenas at issue. At the same time, however, the justices placed a high burden on Congress before it can seek a president's financial and other personal papers. The Court, through Chief Justice Roberts, demanded that Congress in such instances prove that "the subpoena is no broader than reasonably necessary to support Congress's legislative objective" and that "the subpoena advances a valid legislative purpose." These requirements were necessary, Roberts claimed, in order to protect the "President's unique constitutional position."[22]

It is striking to compare the *burden that the Court imposed on Congress*, in order to protect the presidency from possible congressional overreach, *with the extreme deference that the Court showed to the executive branch* two years earlier in upholding the constitutionality of what Trump called the immigration "Muslim ban."[23] In that earlier case, the executive branch's mere assertion that the immigration restriction was needed to protect the national security was enough to insulate the ban from an Establishment Clause challenge despite the president's multiple statements evincing clear anti-Muslim prejudice.[24] The Court in earlier cases involving government policies motivated by animus, including ones approved by voters, Congress, and local governments, had consistently struck down the policies as unconstitutional.[25] But in the Muslim immigration case (*Trump v. Hawaii*), the Court, also through the writing of Chief Justice Roberts, held that the president's animus was constitutionally irrelevant because the executive branch was asserting that the ban was needed to protect national security. It appears, after *Trump v. Hawaii*, that the powers of presidents are so extensive that it allows them to call for the implementation of animus-driven policies, even though the Court, in earlier cases, had made clear that similarly prejudiced policies initiated by voters through ballot referenda, by Congress through statutes, and by local governments through ordinances are unconstitutional. To put it simply, according to the Supreme Court, the president is not subject to the same constitutional prohibitions against prejudiced decision-making that apply to everyone else in the country.

To make matters worse, despite the fact that Congress is a coequal branch of government, *Trump v. Mazars USA* made clear that it is not entitled to anything close to the same level of deference in exercising its authority to gather facts and conduct investigations in order to carry out its constitutional functions that the president enjoys when the executive claims national security is at stake. This double standard is reflected in the *Mazars USA* Court's command that judges rigorously scrutinize Congress's motivations and purposes for issuing subpoenas for documents such as a president's financial records. In short, while the president's motivations and objectives were *irrelevant* to the question of the executive's constitutional authority in *Trump v. Hawaii*, Congress's motivations and objectives were *essential* to the question of its constitutional authority in *Trump v. Mazars USA*.

And what is the reason for applying this unequal standard to a coequal branch of government? According to *Mazars USA*, it is to protect the presidency from congressional overreach and to "safeguard against unnecessary intrusion into the operation of the Office of the President." The congressional subpoenas, Roberts suggested in his majority opinion, may lack any "valid legislative purpose," which might allow the legislature to "exert an imperious control over the executive branch and aggrandize itself at the president's expense, just as the framers feared."[26] In being acutely sensitive to how congressional authority might intrude on the presidency, while largely ignoring how presidential power may intrude on Congress, *Mazars USA* joins a long list of Supreme Court rulings over the last eighty years in which it has protected what it deems to be presidential prerogatives at the expense of congressional authority.[27]

The Court's excessive deference to the exercise of presidential power has been problematic for a long time, but it is particularly troubling in the contemporary era when Congress has been largely sidelined, primarily as a result of its polarization and dysfunction, while the presidency has continued to accumulate unbounded powers. As law professor Sanford Levinson puts it, "the problem with Congress is an institutionalized gridlock that blocks the making of timely and effective public policy. The basic problem with the presidency is the possibility that the occupant of the White House is too unconstrained and can all too easily engage in dramatic exertions of power."[28]

If a president, as Trump and his lawyers claimed, is beyond the reach of the criminal law, that means that impeachment is the only remaining meaningful mechanism available to police and prevent presidential abuses of power, other than a re-election contest in the case of first-term presidents. But after the House of Representatives opened an impeachment investigation following Trump's request, in the summer of 2019, that the president of Ukraine do him the personal and political favor of opening up a criminal investigation of his rival Joe Biden, Trump and his cadre of supporters took the unprecedented absolutist position that if a president, *in his sole discretion*, deems an impeachment investigation to be illegitimate, he can refuse to cooperate with it. Under this absolutist understanding of presidential power, Trump could also prohibit his aides from cooperating in any way with the congressional investigation.[29]

Under Trump's direction, several members of the administration, including the acting White House Chief of Staff, the Secretary of State, and the National Security Adviser, refused to testify before congressional committees investigating the president's attempt to hold up the disbursement of congressionally approved military aide for Ukraine, as well as a White House meeting with the president of Ukraine, in return for a commitment that the Ukrainians would open a corruption investigation of Trump's political rival Joe Biden and his son Hunter. In addition, the administration refused to provide congressional investigators *any* documents related to the Ukraine affair. Although, in their time, Nixon and Clinton defended presidential prerogatives against what they claimed was congressional impeachment overreach, neither contended that a president has the power to unilaterally decide whether the executive branch should cooperate with a congressional impeachment investigation. In fact, Nixon offered to answer interrogatories from and be interviewed by members of the House Judiciary Committee, while Clinton permitted his White House Counsel to testify before the committee and to tell legislators that he was prepared to assist them in performing their constitutional duties.[30]

In contrast, Trump challenged the very authority of Congress to investigate him, while accusing the chairman of the House Intelligence Committee of being a "corrupt" politician who shared with other "human scum" the objective of "running the most unfair hearings in American history."[31] For his part, Trump's White House Counsel deemed the impeachment inquiry unconstitutional, invalid, and a "naked political strategy."[32] And Trump's Attorney General William Barr—who in the past had claimed that Congress lacked the authority to make it a crime for a president to exercise executive powers corruptly and that presidents have the unfettered power to end all law enforcement investigations, even those scrutinizing their own conduct—dismissed the impeachment investigation as nothing more than a political effort to overturn the results of the 2016 presidential election.[33]

In short, Trump and his aides granted themselves the unilateral authority to determine whether an impeachment inquiry was legitimate and therefore claimed the absolute power to determine whether they would cooperate with related congressional investigations. This extreme presidentialist position sought to render impotent the check and balance on executive authority afforded by Congress's impeachment power.

Fortunately, the House of Representatives was able to gather the necessary facts to show that the president used the powers of his office for private, political gain. On July 24, 2019, Mueller testified before Congress detailing the "sweeping and systematic" efforts by the Russian government to interfere with the 2016 election, the numerous contacts between Trump's presidential campaign and Russian operatives, and Trump's efforts to obstruct the investigation. Obviously unchastened by the overwhelming evidence uncovered by Mueller about presidential abuses of power, Trump, less than twenty-four hours later, called Ukrainian president Volodymyr Zelensky urging him to investigate Democratic rival Joe Biden and his son Hunter, the latter of whom had business interests in Ukraine. Trump encouraged Zelensky to work with Rudy Giuliani, Trump's personal attorney, and with Attorney General Barr, in investigating the Bidens.

A few days later, Giuliani met with a top aide to Zelensky in Madrid. Trump's efforts to pressure the Ukrainians to investigate the Bidens came to light when a whistleblower filed a complaint with the inspector general (IG) for the intelligence community.

Several days before Trump's phone conversation with Zelensky, the White House, without public explanation, blocked $391 million in congressionally approved military aid for Ukraine. (A later investigation by the Government Accountability Office concluded that the withholding of the funds violated the Impoundment Act, which, as we saw in Chapter 3, Congress enacted in 1974 in response to Nixon's abuses of presidential power.)[34] The acting ambassador to Ukraine, Bill Taylor, testified at the impeachment hearings that Trump conditioned the release of the military aid on Ukraine investigating the Bidens. Taylor also testified that there was a second channel of American diplomacy with Ukraine, headed by Trump's personal lawyer Giuliani who was not a government official. The purpose of that second channel was to push the Ukrainians to investigate the Bidens, even if it meant undermining the official U.S. policy of supporting Ukraine in its efforts to prevent Russia from occupying more of its territory.[35]

Gordon Sondland, a wealthy hotelier who donated $1 million to Trump's inaugural committee and whom Trump had appointed as ambassador to the European Union, told Congress that he had worked at "the express direction" of the president to pressure the Ukrainians to investigate the Bidens. Explaining that the exchange of favors was a clear "quid pro quo," the ambassador testified that an offer of a White House visit for Zelensky, who had been in office for only three months and highly coveted a meeting with Trump, was conditioned on a Ukrainian investigation of the Bidens. Sondland spent several months trying to broker the deal that would get Trump the Ukrainian investigation of the Bidens that he wanted in return for a White House meeting for Zelensky and the release of almost four hundred million dollars in congressionally approved military aid for Ukraine. Marie Yovanovitch, the former U.S. ambassador to Ukraine, testified about how she had been the subject of a smear campaign led by Giuliani because he viewed her as an impediment to the ultimate objective of persuading the Ukrainians to investigate the Bidens. Following the Giuliani-led smear campaign, Trump fired her from the ambassadorship position. While Yovanovitch was testifying before the House Judiciary Committee, Trump took to Twitter to attack her record as a diplomat, claiming that "everywhere Marie Yovanovitch went turned bad."[36]

In the end, the factual evidence was overwhelming that Trump had abused the powers of his office, leading to his impeachment by the House of Representatives on two counts: the first for abuse of power and the second for obstructing a congressional investigation. But the Republican-controlled Senate refused, first, to call witnesses with direct knowledge of relevant events to testify at the impeachment trial, and, second, to remove Trump from office. Utah's Mitt Romney, the GOP's presidential candidate in 2012, was the only Republican senator who voted in favor of removing Trump from office.[37]

One of the reasons why the powers of the presidency have expanded to such a dangerous degree in recent decades is that members of Congress from the president's party have repeatedly put loyalty to the president above the legislative branch's institutional interests. Unfortunately, for many members of Congress, the short-term political interests of their same-party presidents have prevailed over the long-term interests of the legislative branch they represent.[38] That a president is not only the country's leader but is also understood in modern times to be the head of their political party means that when that party controls one or both federal legislative chambers, Congress behaves "more like a subordinate and deferential arm of the executive branch than like the independent and coequal institution the Founders intended it to be."[39]

Part of the problem is that voters, in particular primary voters, tend to reward members of Congress for being loyal to the president of their party rather than to the institutional interests of Congress. Most voters, perhaps understandably, view questions related to how presidents govern through a partisan "Republican vs. Democrat" lens rather than through an institutional "President vs. Congress" lens. Nonetheless, the fact that not a single congressional Republican criticized Trump for his categorical refusal to cooperate with the impeachment inquiry was both striking and chilling.[40] The congressional Republicans' irresponsible abetting of unchecked presidential powers, one that sought to render Trump immune from Congress's impeachment and removal authority, will only make it easier for future presidents to abuse and exploit those powers. As we saw in Chapter 3, the historical record clearly shows that *presidential power almost always moves in only one direction: toward expansion.*

Within two days of the Senate's acquittal, Trump fired two officials who had complied with the subpoenas issued by the House of Representatives' Judiciary Committee and testified at the impeachment hearings: Gordon Sondland, the wealthy donor whom Trump had appointed as ambassador to the European Union, and Lieutenant Colonel Alexander Vindman, a staff member on the National Security Council.[41]

Two months later, as the country was grappling with and distracted by the tens of thousands of deaths caused by the coronavirus pandemic, Trump also retaliated against Michael Atkinson, the IG for the intelligence community. Trump was furious that Atkinson had complied with his statutory obligation under the Intelligence Community Whistleblower Protection Act by informing the director of national intelligence of the Ukraine whistleblower's complaint. Atkinson had also notified the House Intelligence Committee of the existence of the complaint, as he was required to do under the statute, after the director refused to forward it to Congress.[42] The president did not hide his reasons for firing Atkinson—Trump dismissed the civil servant because the IG "took a fake report . . . to Congress" and because he was "not a big Trump fan." Atkinson responded by pointing out that Trump fired him because he had insisted on carrying out his duties as IG. As Atkinson explained, "it is hard not to think that the president's loss of confidence in me derives from my having faithfully discharged my legal obligations as an independent and impartial inspector general, and from my commitment to continue to do so."[43]

Following Nixon's Watergate abuses of executive power, Congress created inspectors general positions in the 1970s. Legislators tasked these civil servants with the watchdog responsibility of investigating possible corruption, waste, and fraud in federal agencies. Presidents of both parties in the decades that followed recognized the positions' sensitive nature and the need to protect their independence. But Trump chafed at the notion that there were seventy-four federal employees who, as inspectors general, had the responsibility of identifying and investigating possible wrongdoing by his administration, even if those tasks were legislatively mandated. In another brazen abuse of executive power, Trump dismissed *four other IGs (in addition to Atkinson) in a six-week period* during the spring of 2020 because they were investigating possible wrongdoing within the executive branch. The firings received less attention than they otherwise would have because of the mounting deaths and economic devastation wrought by the COVID-19 pandemic.[44]

One of the IGs whom Trump fired was Steven Linick, the State Department's watchdog. Trump fired Linick at the behest of Secretary of State Mike Pompeo. At the time, Linick was investigating possible illegal conduct by Pompeo. Specifically, Linick was looking into the secretary's alleged use of taxpayer money for personal reasons. And, even more problematically from a separation-of-powers perspective, Linick was also investigating the department's authorization of arms sales to Saudi Arabia and the United Arab Emirates that Congress had explicitly prohibited. Trump also fired the Department of Transportation's acting IG who was investigating alleged favoritism in steering taxpayer-funded transportation grants to Kentucky. The department was headed by Elaine Chao, the wife of Republican Senate Majority Leader Mitch McConnell of Kentucky. And Trump fired the Department of Health and Human Services acting IG after she released a report detailing severe shortages of personal protective equipment during the coronavirus pandemic at hundreds of hospitals across the country, a report that contradicted the president's lies that there were no such shortages.[45]

The other IG whom Trump fired was Glenn Fine, the acting Department of Defense IG who was investigating suspected White House manipulation of a $10 billion defense contract for cloud computing services. Amazon was a leading contender for that contract until Trump began objecting to its being awarded to a company led by Jeff Bezos, who also owned the *Washington Post*, a media outlet that Trump repeatedly criticized as a purveyor of "fake news" and as an "enemy of the people."[46] (More on Trump's relentless attacks on the press in Chapter 5.) A council of IGs had recently chosen Fine to chair a panel tasked with monitoring the administration's disbursement of $2 trillion in coronavirus pandemic economic relief funds. But, conveniently for Trump, his abrupt firing of Fine rendered the well-respected civil servant ineligible for that position.[47]

Trump replaced professional and independent IGs with political appointees who were loyal to him. Furthermore, Trump refused to comply with the Inspector General Act's requirement that the president provide Congress with an explanation of the reasons for firing the watchdogs. Instead, Trump simply and generically informed lawmakers that he had lost confidence in the officials. What he did not add was that the reason he had lost confidence in them was because they were carrying out their congressionally mandated investigative responsibilities.[48]

It is worth noting that three of the five IGs whom Trump fired in the spring of 2020 were serving in an acting capacity, that is, without Senate confirmation. By repeatedly and continuously using acting officials, Trump sought systematically to avoid congressional oversight of his appointments. As of February, 2020, Trump had appointed acting officials to twenty-two cabinet and cabinet-level positions for a combined total of 2,700 days of work or about 1 of 9 days across those jobs. On a per-year basis, Trump had acting officials serve more than three times as frequently as did Obama.[49] And no president has ever filled crucial government positions, including the secretary of the Department of Homeland Security and the White House Chief of Staff, with acting officials *for years*. In doing so, Trump was pushing, if not exceeding, the limits of a president's power to appoint acting officials under the Federal Vacancies Act, a statute "meant to serve as a check on a president's ability to utilize gamesmanship to avoid the advice and consent of the Senate for high-level officers."[50]

Trump repeatedly filled vital government positions in this way to increase his control of the executive branch while avoiding the constitutionally mandated mechanism of having his appointees vetted by the Senate. As Trump explained, "I like 'acting' because I can move so quickly. . . . It gives me more flexibility."[51] Three federal courts found that three top administration officials (the acting secretary of the Department of Homeland Security, the acting head of the Citizenship and Immigration Services, and the acting director of the Bureau of Land Management) were all serving in violation of federal law, rulings that the administration brazenly ignored.[52]

The Senate Republicans' acquittal of Trump not only emboldened him to fire IGs who were trying to hold his administration accountable, but it also led him to more blatantly use presidential authority to both target opponents and protect loyalists. The result was an unprecedented and extremely dangerous politicization of the Department of Justice—in the months following Trump's first impeachment, that department, the agency charged with the awesome responsibility of fairly, responsibly, and apolitically enforcing the nation's federal laws, became a powerful tool for advancing the president's personal and political interests.

After the Senate acquitted him, Trump continued his push to have the Department of Justice investigate those who had investigated the links between his 2016 campaign and the Russian government, including FBI director Christopher Wray and special counsel Robert Mueller. Attorney General Barr in 2019 had heeded to Trump's pressure by appointing a special counsel to investigate special counsel Mueller's investigation; Barr did this even though the Department of Justice's IG was already scrutinizing the investigation.[53] The IG ultimately concluded that, as the *New York Times* put it, "FBI officials had sufficient reason to open the investigation into links between Russia and Trump campaign aides in 2016 and acted without political bias."[54]

Trump also stepped up his public campaign to pressure the Department of Justice to drop the prosecution of his former national security adviser Michael Flynn, a prosecution initially spearheaded by Mueller and his team. Flynn in 2017 had pled guilty after admitting he had twice lied to the FBI during its investigation of links between the Russian government and the Trump campaign. For more than two years after Flynn's guilty plea, Trump repeatedly and angrily insisted that Mueller and his team were corrupt and were doing the Democrats' bidding, while contending that he and his loyalists were the victims of a corrupt and deceitful investigation. The president's relentless drum beating eventually had its intended effect: to the dismay of career prosecutors and law enforcement officials, Barr announced in the spring of 2020 that the department was taking the unprecedented step of dropping the charges against Flynn *even though the accused had admitted and pled guilty to having broken the law by lying to federal investigators.* A gleeful Trump immediately took to Twitter calling it "a BIG day for Justice in the USA. . . . Dirty Cops and Crooked Politicians do not go well together!" He also claimed that Flynn was an "innocent man" whom the Obama administration had targeted, conveniently forgetting that Trump had said in 2017, before Mueller's appointment as special counsel, that he had "had to fire General Flynn because he lied to the vice president and the FBI."[55]

The Department of Justice's caving to presidential political pressure by dropping the charges against a former presidential aide who had admitted he committed perjury was so unprecedented that it led Emmet Sullivan, the federal judge overseeing the case, to take an unprecedented step of his own: he appointed a former prosecutor and retired judge to oppose the department's efforts, a decision that was challenged by the administration but upheld by an appellate court.[56] In the end, the issue became legally moot when Trump, after losing his re-election bid, pardoned Flynn.[57]

The Department of Justice under Barr also proved willing to serve as Trump's personal and political agent with regard to the prosecution of Roger Stone, Trump's long-time friend and former campaign adviser. A jury convicted Stone in 2019 of seven felony charges, including witness intimidation and perjury, for obstructing the House Intelligence Committee's examination of interactions between Trump campaign staffers and WikiLeaks (the organization that in years past had disseminated classified U.S. government materials). The committee was investigating whether Trump staffers had sought WikiLeaks's assistance in searching for copies of e-mails from Democratic Party officials that Russian operatives had stolen in efforts to influence the 2016 election. Although Trump was unable to prevent either Mueller from initiating Stone's prosecution or the jury from finding Stone guilty, the president for months repeatedly attacked the legitimacy of the case calling it, among other things, a "disgrace" and a "hoax." Undaunted and unbowed by the president's efforts to protect his friend Stone from their enforcement of federal law, the four career prosecutors in charge of the case recommended to the judge that she sentence Stone to between seven and nine years in prison. Trump immediately and furiously responded to this request by tweeting: "This is a horrible and very unfair situation. The real crimes were on the other side, as nothing happens to them. Cannot allow this miscarriage of justice!"[58]

In yet another unprecedented move, the Department of Justice, in a matter of hours, caved to Trump's public criticisms about the sentencing recommendation as it affected his friend and former campaign adviser. The department did so by hastily filing a new document with the court that disavowed the career prosecutors' recommendation and instead asked the judge to impose whatever sentence she deemed appropriate without a government recommendation of a minimum jail time. This new filing was clearly an attempt by the department to appease a furious president who did not want his friend and confidante to do *any* jail time.[59]

In response to the Department of Justice's abrupt change in position, three of the career prosecutors overseeing the prosecution resigned from the case and the fourth one quit the department altogether. In stark contrast, Trump was elated by the department's softening of its prosecution of Stone, a decades-long friend. "Congratulations to Attorney General Bill Barr for taking charge of a case that was totally out of control," the president tweeted before adding that "evidence now clearly shows that the Mueller Scam was improperly brought & tainted. Even Bob Mueller lied to Congress!"[60] In typical fashion, Trump provided no evidence that Mueller had lied to Congress; in contrast, prosecutors had presented the jury with overwhelming evidence that that was *precisely what Stone had done* in trying to impede and obstruct Congress's investigation of the president.

On the day of Stone's sentencing, the federal judge who oversaw his trial condemned the extent to which the Department of Justice had allowed the case to become politicized. She pointedly noted that Stone "was not prosecuted, as some have complained, for standing up for the president. He was prosecuted for covering up for the president." She added that the "the truth still exists, the truth still matters" in government investigations of wrongdoing. Otherwise, she concluded, "everyone loses." After reciting the extensive criminal behavior engaged in by Stone, which included an effort to intimidate a congressional witness, the judge sentenced the president's former campaign adviser to three-and-a-half years in jail.[61]

Trump immediately lashed out at the judge for what he called a disgraceful miscarriage of justice. Speaking a few hours after the sentencing, Trump argued that Stone should be "exonerated" and intimated that he would pardon Stone if the judge did not agree to a new trial.[62] A few months later, when it seemed clear that Stone was going to prison because Trump could not manipulate the federal courts in the same way he had manipulated the Department of Justice, Trump commuted Stone's prison sentence late on a Friday night.[63] In doing so, the unbounded and unrestrained president did something that not even Richard Nixon had dared to do: he exercised his pardon power to void the prison sentence of a friend and aide. Stone had lied to Congress in a bid to protect Trump from its investigation of links between his 2016 campaign and Russian operatives. Trump then used his presidential authority—first by pressuring the Department of Justice to drop the case, then by pressuring prosecutors to be lenient with Stone, and then by commuting Stone's sentence—in a transparent effort to reward a man who had broken the law several times in order to remain loyal to him.

Two days before Christmas, 2020, and less than a month away from leaving office, Trump outright pardoned Stone (earlier, the president had commuted his sentence). On that same day, Trump pardoned Manafort (the former chairman of his 2016 campaign) and two other former aides whom special counsel Robert Mueller had successfully prosecuted. Trump also pardoned his daughter's father-in-law, who had been convicted of sixteen counts of tax fraud in 2006, as well as three Republican former congressmen—two of whom were early and avid supporters of Trump's presidential ambitions—who had been convicted of corruption. To make matters even worse, in his final hours as president, Trump bestowed dozens of additional pardons, including to his former chief political strategist Steve Bannon, whom federal prosecutors had charged with defrauding investors to help finance Trump's wall along the Mexico–U.S. border, and to Elliott Broidy, a wealthy businessman and leading Trump fundraiser who had pled guilty to violating laws criminalizing covert lobbying on behalf of foreign nations.[64]

According to a tabulation by Jack Goldsmith and Matt Gluck, at least eighty-four of the ninety-four pardons Trump issued by the end of 2020 "had a personal or political connection to the president." As Republican senator Ben Sasse of Nebraska complained, Trump's use of the pardon power was "rotten to the core."[65]

It bears noting that while Trump pardoned friends and allies like Bannon, Flynn, Stone, and Manafort, while raising the possibility of pardoning himself, his children, and his lawyer Rudy Giuliani, a president's pardon powers are limited to violations of federal law and do not constrain a state's sovereign authority to prosecute anyone, including presidentially pardoned individuals, for violating state laws.[66] In addition, as the Supreme Court has held, the Constitution's Double Jeopardy Clause does not prevent "a State [from] prosecut[ing] a defendant under state law even if the Federal Government has prosecuted him for the same conduct under a federal statute."[67] The fact that criminal conduct remains subject to prosecution at the state level independently of how presidents exercise their pardon power constitutes yet another example of how federalist mechanisms and principles, as explored in Chapter 2, can be deployed to limit presidential authority.

There were many other ways in which Trump's Department of Justice acted to advance the president's personal and political interests. For example, several weeks after it refused to ask for any minimum jail time for Stone, the department abruptly dropped a prosecution against Russian firms that had been indicted by Mueller for "a sophisticated scheme to use social media to spread disinformation, exploit American social divisions and try to subvert the 2016 election."[68] And three weeks before Trump commuted Stone's prison sentence, Trump ordered Attorney General Barr to fire Geoffrey Berman, a career prosecutor and the U.S. Attorney for the Southern District of New York.[69] Berman had investigated and jailed Michael Cohen, Trump's former legal fixer, who had testified in court that Trump, while he was running for president in 2016, had directed him to arrange payments, in violation of campaign laws, to two women in order to keep them from speaking publicly about their sexual relations with Trump.[70] At the time the president fired Berman, the prosecutor was overseeing an investigation of Rudy Giuliani, Trump's personal lawyer, for possibly breaking lobbying laws intended to prevent covert foreign influence—in this case, from Ukraine—on the U.S. government. To Trump's chagrin, Berman had filed criminal charges against two of Giuliani's associates and was investigating a state-owned bank in Turkey despite the fact that Trump had pledged to the autocratic Turkish president that he would block the case against the bank.[71]

Trump engaged in many other efforts to use the federal government to advance his personal and political interests. For example, as detailed in devastating detail in a book written by John Bolton, Trump's former National Security Adviser, the president repeatedly expressed interest in having the federal government halt criminal investigations of Chinese and Turkish firms in order, as Bolton put it, to "give personal favors to dictators he liked." (As explored in the next chapter on free speech, the Trump administration unsuccessfully sought to prevent the distribution and sale of Bolton's book.) According to Bolton, the president's actions and statements seemed like "obstruction of justice as a way of life." In addition, Bolton detailed how Trump linked the possible lifting of tariffs imposed by his administration on China to an explicit request of Chinese President Xi Jinping to have his country buy more American agricultural products to help the president with his re-election prospects in farm states.[72] Like the Ukraine affair, this was a quid pro quo offer: a foreign leader would get the American policy he wanted if he agreed to take steps that would benefit Trump politically at home.

Throughout his time in office, Trump and his defenders and enablers contended that there was nothing any entity could do—not Congress, not the special prosecutors' office, not federal or state law enforcement agencies, not federal or state courts—to limit presidential authority in ways that prevented Trump from using the powers of his office however he wanted. They contended, for example, that a president can prevent federal employees from cooperating with congressional investigations; that a president can shut down a criminal investigation of himself or of his political allies whenever he wants; that a president can dangle pardons and intervene in the sentencing of his friends and former aides; that Congress cannot impeach a president for obstruction of justice; that a president can do anything, including the taking or giving of bribes, to help him "get elected, in the public interest," without violating the criminal law or providing grounds for impeachment; that Congress does not have the constitutional authority to impeach a president during an election year; that Congress does not have the constitutional authority to impeach a president during his last weeks in office or to convict an impeached president after he has left office; that the president has complete immunity from all criminal investigations and processes (including grand jury subpoenas issued to third parties that have some affiliation with the president); that the president cannot obstruct justice because he has the unilateral authority to determine what constitutes justice under federal law; that the president has the "absolute right" to do what he wants with the Department of Justice; that the president has the "absolute right" to pardon himself; and that a president could even "shoot someone on Fifth Avenue" or "shoot the Director of the FBI" and not be indicted because of the office he holds.[73]

Trump's abuses of power involving his efforts (1) to obstruct the special counsel's investigation of Russia's interference with the 2016 election; (2) to gain personal, political advantages from Ukraine and other countries while carrying out his official duties as president; (3) to obstruct the exercise of Congress's impeachment and other investigatory powers; and (4) to push the Department of Justice to investigate his political enemies and to protect his political allies from the enforcement of federal law were among his most disturbing and damaging exercises of presidential authority. It was these efforts that therefore received the most attention from the press and the public. But these actions were not the only ways in which Trump's presidency constituted a Madisonian nightmare. Trump attempted to eviscerate separation-of-powers principles in many other ways.

One way he did so was to use the office of the presidency to benefit his family, his companies, and his financial interests. Trump became the first president in the modern era to refuse to disclose his tax returns so that the American public could account for the extent of his wealth and the sources of his income. He also became the first president in recent decades to refuse to divest from his business interests by placing them in a blind trust. In addition, the Department of Justice promoted Trump's personal interests when it conveniently "reversed a half-century of interpretation of the antinepotism law and allowed him to hire his daughter Ivanka and her husband Jared Kushner as his close advisers."[74] (The couple's outside businesses led them to receive more than $80 million in income during Trump's first year in office alone.)[75] While he served as president, Trump's properties "played host to at least thirteen foreign-government sponsored events, 143 foreign government officials, and officials from the state of Maine."[76] Executives of large corporations with regulatory matters before the federal government also spent hundreds of thousands of dollars patronizing Trump properties. This included T-Mobile executives at a time when the Department of Justice was reviewing the company's proposed merger with Sprint and executives from the GEO Group, a private prison company that eventually received large government contracts from the Trump administration. Furthermore, while serving as president, Trump took about five hundred trips (about once every three days) to his properties at a cost to taxpayers—and a financial gain for his businesses—of more than $100 million.[77] A *New York Times* investigation found that revenues at Trump's hotels, golf clubs, and other businesses grew significantly after he became president and that paying customers included more than two hundred foreign governments, foreign companies, domestic corporations, and interests groups, as well as a slew of consultants and lobbyists, all with vested interests in particular federal government policies. As the newspaper explained, "just 60 customers with interests at stake before the Trump administration brought his family business nearly $12 million during the first two years of his presidency. . . . Almost all saw their interests advanced, in some fashion, by Mr. Trump or his government."[78]

The spending of millions of dollars by corporations, foreign governments, and states in ways that financially benefited Trump was challenged in court as violations of the Emoluments Clauses, constitutional provisions aimed at preventing the corruption of federal officials. However, the Department of Justice generally succeeded in blocking the lawsuits on the ground that the challengers lacked legal standing to sue.[79] But the administration's lawyers were considerably less successful in defending Trump's misuse of executive authority to punish sanctuary jurisdictions.

As we saw in Chapter 2, Trump came into office determined to punish sanctuary jurisdictions for refusing to assist the federal government in enforcing immigration laws. Trump put that plan into action by claiming that the administration had the power to place conditions on the disbursement of federal funds independently of Congress. Fortunately, a majority of the federal appellate courts that considered the issue struck down that effort on the ground that it violated bedrock separation-of-powers principles. As one of the courts explained, "the founders of our country well understood that the concentration of power threatens individual liberty and established a bulwark against such tyranny by creating a separation of powers among the branches of government." It then warned that

> if the Executive Branch can determine policy, and then use the power of the purse to mandate compliance with that policy by the state and local governments, all without the authorization or even acquiescence of elected legislators, that check against tyranny is forsaken. The Attorney General in this case used the sword of federal funding to conscript state and local authorities to aid in federal civil immigration enforcement. But the power of the purse rests with Congress, which authorized the federal funds at issue and did not impose any immigration enforcement conditions on the receipt of such funds. In fact, Congress repeatedly refused to approve measures that would tie funding to state and local immigration policies. Nor . . . did Congress authorize the Attorney General to impose such conditions. It falls to us, the judiciary, as the remaining branch of the government, to act as a check on such usurpation of power. We are a country that jealously guards the separation of powers, and we must be ever-vigilant in that endeavor.[80]

Another way in which Trump attempted to eviscerate separation-of-powers principles was through his insistence that the executive branch, over Congress's objection, could build a wall, hundreds of miles in length, along part of the Mexico-U.S. border. For Trump, the wall was "a powerful emblem of his anti-immigration message."[81] As a candidate, Trump promised that, if elected, his administration would build the wall and that Mexico would pay for it. As was obvious to almost everyone, Mexico was never going to pay for the wall. But the bigger political problem for Trump was that although Republicans were in firm control of Congress during his first two years in office, there was little congressional support for the wall. For many conservative Republicans anxious to reduce legal and illegal immigration, building a wall was low on their list of policy priorities.[82]

In 2018, Congress appropriated $1.6 billion for border security, with only a fraction dedicated to wall funding. The House Republican majority, a few days before it ceded control to the Democrats following the midterm 2018 election, added funding for the wall, at the level the president wanted, to a stopgap measure that would keep the federal government open.[83] After the bill failed to receive sufficient support in the Senate, an angry Trump refused to sign legislation to keep the government operating, leading to a shutdown of thirty-five days, the longest in U.S. history.[84] The public largely blamed Trump for the shutdown, forcing him to agree to the government's reopening even though Congress continued to refuse to appropriate all of the wall money he demanded. Bipartisan negotiations with the now Democratic-controlled House ensued, resulting in an allocation of $1.375 billion for the wall. That appropriation was far less than the $5.7 billion necessary to pay for the 234 miles of wall that the president wanted.[85]

Trump, feeling politically boxed in both by an impatient public that would not tolerate another government shutdown and by an uncooperative Congress, signed the appropriation measure. But he then pivoted by claiming that administration lawyers had concluded that, as president, he had the authority to pay for the wall that Congress was refusing to fund by declaring a national emergency at the border. And this was precisely what Trump proceeded to do even though there was, in fact, no such emergency. Conditions had not changed at the Mexican border—the number of individuals attempting to cross it illegally had held roughly constant for several years, and was much lower than it had been twenty years earlier.[86] Although the president and his aides claimed that terrorists were illegally crossing the border, they provided, as usual, no evidence to support the assertion.[87] The only "emergency" was that Congress had refused to provide the president with the money he wanted for the construction of his wall.

The White House asserted that the president's emergency declaration allowed Trump to fund the wall by diverting $3.6 billion that Congress had allocated for other purposes. The move was immediately criticized by Democrats, as well as some Republicans, as an unconstitutional power grab.[88]

Days after Trump used the so-called border emergency to divert congressionally appropriated funds, sixteen states challenged the action in federal court.[89] A few weeks later, private groups and the House of Representatives filed independent challenges against the administration.[90] The lawsuits alleged that

Trump's move was a flagrant violation of separation-of-powers principles because it unconstitutionally diverted congressionally appropriated monies for military projects, drug interdiction, and law enforcement initiatives in order to fund the wall at levels that Congress had explicitly rejected.

The Trump administration justified the diversion of funds to pay for the wall by pointing to the authority granted to the president by the National Emergencies Act (NEA). Ironically, the NEA, as explored in Chapter 3, was a Watergate-era statute *intended to limit the president's authority* to invoke emergency powers and to provide Congress with greater oversight of the process. Prior to the NEA, Congress had not retained for itself the ability to regulate when a president declared a national emergency or when it should be terminated. It was this absence of congressional oversight that had allowed Truman to issue an emergency declaration in 1950 to wage war in Korea without a congressional declaration of war. Truman's Korea emergency declaration was then used by the Johnson and Nixon administrations as a purported legal basis for waging war in Vietnam years later.[91]

The Senate, wanting to better understand the extent to which Congress had granted presidents emergency powers, convened a special committee in 1973 to study the issue of presidentially declared emergencies.[92] The committee found that there were, at the time, three active declared emergencies, in addition to the Korean one from more than twenty years earlier. Incredibly, one of the emergencies still active in 1973 was the banking emergency declared by President Franklin D. Roosevelt the day he took office forty years earlier.[93]

Each declared emergency gave the president access to a huge swath of unchecked powers under almost five hundred federal statutes. According to the Senate committee, the statutes allowed the president to "seize property; organize and control the means of production; seize commodities; assign military forces abroad; institute martial law; seize and control all transportation and communication; regulate the operation of private enterprise; restrict travel; and, in a plethora of particular ways, control the lives of all American citizens."[94]

The committee recommended new legislation, leading to the enactment of the NEA. The new statute was intended to both restrict presidential emergency powers and to provide congressional oversight of their exercise.[95] The NEA prevented presidents from accessing emergency powers by mere proclamation, and instead required them (1) to declare a national emergency as outlined in the Act and (2) to identify the statutory basis for each emergency power they intended to use.[96] Additionally, each state of emergency would automatically end after one year unless the president published a notice of renewal and notified Congress. The act required each chamber to meet every six months to consider a vote terminating the emergency and allowed Congress to do so through a concurrent resolution that was not subject to a presidential veto.[97]

By most accounts, the NEA has not worked as critics of expansive presidential power had hoped.[98] The act has failed to end permanent states of emergency because presidents have bypassed the automatic termination provision by simply renewing the emergency declarations year after year.[99] Presidential declarations of emergencies multiplied under the law. In 2020, there were thirty-eight ongoing states of emergency, compared to only four at the time Congress enacted the NEA. Some of those still-in-place emergencies included one declared by President Carter *forty-one years* earlier in response to the Tehran hostage crisis and another by President Clinton *twenty-five years* earlier following the Cuban military's shooting down of a small, unarmed American airplane in international airspace.[100]

Additionally, the 1983 Supreme Court ruling in *INS v. Chadha* eliminated Congress's authority to terminate an emergency declaration through a concurrent resolution.[101] *Chadha* held that all legally binding congressional action had to be subject to presidential veto review under the Constitution's Presentment Clause. *Chadha* forced Congress to amend the NEA so that a president's emergency declaration could only be terminated through the passage of a joint resolution that was subject to the president's veto, a veto that could only be overturned through a two-thirds majority vote in each chamber. The legislative change necessitated by *Chadha* made it much less likely that Congress would be able to terminate an emergency declaration over the president's objection, thus destroying "the carefully wrought scheme Congress had created in the NEA for sharing power over determining when emergencies existed."[102]

Furthermore, for forty years after it enacted the NEA, Congress did not once bother to do what the statute required: to assess, every six months, whether to terminate a presidential declaration of emergency. The first time Congress did so was in 2019, following Trump's declaration of the supposed Mexico-U.S. border emergency. By a vote of 245-182 in the House and 59-41 in the Senate, Congress voted to terminate Trump's emergency declaration. Trump vetoed the joint resolution, and there were not enough votes to override the veto. Six months later, Congress once again voted to end Trump's emergency declaration with the support of twelve Republican senators, but the president once again vetoed the joint resolution.[103] The administration then proceeded to divert billions of dollars from congressionally approved programs to a congressionally unapproved one: the building of Trump's border wall.[104]

Trump's three immediate predecessors, Clinton (five times), Bush (ten times), and Obama (ten times), had all declared emergencies pursuant to the NEA. But Trump's emergency declaration was unprecedented because *it followed Congress's explicit refusal to authorize the funds in question.* The rationale for granting presidents emergency powers traditionally has been that the executive branch, led by one person, is in a better position to respond quickly and effectively to national emergencies than a slow-moving Congress, which must deliberate and reach compromises among its 535 members before it can legislate. But the decision of whether to appropriate funds for particular purposes is for Congress, and not for the president, to make. By rejecting, for three fiscal years in a row, Trump's requests for border wall funding, Congress made the judgment that allocating more than $5 billion to build a wall was not a proper way of securing the Mexico-U.S. border.

Trump was, of course, entitled to disagree with that policy assessment and to use his bully pulpit as president to put pressure on Congress to change its mind. (As we will see in the next chapter, the term "bully pulpit" took on a different and disconcerting meaning during the Trump era due to his use of the presidency to literally bully, intimidate, and harass opponents, critics, and members of the press.) Trump could have also vetoed the appropriation bills that failed to include wall funding as a way of pressuring Congress to give him what he wanted. But Trump was not constitutionally entitled to override Congress's appropriation-related judgments by tapping into pools of money that Congress had appropriated for entirely different purposes *in bills that he had made legally binding with his signature.* Trump violated a bedrock separation-of-powers principle by exercising the power of the purse, a quintessential legislative function. As a federal court of appeals explained in concluding that Trump's efforts to build the wall by using congressionally appropriated funds in ways the Congress had not authorized was unconstitutional, "the straightforward and explicit command of the [Constitution's] Appropriations Clause means simply that no money can be paid out of the Treasury unless it has been appropriated by an act of Congress. The Clause is a bulwark of the Constitution's separation of powers. It assures that public funds will be spent according to the letter of the difficult judgments reached by Congress as to the common good and not according to the individual favor of Government agents. Without it, the executive would possess an unbounded power over the public purse of the nation; and might apply all its moneyed resources at his pleasure."[105]

Trump administration lawyers claimed that the president has inherent powers to deal with emergencies, which, along with Congress's delegation of power to the president through the NEA, rendered constitutional Trump's reallocation of funds to build the wall. But even if we assume, for the sake of argument, that the Constitution grants presidents a general, unspecified, and unilateral power to declare emergencies as they deem best, on top of the authority granted by the NEA, that declaration cannot constitutionally be used to overrule Congress's *considered and explicit* judgment on how much money to expend in the pursuit of particular policy objectives.[106] Again, that is a decision that the Constitution assigns to Congress and not to the president.

Furthermore, administration lawyers contended that whether the situation at the border constituted a true emergency was a so-called political question, which under Supreme Court doctrine is not amenable to judicial review. Notice that the Trump administration's legal position left the president *as the only source of authority* on the border wall issue, one that could not be appropriately checked by either of the other two branches of government. According to the administration's lawyers, the president's unilateral declaration of emergency allowed him to both override Congress's explicit decision not to fully fund the border wall *and* to preclude all judicial review of that action. As the Constitution's drafters recognized, this type of unchecked executive authority, by either a king or a president, is the very definition of tyranny.

Like his recent predecessors, Trump also repeatedly used presidential directives to unilaterally set policy. For example, on the day he took office, he signed an executive order instructing federal agencies to "exercise all authority and discretion available to them to waive, defer, grant exemptions from, or delay the implementation of any provision or requirement of" Obamacare that would impose a financial cost or regulatory burden on any state, individual, family, as well as health-care providers, insurers, and manufacturers.[107] In addition, like his predecessors, Trump used executive orders to direct administrative agencies to issue regulations to achieve predetermined presidential policy objectives. Examples include an order asking the Environmental Protection Agency (EPA) to unwind Obama's Clean Power Plan with the goal of reviving the coal industry and another directing the agency to issue a rule restricting federal authority to regulate the nation's waterways.[108] Neither the statutory language granting an agency such as the EPA the authority to regulate nor the facts—in this case related to environmental conditions on the ground—justified these regulatory changes. Instead, Trump, like his predecessors, relied on the exercise of unilateral presidential authority to set the policy objectives—another way of putting it would be "to legislate"—and then asked federal agencies to interpret the statutes and the empirical evidence in ways that achieved his preferred objectives.

In many ways, then, Trump's abuses of presidential powers were clear departures from those of his predecessors. For example, in using presidential authority to gain personal, political benefits, in publicly demanding that the Department of Justice prosecute his enemies and benefit his friends, and in refusing to recognize the authority of Congress to investigate his actions and those of his close associates through the constitutional means of impeachment, Trump took claims of presidential power and prerogatives to new heights. But in other ways, Trump's exercise of presidential authority was generally consistent with how most of his recent predecessors had aggressively employed that power by repeatedly and energetically filling the policy voids left by a timid Congress, a deferential Supreme Court, and an indifferent citizenry. Going forward, there are few objectives more important to the future of our constitutional democracy than the reining in of presidential power in domestic affairs.

Presidential Powers in the Progressive Imagination

Ever since the Vietnam War, progressives have worked, to their credit, to limit presidential authority in matters related to armed conflicts abroad and national security at home. It was liberals, for example, who pushed for the War Powers Resolution and for statutory limits in the ability of intelligence agencies to conduct domestic surveillance in the 1970s. Progressives also repeatedly criticized and challenged George W. Bush's expansive understandings of presidential powers following the 9/11 attacks under which he claimed, as explored in Chapter 3, to have the constitutional authority to formulate and implement whichever policies and restrictions he believed, in his sole discretion, were necessary to protect the American people from terrorism.

But progressives prior to the Trump presidency did not, as a political or programmatic matter, prioritize the need to rein in the imperial presidency in domestic affairs. Starting with the New Deal programs of the Franklin D. Roosevelt administration and continuing through the Great Society programs of Lyndon Johnson and the Obama administration's comprehensive reform of the health insurance system, progressives pushed for expansive and expensive federal government programs without worrying too much about whether Democratic presidents, in the pursuit of liberal domestic objectives, were overstepping their constitutional authority.

Indeed, since separation-of-powers principles often serve as, what political scientists call, veto points that make government intervention and regulation more difficult and cumbersome, those on the left generally have not prioritized them in domestic matters. As progressive law professor Jay Wexler puts it, "a system of government with different centers of power is slow and inefficient by design. No one center of power—the president, the Senate, the House, etc.— can do anything bad all by itself, but no center of power can do anything good by itself either. The system makes it difficult for government to solve complex problems like the ones that we face every day in our modern society."[109] Viewed from this perspective, separation-of-powers principles, like the federalist principles explored earlier, can be understood to impede rather than facilitate the federal government's ability to solve pressing national problems such as inadequate access to health care and ongoing environmental threats.

But the multiple ways in which Trump expanded and abused presidential powers should serve as loud wake-up calls for progressives regarding the need to rein in the presidency not only in foreign affairs and national security matters, but in domestic affairs as well. It would be a mistake for progressives to view Trump's misuses of power solely as the actions of an unprincipled and rogue president. Instead, those misuses also reflected the ways in which presidential authority had grown exponentially *before* Trump came to power. And the misuses are likely to repeat themselves in the absence of reforms that seek to oversee and constrain the exercise of presidential authority going forward.

In 2010, law professor Bruce Ackerman published a book, titled *The Decline and Fall of the American Republic*, in which he made a series of predictions about what was likely to happen as a result of the ongoing and relentless expansion of presidential power that had taken place during the preceding decades, long before Trump was elected to office. Almost all of Ackerman's prognostications have come true. After predicting that the current system of nominating presidential candidates, with a significantly reduced role for political party establishments, would lead to the election of charismatic outsiders who would mobilize activists to support extreme programs, Ackerman posited that presidents "will increasingly govern through their White House staff of superloyalists, issuing executive orders that their staffers will impose on the federal bureaucracy even when they conflict with congressional mandates; . . . they will legitimate their unilateral actions through an expansive use of emergency powers, . . . and assert 'mandates from the People' to evade or ignore congressional statutes when public opinion supports decisive action; [and] they will rely on elite lawyers in the executive branch to write up learned opinions that vindicate the constitutionality of their most blatant power grabs."[110]

The fact that Ackerman's predictions—made seven years before Trump became president—all became reality during the Trump presidency illustrates how the expansion of presidential power that preceded Trump was a crucial factor in making his disturbing and dangerous abuses of power possible.

It is true that the Nixon Watergate scandal, which led to a presidential resignation, and the Trump Ukraine affair, which led to a presidential impeachment, shared important similarities. In both instances, the president abused his authority by using presidential powers for personal and political reasons. At the same time, both scandals were, in effect, waiting to happen because both depended on the ascension to the presidency of power-hungry individuals who were willing and able to abuse the extensive accumulation of presidential power that had preceded their time in office. The problem is not only that sometimes authoritarian and deeply flawed individuals become presidents. The problem is more fundamentally that the executive branch, with its far-reaching powers, is led by an office that has relentlessly amassed extensive and excessive amounts of authority since the 1930s. We all bear responsibility for allowing that to happen. And it will be up to all of us to fix it.

For this reason, progressives should make the rolling back of presidential power in domestic matters part of their political agenda regardless of who is president. Going forward, progressives should forcefully and vigorously demand that Congress and the courts take the necessary steps to reverse the dangerous expansion of executive authority that allowed Trump to govern more like a monarch than a president.

The end of the Trump era, with its recurring and dangerous abuses of presidential power, is a good time to focus on reining in presidential power *as a political issue*. This type of political response to bloated presidential power has happened before in American history. It happened after FDR broke norms by pushing to pack the Supreme Court and by running for re-election three times. Congress responded to what were largely perceived as presidential power grabs by, among other things, enacting the Administrative Procedure Act, which required executive branch agencies to follow certain rules and procedures before issuing legally binding regulations, and by proposing the Twenty-Second Amendment to the Constitution that placed a two-term limit on presidents. Similarly, as explored in Chapter 3, Congress in the 1970s enacted laws such as the Ethics in Government Act, the Foreign Intelligence Surveillance Act, and the Inspector General Act in response to the Nixon administration's clear abuses of executive branch authority. Although I believe there should have been, there were no similar congressional responses to presidential power grabs by Ronald Reagan, Bill Clinton, and George W. Bush. But it is my hope that progressives, motivated (if not lacerated) by Trump's abuses of presidential power, will going forward prioritize the need, first, to put in place structural and regulatory mechanisms to limit presidential authority in domestic affairs; and, second, to assess whether proposed federal statutes, regulations, executive orders, and similar measures should be supported not only depending on the substantive policy objectives that they seek to achieve, but also on whether they unduly expand domestic presidential authority.

A good place for progressives to begin is to push to curtail presidents' emergency powers. As explained previously, the National Emergencies Act of 1976 has failed to circumscribe presidential authority arising from unilaterally declared emergencies. A new emergencies statute is needed, one that more rigorously controls the president's power to declare an emergency. Among other things, the statute should terminate presidentially declared emergencies in thirty or sixty days unless Congress votes to approve them.[111] Under current law, a president's emergency declaration remains in place unless Congress votes to terminate the emergency and then is able to muster the two-thirds majority necessary to override the certain presidential veto that would follow the termination. The default position should be the opposite: the emergency declaration should end after a set period *unless Congress acts to extend it*.

The new emergency law should also make clear that the president's emergency powers do not include the authority to reallocate congressionally appropriated monies for programs and projects that Congress has explicitly refused to fund. This would prevent future presidents from arrogating for themselves the power to spend funds in ways that Congress objects, as Trump did to build parts of his border wall. Congress also needs to oversee and limit a series of "secret powers" that presidents have reportedly granted to themselves over the last several decades and that led Trump to boast, rather frighteningly, that "I have the right to do a lot of things that people don't even know about."[112]

It is also important that Congress review, and when appropriate make changes to, the more than one hundred statutes that presently grant presidents special powers following a unilateral emergency declaration. Some critics have suggested that those powers, arising from statutes that have been on the books for decades without any congressional reconsideration, might allow a president, after declaring an emergency due to a threat of war, for example, to seize control of internet traffic in the United States and to order arrests without judicial warrants. In response to these frightening powers, Congress could, as Elizabeth Goitein argues, "repeal the laws that are obsolete or unnecessary. It could revise others to include stronger protections against abuse. It could issue new criteria for emergency declarations [and] require a connection between the nature of the emergency and the powers invoked."[113]

In short, it is vital that Congress carefully consider each of the extensive presidential emergency powers that remain in the statute books, powers that can be unilaterally triggered by a presidential emergency declaration. In conducting that review, Congress should heed the warning of Justice Robert Jackson, who in his famous and brave dissent from the Supreme Court's upholding of Roosevelt's Japanese American internment policy in *Korematsu v. United States*, noted that emergency powers are "like a loaded weapon, ready for the hand of any authority that can bring forward a plausible claim of an urgent need."[114]

Progressives should also push Congress to enact measures aimed at protecting the independence of the Department of Justice from efforts to politicize the most important and consequential decisions that it makes: choosing which individuals to charge with which violations of federal criminal law. There is no plausible disagreement with the proposition that prosecutors must decide whom to charge with a crime in a disinterested manner free from political and personal influences. To state the obvious, the fact that certain individuals are political opponents or critics of the administration in power is not a valid reason for the Department of Justice to investigate them for or charge them with a violation of federal law. Nor is the fact that certain individuals have political, business, or personal ties to powerful members of the administration, including the president, a reason to forego investigations, drop charges, or grant leniency.

Before Trump was elected, there was a relatively strong ethos of prosecutorial independence in the Department of Justice. That ethos, which had been present, to varying degrees, inside the department for decades, was reflected in policies and norms that restricted contacts between the White House and department officials and in internal guidelines adopted in Watergate's wake establishing "the standards for when and against whom the FBI can open an investigation."[115] Prosecutorial independence, as law professors Bruce Green and Rebecca Roiphe point out, is also required by the legal profession's ethical rules, which are judicially mandated.[116] But the combination of (1) Department of Justice guidelines, (2) ethical rules, (3) norms of restraint generally followed by presidents since Watergate, and (4) public opinion proved insufficient in deterring Trump from blatantly and brazenly pressuring the department to target political opponents, weaken and undermine the Mueller special counsel investigation of Russia's interference with the 2016 election, and cease investigating the president's allies and friends. For these reasons, Congress must enact measures that insulate prosecutorial discretion from undue influence by anyone, including the president. By such influence, I mean efforts to have Department of Justice lawyers make prosecutorial decisions tainted by political or personal interests.

To be more specific, Congress should enact a statute making it clear that federal prosecutors represent the interests of the U.S. government and not the president.[117] Congress should also enact a statute prohibiting federal prosecutors from taking certain criteria into account in making prosecutorial decisions, including "the decision maker's personal interest, the interest of a third party, or partisan political advantage."[118] These proposals do not trample on legitimate presidential prerogatives, and therefore do not raise separation-of-powers issues.

Proponents of a unitary understanding of the presidency contend that, as an initial matter, all executive power, including all prosecutorial power, lies exclusively with the president. From this perspective, the president has unfettered discretion on how to delegate it to other members of the executive branch. That is the position that Justice Antonin Scalia took in dissent in the 1988 case of *Morrison v. Olson* when he claimed that Congress's effort to prevent presidents from firing independent prosecutors without cause (that is, without a valid reason) was unconstitutional. But no other justice agreed with Scalia on that point. Instead, the *Morrison* Court concluded that even if prosecutorial power is a governmental function that can be exercised only by the executive branch, it is constitutional for Congress to reallocate prosecutorial authority *within* that branch.[119] The Court also rejected a unitary understanding of the executive branch when it upheld, almost a century ago, the constitutionality of statutorily requiring the president to have a valid reason for firing a commissioner of an independent federal agency such as the Federal Trade Commission.[120] All of this means that it is permissible for Congress to determine that the ultimate decision of whether to prosecute certain individuals for certain crimes should be made according to independent prosecutorial decision-making criteria *even when the president orders that it be done otherwise.*[121]

Although Congress's enactment of laws prohibiting everyone, including the president, from unduly influencing federal prosecutions would not, in my view, raise constitutional problems, they would offer two distinct advantages. First, they would give federal prosecutors statutory grounds for resisting efforts to unduly influence their prosecutorial discretion, even when the source of that influence emanates from the office of the presidency. Second, congressional action would make it more difficult for presidents to claim that they have the unilateral authority to determine who should be prosecuted for which violations of federal law. As Justice Jackson put it in his famous and influential concurrence in *Youngstown Sheet & Tube Co.*, "when the President takes measures incompatible with the expressed or implied will of Congress, his power is at its lowest ebb, for then he can rely only upon his constitutional powers minus any constitutional powers of Congress over the matter."[122]

None of this is to suggest that the president lacks the constitutional authority to determine the policy agenda that shapes prosecutorial priorities. It is for the president, under the Constitution's Article II, to "take care that the laws be faithfully executed." There is nothing problematic with a president requiring the Department of Justice to prioritize, for example, the investigation and prosecution of Medicaid fraud or political corruption in the disbursement of federal funds.[123] At the same time, however, it is within Congress's power to demand that prosecutors, in pursuing the president's prosecutorial priorities, do not make *individualized* decisions on whom to prosecute based on, for example, whether the putative defendants are the president's political allies or foes. It might have been that the importance of protecting prosecutorial independence from undue influence was so obvious before Trump was elected that it did not require congressional codification. But given that Trump repeatedly challenged and undermined the principle of prosecutorial independence by seeking to use the Department of Justice to advance his personal and political interests, it is imperative that Congress respond by codifying that principle into federal law.

It is also necessary for Congress to further safeguard the independence of inspectors general. As noted in a report issued by the U.S. Government Accountability Office following Trump's brazen firings of several government watchdogs in 2020, IGs "serve a critical role in accountability and transparency in government."[124] But under the Inspector General Act of 1978, presidents have complete discretion to fire the watchdogs, with the only limitation being that they must inform Congress of the reason for the termination. (Trump refused to truthfully comply even with that minimum requirement.) Congress should therefore mandate that IGs, like other select federal officials, not be fired except for cause. This would prevent presidents from firing IGs for doing nothing more than carrying out their watchdog functions within executive agencies, which is precisely what Trump did with complete impunity.

Efforts to restrict the president's ability to fire IGs are likely to be constitutionally challenged by future administrations. On the one hand, the Supreme Court's 2020 decision in *Seila Law LLC v. Consumer Financial Protection Bureau*, in which it held that Congress cannot restrict a president's ability to fire the single head of an executive agency—as opposed to the co-heads of an independent agency such as the Federal Trade Commission—might support that challenge.[125] On the other hand, there are compelling arguments for protecting the independence of IGs from presidential overreach given their crucial and unique function in promoting accountability and transparency. At the very least, the question of whether presidents should be permitted to fire IGs for fulfilling their watchdog responsibilities is a debate worth having both inside and outside the courts.

In 2020, Jack Goldsmith and Bob Bauer, senior attorneys in the George W. Bush and Barack Obama administrations respectively, published a book containing several suggestions on how to reform the presidency within constitutional parameters. Among other things, Goldsmith and Bauer called on Congress to prohibit presidents from having any active or supervisory role in the oversight of private businesses. They also suggested that Congress require that presidential candidates, as well as presidents during their terms in office, release their tax returns.[126]

Six weeks before the 2020 election, House Democrats introduced a bill, called the Protecting Our Democracy Act, which also contained multiple proposals for reining in presidential powers. In addition to requiring that IGs be dismissed only for cause, the bill sought, among other things, (1) to mandate that presidential declarations of emergency expire after a certain period of time unless extended by Congress; (2) to amend the federal bribery statute to make explicit that the offering or granting of a presidential pardon or commutation may be a basis for criminal liability under federal law; (3) to toll the statute of limitations for any federal criminal offense committed by the president or vice president, whether before or during their terms in office; (4) to provide a cause of action for Congress to enforce its subpoenas pursuant to expedited judicial review; (5) to expand penalties under the Impoundment Control Act when administration officials impermissibly withhold congressionally appropriated funds; (6) to expand protections for federal whistleblowers, including by further safeguarding their anonymity and by prohibiting any federal official from interfering with their ability to share information with Congress; and (7) to limit the tenure of acting officials who serve without Senate confirmation to 120 days (down from 210 days).[127] It is essential that broad coalitions of progressives support and agitate in favor of these types of reforms, regardless of who is president at any given time, aimed at imposing reasonable limits on presidential and executive branch powers.

More progressives should also join the conservatives who criticize the Supreme Court's repeated unwillingness to require Congress to be more explicit in the policy objectives it wants administrative agencies to pursue. The nondelegation doctrine is supposed to require Congress to provide a minimum degree of policy specificity so that it uses legislation to set the broad contours of federal policies that the executive, in turn, implements. But the last time the Court struck down a statute on improper delegation grounds was almost a century ago.[128] This lack of judicial enforcement of the fundamental separation-of-powers question of which branch legislates and which branch implements has allowed and encouraged Congress to delegate lawmaking authority to executive branch agencies with only the broadest and vaguest of guidance.[129] In doing so, Congress has taken credit for enacting laws directing the executive, for example, to address environmental and public safety problems, without holding itself accountable or responsible for the challenges and difficulties that might arise from the enforcement of those laws. And, just as problematically, the lack of congressional policy guidance has contributed to the relentless expansion of presidential authority.

For several decades now, it has been primarily conservatives who have criticized Congress's willingness to grant the executive branch unbounded lawmaking authority. It is time for more progressives to add their voices, values, and priorities to this criticism.

Conservative Supreme Court justice Neil Gorsuch, in a dissent from a 2019 ruling in which the Supreme Court once again refused to limit Congress's ability to delegate its legislative authority, elaborated on the highly problematic ways in which unbounded delegation expands presidential powers. Gorsuch explained that when Congress refuses to make difficult policy choices and instead assigns that responsibility to the president, it risks making legislation "nothing more than the will of the current President. And if laws could be simply declared by a single person, they would not be few in number, the product of widespread social consensus, likely to protect minority interests, or apt to provide stability and fair notice." To allow Congress to continue to delegate its legislative authority without judicially enforced limits, Gorsuch complained, "serve[s] only to accelerate the flight of power from the legislative to the executive branch, turning the latter into a vortex of authority that was constitutionally reserved for the people's representatives in order to protect their liberties."[130] The crucial problem, identified by Gorsuch and others, is that unbounded delegation of congressional authority contributes to an unbounded presidency.

While many conservatives for years have been raising concerns about the unchecked growth of the administrative state in general, and the demise of the nondelegation doctrine in particular, relatively few progressives before Trump expressed unease about either point. This lack of concern among many progressives about the expansion of executive branch authority through the workings of the administrative state is in some ways understandable given that such an expansion can serve to promote liberal policy objectives such as stricter environmental regulations, stronger workplace protections for employees and product safety measures for consumers, and expansive federal health-care and welfare programs. Even after Trump became president, some progressives continued to defend the nondelegation doctrine's dormancy, believing that its return to life would constitute an existential threat to the administrative state.[131]

But it is time for progressives to recognize that the impotence of the nondelegation doctrine has contributed in crucial ways to the expansion of presidential power, an expansion that, when in the wrong hands, represents a grave threat to our democracy. Forcing Congress to legislate with greater specificity on what the government's policy objectives should be would still leave administrative agencies with significant discretion to deploy their expertise in crafting and implementing regulations. It is neither advisable nor possible for Congress to try to determine, for example, how many parts per million of a given particulate can end up in drinking water without threatening public health or whether a new form of medical treatment should be covered by Medicare and Medicaid. Only administrative agencies can effectively and efficiently make those types of fact-intensive decisions. Nonetheless, it is essential for Congress, prodded by the courts if necessary, to be more specific in detailing the general objectives that federal agencies should pursue through the issuance of regulations. Otherwise presidents will continue to expand their powers by filling the vacuum created by Congress's failure to provide more guidance to administrative agencies. As explained in Chapter 3, this is precisely what presidents from both parties have done since the 1980s—they have repeatedly directed agencies to regulate in ways that are intended to achieve presidential policy objectives rather than congressional ones.

Some on the left may argue that progressive causes, as a whole, are better served by judicially unrestricted congressional delegation that gives administrative agencies expansive discretion to adopt, for example, stringent environmental and public health regulations. But unbounded legislative delegation engenders three significant types of costs for progressives. First, the same discretion that allows a progressive administration to *expand* the federal government's regulatory reach in policy areas such as those of environmental protection and consumer safety permits a conservative administration to *restrict* that reach. Second, unbounded delegation allows conservative administrations to expand the scope of federal government regulations in areas such as immigration, national security, and law enforcement in ways that threaten progressive policy objectives.

And third, unrestricted congressional delegation to the executive branch, as already explained, strengthens the imperialist domestic presidency. Progressives, therefore, should not assume that the dormancy of the nondelegation doctrine is a good thing for progressive causes and movements.

I recognize that to argue in favor of reviving the nondelegation doctrine is not the same as explaining what its substantive content should be and how the courts should enforce it. The devil, in this case, is indeed in the details, and I cannot in this book provide those details.[132] My objective here is more modest: to persuade progressives to further engage with the question of when Congress impermissibly delegates legislative authority because, as law professor Martin Redish puts it, "in a time [when] the executive branch continues to grow in size and strength, reviving the nondelegation doctrine has become more important than ever."[133]

Progressives should not only encourage the courts to place some limits on Congress's ability to delegate legislative authority, but they should also push Congress to delegate less of it, even if not constitutionally required to do so by the courts. Admittedly, it has been difficult enough, due to increasing hyperpartisanship and dysfunction, to get Congress to do any important legislating since the 1990s, much less to legislate with greater specificity.[134] But progressives must try anyway because a Congress that is more assertive in setting policy through legislation is essential to constraining presidential power going forward. As law professor Burt Neuborne explained in 2019, "when progressives get back in power, it will be time to stop governing through short-term presidential orders and executive regulations, even when we control the presidency. It's long past time to put Congress back to work as the principal architect of new law. Not only does a congressional statute more accurately reflect the will of the people, but statutes can't be turned on and off every time there is a new president. It's time to elect people to the House and Senate who are willing to shoulder Congress's separation-of-powers burden to make the law, rather than giving away that power to the president—of either party."[135]

Trump was able to abuse presidential powers and undermine our constitutional democracy not only because he was an arrogant, autocratic, and corrupt leader, but also because the powers of the office of the presidency, before he was elected, had become dangerously unbounded and unrestrained. But restricting the presidency's authority will not be easy, especially once Trump's abuses of power begin to recede into history. Indeed, it was only seven years after Nixon resigned in ignominy in 1974 that a president (Ronald Reagan) came into office determined to "restore" the supposed loss of presidential authority that resulted from modest Watergate-era reforms. We can therefore safely expect future presidents, both Democratic and Republican, to resist efforts to curtail their powers. In addition, progressives may not find the political will or courage to push for restricting presidential authority when there is a liberal like Joe Biden in the White House. And we can expect fierce resistance to such restrictions from most conservatives, as we saw during the Trump years, when there is a Republican president. Indeed, while many Republicans since the Reagan years have claimed to be deeply committed to cutting back activist government, many have been equally committed to defending presidential power and prerogatives when there is a Republican in the White House.

It will take significant discipline and commitment by progressives to support limiting presidential powers, especially during the terms of liberal presidents. An important contributor to the expansion of presidential power has been the tendency of Democrats and Republicans alike to conveniently forget or minimize the dangers of unilateral presidentialism when there is someone to their liking in the White House. As Gene Healy explains, "upon assuming power, the former out-party typically abandons its criticisms of unilateralism; the ability to make law by executive order, to order military action without congressional approval, to tap phones and read e-mail without securing a warrant—all such powers seem far more enticing when one's friends are at the helm."[136]

Although it will not be simple or easy, progressives should prioritize reining in presidential power in domestic affairs as a political issue, adding that objective to traditional liberal concerns such as economic justice, civil rights protections, and reproductive freedoms. Progressives should assess whether particular candidates for elected federal offices, including for the presidency, merit support in part depending on whether the candidates believe that presidential powers need to be curtailed. In addition, progressives going forward should determine whether to support particular statutes, regulations, executive orders, and similar measures depending not only on their substantive policy goals, but also on whether they unduly expand domestic presidential powers. Finally, progressives in the post-Trump years should support reforms that reasonably seek to limit presidential powers.

Defenders of expansive presidential powers will continue to rely on two main arguments to oppose efforts to curtail presidential authority. One claim is that limits on that authority are dangerous because they impair the president's ability to engage in effective and efficient decision-making. Presidentialists repeatedly point out that, unlike Congress, which cannot act in the absence of deliberation and compromise (both of which take time), the president, as the sole head of the executive branch, can act quickly and decisively to address problems and crises as they arise. As the political scientist Andrew Rudalevige puts it in summarizing the claim, "the structural advantages of the executive—unity, decision, dispatch—are well suited to overcoming fragmentation in other parts of the government. Where fast, unified action is necessary, the president is the only actor in our political system who can provide it."[137]

A second objection is that limits on presidential authority are anti-democratic because the president is the only elected official who is accountable to the entire country. This makes presidents particularly sensitive to the nation's majoritarian preferences, while allowing them to consider the interests and priorities of the entire nation rather than subsections of it, whether regional, social, or economic.

There is some merit to both of these arguments. As a result, it is important to make sure that presidential powers are not curtailed to such an extent that the presidency becomes weak and ineffective. Even Arthur Schlesinger, whose volume *The Imperial Presidency* is likely the most influential book critical of presidential powers ever published in the United States, recognized the importance of not emasculating the presidency through reforms. As he put it, we need to make sure that "revulsion against inordinate theories of presidential power [do not] produce an inordinate swing against the Presidency and thereby do essential damage to our national capacity to handle the problems of the future. The answer to the runaway Presidency is not the messenger-boy Presidency. The American democracy must discover a middle ground between making the President a czar and making him a puppet." The key, Schlesinger explained, is to devise "a strong presidency within an equally strong system of accountability."[138]

But it seems to me that there is little danger, anytime soon, of making the presidency weak or powerless. The fundamental separation-of-powers challenge that the nation confronts is not that the presidency is in danger of being rendered impotent and ineffective by the other two branches of government. Instead, the essential problem is the exact opposite: as the Trump years showed, presidential powers have become so far-reaching and wide-ranging that they threaten the very future of the democracy. It is for this reason that progressives should prioritize scaling back presidential authority not only in issues related to armed conflicts abroad and national security at home, but in domestic policy matters as well.

PART III
PRINCIPLES MATTER: THE FIRST AMENDMENT

5

The First Amendment During the Trump Era and Beyond

At first glance, the contention that the First Amendment should matter to progressives may seem so obvious as to be trite. After all, there seems to be a wide consensus in the United States about the fundamental importance of the freedoms of speech, the press, and assembly, and of the rights to exercise religion and petition the government, all of which are protected by the amendment. Despite this apparent consensus, there are two principal reasons why it is both appropriate and necessary to remind progressives of the First Amendment's importance. First, some progressives, especially in the years leading up to Trump's election, had grown increasingly skeptical of certain expansive understandings of the First Amendment that, for example, prohibit the regulation of hate speech, protect the free speech rights of corporations, and shield businesses owned by religious conservatives from laws that protect LGBTQ people from discrimination. Second, the autocratic ways in which Trump governed highlighted and made palpable the crucial importance of the First Amendment rights to free speech and of the press in both restraining government abuses of power and protecting the ability of individuals and groups to oppose and dissent from government policies and priorities.

The Trump years served as a reminder of the First Amendment's vital role in protecting democratic institutions, self-governance, and the right to dissent, a role that many Americans of all political stripes, in the decades leading up to Trump's election, generally had taken for granted and, therefore, had become somewhat complacent about. There is nothing like a challenge to widely shared principles to encourage further thinking about, and deeper appreciation for, them. It is important that progressives, going forward, do not allow what in this chapter I call "First Amendment skepticism" to grow to the point that it undermines the amendment's ability to shield democratic processes, dissenters, and vulnerable groups from autocratic government officials in the Trump mold. This is not to suggest that the First Amendment worked perfectly in deterring or preventing all of Trump's multiple abuses of power. But it is to suggest that First Amendment protections, whether explicitly enforced through the courts or not, helped curtail some of his autocratic policies and practices.

Principles Matter. Carlos A. Ball, Oxford University Press. © Carlos A. Ball 2021.
DOI: 10.1093/oso/9780197584484.003.0006

Progressive First Amendment Skepticism: A Brief Look

Progressives in recent decades have disagreed among themselves on some important First Amendment issues. Some individuals on the left, whom I will call "civil libertarian progressives," generally believe that free speech rights should almost always trump other constitutional values, including equality. As a result, these progressives tend to view speech rights in more absolute terms than others on the left. Civil libertarian progressives consider the right to free speech to be a foundational one that makes democracy and the enjoyment of most other individuals rights possible. For these progressives, expansive free speech rights protect autonomy, self-determination, and self-governance. A free and unfettered "marketplace of ideas," it is argued, also promotes the search for truth and greater tolerance for diverse views and perspectives. Civil libertarian progressives believe it is important to protect the free speech rights of even those who engage in hateful speech (as long as, for example, the expression is not intended and likely to incite imminent harm). By protecting the speech we hate, civil libertarians argue, we ensure that the speech rights of everyone are respected.[1]

In contrast, others on the left, whom I will call "egalitarian progressives," view free speech rights in less absolute terms by contending that free speech protections must be cabined by principles of inclusion, dignity, and, above all else, equality. For these progressives, the foundational value is not liberty, but instead is equality. Egalitarian progressives are also critical of the notion of a "marketplace of ideas"—to treat speech as a "commodity," it is argued, allows those with greater power and wealth to gain enhanced access to the purported marketplace, repeatedly and harmfully drowning out the voices of the subordinated, disenfranchised, and the poor. Egalitarian progressives generally welcome government efforts to level the speech playing field by making it possible for the less powerful and less wealthy to be heard by, for example, limiting the private financing of electoral campaigns. Egalitarian progressives also call for restrictions on the free speech rights of racists, anti-Semites, misogynists, pornographers, and others who engage in hateful speech. Egalitarian progressives argue that hate speech, generally defined as speech that demeans racial, religious, sexual, and gender minorities by questioning their equal status in society, tangibly harms members of minority groups, interferes with their rights to autonomy and self-determination, and makes democracy and meaningful self-governance impossible.[2]

The disagreements between the two progressive camps came to a head in the Trump era's first summer during events surrounding a "Unite the Right" rally held by white supremacists in Charlottesville, Virginia, that resulted in the brutal murder by a neo-Nazi of Heather Heyer, a leftist counterprotestor. Earlier that summer, a group of white nationalists had held two rallies in the center of Charlottesville protesting the city's planned removal of a statute of Robert E. Lee from a public park. The white nationalists then planned a third rally, to be held in August, this time supposedly to demand the recognition of free speech rights that the organizers claimed were threatened by city officials and counterdemonstrators.[3]

No organization has defended civil libertarian progressive values more extensively, consistently, and effectively than the American Civil Liberties Union (ACLU). In the mid-1970s, the group represented Nazis who wanted to march in Skokie, Illinois. The Nazis targeted Skokie because of the large number of Jews, some of whom were Holocaust survivors, who lived there. Although the Nazis, in the end, chose not to march in Skokie after they were permitted to congregate in the Chicago park where they initially had hoped to march, the ACLU successfully persuaded the courts that the Nazis had a First Amendment right to parade down the streets of a majority-Jewish town like Skokie. The ACLU's free speech advocacy on behalf of Nazis was extremely controversial and led tens of thousands of its members to resign. But the organization stuck to its civil libertarian principles by arguing that the efforts to silence the Nazis constituted a greater threat to freedom than allowing a few deeply misguided and prejudiced individuals to publicly express their hateful anti-Semitic messages. As the ACLU saw it, the Nazis in Skokie wanted to engage in political speech and the Free Speech Clause protects *all* such speech, even the vilest and most abhorrent kind. The best way of protecting everyone's free speech rights, the ACLU claimed, was by protecting the speech we most despise.[4]

The ACLU's decision to legally represent the white supremacists who wanted to march in Charlottesville in 2017 led to similar disagreements among progressives. As they had done forty years earlier in the context of the Skokie march, egalitarian progressives rejected the notion that the First Amendment should protect hateful speech that is intended to deny the equal moral worth and basic human rights of traditionally subordinated and marginalized minorities. Egalitarians argued that by defending the rights of white supremacists to march in Charlottesville, the ACLU's lawyers and other civil libertarian progressives were aiding and abetting the further entrenchment of hateful racism and anti-Semitism in American society.[5]

What actually transpired on August 12, 2017, illustrated and reinforced the concerns of egalitarian progressives who challenge the civil libertarian premise that it is generally possible to distinguish between constitutionally protected racist speech and unprotected racist violence. After a court, pursuant to an ACLU request, ordered city officials to permit the white supremacists to march in the park near downtown that contained the Robert E. Lee statute, a group of about one hundred neo-fascists entered the park holding tiki torches and chanting "Blood and Soil!," a German Nazi slogan used during Hitler's rise to power. The marchers were supported by a group of men wearing militia uniforms and armed with semi-automatic weapons who stood at the park's entrance blocking admission to others who wanted to enter. Shortly after the march began, another group of white supremacists physically assaulted Dre Harris, an African American man, several blocks away. A large group of counterprotestors responded to Harris's assault by converging in the area near the attack. The sight of a large group of cheering leftist counterprotestors angered James Fields Jr., a twenty-year-old white supremacist who was driving nearby. Fields suddenly and violently rammed his automobile into the group of counterprotestors, pushing several to the ground. Fields reversed his vehicle and then slammed into the crowd again, striking more people. One of those hit was a thirty-two-year-old woman by the name of Heather Heyer. An ambulance rushed Heyer to a hospital; she died a few hours later due to blunt-force injuries to her chest. The violent clashes in Charlottesville that day resulted in dozens of injuries. In addition, two state troopers, who were monitoring the demonstrations, died when their police helicopter crashed.[6]

Two days later, a Ku Klux Klan leader in North Carolina said he was "glad" that Heyer had died. He added that "they were a bunch of Communists out there protesting against somebody's freedom of speech, so it doesn't bother me that they got hurt at all." In stark contrast, elected officials across the country uniformly reacted in horror and condemned the violence in Charlottesville, placing the blame exclusively where it belonged: with the white supremacists. The striking exception was Donald Trump: the president, in addressing Heyer's death, claimed that there were "some very fine people on both sides" and that "there's blame on both sides" for the violence.[7]

For many egalitarian progressives, the white supremacist violence in Charlottesville confirmed their view that the distinction that civil libertarians make between hateful speech and hateful violence is a problematic and tenuous one. Following Heyer's murder, some progressives called on the ACLU to stop representing white supremacist organizations.[8] The civil liberties group responded by condemning the violence and announcing that it would no longer represent protestors who intended to bring weapons to their rallies.[9] But the ACLU remained committed to its absolutist position in defending the constitutionally protected status of hate speech that falls short of true threats or incitements to violence. As David Cole, the organization's legal director, explained two weeks after the events in Charlottesville, in the hate speech context, "it is virtually impossible to articulate a standard for suppression of speech that would not afford government officials dangerously broad discretion and invite discrimination against particular viewpoints."[10]

Disagreements between egalitarian and civil libertarian progressives over the issue of hate speech have also flared as a result of a handful of well-publicized disputes involving controversial right-wing speakers on college campuses. Civil libertarian progressives have joined conservatives in criticizing students and faculty who object to having guest speakers on university campuses who claim, for example, that white people are genetically more intelligent than people of color, or that men's brains are better suited for science and math than women's, or that transgender individuals are mentally disturbed. The proper functioning of universities as forums for academic freedom, civil libertarian progressives argue, require that campuses be open to all invited speakers, even those with vile, demeaning, and offensive beliefs. Rather than banning offensive and hateful speakers, progressives should challenge their assertions through counterspeech by exposing their empirical claims as factually wrong and their normative claims as morally objectionable. The best solution to offensive speech on university campuses, civil libertarian progressives insist, is not to ban it, but to confront it through more speech.[11]

But egalitarian progressives assert that civil libertarians fundamentally misunderstand the nature of higher education and academic freedom. Universities repeatedly and uncontroversially restrict speech in multiple ways, including when deciding whom to hire as faculty and what to teach in classrooms. The main objective of a university is to pursue knowledge and truth, not to serve as an open forum for all ideas and claims. This means that a public university, for example, can deny degrees to graduate students in the sciences who insist in defending false claims about climate change as part of their schoolwork without violating the First Amendment. Similarly, a public university can refuse to hire Holocaust deniers as faculty members even if the First Amendment does not permit the government to criminally penalize them for that denial. As a result, despite all of the hand-wringing by conservatives and civil libertarians about the supposed free speech crisis on American campuses, egalitarian progressives argue that the relatively small number of instances in which students and faculty have objected to outside speakers due to their racist, misogynist, anti-Islamist, or anti-LGBTQ views do not raise the type of existential threat to First Amendment principles and values that conservatives and civil libertarians claim.[12] Egalitarian progressives generally believe that the harm that hate speech inflicts on members of vulnerable minorities on America's campuses, by questioning their basic right to be part of educational communities, justifies denying white supremacists, misogynists, Islamophobes, homophobes, and other similar speakers the imprimatur of legitimacy that comes with speaking at an institution of higher learning.[13]

One of the most prominent defenders of egalitarian free speech positions in recent decades has been law professor Catharine MacKinnon. In the 1980s, MacKinnon and fellow feminist Andrea Dworkin spearheaded a campaign to persuade legislators to ban hardcore pornography that subordinates women by, for example, presenting them as sexual objects that enjoy being raped or that are subjected to mutilation and other forms of physical violence. After Indianapolis adopted such a law in 1984, a federal appellate court struck it down on the ground that it constituted a form of "thought control" because it required the government to approve how women could be portrayed in sexual encounters in books and films.[14]

Undaunted, MacKinnon continued to insist that free speech interests should not be used to void legislative efforts aimed at protecting women and racial minorities from tangible harms caused by subordination and humiliation. MacKinnon and other egalitarian progressives argue that civil libertarians are mistaken in claiming that the First Amendment can serve as a *neutral* bulwark of protection for all views and perspectives. Instead, egalitarian progressives argue, the First Amendment has been weaponized by those on top of racial, gender, and economic hierarchies to protect their many privileges, while simultaneously reinforcing conditions of inequality and relationships of subordination for minorities.[15] As MacKinnon explained in a 2019 essay,

> the First Amendment over the last hundred years has mainly become a weapon of the powerful. Legally, what was, toward the beginning of the twentieth century, a shield for radicals, artists and activists, Socialists and pacifists, the excluded and the dispossessed, has become a sword for authoritarians, racists and misogynists, Nazis and Klansmen, pornographers and corporations buying elections. In public discourse, freedom of speech has gone from protection for dissenters from dominant power to a claimed protection of those with dominant power, of their hierarchical position, of hierarchy itself. It has gone from an entitlement of structurally unequal groups to expose their inequality and seek equal rights to a claim by dominant groups to continue to impose their hegemony.[16]

Although progressives have disagreed among themselves on issues related to hate speech regulations and pornography restrictions, they generally have been united in emphasizing equality principles over free speech values in other ongoing First Amendment controversies. For example, with a few exceptions (perhaps the ACLU most prominently), progressives have decried the Supreme Court's 2010 ruling in *Citizens United v. Federal Elections Commission* striking down regulations limiting the ability of corporations to spend company funds to influence elections in the weeks leading up to voting.[17] According to most progressives, *Citizens United* reinforced a troubling feature of our democracy: the ways in which wealthy institutions and individuals exert undue influence on who gets elected and, after elections, on the setting of government policies. From this perspective, for-profit corporations should not be permitted to use the enormous amounts of money the law allows them to amass to distort our democracy by drowning out the voices—and discouraging the participation in elections—of those with significantly fewer financial resources. Progressives generally argue that limiting the ability of wealthy corporations to use their successes in the economic sphere to dominate the political sphere promotes rather than threatens a truly robust and ideologically diverse exchange of ideas.[18]

In addition, progressives generally have criticized the claim that the First Amendment, in both its protections for freedom of speech and of religion, exempts religious employers, business owners, and landlords from the application of laws that protect LGBTQ individuals from discrimination. As most progressives see it, the First Amendment should not be understood to grant participants in commercial activities the constitutional right to discriminate. Such an expansive understanding of the First Amendment, many progressives argue, threatens the constitutional underpinning and effectiveness of the nation's civil rights laws.[19]

Progressives have also criticized the ways in which the Supreme Court in the last few decades has protected the free speech rights of powerful entities and individuals (such as corporations and the rich) while restricting the First Amendment rights of government employees, public school students, and those who seek to use government property—beyond traditional public forums such as public streets and parks—to engage in speech.[20] This point is made, in admirable detail, by law professor Ronald Krotoszynski in his book *The Disappearing First Amendment*. Among other things, Professor Krotoszynski elaborates on the relationship between wealth and free speech rights sanctioned by Supreme Court rulings in recent years. As he notes, if you rely on your own property and assets to speak by, for example, spending millions of dollars to support or oppose the election of particular candidates,

> then your speech rights have never been more robust—the world is your oyster. On the other hand, however, if you lack property, your speech rights are subject to very broad forms of government discretion to make public property available for the use of impecunious citizens—or to withhold access. All citizens have a theoretical right to speak, but enjoy the ability to speak in practice only if they possess the means of doing so without government aid or support. This unregulated free-market approach to allocating First Amendment rights has profound, and quite negative, implications for the marketplace of ideas—and especially for democracy and democratic participation by ordinary citizens.[21]

The notion that the First Amendment in contemporary times serves the interests of the rich and the powerful at the expense of the poor and minorities seems to be shared by a growing number of progressives. Lawyer and journalist Lincoln Caplan encapsulated that view when he argued in 2015 that "the most fervent champions" of free speech today "are not standing up for mistrusted outliers . . . or for the dispossessed and the powerless." Instead, much of contemporary free speech advocacy does "the bidding of insiders—the super-rich and the ultra-powerful, the airline, drug, petroleum, and tobacco industries, all the winners in America's winner-take-all society." Caplan added that in a society where the "gap between the haves and have-nots has grown [to] extreme [levels], the haves have seized free speech as their cause—and their shield."[22]

In short, many progressives in the years leading up to the Trump era had grown increasingly skeptical of broad understandings of First Amendment rights when they conflict with the pursuit of equality. Some of this skepticism resulted from the courts' repeated willingness to provide constitutional protection to hate speech, an issue that has divided progressives. But some of the skepticism arose in other contexts, such as corporate speech, campaign financing, and anti-discrimination law, in which progressives generally have been unified in defending more circumscribed understandings of First Amendment rights in order to advance the equality interests of vulnerable minorities and the less affluent.

For purposes of this chapter, I assume that the First Amendment skepticism of many progressives, which I have briefly summarized, is correct and appropriate. I proceed under this assumption because my objective here is neither to criticize nor defend that skepticism. Instead, my claim is that even if the skepticism is well-founded and justified, the ways in which Trump governed should serve as crucial reminders to progressives of why robust First Amendment rights continue to matter. The Trump years showed how and why First Amendment safeguards, including those prohibiting the government from regulating speakers on the basis of their viewpoints and the right not to be retaliated against for engaging in protected speech, can play a crucial role in protecting democratic institutions, government critics, and the free press from autocratic officials. It is therefore important that the First Amendment skepticism expressed by a growing number of progressives not expand to the point that, going forward, it undermines or weakens the amendment's fundamental ability to protect those who resist autocratic government officials in the Trump mold.

Trump's Autocratic Contempt for the First Amendment

It is possible to write an entire book exploring the ways in which Trump targeted rights to freedom of speech, of the press, and to peaceably assemble during his years in office.[23] In this section, I provide a representative sample of those attacks, paying particular attention to Trump's actions and statements that encouraged violence against critics and protestors; questioned the legitimacy, integrity, and motivations of the press; and served as, or called for, government retaliation against those who dared criticize him or his administration.

During the 2016 presidential campaign, small groups of protestors regularly attempted to interrupt Trump's speeches. Most candidates for elected office, when confronted by hecklers in public venues, usually remain silent during the short time it takes security personnel to remove jeering protestors. But candidate Trump repeatedly responded to the interruptions by lashing out at his hecklers, frequently encouraging his followers to physically assault them. For example, on the day of the 2016 Iowa caucus, Trump urged his supporters at a Cedar Rapids rally to "knock the crap" and "knock the hell" out of protestors while promising to pay the attackers' legal fees. Later that month, at a rally in Las Vegas, Trump complained that security guards were being too gentle on a protestor while escorting him out of the premises. "I'd like to punch him in the face," Trump screamed into the microphone as his admirers cheered him on. At other times, Trump responded to a heckler by stating "I'll beat the crap out of [him]" and "maybe he should have been roughed up." On one occasion, after his supporters had kicked and punched an African-American Black Lives Matter activist who interrupted a Trump rally in Birmingham, Alabama, Trump told Fox News that "maybe he should have been roughed up, because it was absolutely disgusting what he was doing."[24]

At his rallies, candidate Trump repeatedly mocked "and made sport of the reporters who stood in fenced-off areas during his speeches, often whipping up the crowd against them."[25] Trump also frequently laced his verbal attacks on protestors with attacks on the press. For example, at a rally in Louisville, Kentucky, he used a sarcastic voice to urge his supporters not to physically attack protestors in the arena and then followed up with this explanation: "See, if I say, 'Go get him,' I get in trouble with the press, the most dishonest people in the world."[26] A group of Trump's supporters then "assaulted, pushed and shoved" the protestors, one of whom "was punched in the stomach."[27]

Trump's encouragement of violence and his attacks on the press continued unabated after taking office. In 2017, he "tweeted a video showing him pummeling a figure superimposed with [CNN's] logo, a cartoon depicting a 'Trump train' hitting a person labeled as CNN, and a doctored photo of him with a CNN blood smear on the bottom of his shoe."[28] In 2018, Trump praised Greg Gianforte, a Republican who, while running for Montana's seat in the House of Representatives, assaulted Ben Jacobs, a *Guardian* reporter. Gianforte physically attacked the journalist after he had asked the candidate a question about the Republicans' position on health care. Gianforte was eventually convicted of a misdemeanor assault charge for throwing Jacobs to the ground and punching him several times. At a rally in Montana a few days before the 2018 midterm election, Trump praised Gianforte by stating that "any guy that can do a body slam, he is my type."[29] During the 2020 election campaign, Trump described an incident in which the Minneapolis police, during a Black Lives Matter protest, fired a rubber bullet into the knee of MSNBC journalist Ali Velshi—whom the president called "an idiot reporter"—as "the most beautiful thing. It is called law and order."[30]

By encouraging violence against critics and the media alike, Trump displayed his disdain for free speech principles and contempt for the role of the free press in holding government officials accountable. Less than three weeks into his presidency, Trump called media outlets such as the *New York Times*, CNN, and NBC News "the FAKE News media" and accused them of being "the enemy of the people," charges he repeated hundreds of times in the months and years to come.[31] Following the examples of autocratic leaders in countries such as China, Hungary, Russia, and Venezuela, Trump equated the independent press's efforts to hold administration officials accountable with threats to the nation's interests. At different times, President Trump called journalists "unpatriotic," "corrupt," "crazy," "losers," "troublemakers," "unfair," "scum," "disgusting," "sleaz[y]," "slime," "phony," "crooked," "biased," "garbage," "crazy," "sick," and "among the most dishonest human beings on earth."[32] According to John Bolton, Trump's National Security Adviser, Trump once privately called journalists "scumbags" and said that they "should be executed."[33]

Trump also questioned journalists' patriotism, not only by calling them the "enemies of the American people," but by also claiming that media members (except those from friendly outlets such as Fox News and the Sinclair Broadcast Group) were "distorting democracy in our country" while "trying to take away our history and our heritage."[34] When asked by a journalist why he was so relentlessly harsh in attacking the press, Trump stated that his goal was to make the public skeptical about the media's integrity and legitimacy in order to immunize himself from criticism and disapproval: "I do it to discredit you all and demean you all, so when you write negative stories about me no one will believe you."[35]

Trump's characterization of the mainstream media was embraced by a significant number of Republicans. A 2018 poll found that an astonishing 48 percent of Republicans agreed with Trump that the press was the enemy of the people. An almost equal percentage of the polled Republicans agreed with the proposition that "the president should have the authority to close news outlets engaged in bad behavior." And almost a quarter (23 percent) of Republicans believed that "President Trump should close down mainstream news outlets, like CNN, the *Washington Post*, and the *New York Times*."[36]

According to PEN America, a non-profit association of writers and media professionals that defends the free speech rights of journalists in the United States and abroad, Trump during his first two years in office "sent 1,339 tweets about the media that were critical, insinuating, condemning, or threatening.

These communications frequently single[d] out news organizations or individual journalists who the President believes have criticized his Administration."[37] A typical Trump tweet about the media came in late 2018 when he wrote that "a very big part of the Anger we see today in our society is caused by the purposely false and inaccurate reporting of the Mainstream Media that I refer to as Fake News. It has gotten so bad and hateful that it is beyond description. Mainstream Media must clean up its act, FAST!" Trump sent this message to his millions of Twitter followers twenty-four hours after one of his supporters mailed sixteen pipe bombs to prominent Democrats and media outlets.[38]

Trump's attacks on the media intensified in 2019. He used the term "fake news" an astounding 273 times in 2019, a 50 percent increase from the year before. He also tweeted that the press was "the enemy of the people" twenty-one times, up from sixteen the year before. In addition, during 2019, he accused the *New York Times* of "treason." And Trump ended the decades-long tradition of White House daily briefings by the press secretary. Sarah Huckabee Sanders, Trump's press secretary, failed to hold a traditional press briefing between March 2019 and April 2020, when she left office. During that long period, she rarely spoke in public, except for appearing on Trump-friendly Fox News and local television stations owned by the politically conservative Sinclair Broadcasting Group.[39]

In addition to accusing the mainstream media of bias, dishonesty, and a lack of patriotism, Trump sought to punish specific press organizations and journalists that covered him in ways he disapproved by denying them access. During the 2016 campaign, Trump blacklisted about a dozen news organizations by preventing them from covering campaign events and riding on his press plane. After he became president, reporters whom the administration deemed objectionable because they wrote negative stories were "forcibly barred from an administrative agency meeting [and] . . . excluded from press briefings."[40] Trump also asserted that *Washington Post* reporters "shouldn't even be allowed on the grounds of the White House."[41] In addition, the president had four American journalists barred from covering a dinner with the North Korean leader because he was not happy with their reporting.

The denial of access to a journalist that received the most attention during the Trump years followed a tense exchange between the president and Jim Acosta, CNN's chief White House correspondent, during a press conference in 2018. After Acosta asked Trump a question about the administration's immigration policies that angered the president, Trump called the reporter a "rude, terrible person" and scolded him by saying that "you should let me run the country— you should run CNN." Several hours later, the administration revoked Acosta's press credentials, denying him access to the White House and the president's staff. (Press secretary Huckabee Sanders falsely claimed that Acosta had forcibly placed his hands on a White House employee during the press conference.)

CNN sued the administration, and several days later, a federal judge ordered the government to restore Acosta's credentials. The judge reasoned that the administration lacked criteria for revoking press credentials, allowing it to do so in arbitrary and capricious ways. The following year, a federal court of appeals upheld a lower court's order requiring the White House to reinstate the press credentials of Brian Karem, a *Playboy* reporter and CNN political analyst, after the administration revoked them following a heated verbal exchange between the journalist and a former Trump aide at a White House event.[42]

Trump was, by no means, the only administration official who attacked the press. A few weeks after the House of Representatives impeached Trump for the first time, an NPR reporter, during a one-on-one interview with Secretary of State Mike Pompeo, asked him a question about Trump's firing of Marie Yovanovitch, the U.S. ambassador to Ukraine, a dismissal that became a crucial aspect of the impeachment investigation. Pompeo, angered by the question, abruptly ended the interview and then later in his office screamed at the reporter for several minutes in an obscenity-fueled rant. Ironically, Pompeo the next day issued a statement calling the media "unhinged," a characterization that perfectly described his reaction to the journalist's question. And echoing Trump's anti-media tirades, the secretary added that "it is no wonder that the American people distrust many in the media when they so consistently demonstrate their agenda and their absence of integrity." In obvious retaliation against NPR, the State Department a few hours later announced it was prohibiting the radio network's diplomatic correspondent from traveling on the secretary's government airplane on his next trip abroad.[43]

As part of Trump's organized, methodical, and concerted scheme to undermine the media's work product and reputation by accusing it of lying and of disloyalty to the nation, he on several occasions threatened to modify libel protections with the goal of making it easier to win high monetary awards in defamation cases brought against newspapers, magazines, television networks, and book publishers.[44] One of those threats—in which he called libel laws a "sham" and a "disgrace"—followed the publication by author Michael Wolff of an unflattering book about the administration.[45] A few days before this particular attack by Trump on libel laws, his personal lawyer had sent the book's publisher a cease and desist letter demanding that the book be removed from bookstores and that it apologize to the president. (The publisher did neither.)

Similarly, the administration in 2020 unsuccessfully sought a prior restraint from a federal judge in an effort to prevent the sale of a damaging book written by John Bolton, Trump's former National Security Adviser.[46] The book detailed several ways in which the president used trade policies and criminal investigations to promote his personal and political interests. Attorney General William Barr's Department of Justice subsequently opened a criminal investigation of Bolton and his publisher based on the contention that the book disclosed classified information.[47] As the *New York Times* explained, Barr's "aggressive move is the latest instance in which the Justice Department under [his] watch has appeared to wield its law enforcement power in ways that align with Mr. Trump's views of perceived political allies or adversaries."[48]

The career official whose job it was to review Bolton's book before it was published later disclosed that Trump's aides had pressured her to prioritize the president's personal and political interests in blocking the book over the public's interests and the even-handed application of the rules regarding what national security officials can publicly reveal after leaving their government jobs. When the career civil servant refused to sign a declaration against Bolton that included false assertions, Trump officials punished her by denying her a permanent position in the White House and reassigning her.[49]

Also in 2020, the Trump re-election campaign sent cease and desist letters to television stations across the country after they aired an ad, paid for by a Democratic super PAC, criticizing the administration's response to the coronavirus. In the letter, the campaign threatened to sue the stations for defamation and to ask the Federal Communications Commission (FCC) to revoke their licenses. The campaign also wrote a letter to CNN demanding it retract and apologize for reporting on a poll showing that more voters supported Democratic candidate Joe Biden than the president. At around the same time, the campaign sued the *New York Times* and the *Washington Post* for defamation because the newspapers had published opinion articles tying the 2016 Trump campaign to Russian government interference with the election. The Trump campaign also sued a Wisconsin television station for airing a commercial by a liberal super PAC contending that the president had deemed the coronavirus to be a "hoax" when he stated, in February, 2020, that the federal government had the epidemic "totally under control" and that "the coronavirus, this is their [Democrats'] new hoax."[50]

Trump also targeted owners of media outlets he deemed critical of him. For example, he urged the Postal Service to double the delivery rates charged to Amazon, a company then led by Jeff Bezos, who also owned the *Washington Post*. Trump repeatedly complained about the *Post*'s coverage of him, claiming that it was the purveyor of "fake news" and that it was Bezos's "lobbyist weapon."[51] As part of his anti-Bezos campaign, Trump accused the Postal Service of giving Amazon a sweet deal by charging shipping rates that the president claimed were too low.[52] In 2018, Trump issued an executive order directing the agency to consider raising "the pricing of the package delivery market."[53] Sure enough, the Postal Service six months later announced a 12-percent increase for the shipping service used by Amazon. And in the summer of 2020, as the country was grappling with the COVID-19 epidemic, Trump threatened to veto a coronavirus relief bill if it included funds to help the Postal Service handle mail-in ballots during the upcoming election. This was part of the president's coordinated attack on the right to vote, the expansion of the franchise to as many citizens as possible, and the legitimacy and accuracy of the presidential election.[54]

Trump also went after the owner of another media outlet that he despised: CNN. At an election rally in 2016, candidate Trump denounced the then proposed merger between AT&T and Time Warner, the owner of CNN. He claimed that the news network was part of the media "power structure" that was actively seeking to suppress his voters. Trump promised that the proposed merger was "a deal we will not approve in my administration." After Trump became president, he asked the Department of Justice to investigate the merger. Trump's objective was to punish CNN in order, as a *New York Times* editorial explained, "to force a sale of the news organization to owners that will strip away its editorial independence and turn it into a house organ of the Trump administration."[55]

In November 2017, the Department of Justice filed an antitrust lawsuit against the merger, the federal government's first challenge in fifty years of a so-called vertical merger (that is, a merger involving companies at different levels in the chain of distribution and that, therefore, do not compete with one another). The federal government lost its lawsuit at trial the following year. In contrast to its effort to block a merger by CNN's corporate owner, the administration praised the horizontal, and therefore, from an antitrust perspective, much more problematic merger of two competitors in the entertainment business: the Walt Disney Company and Twenty-First Century Fox. The executive chairman of the latter was Rupert Murdoch, the chairman and CEO of the News Corporation, the owner of Trump-friendly Fox News.[56]

Trump also threatened to revoke the broadcasting licenses of television networks whose reporting he disliked. (Although the FCC does not issue broadcast licenses to networks, it does issue them to their local affiliates.) In 2017, Trump tweeted that "with all of the Fake News coming out of NBC and the Networks, at what point is it appropriate to challenge their License?" He warned that the networks' "licenses must be challenged and, if appropriate, revoked." Later that same day, Trump complained at a press conference about an NBC News report that he disliked by stating that it was "frankly disgusting the way the press is able to write whatever they want to write," adding that "people should look into that." The following year, Trump suggested that NBC and other networks' coverage "should be tested in courts" because the networks "only defame & belittle" in ways that showed collusion.[57]

In 2020, about six months before voters went to the polls to decide whether he should be re-elected, Trump used his Twitter account to falsely accuse Joe Scarborough, a host of an MSNBC morning cable news show, of murdering a member of his congressional staff in 2001 while serving as a Republican congressman. According to media reports, Trump was angry at Scarborough for his critical coverage of the administration's woeful response to the COVID-19 epidemic and to the public health and economic devastation that it wrought. Trump called on prosecutors to criminally investigate Scarborough, suggesting, without providing any proof, that the news show host may have killed the female aide after having had an affair with her. But, as a *Wall Street Journal* editorial explained, "there's no evidence of foul play, or an affair with the woman, and the local coroner ruled that the woman fainted from an undiagnosed heart condition and died of head trauma." Trump's insinuating lies about a media critic—going so far as to accuse him of *murder*—seemed intended to distract the public at a time when the country was surpassing the grim milestone of one hundred thousand COVID-19 deaths, only three months after Trump had predicted that the virus would soon disappear on its own.[58]

Although Trump was by no means the first president to complain of unfair and biased press coverage, he took his criticisms of the media to new and dangerous levels by questioning its legitimacy and its role in promoting government transparency and accountability. As law professor Tim Zick put it in 2019, "the public labeling of the press as 'the enemy of the people,' the transparent and intentional effort to undermine the credibility of the press, and the threats to use the power of the presidency to punish or deter critical reporting are all unique attributes of this presidency."[59]

With the exception of Richard Nixon, presidents in recent decades seemed to recognize that ongoing scrutiny and criticism by political opponents and the press were part of the price to pay for the tremendous powers that came with the presidency. But Trump never conceded the legitimacy or appropriateness of *any* scrutiny or criticism, whether it originated in the political opposition, critics, or the media.

Throughout his time in office, Trump took concrete steps to silence critics, both inside and outside the administration. The president repeatedly targeted, intimidated, and, in many cases, ordered fired or transferred federal employees who raised questions about possible wrongdoing by administration officials. For example, while the former U.S. ambassador to Ukraine, Marie Yovanovitch, was testifying before the House of Representatives' Judiciary Committee during the first impeachment hearings, Trump took to Twitter to attack her integrity and competency, a condemnation she acknowledged during her testimony was "very intimidating."[60] Only two days after the Senate acquitted him, Trump fired Gordon Sondland, the U.S. ambassador to the European Union, because he had complied with a congressional subpoena to testify at the impeachment hearings.[61] Trump also removed Lieutenant Colonel Alexander Vindman, a decorated Iraq War veteran, from the National Security Council for the same reason.

Vindman, who was escorted out of the White House by security guards, retired from the military a few months later after "the White House had made clear to the Pentagon that President Trump did not want [him] promoted" even though there was no reason, other than his complying with the congressional subpoena, for the denial. According to the *New York Times*, "Mr. Trump's allies at the White House asked Pentagon officials to find instances of misconduct by Vindman that would justify blocking his promotion," but neither the Secretary of Defense nor the Army Secretary was able to produce any such evidence.[62] Nonetheless, knowing that he had no viable future in the military because of Trump's attacks, Vindman retired.

In addition, Rick Bright, the head of the federal agency in charge of over-seeing the development of a coronavirus vaccine, was removed from his post in April 2020 after calling for a rigorous vetting of an anti-malaria drug that Trump falsely claimed cured COVID-19 and for exposing what he alleged was cronyism and corruption at the Department of Health and Human Services.[63] Bright later testified before a House of Representatives committee, charging that the administration's incompetent response to the coronavirus had cost lives.[64] An investigation by the Office of the Special Counsel, the federal agency tasked with protecting federal whistleblowers, concluded that there were reasonable grounds to believe that the Trump administration had ousted Bright from the government research agency combating the coronavirus because he had disclosed information in the best interests of the American public within the meaning of the Whistleblower Protection Act.[65]

Furthermore, as detailed in Chapter 4, Trump fired several inspectors general for investigating alleged corruption and illegal acts by administration officials.[66] One of the individuals Trump fired was the State Department's inspector general who was, at the time of his dismissal, pursuing an investigation into possible misuse of taxpayer money by Secretary of State Mike Pompeo.[67] Finding that the administration was making it impossible for him to do his job of investigating possible wrongdoing by Pompeo, the replacement inspector general resigned after only three months on the job.[68]

Trump also repeatedly went after critics outside the federal government. One of his administration's first official acts was to criminally charge a group of protestors at his inauguration. The individuals in question had been "kettled" by law enforcement officials in riot gear in ways that physically restricted their movement on public streets in Washington, D.C. (Kettling also became a common tactic used by overly aggressive police officers during the weeks of na-tionwide protests that followed the 2020 killing of George Floyd by a Minneapolis police officer.)[69] After a handful of inauguration protestors threw rocks at po-lice officers and broke windows, the Department of Justice charged more than two hundred individuals, including nine journalists trapped in the kettled zone, with "conspiracy to riot." As part of a concerted effort to harass and intimidate anti-Trump protestors, law enforcement officials sought unprecedented access to records detailing the defendants' use of the internet prior to the inauguration. In particular, investigators "sought to force an internet hosting company and Facebook to turn over identifying and other information concerning visitors to anti-Trump websites used for organizing the protests."[70]

A handful of the protestors pled guilty, but the majority demanded trials. In the end, the government dismissed all the remaining charges after it lost the first of several planned trials. (One of the defendants acquitted at that trial was a photojournalist.)[71] Although the prosecution fell apart in the courtroom, the defendants generally believed the federal government had accomplished its objective of silencing and deterring protestors. As several of the defendants told journalist P.E. Moskowitz, the government's "calculus was, either [it] was going to win the trial and set a new precedent against protest or lose the trial but scare 200 activists off the streets of D.C., and possibly scare protestors across the country into thinking twice before heading down to any march."[72]

There were many other ways in which Trump targeted his critics. For example, he retaliated against John Brennan, a former CIA director under Obama and MSNBC contributor, by revoking his security clearance after he criticized the president's national security policies. Trump also threatened to revoke the clearances of Susan Rice (a former national security adviser under Obama and an outspoken Trump critic); James Comey (a former FBI director whom Trump fired for not blocking his agency's investigation of Trump campaign contacts with Russian operatives during the 2016 election); and Andrew McCabe (a former deputy director of the FBI whom Trump had hounded out of office by, among other things, demanding that he be fired, the day before he would have been eligible to retire with a full pension, for his role in the Russia investigation).[73] The day after Trump revoked Brennan's security clearance, retired Admiral William McRaven, who oversaw the Joint Special Operations Command during the time of the raid that killed Osama bin Laden and who had never before ventured into political matters, wrote an op-ed in the *Washington Post* asking Trump to revoke his security clearance. McRaven explained that he would deem the revocation "an honor" because it would allow him to add his name "to the list of men and women who have spoken up against your presidency."[74]

Trump also barred several individuals critical of him from his Twitter account. In a successful lawsuit filed by some of the targeted individuals and the Knight First Amendment Institute at Columbia University, the "government concede[d] that [the individuals were] blocked after posting replies in which they criticized the President or his policies and that they were blocked as a result of their criticism." A federal court of appeals eventually held that the blocking of the critics violated the Free Speech Clause because it constituted discrimination against speakers based on their viewpoints.[75]

The administration also returned Michael Cohen, Trump's former legal fixer and later accuser and critic, to prison because he refused to agree not to publish a book or post on social media. Cohen had pleaded guilty to violating campaign finance laws and other crimes as part of his efforts to arrange hush payments, at Trump's direction, to two women to keep them from speaking publicly about their sexual relations with Trump. Cohen was writing a book in prison that, among other things, provided an insider's account of Trump's lifelong racism, anti-Semitism, and lying. Due to the coronavirus, the federal Bureau of Prisons had granted Cohen a supervised release from prison that required him to be confined to his home. But federal officials one day abruptly demanded that Cohen waive his First Amendment rights to publish a book and post on social media as a condition of his continued release. When Cohen refused to sign the agreement, officials handcuffed him on the spot and returned him to prison. Cohen sued the administration, leading a federal judge to conclude, a few days later, that the decision by the Bureau of Prisons to send Cohen back to jail was "because of his desire to exercise his First Amendment rights to publish a book and to discuss anything about the book or anything else he wants on social media and with others." The judge held that the government's actions constituted unconstitutional retaliation for exercising free speech rights and ordered that Cohen be returned to home confinement.[76]

Trump also repeatedly threatened to use government authority to target critics and others who displeased or annoyed him. For example, in typical autocratic fashion, Trump threatened to have the Department of Justice criminally investigate some of his political opponents, including Hillary Clinton, his former rival in the 2016 election, and Debbie Wasserman Schultz, the former chairwoman of the Democratic National Committee.[77] Weeks before the 2020 election, Trump repeatedly pressured the Attorney General to bring criminal charges against former President Obama and Democratic presidential candidate Joe Biden.[78]

Trump also called for individuals who burn the American flag as a political statement to be jailed and stripped of their citizenship.[79] In addition, the president suggested that federal officials investigate Google, accusing the company, without proof, of designing its internet search algorithm in ways that were purposefully biased against him by favoring stories that made him "look bad."[80] Furthermore, after a group of universities both criticized his administration's attempted revocation of visas for foreign students during the coronavirus pandemic and sued the government to stop the revocation, Trump responded by ordering the Treasury Department to investigate the universities' tax-exempt status because too many of the schools, he claimed, "are about Radical Left Indoctrination, not Education."[81] And, proving that no criticism was too minor or trivial to go unaddressed, Trump called on federal agencies such as the Federal Elections Commission and the Federal Communications Commission to investigate the NBC comedy show *Saturday Night Live*, along with other late-night shows, for mocking him and his presidency.[82]

Another representative example of Trump's disdain for free speech rights involved his repeated attacks on a handful of National Football League (NFL) players who chose to silently kneel rather than stand during the playing of the national anthem before games to bring attention to the issue of police brutality and racism. Trump accused the players of being unpatriotic and called on team owners to fire them. At a 2017 rally in Alabama, the president urged team owners to respond to a kneeling player by saying "Get that son of a bitch off the field right now. Out! He's fired. He's fired!" Trump also threatened to "look into" the NFL's "massive tax breaks" and the federal government's long-standing granting to the league of an antitrust exemption if the owners did not ban the pre-game kneeling. Shortly thereafter, the league, clearly intimidated by the president's attacks and threats, announced that it would begin fining teams that allowed players to kneel during the playing of the national anthem. It would take more than two years, and the nationwide Black Lives Matter protests of 2020, for the league, a hugely wealthy and powerful organization, to muster the courage to ignore the president's repeated attacks by declaring that it now supported players who chose to kneel as a way of protesting police brutality and racism.[83]

It is no coincidence that most of the NFL players whom Trump targeted for expressing their views on police brutality were people of color. Although Trump attacked and threatened critics across the board, he was particularly hateful and malicious toward people of color, women, religious minorities, and the disabled, exposing his raw racism, misogyny, Islamophobia, and disability phobia, among other prejudices.

Trump's hateful comments about some of his political opponents and critics were consistent with his prejudiced comments about ethnic and religious minorities. For example, the president called Haiti, El Salvador, and certain African nations "shitholes countries," while complaining that the United States should allow more immigration from what he deemed to be exemplary countries like Norway.[84] He also claimed that all Haitian immigrants "have AIDS" and that Nigerian immigrants, after experiencing the standard of living in the United States, would never "go back to their huts."[85] In addition, Trump claimed that Mexican immigrants brought crime with them and were "rapists" and "animals," and that a federal judge—who was presiding over a lawsuit against Trump University by former students which asserted that they had been defrauded— could not be impartial because of his Mexican ancestry.[86] In 2019, while calling for a wall along the southern border, he claimed that the nation was being invaded by immigrants who were committing stabbings, rapes and beatings and that "day after day, precious lives are cut short by those who have violated our borders."[87]

Trump also contended that "in our inner cities, African Americans, Hispanics are living in hell because it's so dangerous. You walk down the street, you get shot." In seemingly distinguishing between racially segregated neighborhoods in Chicago, Trump stated that "there's one Chicago that's incredible, luxurious and all, and safe. There's another Chicago that's worse than almost any of the places in the Middle East."[88] During the 2020 election campaign, Trump presented himself as the defender of white identity and repeatedly claimed that the safety of "suburban housewives" (read: white women) was threatened by residents of low-income housing (read: people of color) built in the suburbs.[89] And while debating his opponent Joe Biden on national television, Trump refused to condemn white supremacists.[90]

Trump's attacks on critics who belonged to minority groups was as frequent as they were malicious and insidious. In 2019, for example, he stated that four first-term congresswomen of color, who were among his most prominent, visible, and unsparing critics, should "go back and help fix the totally broken and crime infested places from which they came." He added that it was "so interesting to see 'Progressive' Democrat Congresswomen, who originally came from countries whose governments are a complete and total catastrophe, the worst, most corrupt and inept anywhere in the world (if they even have a functioning government at all), now loudly and viciously telling the people of the United States, the greatest and most powerful Nation on earth, how our government is to be run."[91] Three of the four congresswomen whom Trump attacked in this way— Representatives Alexandria Ocasio-Cortez of New York, Ayanna Pressley of Massachusetts, and Rashida Tlaib of Michigan—were born in the United States. The fourth representative—Ilhan Omar of Minnesota—was born in Somalia, and, like the three others, is a U.S. citizen.

Trump also made racist comments about Baltimore, a majority Black city, in attacking Elijah Cummings, an African American congressman from Maryland. As chairman of the House's Oversight Committee, Cummings was charged with investigating several of the administration's worst abuses of power, including its policy of separating immigrant children from their parents at the Mexico-U.S. border. Trump responded to Cummings's questioning of immigration officials about the barbaric separation policy at a congressional hearing by claiming that the congressman did not have the right to criticize the administration because Cummings's hometown of Baltimore was a "disgusting, rat and rodent infested mess."[92]

After the African American basketball star LeBron James, while being interviewed on CNN by Don Lemon, a Black journalist, criticized Trump for pitting Americans against one another, the president mocked James's intelligence while calling Lemon "the dumbest man on television." During a three-day period in 2018, Trump attacked three different female African American journalists, calling one "stupid," another "a loser," and the third "racist." He also claimed that the Black congresswoman Maxine Waters, one of his most vociferous congressional critics, was "an extraordinarily low IQ person." In addition, he called Omarosa Manigault Newman, an African American woman who had worked for him as a White House aide before resigning and becoming a critic, "a crazed, crying lowlife" and a "dog." Within hours of being selected as the first woman of color to be the vice-presidential candidate of a major party, Trump called Kamala Harris "angry," "horrible," and "nasty."[93]

After Megyn Kelly, a Fox News reporter who was moderating a GOP presidential debate in 2015, asked Trump whether he had the temperament to be president given that he had called women "fat pigs, dogs, slobs, and disgusting animals," Trump called her a "bimbo" who had "blood coming out of her eyes, blood coming out of her wherever." The president also mocked professor Christine Blasey Ford at a rally because, in claiming that Trump's Supreme Court nominee Brett Kavanaugh had sexually assaulted her when she was fifteen years old, at someone else's home in 1982, she could not remember whether the attack had taken place upstairs or downstairs. And he mocked reporter Serge Kovaleski, who has arthrogryposis, by flapping his arms to imitate the journalist's congenital joint condition; the mocking followed Kovaleski's complaint that Trump had lied when he claimed that one of the reporter's *Washington Post* articles supported Trump's lie that thousands of Muslims in New Jersey had publicly cheered from their rooftops after terrorists killed more than 2,600 people in the attacks on the World Trade Center on 9/11.[94]

One of the ways in which Trump attempted to escape accountability and undermine freedom of speech and of the press was through his constant lying. The pursuit of truth is one of the traditional justifications in American jurisprudence for protecting the freedom of speech. As Justice Oliver Wendell Holmes Jr. famously explained in 1919, when people "have realized that time has upset many fighting faiths, they may come to believe even more than they believe the very foundations of their own conduct that the ultimate good desired is better reached by free trade in ideas—that the best test of truth is the power of the thought to get itself accepted in the competition of the market, and that truth is the only ground upon which their wishes safely can be carried out."[95]

Trump's incessant lying revealed, most obviously, his utter disdain for the truth—but it also revealed his contempt for freedom of speech and of the press. As Susan Hennessey and Benjamin Wittes explained in 2020, Trump "makes newspapers choose between cataloguing his lies and giving up on accountability—newspapers he then accuses of making up sources and purveying 'fake news.' He lies about policy, about ethics matters, about his enemies and opponents, and about his personal behavior. He [even] lies routinely about his prior lies." All of that lying was intended to obfuscate, frustrate, and confuse, making it "impossible for the press and the public to effectively filter for his dishonesty." The lying was so persistent and insidious that it rendered *any one lie*, regardless of its magnitude, purpose, or consequences, essentially immune to correction and perhaps even to reproach. As Hennessey and Wittes put it, "Trump is surely the first to so pervade presidential communication with lies . . . as to make factual correction of any one misstatement an irrelevant raindrop in a typhoon."[96] The constant lying, including about well-known and irrefutable facts, was a strategic ploy by Trump to undermine efforts to hold him and his aides accountable for how they governed. As the political scientist James Pfiffner explains, "if there are no agreed upon facts, then it becomes impossible for people to make judgments about their government. Political power rather than rational discourse then becomes the arbiter."[97]

Twitter was Trump's favorite medium for disseminating attacks and spreading lies. For most of Trump's presidency, Twitter resisted pressure from critics to respond to Trump's hateful and deceitful tweets. But the social media company changed course in the spring of 2020 when it attached, for the first time, warnings to two Trump tweets which falsely claimed that California's use of mail-in ballots would lead to voter fraud and the rigging of the upcoming presidential election. Twitter's warnings, which encouraged users "to get the facts" about voting by mail, infuriated the president. He immediately accused the company of "interfering" with the 2020 election and of "stifling" free speech. Two days later, Trump retaliated by signing an executive order targeting big internet companies, such as Twitter, Google, and Facebook, by seeking to deprive them of legal immunity for content posted by third parties. (We will explore the executive order's constitutionality in the next section.)[98]

Trump's assaults on the exercise of First Amendment rights reached their apogee during the nationwide Black Lives Matter protests that followed the killing of George Floyd, an African American man, by a white Minneapolis police officer in May 2020. Floyd died of asphyxiation after the officer pinned him on the ground with the full weight of his body for almost nine minutes despite Floyd's repeated and panicked complaints that he was unable to breathe. Floyd's killing was one of many instances, over the previous years and decades, of police officers committing horrifying acts of physical violence on people of color. Just in the days before Floyd's death, for example, a former police officer and his son shot and killed Ahmaud Arbery, a Black man who was jogging near his home in Georgia. At around the same time, Louisville police officers killed an African American woman by the name of Breonna Taylor by shooting her at least eight times while she lay on her bed at home. The out-of-control shooting followed the police's bursting into Taylor's home, in the middle of the night, to enforce a no-knock warrant issued for someone else.[99]

The killings of Floyd, Arbery, and Taylor took place a few months after the coronavirus epidemic hit the country. The epidemic, which killed more than one hundred thousand Americans in its first few months, had a disproportionately devastating toll on communities of color. The endemic police brutality targeting African Americans, coupled with the systemic racism that denied people of color adequate jobs, education, and health care, led millions of people across the country—in more than 2,500 cities and towns in all 50 states—to take to the streets in May and June of 2020 to demand an end to racist state violence and other forms of institutional racism. Although a small minority of individuals used the protests as an excuse to destroy or steal property, the vast majority of the 2020 Black Lives Matter rallies and marches—which averaged about 140 a day during their first two months—were peaceful exercises of First Amendment rights. According to one estimate, there were no individuals harmed or property damaged in 93 percent of Black Lives Matter protests in the United States in 2020.[100]

As Trump had done at other crucial and difficult moments during his presidency, he chose to stoke animosity and inflame passions rather than try to unite the country and help heal its wounds. A few days after Floyd's death, Trump characterized protestors as "thugs." He also encouraged the police to use violence by tweeting an infamous segregationist phrase used by a racist Miami police chief in the late 1960s: "when the looting starts, the shooting starts." Twitter responded by attaching a warning to Trump's tweet informing users that it violated its posting policies because it glorified violence. A month later, Twitter attached another warning to a Trump tweet that threatened to use "serious force" against Black Lives Matter protestors in Washington, D.C.; according to the social media company, the tweet violated its policy against messages that threatened "harm against an identifiable group."[101] Several months later, after Trump instigated the violent attack on the Capitol by his supporters in a failed effort to stop the certification of Biden's electoral victory, Twitter permanently banned Trump from its platform.[102]

Before further exploring Trump's actions and statements related to the Black Lives Matter protests that followed Floyd's death, it is worth noting that Trump earlier had called for or condoned violence by either the government or his supporters. For example, as already noted, as a candidate in 2016, he encouraged his supporters to physically attack individuals who protested at his rallies. Also, as explained earlier, following a white supremacist's brutal murder of a peaceful counterprotestor during the Charlottesville "Unite the Right" march in 2017, Trump claimed that "there were some very fine people on both sides." Also in 2017, while speaking to cheering police officers on Long Island, New York, the president urged them not to "be too nice" when throwing "thugs into the back of a paddy wagon," comments that were widely understood as encouraging law enforcement officials to physically mistreat detainees.[103] Also, during the coronavirus lockdowns, Trump took to Twitter to urge his supporters to "LIBERATE" states led by Democratic governors in which "your great 2nd Amendment . . . is under siege." A few days later, armed protestors descended on the Kentucky, Michigan, and North Carolina state houses demanding that legislators force governors to lift their stay-at-home orders.[104] It was hardly surprising, therefore, when Trump resorted to calls for state-sponsored violence in response to the Black Lives Matter protests.

Trump's militarized response to the Black Lives Matter protests were consistent with his prior comments on how government officials should treat progressive protestors. As a candidate in 2016, Trump had praised the Chinese government for its brutal attack on the 1989 Tiananmen Square protestors (whom Trump called "rioters") that resulted in the Chinese military murdering hundreds of demonstrators.[105] A few months after becoming president, Trump reversed an Obama policy that had sought to deny local police departments access to military surplus supplies, including grenade launchers, military vehicles, and bayonets. The Obama administration had instituted the policy due to a concern that militarized police responses to protests were disproportionally targeting communities of color while threatening free speech rights.[106] But the Trump administration had no such qualms about the impact of militarized policing on people of color or anyone else. According to Attorney General Jeff Sessions, the Obama rule placed artificial and unnecessary restrains on law enforcement. In its first three-and-a-half years in office, the Trump administration disbursed close to a billion dollars in surplus military equipment to police departments throughout the country.[107]

Trump's calls for violent or threatening responses by his followers reached their peak of recklessness on January 6, 2021, fourteen days before he left office. After weeks of methodically stoking rage among many of his supporters by falsely claiming that he had won in a "landslide" election that "the other side" was "trying to steal," Trump organized a rally in front of the White House on the morning that Congress was scheduled to certify the results of the presidential election. During the rally, Trump gave a speech riddled with violent imagery and angry calls to fight harder "to take back our country" against those who were trying to "steal the election." Trump warned his angry and agitated audience that "our country has had enough, we will not take this anymore." The president also claimed that "Republicans are constantly fighting like a boxer with his hands tied behind his back" and that "we're going to have to fight much harder" against "bad people." He added that "when you catch someone in a fraud, you are allowed to go by very different rules." He also told his restless audience, after urging them to go to the Capitol to "stop the steal," that "if you don't fight like hell, you're not going to have a country anymore."[108]

Within minutes of the start of Trump's speech, hundreds of his supporters began storming the Congress as part of an insurrectional mob whose clear purpose was to violently prevent legislators from certifying Biden's election to the presidency. The attack resulted in the deaths of five people, injuries to dozens of police officers, and repeated threats of violence against scores of elected officials, including Vice President Mike Pence, who had to hide in fear of being attacked. It was not until several hours after the violent mob of Trump supporters first began running amok in the halls and on the grounds of Congress that the president finally issued a video statement in which he repeated his false claim that Democrats were trying to steal the election and asked those who stormed the Capitol to stop the violence after calling them "patriots" and telling them that "we love you, you are very special." A week later, the House of Representatives impeached Trump for a second time, this time for inciting an insurrection against the U.S. government.[109]

In the same way that Trump encouraged his followers to respond to political opponents in violent or threatening ways, he called on law enforcement agencies to respond violently to demonstrations on behalf of racial justice. The day after he warned that looting as part of the protests would lead to shooting, Trump stated that if Black Lives Matter protestors who were congregating on a daily basis in Lafayette Square, a small park across from the White House, breached the White House perimeter, they would "be greeted with the most vicious dogs, and most ominous weapons." Trump also threatened to invoke the Insurrection Act of 1807 to send military active-duty troops into cities without first seeking the approval of mayors or governors.[110]

According to Trump, state and local officials were not being sufficiently aggressive in confronting protestors. Yet, the reality was very different: law enforcement officials in many parts of the country were antagonistically and violently confronting peaceful protestors who were doing nothing more than exercising their First Amendment rights in demanding an end to police brutality and systemic racism in America. The police's militarized response to the marches and protests was evident in a *New York Times* study which found that at least ninety-nine police departments—many of them in large cities—had used tear gas to disperse Black Lives Matter demonstrators during the three weeks following George Floyd's murder, despite the fact that the Chemical Weapons Convention bans the use of the gas in times of war.[111]

The peaceful nature of the vast majority of the protests did not prevent Trump from calling protestors "terrorists" and urging governors "to deploy the National Guard in sufficient numbers that we dominate the streets." During remarks from the Rose Garden on June 1, 2020, he told Americans that he was their "president of law and order" and warned that if governors and mayors did not take the necessary steps to protect their residents, he would "deploy the United States military and quickly solve the problem for them." In addition, Trump announced he was "dispatching thousands and thousands of heavily armed soldiers, military personnel, and law enforcement officers to stop the rioting, looting, vandalism, assaults and the wanton destruction of property" in Washington, D.C.[112]

As Trump was speaking, heavily armed federal law enforcement officers in riot gear used tear gas and flash grenades to push and shove peaceful protestors out of Lafayette Square. The press would later report that the White House ordered the clearing of the Black Lives Matter protestors in order to provide the president with a photo opportunity. After the anguished screaming of the protestors ceased and the tear gas cleared, Trump and some of his aides, including the Attorney General, the Secretary of Defense, and the chairman of the Joint Chiefs of Staff in military combat fatigues, walked to a nearby church that had been the site of a small basement fire set by looters a few days before. After he arrived at the church, the self-acclaimed "law and order" president posed for photographers while holding a Bible in the air. Trump and his entourage then headed back to the White House, while "the police and other forces pursued demonstrators around the capital the rest of the evening, with military helicopters even swooping low overhead in what were called shows of force."[113]

Six weeks after his administration ordered the use of tear gas and flash grenades to disperse peaceful protestors near the White House so that the president could take a seventeen-minute stroll and pose for photographers while holding up a Bible, Trump ordered federal law enforcement agents, including officials from Customs and Border Protection and from Immigration and Customs Enforcement, dressed in camouflage and tactical gear, to patrol the area around the federal courthouse in Portland, Oregon. The area had been the site of fifty consecutive days of protests. Although some protestors had committed acts of vandalism, the protests had been generally peaceful, and before the deployment of federal troops, they were becoming more muted and less well-attended. But Trump's ultimate objective was not to have the protests lose steam; instead, he wanted to use the protests for political advantage by claiming that large cities controlled by liberal Democrats were violent and dangerous places. At one point, he even absurdly claimed that Portland had become more violent than Afghanistan. Trump's deployment of militarized law enforcement agents in Portland, and his threats to do the same in cities such as Chicago and Oakland, provided the backdrop that he wanted for his re-election campaign's "law and order" commercials that began running at around the same time.[114]

The federal agents deployed in Portland in the summer of 2020 did not wear identifying markers or names on their military-style uniforms. These anonymous agents in full military gear attacked demonstrators violently and viciously by beating people up with batons, shooting projectiles at protestors, detonating tear gas containers, and abruptly pulling protestors into unmarked vans without identifying themselves or explaining their actions.[115] One of the protestors who was whisked away by federal law enforcement officials in an unmarked van and detained for two hours, without an explanation, stated after being released that "it felt like I was being hunted for no reason. It feels like fascism."[116]

According to a federal court, a video of a July 29, 2020, incident in Portland showed "federal agents firing tear gas and less lethal munitions" at journalists. The court found that "there was no one nearby on the street but numerous federal enforcement officers and six journalists when the munitions were deployed." At other times, federal agents fired flashbang grenades and 40 mm rubber bullets at journalists. The court concluded that "at least some of the federal officers" deployed in Portland "had intentionally targeted journalists and legal observers in retaliation for their news-reporting efforts."[117]

The presence of federal troops in their city energized and angered many Portland residents. As often happens when First Amendment rights are under attack, the number and energy level of protestors in Portland and in other cities grew significantly after Trump again chose to militarize the federal government's response to the Black Lives Matter demonstrations. Facing mounting criticism about its thug-like law enforcement tactics in Portland, the administration relented after about two weeks by returning the responsibility for maintaining peace and order near the federal courthouse to state and local officials.[118]

The First Amendment as a Constraint on Trump's Autocracy

Trump's attacks on First Amendment rights can be divided into three broad categories. The first category consisted of offensive, malicious, and frequently hateful and false statements attacking the legitimacy, integrity, and motivations of both critics and the press. It could be argued that Trump's attacks in this vein violated rights to freedom of speech because they chilled the expression of those who were critical of the administration's policies. The problem with this claim, however, is that the Supreme Court has made it clear that the Free Speech Clause does not place limits on government speech, including that of government employees speaking in their official capacities.[119] The reason why the Free Speech Clause is inapplicable to government speech is that the government could not function properly and effectively if it lacked the constitutional authority to prefer some state-sponsored messages over others or if it had a constitutional obligation to present the public with countervailing views. In short, when the government speaks, it can favor certain viewpoints over others, a power that the Free Speech Clause almost always denies the state when it regulates the speech of non-government actors.[120]

It could also be argued that the vicious and personal nature of Trump's attacks on critics and the press means that at least some of his statements cannot reasonably be considered government speech. But if the statements in question are not considered government speech, then they would likely be deemed constitutionally protected political speech. Even if we were to assume, to use just one example, that when Trump attacked the NFL players of color who chose to kneel during the playing of the national anthem by calling them "unpatriotic" and "weak and out of control," he was not communicating or pursuing government policy and therefore was not engaging in government speech, the verbal attacks would nonetheless be protected by the First Amendment. The Supreme Court has made it clear that offensive, malicious, and even false statements regarding issues of public concern are constitutionally protected. In doing so, the Court has reasoned that we all have an obligation to "tolerate insulting, and even outrageous, speech in order to provide adequate breathing space to the freedoms protected by the First Amendment."[121] If, as the Court has held, the Free Speech Clause protects, for example, the rights of protestors to stand near the private funeral of a deceased marine holding signs stating "Thank God for Dead Soldiers" and "God Hates Fags," then it is likely that even Trump's most malicious and hateful statements about his critics and the press were constitutionally protected.[122]

In short, if Trump's many malicious and deceitful statements attacking his critics and the press had been challenged, it is unlikely that the First Amendment, as interpreted by the Supreme Court, would have either required or allowed restrictions on Trump's speech. In contrast, the First Amendment did constrain Trump in a second category of cases, that is, when the administration followed up his verbal attacks with policies or actions targeting critics and the press. While Trump was free to verbally disparage and attack critics and the media alike, the Constitution prohibited him and his administration from *retaliating* against them for exercising their First Amendment rights. For example, as a federal court of appeals recognized, it was unconstitutional for officials to block Trump's critics from the Twitter account that he used regularly to communicate with the public as president.[123] Furthermore, while Trump was free to call members of the mainstream press "dishonest," "scum," "corrupt, "the enemy of the people," and purveyors of "fake news," among other epithets, the administration, as the courts ruled, could not bar particular journalists from the White House simply because they had angered the president or his staff.[124] In addition, the administration got nowhere when it attempted to persuade a federal judge to prohibit the distribution and sale of John Bolton's book, which was highly critical of Trump and the ways he governed.[125] And a federal judge quickly stepped in when the administration tried to coerce Michael Cohen, Trump's former legal fixer turned critic, into not writing a book about Trump while he was in prison. After the judge ruled that the government's efforts were likely unconstitutional, the administration agreed to drop its attempt to condition Cohen's release on his promise not to publish books or post on social media.[126] In short, courts used the First Amendment to block repeated efforts by the Trump administration to retaliate against critics.

Similarly, the Trump campaign's efforts to sue media outlets like the *New York Times* and the *Washington Post* for libel, after they published opinion articles linking the 2016 campaign with Russian efforts to interfere with the presidential election, were significantly limited by the First Amendment. As the Supreme Court had held more than fifty years earlier in *New York Times v. Sullivan*, public officials have to meet a high constitutional standard before winning libel suits— the Free Speech Clause requires them to establish that the defendants acted with "actual malice," that is, with knowledge that the statements in question were false or with reckless disregard as to their possible falsity.[127] Furthermore, the newspaper articles legally challenged by the Trump campaign were opinion pieces on issues of public concern based on widely reported facts, a type of expression that is entitled to the highest level of protection under the Free Speech Clause.

Although the issue was not litigated during the Trump years, it is clear that the First Amendment prohibits the government from retaliating against a company because it is led by someone who also owns a media outlet that is critical of the president. This seems to be precisely what happened when the Postal Service, following Trump's repeated haranguing, suspiciously raised shipping charges paid by Amazon, a company then led by the same person, Jeff Bezos, who owns the *Washington Post*. Similarly, although courts did not address the issue, it is likely that Trump's retaliatory executive order seeking to punish Twitter after the social media company exercised its free speech rights by attaching warnings to some of Trump's tweets violated the corporation's First Amendment rights.

If Amazon had challenged the Postal Service's raising of its shipping fees following Trump's denunciation of Bezos and the *Washington Post*, the administration likely would have attempted to articulate a neutral and legitimate reason for the price hike in order to insulate it from constitutional challenge. This was essentially what happened when the Supreme Court in *Trump v. Hawaii* deemed the president's clear Islamophobic statements and prejudice to be constitutionally irrelevant because the government had professed to have neutral and legitimate reasons for instituting what Trump called an immigration "Muslim ban."[128] But one would hope that had Twitter challenged Trump's executive order, courts would have rejected efforts by government lawyers to defend its constitutionality on the ground that it was not intended to be retaliatory. This is because the timing of Trump's order—coming *two days* after Twitter angered the president by, for the first time, questioning the veracity of some of his tweets—can leave little doubt as to its purpose: to punish Twitter for exercising its free speech rights. (The executive order also targeted other large internet companies such as Facebook and Google, which Trump had repeatedly accused of being biased against conservatives.) The president left no doubt regarding his intent when he warned, shortly before issuing the executive order, that Republicans would "strongly regulate" social media companies or "close them down" if they "continued to silence conservative voices."[129]

As law professor Tim Wu noted at the time, Trump's executive order violated the First Amendment because it constituted an official reprisal for Twitter's protected speech (that is, its warning users about the factual falsity of some of Trump's tweets). Wu correctly argued that to treat the order as the basis of any government action would "grant the president an alarming authority he is not supposed to have: to use the power of the state against speech with which he disagrees."[130] The Supreme Court has made it clear that "the First Amendment prohibits government officials from retaliating against individuals for engaging in protected speech."[131]

Furthermore, Trump's executive order targeting Twitter—it mentioned the company six times—was problematic not only because it trampled on free speech rights, but also because it constituted another example of Trump's dangerous efforts to expand presidential authority in ways that were inconsistent with clear congressional enactments of policy. The legal immunity that Trump wanted revoked had been granted by Congress to internet companies through section 230 of the Communications Decency Act of 1996. That provision generally exempts internet platforms from legal liability for materials posted by third parties. Since the immunity is statutorily based, only Congress has the constitutional authority to rescind or modify it. In directing executive agencies to rescind or modify the liability immunity, Trump not only violated free speech principles but also separation-of-powers ones.

As we saw in Chapter 4, Trump repeatedly and aggressively sought to expand the powers of the presidency in ways that transgressed on congressional authority. It is therefore not particularly surprising that, in retaliating against Twitter and other social media companies, Trump claimed that the executive branch had the unilateral authority to implement his policy choices over those of Congress. The same autocratic leader who consistently attempted to undermine the constitutional system of checks and balances did not hesitate to contend that he had unbounded executive power to target and punish critics. As professor Zick notes, "the authoritarian urge to punish . . . critics is a natural byproduct of expansive executive power, and [Trump] aggressively pushed the boundaries of executive" authority.[132]

We have so far explored two categories of Trump's attacks on free speech rights. The offensive, malicious, and frequently hateful and false statements that made up the first category of attacks were either not restricted by the First

Amendment (as government speech) or were protected by it (as political speech). At the same time, the administration's retaliatory actions against those engaging in protected speech that make up the second category of Trump's attacks violated the First Amendment. But there was a third category of Trump's attacks on First Amendment rights that fell in a constitutional gray area between, on the one hand, malicious, hateful, and false statements, which are not constitutionally prohibited, and on the other hand, the adoption of retaliatory government policies, which is constitutionally proscribed. This third category consisted of *threats* of retaliation.

The administration frequently failed to follow through on Trump's repeated threats of retaliation against critics and the media. For example, there is no publicly available evidence that the Department of Justice criminally investigated Hillary Clinton or the former chairwoman of the Democratic Party, as President Trump urged it to do. There is also no indication that the FCC considered revoking the licenses of ABC, CBS, and NBC affiliates despite Trump's threats to punish networks because their news divisions were disseminating what the president deemed to be "fake news."

In addition, the government did not seek to remove the NFL's antitrust exemption or its "massive tax breaks" (as Trump called them) as a way of pressuring the league to clamp down on its players who kneeled during the national anthem to bring attention to the issue of police brutality and racism. Furthermore, the administration did not take any steps to modify libel law as Trump threatened to do several times. (It is not clear, in any event, how the administration could have modified libel law in the ways that Trump wanted given that it is a creature of state (not federal) law, as limited by constitutional doctrine determined by the courts.) There were also apparently no FCC investigations of network affiliates for broadcasting ads paid by a Democratic super PAC or of the producers of *Saturday Night Live* for the show's parodies of Trump. In addition, nothing seems to have come from the Trump-ordered investigations of universities that challenged his administration's efforts to revoke foreign students' visas during the coronavirus pandemic. And there is no evidence that the federal government investigated, or pressured Florida law enforcement officials to investigate, journalist Joe Scarborough for the death of his aide almost twenty years earlier. In addition, it does not appear that the administration followed through on Trump's threat to strip protestors who burned American flags of their U.S. citizenship.

It could be argued, on the one hand, that Trump's threats of retaliation against critics and members of the press for exercising their First Amendment rights, even when not translated into specific government action, sufficiently threatened, burdened, or chilled the exercise of those rights so as to effect constitutional violations.[133] On the other hand, it can be argued that the unrealized threats were closer to Trump's offensive and malicious statements that were not accompanied by threats of retaliation, which, as already explained, are beyond judicial review under the First Amendment.[134] But however that question is best answered, it is worth emphasizing that *Trump administration officials repeatedly failed to implement many of the president's threats of retaliation against critics and the press.* It is likely that the First Amendment played an important role in that failure to act.

Unlike in matters related, for example, to immigration and the environment, in which administration officials continually translated Trump's punitive, misleading, or problematic rhetoric into government regulations, officials took relatively few explicit steps to translate the president's virulent anti-press and anti-dissent rhetoric into government policy or actions. The retaliatory threats that *were* actualized into government action—such as the banning of critics from Trump's Twitter account and the barring of certain reporters from the White House—were quickly and successfully challenged in the courts. But with *unrealized* retaliatory threats, there were no specific government actions to challenge in the courts. Yet, the absence of litigation should not obscure the role that the First Amendment likely played in preventing the adoption of a slew of policies aimed at silencing critics and muzzling the press.

There are several reasons that might help explain the administration's failure to follow through on many of Trump's retaliatory threats aimed at critics and the press. One might be that more sensible (than Trump) administration officials realized that attempts to implement the president's retaliatory threats would stir further political opposition and backlash against the administration. But it is also likely that the more sensible officials understood, in ways that Trump apparently did not comprehend or care about, that the First Amendment significantly constrained the government's ability to retaliate against critics and the press. In this way, the First Amendment served as a "background constraint" on autocratic government action by preventing many of Trump's threats aimed at discouraging critics and the press from exercising their First Amendment rights from being actualized into government policies and practices.

Trump would have been much more successful in trampling on First Amendment rights were it not for the wide consensus, likely shared by the administration's lawyers, that those rights robustly protect political speech in general and the ability of both opponents and the media to criticize government policy and officials in particular. There can be no doubt that the subjects of Trump's retaliatory threats—everyone from the kneeling NFL players to the opposition-party officials whom Trump wanted the Department of Justice to criminally investigate to the executives of news network that disseminated critical stories of the administration—were engaging in constitutionally protected political speech. That type of speech, the Supreme Court has held, "is the essence of self-government," is "indispensable to decisionmaking in a democracy," and serves to protect the "unfettered interchange of ideas for the bringing about of political and social changes desired by the people."[135] Furthermore, as the Court explained in *New York Times v. Sullivan*, the suggestion that government critics can be punished for their criticism "strikes at the very center of the First Amendment."[136] This means that even Trump-appointed judges would have been highly skeptical of efforts, for example, to deny broadcasters licenses or to target the producers of *Saturday Night Live* because they aired criticisms or parodies of the president.

None of this is to suggest, of course, that the First Amendment worked perfectly or seamlessly to deter or address all abuses of power by the Trump administration. The deployment of militarized federal law enforcement personnel to violently break up the peaceful Black Lives Matter protest in front of the White House on June 1, 2020, and to occupy the streets of Portland, Oregon, a few weeks later, are two deeply troubling examples of the ways in which the Trump administration trampled on First Amendment rights without being restrained either by Congress or the courts. But while the First Amendment did not work perfectly during the Trump years in curbing government abuse, the number and negative impact of Trump's autocratic policies and practices would have been significantly greater had the amendment not explicitly (in the case of implemented retaliations against critics and the media) and implicitly (in the case of unrealized retaliations against the same) helped to constrain his power as president.

The Exercise of Free Speech Rights and Press Freedoms During the Trump Years

As noted earlier, some progressives have grown increasingly critical of certain expansive understandings of First Amendment rights, some of which have been adopted by the courts. Progressive First Amendment skepticism has been particularly prevalent on issues related to corporate speech rights and to the claim, defended by many conservatives, that the Constitution grants religious business owners, employers, and landlords exemptions from LGBTQ anti-discrimination laws. In addition, egalitarian progressives have repeatedly and forcefully questioned the constitutional protection that American courts have granted to hate speech. At its most fundamental level, the First Amendment skepticism is grounded in the concern that, in some areas, free speech rights are being used to undermine the attainment of equality objectives. To put it simply, some progressives on some issues have come to view the First Amendment as an impediment to, rather than a facilitator of, equality.

As I also noted earlier, my objective here is neither to criticize nor defend progressive First Amendment skepticism. Instead, my claim is that even if that skepticism is well-founded and justified, the ways in which Trump governed should serve as crucial reminders to progressives of why robust First Amendment protections continue to matter. The Trump years showed how and why First Amendment principles and rights can play a vital role in protecting democratic values, government critics, and the press from autocratic officials. Those principles and rights include (1) the granting of robust protections for political speech, broadly defined; (2) the requiring that the government, when it regulates expression, remains strictly neutral regarding speakers' viewpoints; and (3) the prohibiting of government retaliation against dissenting or unpopular speech. The viability and successes of progressive movements and causes going forward partly depends on not allowing progressive First Amendment skepticism to expand to the point that it undermines or weakens these types of fundamental free speech principles and rights.

The exercise of the right to dissent, protected by the First Amendment, was crucial during the Trump era. During those difficult and frightening years, progressives repeatedly exercised their First Amendment rights to organize, assemble, petition, and agitate against a long list of highly problematic policies, many of which targeted vulnerable communities and populations. For example, there was widespread outcry and criticism following the implementation of the Trump administration's barbaric policy of separating immigrant children from their families at the Mexico-U.S. border as a way of discouraging further immigration. The administration, battered by the public uproar and condemnation, rescinded the zero tolerance policy that led to the separation of approximately 5,500 minors from their families and that a federal court deemed to be "egregious," "outrageous," and sufficient to "shock the conscience."[137] (It took months for the administration to return most of the children to their families. Even so, by the end of 2020, the federal government had failed to locate the parents of 545 children it had disgracefully separated from their families.)[138] Political activism and organizing on behalf of Dreamers also continued throughout the Trump years, helping to maintain public attention on their plight and the compelling arguments in favor of allowing them to remain in the country.[139]

It is true, of course, that the exercise of First Amendment rights in opposition to the Trump administration's countless problematic and harmful policies and actions, including those that were harshly anti-immigrant, did not always (or even most of the time) prevent their implementation. Clearly, the mere exercise of First Amendment rights to express dissenting views does not guarantee policy results. But the exercise does allow for political organizing and mobilizing that, especially over time, can lead to reforms and changes in policies.

The importance of the First Amendment for progressive movements and causes was also evident in the massive protests, centered around the demands of the Black Lives Matter movement, which broke out nationwide following the killing of George Floyd by a Minneapolis police officer in May of 2020. Despite Trump's efforts to threaten, intimidate, and silence Black Lives Matter protestors, the marches and rallies demanding an end to police brutality and systemic racism continued unabated across the country for weeks. The Black Lives Matter demonstrations of 2020 likely constituted the largest protest movement in the nation's history.[140]

Trump's militarized response to the generally peaceful exercise of First Amendment rights—including the use of federal law enforcement troops to clear Lafayette Square, in Washington, D.C., of protestors on the evening of June 1, 2020, and to attack demonstrators on the streets of Portland, Oregon, several weeks later—only emboldened protestors to double-down in their efforts to publicly and forcefully demand both justice for the victims of police abuse and structural reforms to the economy and the criminal justice system. In doing so, the protests articulated powerful dissenting messages from the type of "law and order" policies, strongly supported by Trump through the years, that have resulted in state-sponsored violence against people of color. The protests also sent a powerful countervailing message of opposition to the racist policies and rhetoric that Trump promoted and defended while in office. The rallies, marches, and vigils raised awareness about the continued invidious impact of structural racism in the country in ways that helped move public opinion to the left on issues related to discrimination, inequality, and policing.[141]

There was also a wide consensus, even among some Republican officials, that Trump had acted improperly in militarizing the government's response to Black Lives Matter protestors, in lashing out at their exercise of First Amendment rights, and in repeatedly failing to distinguish between the vast majority of peaceful demonstrators and the relatively small number of individuals who had committed illegal acts during the protests. For a growing number of Americans, it was the protestors who were acting patriotically in exercising their First Amendment rights to express their dissenting views, and it was the president and members of his administration who were on the wrong side of the Constitution in seeking to stifle and silence dissent.[142]

The Black Lives Matter protests, which became inextricably linked with the expression of anti-Trump voices and viewpoints, showed the continued importance to our democracy of public places—including streets, sidewalks, and parks—as free speech zones. There has been considerable discussion in recent years about how the internet and social media sites have become the new public square. As the Supreme Court explained in 2017, these platforms "provide perhaps the most powerful mechanisms available to a private citizen to make his or her voice heard. They allow a person with an Internet connection to become a town crier with a voice that resonates farther than it could from any soapbox"[143] But even with modern technology and new forms of communication, there is something uniquely powerful about thousands of people "hitting the streets" to express their dissatisfaction with and opposition to government policies and the status quo. Well-attended public protests by angry and frustrated citizens capture the attention of government officials, the press, and the broader public in ways that social media posts, Facebook "likes," and retweets, even in large numbers, have a difficult time replicating. Among other things, the Black Lives Matter protestors powerfully communicated the depth of their commitment to their civil rights cause by risking both police violence and exposure to the coronavirus in order to publicly demand an end to centuries of systemic racism in America.

The Trump years also highlighted the vital role that a free press plays in our democracy. The press has been battered in recent decades by technological changes that have shifted billions of advertising dollars from newspapers, magazines, and television stations to a handful of social media giants like Google and Facebook. For many years now, countless media outlets have been hemorrhaging money and employees. Hundreds of print publications, both large and small, have either closed altogether or shifted their publication entirely online, making it difficult for them to survive economically. Also, as society has become more politically polarized, activists on both the right and the left have repeatedly attacked the mainstream media, accusing it of being biased and dishonest, charges that have tarnished its reputation among members of the public.[144]

In his quest for the presidency in 2016, Trump correctly determined that there were millions of votes to be gained by challenging the honesty, integrity, and motivations of the mainstream press. Trump portrayed himself as the only candidate strong and brave enough "to protect" the country from media outlets that were "the enemy of the people" and purveyors of "fake news." After he was elected to office, as we have seen, Trump increased the frequency and harshness of his attacks on the media. The president's attacks were intended to challenge, silence, intimidate, and weaken media organizations and journalists whose primary and most important responsibility is to keep the American public informed about what its government is doing and why. A president who repeatedly lied to the public, on matters big and small, was not interested in promoting either transparency or accountability, precisely the two main objectives behind the proper workings of a free press.

To their immense credit, many media organizations and journalists insisted and persevered in carrying out their responsibilities despite Trump's relentless, aggressive, and vitriolic attacks on them. As a general matter, newspapers, magazines, and television news networks refused to be cowed by Trump—in the face of his repeated attacks, the press kept at it, doing its best to keep the public informed about the administration's policies, plans, and objectives. The media also generally continued to do what it had attempted to do since at least the Watergate years—investigating and exposing government malfeasance and abuses of power. For example, some media outlets comprehensively tracked, exposed, and challenged Trump's innumerable lies, on matters both big and small.[145] The media also closely covered the events behind the Ukraine scandal that led to Trump's first impeachment. Had it not been for a generally vigilant press that was determined to carry out its responsibility of bringing greater transparency and accountability to how the country was being governed, Trump's abuses of power would undoubtedly have been even more extensive and pernicious than they were.

In many ways the mainstream media's efficacy in carrying out its oversight function was reflected in Trump's relentless attacks on its honesty and motivations. Trump was not critical of the media writ large; instead, he lambasted press outlets when they failed to cover him and his administration in praiseworthy and positive ways. At the same time, Trump commended and rewarded with interviews media outlets and journalists that were willing to serve as his boosters and defenders. For example, Trump generally professed his admiration and appreciation for Fox News, except on the rare occasion when the right-wing news network reported stories in ways that he perceived to be critical of him; on those occasions, he ferociously attacked the network like he did any other source of criticism.[146] In short, Trump demanded that the media be completely loyal to him and his administration (and, to a lesser extent, to the Republican Party); for Trump, nothing less than glowing and fawning coverage was acceptable. In making such demands, Trump attempted to undermine the essential purpose of a free press, which exists to serve the public's interests rather than those of government officials.

Trump ultimately failed in his calculated campaign to intimidate and co-opt the mainstream press. At the same time, it would be naïve to believe that the media succeeded in exposing every instance of corruption and abuse of power by Trump and his administration. It is very likely that given what we know of how Trump governed, of his lack of morals and scruples, and of his willingness to put his personal and political interests above all else, that the president and his administration committed abuses of power and engaged in types of corruption that have yet to come to light. Those abuses are likely to trickle out in the years and decades to come, perhaps as much as a result of the work of historians as of that of journalists.

It can also be argued that the media sometimes paid *too much* attention to Trump's every tweet and comment, perversely amplifying the impact and harm of his deliberately malicious, offensive, and false statements. As professor Zick noted in 2019, "a new dysfunctional symbiosis has emerged, one in which the media rely on Trump to create content that draws viewers and readers and the president simultaneously conducts his 'war' on the press for political gain. . . . As the past few years have demonstrated, constantly reacting to every public statement [Trump] makes is a pernicious trap" for the press.[147] And yet, despite both Trump's attacks and the media's failings, the free press survived the Trump years.

As a general matter, then, both Trump's critics and the media "generally stood their ground in the face of [his] attacks" by refusing to be silenced and cowed.[148] It is not at all clear that that positive outcome, for the nation and for its democratic institutions, would have occurred had Trump and his administration not been restrained by the First Amendment. That restraint, as we have seen, was both explicit (in prohibiting the administration, for example, from barring critics from Trump's Twitter account and probing journalists from the White House) and implicit (in helping to prevent the turning of many of Trump's attacks and threats against critics and the press into government policy or action). Those restraints resulted directly from the courts' long-standing protections for political speech and for the right of individuals to criticize and of the press to scrutinize government officials and policies.

It is important for progressives to keep all of this in mind when conservative activists, commentators, and journalists aggressively critique, attack, and condemn future liberal presidents and their policies. Progressives may be tempted then to soften their support for First Amendment protections because they may deem them as impeding rather than promoting progressive political objectives. But progressives should resist that temptation by remembering how crucial the freedoms of speech and of the press were in constraining the harms to both our democratic system and the public's welfare caused by Trump's autocratic governance. As bad as Trump's abuses of power were, matters would have been considerably worse without the First Amendment.

Looking to the Future: The Case of Hate Speech Regulations

The question of hate speech and its regulation seems particularly pertinent in thinking about the intersection of the Trump years, the First Amendment, and progressive priorities. One reason for the high relevance is that Trump frequently engaged in hateful speech himself, both as a presidential candidate and as president. Another reason is that the nationwide Black Lives Matter protests that exploded across the country at the end of Trump's term in office targeted, among other things, the institutional racism that is frequently reflected in racist language, rhetoric, and symbolism, including in the honoring of the Confederacy through monuments on public property. Although the question of how best to regulate hate speech is a complicated one that I cannot fully address here, it is worth exploring how the Trump years might impact the ways in which progressives think about hate speech regulations going forward.

There are different ways of defining hate speech, but generally speaking it is understood to entail speech that intentionally seeks to insult, degrade, or demean individuals based on race, color, or ethnicity. Many proponents of hate speech regulations also include within its definition speech that targets individuals on the basis of religion, gender, and sexual orientation. The laws of most Western democracies, including those of the United Kingdom, Germany, France, and Canada, criminalize hate speech to varying degrees.[149] But in the United States, the Free Speech Clause, as interpreted by the Supreme Court, prohibits the government from criminalizing hate speech that falls short of constituting either true threats of harm to particular individuals or incitements to engage in imminent and violent conduct.[150]

As noted earlier, egalitarian progressives in the United States have for decades been pushing for greater regulation of hate speech. Supporters of such regulations can point to Trump's hateful rhetoric, including his attacks on people of color, women, and Muslims, to support their claims that hate speech harms members of vulnerable minorities by seeking to render them second-class citizens. This is especially true when the president, the most powerful person in the country, engages in hate speech himself.

In using the Trump era to support calls for greater hate speech regulations, proponents can also point to the disturbing increase in racist, anti-Semitic, and anti-Muslim hate crimes during Trump's term. The number of hate crimes reported to the FBI by state and local law enforcement agencies increased by 17 percent during Trump's first year in office.[151] And according to the Anti-Defamation League (ADL), anti-Semitic incidents during that year increased by an astonishing 60 percent.[152] The year 2019 saw the highest number (2,107) of anti-Semitic incidents in the United States in the forty years since the ADL began tracking hate crimes. And the Trump years of 2018 (2,066 incidents) and 2017 (1,986 incidents) constituted the third and fourth highest, respectively.[153]

Furthermore, anti-Muslim hate crimes in the United States doubled during the Trump presidency, compared to the presidencies of Barack Obama and George W. Bush.[154] One study conducted in 2019 found that hate crimes in counties that had hosted a Trump campaign rally in 2016 increased by more than 200 percent after Trump became president. As the authors put it, "it is hard to discount a 'Trump effect' when a considerable number of these reported hate crimes reference Trump."[155] The authors of another study concluded that the data showed "compelling evidence" that Trump's inflammatory rhetoric and his election to office likely "fueled the hate crime surge."[156]

The hate crimes during Trump's presidency included the Charlottesville murder during the "Unite the Right" rally in 2017; the 2018 shooting, by a neo-Nazi who posted anti-immigrant screeds online, at the Tree of Life Synagogue in Pittsburgh that killed eleven people; and the 2019 massacre at a Walmart in

El Paso, Texas, in which a white supremacist killed twenty-two people, most of whom were Latinx. In 2019, according to the FBI, "more murders motivated by hate were recorded than ever before."[157]

Proponents of hate regulations can point to not only the increase in hate crimes that followed Trump's election, but also to the ways in which Trump's racist rhetoric emboldened white supremacists to more forcefully and publicly express their hatred. As law professor Jeannine Bell explains, "what was most compelling about the new hate activity was the rise of a new, open presence of extremists—those ideologically committed to White supremacy. For decades, racial extremists—members of organized hate groups and others ideologically attached to the tenets of White supremacy—had lived in the shadows. After Trump's election, racial extremists stepped into the light."[158] According to the white supremacist leader Robert Spencer, speaking shortly after the 2016 election, America belonged to white people, a race of "conquerors and creators" who had been marginalized but that now, because of Trump's election, were "awakening to their own identity." Spencer made these remarks at a gathering, in a Washington, D.C., hotel, of more than two hundred white nationalists, many of whom stood with outstretched arms in Nazi salutes as he spoke.[159] David Duke, a former Grand Wizard of the Ku Klux Klan, said of the Unite the Right Rally in Charlottesville in 2017 that "we are determined to take our country back. We are going to fulfill the promises of Donald Trump."[160]

Civil libertarian critics of hate speech regulations frequently note that countries which have adopted them continue to experience hate crimes and rhetoric; this shows, critics contend, that the regulations are ineffective, at best, and counterproductive, at worst.[161] But the fact that hate crimes and rhetoric continue unabated, and have recently increased, in the United States suggests that responding to hate speech with counter speech rather than with regulation, as civil libertarians demand, is equally ineffective. Given the intractability of institutionalized racism, the frequency of hate crimes, and the prevalence of hateful rhetoric in the United States, it is understandable for egalitarian progressives to be skeptical of the notion that an unfettered "marketplace of ideas," where everyone is free to express their viewpoints no matter how hateful of and demeaning to others, is the best way of mitigating and preventing the harms engendered by, for example, racist, anti-Semitic, and anti-Muslim hate speech.

Civil libertarians argue that the link between hate speech and actual, tangible harms to individuals is too attenuated or unproven to justify its regulation.[162] But it is not clear that the link between other forms of speech that *can* be punished under the Constitution and actual harms is any less attenuated than it is in the context of hate speech. Indeed, the Supreme Court deems certain forms of speech to be unprotected by the First Amendment even though the harms engendered by them are rather vague, general, and unspecified. For example, under current law, obscenity can be constitutionally criminalized to protect the community from vague harms associated with violations of its standards of decency (whatever that means).[163] In addition, liability for libel can sometimes attach to false statements in order to protect individuals from reputational harms that are frequently difficult to quantify with much precision.[164] Furthermore, the providing of "material support" to foreign groups that the U.S. government classifies as terrorist organizations can be criminalized under the First Amendment, on rather vague national security grounds, even when the support entails nothing more than *political speech* aimed at persuading those organizations to peacefully accomplish their goals.[165] Egalitarian progressives can argue, with compelling justification, that courts subject hate speech regulations to an unjustifiably greater level of scrutiny, and to an excessively demanding standard of proof on the question of harm, than other forms of speech regulations that pass constitutional muster.

In defending hate speech regulations, the legal philosopher Jeremy Waldron emphasizes the social harm suffered by minorities when others question their status as equal citizens in society based on characteristics such as race and ethnicity. Every member of a democratic society, Waldron argues, has a basic entitlement to be regarded as an equal member in good standing. Part of that entitlement includes a right not to have others challenge their equal standing based on their membership in a minority group.[166]

As a presidential candidate and later as president, Trump repeatedly questioned the equal standing in society of certain minority groups. For example, he did that when he claimed that Mexican immigrants were criminals and rapists, and that a federal judge could not be impartial because of his Mexican heritage.[167] He did that when he claimed that four congresswomen of color, all of whom were American citizens and three of whom were born in the United States, should go back to their home countries "and help fix the totally broken and crime infested places from which they came."[168] He did that when he claimed that several Black-majority countries were "shitholes" and that the United States should restrict immigration from them while encouraging immigration from countries like Norway.[169] He did that when he associated the Muslim faith with terrorism and violence, while claiming that the religion itself represented a threat to the country.[170] In part because of the vitriolic and malicious nature of his statements and in part because of the awesome powers of the presidency, Trump's hate speech crystalized the ways in which such speech threatens the equal human dignity and civic status of individuals based solely on their membership in certain minority groups.

In sum, an understandable progressive response to Trump's relentless use of hate speech would be to more forcefully push for the types of hate speech regulations that are currently in force in most other Western democracies. Although American courts are unlikely, in the near term, to uphold the constitutionality of those regulations, progressives could continue both to ag-itate for them and criticize judges for blocking them. At the same time, how-ever, the ways in which Trump governed also provide progressives with good reasons for proceeding cautiously in pushing for new hate speech regulations. In considering such regulations in the post-Trump era, progressives should keep in mind the likelihood that future autocratic leaders and right-wing officials will use them to clamp down on progressive speech and to target (or at least leave un-protected) speech by traditionally vulnerable minorities.

Speech regulations, such as those included in criminal statutes and in the codes of conduct of public universities, are ultimately interpreted and enforced by government officials and school administrators. If those who enforce hate speech regulations are genuinely concerned with protecting the equal standing of all members of society, while remaining cognizant of the need to apply the rules carefully and prudently in order not to inappropriately squelch political speech and the right to dissent, then it is possible that the regulations will work in the ways their proponents intend.

But the Trump years showed how both democracy and equality can be threat-ened when the levers of government power fall into the hands of individuals who are committed to undermining democratic institutions, silencing and intimi-dating critics, and targeting vulnerable minorities. It is therefore important for progressives to consider how hate speech regulations, even when drafted and adopted with the best of intentions, may be used by non-progressive government officials to advance right-wing policy objectives and the personal interests and vendettas of autocratic leaders in the Trump mold. It is certainly not beyond the realm of possibility that such officials will interpret, implement, and apply hate speech regulations in ways that protect majority groups and target vulnerable minority ones.

It is worth remembering, in considering how hate speech regulations may be maladministered by non-progressive officials, that a significant number of conservatives insist that racism against African Americans is largely a thing of the past. Many of these conservatives also believe that race-conscious reform measures, such as affirmative action policies, aimed at addressing the ongoing effects of the nation's racist history, are themselves racist because they purport-edly discriminate against whites.[171] Indeed, a 2019 poll found that 69 percent of Republicans believed that discrimination against white people was just as much of a problem as discrimination against racial minorities.[172] If officials who im-plement and administer hate speech regulations generally share these types of views—as is likely to happen in some parts of the country and at the federal level under a future autocratic, right-wing administration in the Trumpian mold—then it is not unrealistic to expect that the officials will more quickly and rigor-ously proscribe speech that they deem to be anti-white than anti-Black.

Similarly, many of the conservatives who endorsed (or did not object to) Trump's deeply prejudiced statements equating the Muslim faith with terrorism, violence, and a "hatred" of America, are the same people who contend that Christianity in the United States is constantly under attack. These attacks are evident, it is claimed, in efforts to enforce LGBTQ anti-discrimination laws against those who have religious objections to same-sex marriage and to transgender rights. From this perspective, it is Christian conservatives who are the victims of state-sponsored discrimination. Many religious conservatives also complain that the ban on prayer in the schools, the removal of Christian symbols from public property, and the push to celebrate the "holidays" rather than Christmas are all part of organized secular and multicultural attacks on Christianity. Before pushing for hate speech regulations, therefore, progressives should keep in mind the real possibility that some officials in some parts of the country will likely use those regulations as legal mechanisms to protect majoritarian Christianity from criticism and to target the speech of members of religious minorities and atheists.

In short, officials can enforce hate speech regulations against Black Lives Matter and Palestinian rights activists, to give just two examples, just as readily as they can against white nationalists and homophobes.[173] As a result, in considering whether to push for hate speech regulations, progressives should account for the likelihood that some officials will use the regulations to target progressive opinions and minority groups.

The ways in which hate speech regulations have been actually enforced confirms that concerns about possible maladministration—by which I mean, in this context, their misuse against minority groups and voices—are legitimate and should give progressives pause. For example, during the approximately eighteen months in which a University of Michigan hate speech regulation was in effect in the late 1980s, before a federal court struck it down as unconstitutional under the First Amendment, "there were more than twenty cases of whites charging blacks with racist speech."[174] Furthermore, the only two students who were ultimately punished by the university for engaging in racist speech were sanctioned for speech that was "communicated by or on behalf of black students."[175]

The application and enforcement of hate crimes regulations in other Western democracies illustrate how readily they can be enforced against progressive voices. While the regulations have been used to outlaw and punish, for example, racist, Islamophobic, anti-Semitic, and homophobic speech, officials have also sometimes used them to silence progressives, including members of minority groups. In 2015, for example, France's highest court upheld the criminal hate speech conviction of twelve Palestinian rights activists for wearing T-shirts that stated "Long live Palestine, boycott Israel." Several years earlier, Palestinian rights activists had been convicted of "inciting racial hatred" for placing boycott stickers on Israeli fruits in French supermarkets. Also in France, the head of the Paris chapter of ACT UP, the AIDS advocacy group, was fined for calling the president of a conservative organization a "homophobe."[176]

In 2012, a Muslim teenager in Britain who was angered by Western military killings of noncombatants in Afghanistan was charged with a hate speech crime after he wrote the following on his Facebook page: "All soldiers should DIE & go to HELL! THE LOWLIFE FUCKING SCUM! gotta problem go cry at your soldiers grave & wish him hell because that where he is going." Although the teenager was eventually able to avoid a jail term for what a police spokesperson described as his failure "to make his point very well," he was nonetheless subject to a months-long criminal investigation and had to pay a fine. This misuse of Britain's hate speech law led a critic to argue that the teenager was "the latest victim of a concerted effort to redefine racism as anything that could conceivably offend white people."[177]

One of the more powerful—and, in my view, correct—points that many progressives make about racism in the United States is that its devastatingly harmful effects are not limited to those caused by the actions and statements of a few prejudiced individuals; instead the evil of racism is intrinsic to the ways in which our nation's most important governmental, economic, and educational organizations exercise their power and authority. The concept of systemic or institutional racism holds that racism is embedded in both the substantive policies and the decision-making processes of the nation's most powerful institutions, including law enforcement and other government agencies, large corporations, and private and public universities.[178] Progressive critiques of racism in the United States also frequently emphasize and expose the prevalence and invidiousness of unconscious racial biases that afflict just about everyone, albeit to different degrees, and that are therefore found throughout society.[179]

It is crucial to keep the phenomena of structural racism and unconscious biases in mind when considering the advisability of hate speech regulations.[180] Those regulations, if enacted, will be enforced through government and legal structures that, according to many progressives, are intrinsically racist. In addition, the officials doing the enforcing will be subject to the conscious and unconscious racial biases that rightfully trouble many progressives. Given all of this, it is unlikely that the enforcement of hate speech regulations in the United States can be done in ways that are not, at least some of the time, distorted by institutional racism and other forms of structural prejudices. This danger of maladministration is then heightened significantly when speech enforcement mechanisms may fall under the control of right-wing, racist, and autocratic officials in the mold of Donald Trump.

It is true that, if conservative judges enforce the First Amendment principle of viewpoint neutrality, which prohibits the government from regulating speech due to its ideological content, in assessing the constitutionality of the misuse of hate speech regulations to target minority-group or progressive speech to the same extent that they have been willing to do so in the contexts of corporate or religious speech, then it is possible that some of the worst consequences, for progressives, of the possible maladministration of hate speech regulations will be avoided. But the point is that if progressives expect conservative judges to use the principle of viewpoint neutrality to protect minority-group and left-wing speech (as progressives expected during the Trump years), then progressives have to be willing to defend the same principle as applied to the regulation of anti-egalitarian and right-wing speech. Otherwise, progressives would be left in the problematic position of embracing situational constitutionalism by defending viewpoint neutrality, as a core First Amendment principle, when it is politically convenient and attacking or ignoring it when it is not.

Law professor Vincent Blasi argues that in determining the proper scope of First Amendment rights, it is crucial to think about which protections would be most effective when the threats to democratic institutions and free expression by government officials are at their greatest. As Blasi puts it in defending what he calls a "pathological understanding" of free speech protections, "the overriding objective at all times should be to equip the First Amendment to do maximum service in those historical periods when intolerance of unorthodox ideas is most prevalent and when governments are most able and most likely to stifle dissent systematically. The First Amendment, in other words, should be targeted for the worst of times."[181] Similarly, when considering whether to push for hate speech regulations in the United States, progressives should keep in mind that the levers of power in democratic societies frequently change hands and that, at any given time, those enforcing the regulations may be committed to *both* targeting minorities and squelching progressive speech. Hate speech regulations, properly enforced, may very well be effective in protecting vulnerable minorities from harm without impermissibly burdening free expression. But progressives, in deciding whether to push for such regulations, should account for the likelihood that they will be improperly enforced.

James Madison famously wrote in *The Federalist Papers* that "if men were angels, no government would be necessary."[182] As law professor Frederick Schauer notes, something similar can be said of the First Amendment: if angels controlled government, we would not need the amendment. As Schauer explains, "the First Amendment's foundations lie not with ideal aspirations, but instead with the kind of arguably necessary pessimism that Madison's famous line captures. Not only the First Amendment, but also the very idea of a principle of freedom of speech, is an embodiment of a risk-averse distrust of decisionmakers." Schauer adds that "once we understand this, we are able to understand as well that the First Amendment is not the reflection of a society's highest aspirations, but rather of its fears, being simultaneously the pessimistic and necessary manifestation of the fact that, in practice, neither a population nor its authoritative decisionmakers can even approach their society's most ideal theoretical aspirations."[183]

It is unlikely that progressives who express First Amendment skepticism in several important policy contexts—from corporate free speech rights, to the application of LGBTQ anti-discrimination laws, to the regulation of hate speech—will fall for romanticized or idealized notions of the First Amendment as an embodiment of the nation's highest principles and aspirations. After all, these progressives have strongly opposed, as they see it, efforts by conservative leaders, judges, and activists to weaponize the amendment by deploying it as an anti-egalitarian tool. At the same time, however, the Trump years made progressives keenly and painfully aware of how an autocratic and pathological (to use Blasi's term) government can threaten democratic institutions and values, as well as vulnerable minorities. This awareness should make strong and robust First Amendment protections highly relevant to progressive movements and causes going forward.

I have argued throughout this book that progressives should systematically think about constitutional principles and values in ways that will most effectively help prevent abuses of power by future autocratic leaders in the Trump mold. After all of the vitriolic and hateful speech engaged in by both Trump and many of his most loyal supporters, some progressives may reasonably believe that hate speech regulations are even more necessary, going forward, than they were before Trump was elected to office. But the ways in which Trump governed also raise troubling questions about how those regulations might be implemented and enforced by right-wing government officials. Although, again, my objective here is not to try to answer definitively whether or how to regulate hate speech, progressives need to think carefully about what might happen if hate speech regulations were to fall, so to speak, in the wrong hands.

One of the crucial lessons that emanated from the Trump era is how attacks on free speech rights by government officials, especially the president of the United States, can be a powerful means of political and social suppression. Trump repeatedly deployed or threatened to deploy federal government authority to suppress speech that (1) questioned or criticized his administration, (2) fulfilled the media's professional and social responsibilities, or (3) expressed left-of-center viewpoints and perspectives. The arguments made by many progressives about the need to incorporate egalitarian considerations into First Amendment doctrine are, in my view, generally powerful and persuasive.[184] But in pushing to make the First Amendment a more egalitarian constitutional provision, progressives should not lose sight of the fact that giving government officials the power to regulate expression is a potentially dangerous step even when done with the best of intentions, including, for example, to protect vulnerable minorities from hatred or to allow less well-funded voices to be heard during electoral campaigns. As suggested by Blasi's pathological perspective on the First Amendment, hate speech laws and other forms of speech regulations that grant government officials the power to prohibit certain forms of expression need to be considered partly in light of how they may be enforced in the worst of times.

In a provocative and thoughtful essay titled "Can Free Speech Be Progressive?," law professor Louis Seidman claims that free speech protections, as reflected in contemporary First Amendment principles and doctrine, are intrinsically incompatible with progressives' political objectives. According to Seidman, there is an irreconcilable conflict between the regulatory and redistributive policies that progressives demand and the libertarian free speech principles and doctrine, strongly defended by contemporary courts, that are both skeptical of government intervention and protective of existing patterns of property and wealth distributions. Seidman also argues that current free speech law, with its purported emphasis on promoting as much expression as possible, is incapable of coping with the serious contemporary problem, fueled by the internet and social media, of "too much speech." The fact that anyone with an internet connection can say anything to anyone about anyone at any time, Seidman compellingly argues, gives control and influence, as a practical matter, not to speakers but to the powerful for-profit corporations, such as Facebook and Google, that aggregate the speech of others.[185]

Although Seidman raises vital questions about how First Amendment doctrine and priorities mesh with progressive objectives, I am less pessimistic than he is about the value of free speech protections, as understood and applied in the United States, to progressive causes. In fact, I have written another book about how the LGBTQ rights movement, in the decades following Stonewall, was able to use First Amendment rights of free speech and association—at a time when sexual minorities enjoyed no legally recognized rights to either equality or privacy—to better understand their sexuality, to find each other and form identity-based bonds, to highlight and criticize discriminatory government policies and social norms, and to organize politically in order to provide LGBTQ people with many of the legal rights and protections long available to heterosexuals and cisgender individuals. To put it simply, for LGBTQ Americans, free speech came first, and equality second.[186]

But regardless of whether Seidman's pessimism about the value of the First Amendment to progressives is warranted, even he concedes that it can protect progressives "against the possibility of catastrophic outcomes" and "the total annihilation of progressivism."[187] Seidman does not define either "catastrophic outcomes" or "total annihilation," but it seems to me that both phrases accurately describe what *would have happened to progressive movements and causes* had the First Amendment not served as an explicit and implicit restraint on Trump's ability, as president of the United States, to target, silence, intimidate, and harass political opponents, critics, and the press. Preventing those outcomes was of the highest importance to progressives and, more fundamentally, to the very survival of democracy and its institutions during the Trump years. In my view, this powerfully confirms that the First Amendment should matter a great deal to progressives.

Going forward, progressives should continue to challenge and dispute some of the ways in which current First Amendment doctrine insufficiently accounts for equality-based interests behind, for example, (1) protecting vulnerable minorities from discrimination and harm; (2) regulating the economic marketplace to minimize the instability, disruptions, and harms caused by unfettered capitalism; and (3) redistributing wealth and income to reduce social and economic inequality. But there are certain core principles embedded in First Amendment doctrine, such as prohibiting the government from regulating speech differently based on the viewpoints expressed and from retaliating against those who engage in protected speech, that progressives, with the Trump era in mind, should strongly value and support.

The Trump years showed progressives why they should not give up on the First Amendment, even when it can be reasonably argued that the Supreme Court is generally interpreting free speech protections in ways that advance the interests of the powerful and the wealthy over the poor and marginalized. As I have noted, my point is not that the First Amendment worked perfectly in restraining Trump's abuses of power. But the First Amendment was nonetheless of considerable assistance to progressives in resisting and opposing Trump and his misguided, harmful, and discriminatory policies. Contemporary First Amendment doctrine, even with all of its flaws and limitations, proved crucial to progressives during the Trump years because, to put it succinctly, it helped keep an autocratic right-wing president from governing like a dictatorial one.

Epilogue

The summer of 2020 was a harrowing time for the nation in general and for progressives in particular. The Trump administration's incompetent response to the coronavirus epidemic helped fuel a frightening spike in new cases, especially in the South and the West. The administration's promotion of militarized and violent responses to peaceful Black Lives Matter protests led to repeated confrontations between citizens and federal law enforcement troops in Washington, D.C., and Portland, Oregon. Trump, who was consistently behind in the election polls, further sowed chaos and fear by baselessly claiming that states controlled by Democrats were turning to voting-by-mail procedures to steal the election. While otherwise seeking to minimize the virus's impact, Trump also suggested that the presidential election might have to be suspended due to the epidemic. Furthermore, the president refused to commit to accepting the election's results, reserving for himself the right to determine whether the election was fair.[1]

As if all of this were not troubling enough, progressives were also anxious about what the Supreme Court, now firmly in control of conservative justices following Trump's appointment of Neil Gorsuch and Brett Kavanaugh, might do. (Trump's appointment of a third justice, Amy Coney Barrett, following the death of Ruth Bader Ginsburg, did not occur until several months later.) As a presidential candidate in 2016, Trump had made clear that appointing judges committed to pursuing a conservative political agenda was a top priority. As president, Trump consistently derided the notion of judicial independence while making it clear that he expected loyalty from his judicial appointees.[2] Progressives were therefore understandably concerned, as the end of the Supreme Court's 2019–2020 term approached, that a conservative-dominated Court would rule, for example, that a sitting president could not be investigated by state officials for alleged criminal conduct engaged in before elected to office, that Title VII of the Civil Rights Act of 1964 did not protect LGBTQ people from employment discrimination, and that Louisiana could enact an abortion law that would close all but one abortion clinic in the state.

In the end, however, the conservative-dominated Court in 2020 did none of those things. Instead, the Court relied on the principle that the president is not above the law to allow the Manhattan District Attorney's Office to continue its criminal investigation of Trump and his businesses.[3] It also relied on the

Principles Matter. Carlos A. Ball, Oxford University Press. © Carlos A. Ball 2021.
DOI: 10.1093/oso/9780197584484.003.0007

textualist principle that the meaning of a statute's words should control its interpretation to hold that Title VII's prohibition of discrimination "because of sex" protected LGBTQ people from employment discrimination.[4] And the Court relied on the principle of *stare decisis*, which presumes that precedents should control the outcomes of similar disputes, to strike down the Louisiana abortion law four years after it had done the same to a nearly identical Texas law.[5]

Progressives celebrated all of these outcomes and generally praised the Court for sticking to principles. Of course, it is relatively easy to support principled judicial decision-making when it leads to preferred political or policy results. It is much more difficult to stick to principles when their application leads to disfavored outcomes; it is those situations that require the making of the frequently tough choice between abiding by principles and pushing for preferred results.

I have argued in this book that progressives, in the long run, have more to gain than to lose by generally defending and supporting constitutional principles associated with federalism, separation of powers, and free speech. In those difficult instances when principles and preferred policy outcomes are in tension, I suggest that progressives follow this rule of thumb: if a constitutional principle was worth deploying to resist Trump's harmful policies and autocratic governance, then the principle is likely worth defending in the post-Trump era even if it makes the short-term attainment of progressive objectives more difficult. This is because, as I have argued in this book, progressive causes and movements, over the *long run*, are more likely to gain than to lose from the application of that principle.

Examples of principles worth defending, and rendered highly salient to progressives by the Trump era, include the federalist anti-commandeering principle that prohibits the federal government from mandating that states assist in the pursuit of federal objectives and in the enforcement of federal laws; the separation-of-powers principle that prohibits the president from using federal money for projects and programs that Congress has refused to fund; and the separation-of-powers principle that the executive branch cannot set conditions on recipients of federal funds that Congress has not authorized. If these principles were worth defending while Trump was in office, then they are likely worth defending going forward regardless of the ideology or character of any given president.

It bears emphasizing that all of these principles are substantively neutral, by which I mean that they restrict the authority of the federal government's executive branch regardless of any given administration's substantive policy preferences. For example, the anti-commandeering doctrine applies equally regardless of whether the federal government is seeking to strictly enforce gun safety regulations or immigration laws. And the principle that a president cannot spend federal dollars for projects that Congress has refused to authorize applies regardless of whether the president wants to use the money to build a wall along the Mexico-U.S. border or to house the homeless.

It will be tempting, following Biden's defeat of Trump, for progressives to try to put the traumatic and harrowing Trump years behind them by worrying and fretting less about the implications of his policies and of how he governed. A strong sense of relief that the democracy seemed to have survived Trump may lead some progressives and others to try to minimize or forget the threats that his presidency presented to democratic institutions, the nation's welfare, and traditionally vulnerable minorities. But progressives should keep in mind that, as Susan Hennessey and Benjamin Wittes wrote before the 2020 election, "in an atmosphere of intense polarization, in which hating and defeating the other side is the only virtue, it seems reasonable to expect that even in failure, aspects of [Trump's] experiment will influence future presidents. And it seems imprudent to bet against some enterprising politician attempting a more sophisticated Version 2.0 of the entire undertaking."[6] That enterprising politician may even be Trump himself, given that he will be eligible to run for another presidential term and that the Senate failed to convict him following his second impeachment.

Progressives must be prepared for the possibility of a future president in the Trump mold by continuing to defend the constitutional principles that they endorsed and championed during the Trump era. Those principles consist of not only the ones that progressives have valued for decades, including those related to equality, privacy, and the fundamental right to vote, but also the structural constitutional principles that progressives had generally ignored or underemphasized before the Trump presidency, but which became crucial to them in resisting it.

It will also be tempting for progressives to dispense with concerns about expansive presidential powers when there is a liberal in the White House. Indeed, the day after Biden became president, law professor Eric Posner, a defender of robust presidential powers, wrote an op-ed in *The New York Times* urging progressives to support a strong presidency on the ground that Democrats benefit more often from the exercise of unilateral presidential authority than Republicans.[7] But, as I have argued in this book, progressives should weigh the benefits of short-term policy gains that may be attained through the exercise of unilateral presidential power against both the likelihood that the gains will be fleeting due to changes in who controls the presidency and the danger that a future president in the Trump mold will unilaterally exert presidential powers in ways that fundamentally challenge both democratic and progressive values and objectives. This does not mean that all unilateral exercise of presidential power is necessarily problematic; but it does mean that such exercise should be carried out prudently and carefully, with an eye on how similar claims of unilateral power may be abused by future autocratic and irresponsible presidents.

Going forward, progressives should make the placing of reasonable limits on presidential power in domestic matters one of their political and policy priorities. Realistically, progressives will be significantly more likely to succeed in pushing for those limits when there is an amenable Democrat in the White House. Indeed, the combination of an amenable Democratic president and Republican control of one or both of Congress's chambers may be particularly conducive to placing reasonable limits on presidential authority, in part, because congressional Republicans will be substantially more willing to support limits on presidential powers when there is a Democrat, rather than one of their own, in the White House.

At the same time, progressives will undoubtedly continue to push for the attainment of progressive policy objectives, such as addressing systemic racism, reducing social and economic inequality, and promoting reproductive freedoms. Progressive drives in these policy areas are particularly likely when the chances of success are higher, which at the federal level means when Democrats control both the presidency and Congress. There is nothing problematic, of course, about progressives emphasizing progressive policy objectives, but it should be done while respecting the structural constitutional principles and robust free speech protections that proved to be so crucial to progressives in resisting the Trump administration. Progressives need to consider not only which substantive policies they should demand of Democrats when they control the federal government's political branches, but also how best to enact and implement measures aimed at protecting democratic institutions and traditionally vulnerable minorities when those branches fall into the hands of individuals who are ideologically opposed to progressive values and objectives.

There is a relatively recent precedent for this type of dual approach. After the 1976 federal elections that followed Richard Nixon's resignation, Democrats gained control of the presidency to go along with their majorities in both houses of Congress. In the years that followed, a Democratic Congress passed, and President Jimmy Carter signed, several laws, including the Ethics in Government Act and the Inspector General Act, intended to limit presidential and executive branch power grabs. Although those reforms, as explored in Chapter 4, proved generally ineffective in constraining Trump's relentless abuses of power, they demonstrate that it is possible to impose reasonable limits on presidential power even when one party controls both the presidency and Congress. In other words, instituting structural reforms that limit presidential powers is possible even when they first constrain the authority of a president who is of the same party as the majorities in Congress. To their immense credit, it was primarily progressives, supported by moderate conservatives and government reformers, who pushed for the post-Watergate government reforms. In the post-Trump years, it should also be progressives who are in the vanguard of efforts to institute and implement structural mechanisms and reforms that will make it more difficult for future presidents, regardless of their political ideology or policy priorities, to abuse the powers of their office in the ways that Trump repeatedly did.

The temptation to "move on" from Trump may also spring from the fact that, as harmful as his governance was for democratic institutions, the nation's welfare, progressive values, and traditionally subordinated minorities, that governance, as is almost always the case, could have been even more dangerous and more autocratic. Similarly, it may be tempting to point to Trump's seeming incompetency in attaining some of his policy objectives to minimize the extent to which he constituted a threat to the nation and its democratic values. But even if Trump's incompetency to some extent blunted the impact of his abuses of power, we may not be so "lucky" the next time around—the only thing more frightening than a seemingly incompetent autocrat is an actually competent one.

Acknowledgments

This project, especially the separation-of-powers materials, benefited from many informal conversations through the years with my Rutgers colleague and *tocayo* Carlos Gonzalez, often as we were getting ready to go teach our respective constitutional law classes. I thank him for his suggestions and support, including at a pre-COVID-19 lunch in which he helped me figure out what I wanted to say about presidential powers. Chapter 5 benefited from insightful comments and suggestions from Tim Zick, while Steve Gold methodically and thoughtfully gave me feedback on Chapter 2. Thank you as well to the Oxford University Press's anonymous peer reviewers for their suggestions on how best to frame the project, including which topics not to tackle. I also thank my editors Jamie Berezin and David Lipp.

Thanks as well to Rutgers Law School and its Co-Dean David Lopez for their support. A research fund generously financed by former Rutgers Law School Dean Peter Simmons helped with some of the research costs associated with this project. Ruby Kish provided crucial research assistance in the writing of Chapter 2.

I presented sections of this book at faculty workshops at Penn State Law School, Rutgers Law School, Seton Hall Law School, and the University of Illinois College of Law. Thank you to the more than one hundred professors and others who attended the workshops and for the many generous comments and suggestions on how to improve the manuscript.

I began working on this project in the summer of 2019, more than halfway through the Trump presidency. One reason for writing the book was to attempt to do something productive in the face of the Trump administration's almost daily abuses of government power and democratic institutions, as well as its repeated threats to the well-being of immigrants, people of color, and other vulnerable minorities. But immersing myself in the details and implications of those abuses and threats was sometimes emotionally challenging and draining. I would not have been able to complete the book without the unceasing love and support of my husband Richard, my daughter Ema, and my son Sebastian. I also benefited immensely from the years-long friendships of the individuals to whom this book is dedicated. The joy, laughter, and companionship that they bring to my life were fortifying in and essential to the writing of this book.

Notes

Introduction

1. Nick Corasaniti, "Democrats in New Jersey Have a Firm Grip on Power. They Want Even More," *New York Times*, December 13, 2018; Editorial, "New Jersey Democrats Play Power Games Too," *New York Times*, December 14, 2018; "New Jersey's Redistricting Reform Legislation (S.C.R. 43/A.C.R. 205): Republican Gerrymanders, Democratic Gerrymanders, and Possible Fixes," Princeton Gerrymandering Project, December 5, 2018, https://election.princeton.edu/wp-content/uploads/2018/12/Princeton-Gerrymandering-Project-Analysis-of-S.C.R.-43-A.C.R.-205-5-December-2018-1.pdf.
2. For an analysis of partisan gerrymandering, see Laura Royden & Michael Li, *Extreme Maps* (Brennan Center for Justice, 2017).
3. Rucho v. Common Cause, 139 S. Ct. 2484 (2019); Gill v. Whitford, 138 S. Ct. 1916 (2018).
4. Mark Stern, "The 2018 Election Was a Body Blow to Partisan Gerrymandering," *Slate*, November 7, 2018; Steve Harrison, "With Focus on Redistricting, Democrats Place New Emphasis on Statehouses," *NPR*, August 7, 2020.
5. Kevin Drum, "Three Cheers for New Jersey's Appalling Gerrymandering Law," *Mother Jones*, December 13, 2018.
6. Colleen O'Dea, "Dems' Decision to Push Ahead with Redistricting Bill Has Blue Base Fighting Mad," *NJSpotlight*, December 6, 2018; Mark Stern, "How Progressive Activists Killed New Jersey Democrats' Gerrymandering Scheme," *Slate*, December 17, 2018; Nick Corasaniti, "After Backlash, Democrats in New Jersey Rethink Redistricting Plans," *New York Times*, December 16, 2018.
7. I borrow the term "situational constitutionalism" from J. Richard Piper, "Situational Constitutionalism and Presidential Power: The Rise and Fall of the Liberal Model of Presidential Government," *Presidential Studies Quarterly*, vol. 24 (1994), pp. 577–596.
8. Sanford Levinson, *Our Undemocratic Constitution: Where the Constitution Goes Wrong* (New York: Oxford University Press, 2006).
9. Lisa Miller, "Amending Constitutional Myths," *Drake Law Review*, vol. 67 (2018), pp. 947, 955. Mark Graber defends a similar claim in "Social Democracy and Constitutional Theory: An Institutional Perspective," *Fordham Law Review*, vol. 69 (2001), p. 1969.
10. I return to this issue in Chapter 2.
11. I return to these issues in Chapters 2 and 3.

12. Jacob Hacker & Paul Pierson, *Let Them Eat Tweets: How the Right Rules in an Age of Extreme Inequality* (New York: Liveright, 2020); Stuart Stevens, *It Was All a Lie: How the Republican Party Became Donald Trump* (New York: Knopf, 2020).

13. The Constitution's Preamble reads as follows: "We the people of the United States, in order to form a more perfect union, establish justice, insure domestic tranquility, provide for the common defence, promote the general welfare, and secure the blessings of liberty to ourselves and our posterity, do ordain and establish this Constitution for the United States of America."

14. Lawrence Lessig, *They Don't Represent Us: Reclaiming Our Democracy* (New York: Dey Street Books, 2019); Levinson, *Our Undemocratic Constitution*. See also Chris Edelson, "How to Keep the Republic (Before It's Too Late): Why a New Constitution Is Necessary to Strengthen Liberal Democracy in the United States," in *Presidential Leadership and the Trump Presidency: Executive Power and Democratic Government*, p. 121. Charles Lamb & Jacob Neiheisel, eds. (New York: Palgrave, 2019).

15. There is an extensive literature on recent autocratic governance. See, for example, Anne Applebaum, *Twilight of Democracy: The Seductive Lure of Authoritarianism* (New York: Doubleday, 2020); Steven Levitsky & Daniel Ziblatt, *How Democracy Dies* (Crown: New York, 2018).

Chapter 1

1. Garcia v. San Antonio Metropolitan Transit Authority, 469 U.S. 528 (1985); United States v. Darby, 312 U.S. 100 (1941).

2. This chapter focuses on the distribution and sharing of power between the federal and state governments. There is, of course, a third level of government of immense importance: local government. I cannot in this book address local government issues. There is an extensive literature on the power, benefits, and accomplishments of progressive localism. See, for example, Richard Schragger, *City Power: Urban Governance in a Global Age* (New York: Oxford University Press, 2016).

3. Some scholars have argued that federalism has much to offer progressives. A leading scholar of progressive federalism is Heather Gerken. For some of her articles on the topic, see "Federalism 3.0," *California Law Review*, vol. 105 (2017), p. 1695; "A New Progressive Federalism," *Democracy*, Spring (2012), available at https://democracyjournal.org/magazine/24/a-new-progressive-federalism/. See also Burt Neuborne, *When at Times the Mob Is Swayed: A Citizen's Guide to Defending our Republic* (New York: New Press, 2019), ch. 9; Ernest Young, "Welcome to the Dark Side: Liberals Rediscover Federalism in the Wake of the War on Terror," *Brooklyn Law Review*, vol. 69 (2004), p. 1277.

4. New State Ice Co. v. Liebmann, 285 U.S. 262, 311 (1932) (Brandeis, J., dissenting). The taxonomy of arguments in favor of federalism is derived from Erwin Chemerinsky, *Constitutional Law: Principles and Policies* (New York: Wolters Kluwer, 6th edition, 2019), pp. 336–339.

5. Gregory v. Ashcroft, 501 U.S. 452, 458 (1991).

6. C. Vann Woodward, *The Strange Career of Jim Crow* (New York: Oxford University Press, 1974); Paul Lombardo, *Three Generations, No Imbeciles: Eugenics, the Supreme Court, and* Buck v. Bell (Baltimore: Johns Hopkins University Press, 2008).

7. Nancy Knauer, "The COVID-19 Pandemic and Federalism: Who Decides?," *N.Y.U. Journal of Legislation and Public Policy*, vol. 23 (2021), p. 1.

8. Akhil Reed Amar, *America's Constitution: A Biography* (New York: Random House, 2005), p. 250.

9. Amar, *America's Constitution*, pp. 25–26; Article III, Articles of Confederation (1781).

10. George Van Cleve, *We Have Not a Government: The Articles of Confederation and the Road to the Constitution* (Chicago: University of Chicago Press, 2017), p. 285.

11. See, for example, Amar, *America's Constitution*; Michael Klarman, *The Framers' Coup: The Making of the United States Constitution* (New York: Oxford University Press, 2016).

12. It was not until the twentieth century that the U.S. Supreme Court began applying the Bill of Rights to the states through its interpretation of the Fourteenth Amendment's Due Process Clause, a process known as "incorporation." Chemerinsky, *Constitutional Law*, pp. 545–551.

13. Tenth Amendment, U.S. Constitution.

14. Eric Foner, *The Second Founding: How the Civil War and Reconstruction Remade the Constitution* (New York: W.W. Norton & Co., 2019), p. 2.

15. Sean Wilentz, *No Property in Man: Slavery and Antislavery at the Nation's Founding* (Cambridge, MA: Harvard University Press, 2018), pp. 25–41; Arthur Zilversmit, *The First Emancipation: The Abolition of Slavery in the North* (Chicago: Chicago University Press, 1967).

16. Matthew Desmond, "In Order to Understand the Brutality of American Capitalism, You Have to Start on the Plantation," *New York Times Magazine*, August 18, 2019, p. 32.

17. Edward Baptiste, *The Half Has Never Been Told: Slavery and the Making of American Capitalism* (New York: Basic Books, 2014).

18. Andrew Delbanco, *The War Before the War: Fugitive Slaves and the Struggle for America's Soul from the Revolution to the Civil War* (New York: Penguin Press, 2018).

19. Delbanco, *The War Before the War*, p. 169.

20. The most detailed analysis of Personal Liberty Laws remains Thomas Morris, *Free Men for All: The Personal Liberty Laws of the North, 1780–1861* (Baltimore: Johns Hopkins University Press, 1974). See also H. Robert Baker, Prigg v. Pennsylvania: *Slavery, the Supreme Court, and the Ambivalent Constitution* (Lawrence: University Press of Kansas, 2012), ch. 4.

21. Paul Finkelman, "Story Telling on the Supreme Court: *Prigg v. Pennsylvania* and Justice Joseph Story's Judicial Nationalism," *Supreme Court Review*, vol. 1994 (1994), pp. 247, 250.

22. Baker, *Prigg v. Pennsylvania*, pp. 102–104.

23. For an explanation of why Margaret Morgan may have been a free resident of Pennsylvania, and perhaps even free under Maryland law, see Baker, *Prigg v. Pennsylvania*, pp. 104–108. See also Paul Finkelman, *Supreme Injustice: Slavery in the Nation's Court* (Cambridge, MA: Harvard University Press, 2018), pp. 158–160.

24. Baker, *Prigg v. Pennsylvania*, pp. 112–113.

25. Finkelman, *Supreme Injustice*, p. 141.

26. Baker, *Prigg v. Pennsylvania*, ch. 7.

27. Prigg v. Pennsylvania, 41 U.S. 539 (1842).

28. For a summary of Story's antislavery views before *Prigg*, see Finkelman, *Supreme Injustice*, pp. 112–130. On Story's strong views about the pre-eminence of the federal government over the states, see Finkelman, *Story Telling on the Supreme Court*.

29. *Prigg*, 41 U.S. at 623.

30. *Prigg*, 41 U.S. at 624.

31. Finkelman, *Supreme Injustice*, pp. 164, 170.

32. *Prigg*, 41 U.S. at 615–616.

33. Paul Finkelman, "Sorting out *Prigg v. Pennsylvania*," *Rutgers Law Journal*, vol. 24 (1993), p. 646, n. 208.

34. Finkelman, *Story Telling on the Supreme Court*, p. 288.

35. Delbanco, *The War Before the War*, pp. 181–182. On the second generation of Personal Liberty Laws, see Sandra Rierson, "Fugitive Slaves and Undocumented Immigrants: Testing the Boundaries of Our Federalism," *University of Miami Law Review*, vol. 74 (2020), pp. 598, 627–630.

36. Paul Finkelman, "States' Rights, Southern Hypocrisy, and the Crisis of the Union," *Akron Law Review*, vol. 45 (2012), pp. 449, 454.

37. Finkelman, *States' Rights*, p. 455. See also Commonwealth v. Aves, 35 Mass. 193 (1836).

38. Finkelman, *States' Rights*, p. 472.

39. Scott v. Sandford, 60 U.S. 393 (1857).

40. Wilentz, *No Property in Man*, p. 249.

41. Jeffrey Schmitt, "Courts, Backlash, and Social Change: Learning from the History of *Prigg v. Pennsylvania*," *Penn State Law Review*, vol. 123 (2018), pp. 103, 133.

42. Finkelman, *States' Rights*, p. 458.

43. Rierson, *Fugitive Slaves and Undocumented Immigrants*, pp. 632–635.

44. For a discussion of Personal Liberty Laws enacted by northern states following the Fugitive Slave Act of 1850 and the Kansas-Nebraska Act of 1854, see Rierson, *Fugitive Slaves and Undocumented Immigrants*, pp. 638–642. It bears noting that some northern states moved in the opposite direction by attempting to *exclude* free African Americans. For example, "by 1851 whites in Indiana and Illinois created new state constitutions and passed laws completely barring any further free African-Americans from entering the states." Anna-Lisa Cox, "Black Pioneers Not Welcome Here," *New York Times*, September 22, 2019.

45. Delbanco, *The War Before the War*, p. 345.

46. Ableman v. Booth, 62 U.S. 506 (1858).

47. Ex Parte Bushnell, 9 Ohio St. 77 (1859).

48. Baker, *Prigg v. Pennsylvania*, p. 170.

49. Finkelman, *States' Rights*, p. 452.

50. Finkelman, *States' Rights*, p. 471.

51. For skepticism of the idea that Story intended *Prigg* to be an anti-slavery opinion, see, for example, Don Fehrenbacher, *The Slaveholding Republic: An Account of the United States Government's Relations to Slavery* (New York: Oxford University Press, 2001), pp. 220–221. For the possibility that Story believed that *Prigg* would have significant anti-slavery implications, see, for example, Leslie Friedman Goldstein, "A 'Triumph of Freedom' After All? *Prigg v. Pennsylvania* Re-Examined," *Law and History Review*, vol. 29 (2011), pp. 763, 766–768.

52. Printz v. United States, 521 U.S. 898 (1997). See also New York v. United States, 505 U.S. 144 (1992).

53. *Printz*, 521 U.S. at 939 (Stevens, J., dissenting). It is worth noting that the dissent's rejection of the anti-commandeering principle did not go so far as to suggest that Congress could require state *legislatures* to legislate in certain ways. See also Murphy v. National Collegiate Athletic Association, 138 S. Ct. 1461 (2018).

54. *Declaration of the Immediate Causes Which Induce and Justify the Secession of South Carolina from the Federal Union* (Charleston, SC, 1860).

55. Amar, *America's Constitution*, pp. 35–36.

56. Eric Foner, *Reconstruction: America's Unfinished Revolution, 1863–1877* (New York: Harper & Row, 1988), pp. 142–153, 158–162.

57. Foner, *The Second Founding*, p. 17.

58. Foner, *Reconstruction*, p. 250.

59. Foner, *Reconstruction*, p. 251.

60. Foner, *Reconstruction*, pp. 425–444.

61. Foner, *Reconstruction*, p. 456 (quoting Lyman Trumbull, Republican Senator from Illinois).

62. On the legislative history of the Civil Rights Act of 1975, including the question of whether it should apply to public schools, see Michael McConnell, "Originalism and the Desegregation Decisions," 81 *Virginia Law Review*, vol. 81 (1995), pp. 947, 984–1049.

63. Foner, *Reconstruction*, pp. 581–582.

64. The Civil Rights Cases, 109 U.S. 3, 11, 15, 19 (1883). See also U.S. v. Cruikshank. 92 U.S. 542 (1876).

65. The Slaughterhouse Cases, 83 U.S. 36, 74–80 (1872).

66. Woodward, *The Strange Career of Jim Crow*, p. 6. See also Henry Louis Gates Jr., *Stony the Road: Reconstruction, White Supremacy, and the Rise of Jim Crow* (New York: Penguin Press, 2019).

67. Plessy v. Ferguson, 163 U.S. 537 (1896).

68. Steven Levitsky & Daniel Ziblatt, "Why Republicans Play Dirty," *New York Times*, September 21, 2019.

69. Vann Woodward, *The Strange Career of Jim Crow*, p. 85.

70. Shelby County v. Holder, 570 U.S. 529 (2013).

71. Foner, *Reconstruction*, p. 586.

72. See, for example, Lochner v. New York, 198 U.S. 45 (1905) (maximum work hours); Morehead v. New York, 298 U.S. 587 (1936) (minimum wage); Weaver v. Palmer Brothers Co., 270 U.S. 402 (1926) (consumer protection).

73. See, for example, Carter v. Carter Coal Co., 298 U.S. 238 (1936) (wages and hours protections); Hammer v. Dagenhart, 247 U.S. 251 (1918) (child labor).

74. *Hammer*, 247 U.S. at 533.

75. Erwin Chemerinsky, *We the People: A Progressive Reading of the Constitution for the Twenty-First Century* (New York: Picador, 2018), p. 113.

76. Carter v. Carter Coal Co., 298 U.S. 238 (1936).

77. Railroad Retirement Board v. Alton R.R. Co., 295 U.S. 330 (1935); A.L.A. Schecter Poultry Corporation v. United States, 295 U.S. 495 (1935); United States v. Butler, 297 U.S. 1 (1936).

78. See, for example, NLRB v. Jones & Laughlin Steel Corp., 301 U.S. 1 (1937) (protecting collective bargaining); United States v. Darby, 312 U.S. 100 (1941) (wages and hours regulations); Wickard v. Filburn, 317 U.S. 111 (1942) (agricultural prices support).

79. United States v. Lopez, 314 U.S. 549 (1995).

80. Michael Schulyer, "A Short History of Government Taxing and Spending in the United States" (Tax Foundation, February 19, 2014).

81. Jeneen Interlandi, "Why Doesn't the United States Have Universal Healthcare? The Answer Begins with Policies Enacted After the Civil War," *New York Times Magazine*, August 18, 2019, p. 45.

82. Interlandi, "Why Doesn't the United States Have Universal Healthcare?"

83. Brown v. Board of Education, 347 U.S. 483 (1954).

84. Richard Kluger, *Simple Justice: The History of* Brown v. Board of Education *and Black America's Struggle for Equality* (New York: Vintage, 2004), p. 717.

85. *Race Relations Law Reporter*, vol. 1 (1956), p. 239.

86. *Race Relations Law Reporter*, vol. 1 (1956), p. 116. The legislatures of six other southern states—Alabama, Florida, Louisiana, Mississippi, South Carolina, and Virginia—issued similar "interposition and nullification" resolutions.

87. *Race Relations Law Reporter*, vol. 1 (1956), p. 418.

88. Harvie Wilkinson, *From* Brown *to* Bakke: *The Supreme Court and School Integration, 1954–1978* (New York: Oxford University Press, 1979), pp. 82–83; Griffin v. County School Board, 377 U.S. 218 (1964).

89. James Patterson, Brown v. Board of Education: *A Civil Rights Milestone and its Troubled Legacy* (New York: Oxford University Press, 2001), pp. 100–101; Green v. County School Board, 391 U.S. 430 (1968).

90. On pupil placement laws, adopted by every southern state, see Michael Klarman, *From Jim Crow to Civil Rights: The Supreme Court and The Struggle for Racial Equality* (New York: Oxford University Press, 2004), pp. 329–331; 358–359.

91. Patterson, *Brown v. Board of Education*, p. 108.

92. Shuttlesworth v. Birmingham Board of Education, 358 U.S. 101 (1958); Kelley v. Board of Education of Nashville, 270 F.2d 209 (6th Cir.), affirmed by 361 U.S. 924 (1959).

93. Klarman, *From Jim Crow to Civil Rights*, pp. 324–325; Patterson, *Brown v. Board of Education*, pp. 80–82.

94. On the Manifesto, see Kyle John Day, *The Southern Manifesto: Massive Resistance and the Fight to Preserve Segregation* (Jackson: University Press of Mississippi, 2015).

95. Patterson, *Brown v. Board of Education*, p. 113.

96. Carlos A. Ball, *The First Amendment and LGBT Equality: A Contentious History* (Cambridge, MA: Harvard University Press, 2017), pp. 169–174.

97. Civil Rights Act of 1964, S. Rep. 88–872, 88th Cong., 2d Sess. (1964), p. 79.

98. Equal Employment Opportunity Act of 1963, 88th Cong., 1st Sess. (1963) (views of Representatives David Martin and Paul Findley), p. 20.

99. Civil Rights Act of 1964, H.R. Rep. 88–914, 88th Cong., 2d Sess. (1964) (minority report).

100. William Riker, *Federalism: Origin, Operation, Significance* (Boston: Little Brown, 1964), pp. 140, 155.

101. Edward Rubin & Malcolm Feeley, "Federalism: Some Notes on a National Neurosis," *UCLA Law Review*, vol. 41 (1994), pp. 903, 909.

102. Shelby County v. Holder, 570 U.S. 529 (2013); Austin Graham, "Unstable Footing: *Shelby County*'s Misapplication of the Equal Footing Doctrine," *William & Mary Bill of Rights Journal*, vol. 23 (2014), p. 301.

103. See, for example, Allan Lichtman, *The Embattled Vote in America* (Cambridge, MA: Harvard University Press, 2018), pp. 197–215; Andrew Cockburn, "Election Bias: The New Playbook for Voter Suppression," *Harper's Magazine*, January, 2020, p. 69.

104. For other examples of federal policies that further entrenched discrimination, injustice, and inequality, see Richard Rothstein, *The Color of Law: A Forgotten History of How Our Government Segregated America* (New York: Liveright, 2017); Vann R. Newkirk II, "This Land Was Our Land: How Nearly 1 Million Black Farmers Were Robbed of Their Livelihood," *The Atlantic*, September 2019, p. 74.

105. Baehr v. Lewin, 852 P.2d 44 (Haw. 1993). For an account of the background and aftermath of the Hawaii same-sex marriage lawsuit, see Carlos A. Ball, *From the Closet to the Courtroom: Five LGBT Rights Lawsuits that Have Changed Our Nation* (Boston: Beacon Press, 2010), ch. 4.

106. Goodridge v. Department of Public Health, 798 N.E.2d 941 (Mass. 2003); In re Marriage Cases, 43 Cal. 4th 757 (Cal. 2008); Kerrigan v. Commissioner of Pub. Health, 957 A.2d 407 (Conn. 2008); Varnum v. Brien, 763 N.W.2d 862 (Iowa 2009).

107. Ball, *The First Amendment and LGBT Equality*, pp. 235–238.

108. William Eskridge Jr. & Christopher Riano, *Marriage Equality: From Outlaws to In-Laws* (New Haven, CT: Yale University Press, 2020).

109. For the role that child-based arguments played in legal and policy debates over same-sex marriage, see Carlos A. Ball, *Same-Sex Marriage and Children: A Tale of History, Social Science, and Law* (New York: Oxford University Press, 2014).

110. Ernest Young, "Exit, Voice, and Loyalty as Federalism Strategies: Lessons from the Same-Sex Marriage Debate," *University of Colorado Law Review*, vol. 85 (2014), p. 1133.

111. United States v. Windsor, 570 U.S. 744 (2013); Obergefell v. Hodges, 576 U.S. 644 (2015).

112. Heather K. Gerken, "*Windsor*'s Mad Genius: The Interlocking Gears of Rights and Structure," *Boston University Law Review*, vol. 95 (2015), pp. 587, 597–598.

113. A handful of liberal municipalities in the 1970s, including West Hollywood, California, and Madison, Wisconsin, were the first jurisdictions in the United States to adopt laws prohibiting discrimination on the basis of sexual orientation.

114. Bostock v. Clayton County, 140 S. Ct. 1731 (2020); Kerith Conron & Shoshana Goldberg, "LGBT People in the U.S. Not Protected by State Non-Discrimination Statutes" (Williams Institute, April 2020).

115. Nancy Knauer, "LGBT Equality Gap and Federalism," *American University Law Review*, vol. 70 (2020), p. 1.

116. Carlos A. Ball, *The Queering of Corporate America: How Big Business Went from LGBTQ Adversary to Ally* (Boston: Beacon Press, 2019).

117. According to data from the General Society Survey, more than 60 percent of Democrats in 2016 supported the legalization of marijuana, while only 40 percent of Republicans did. And, although a majority of Americans support a federalist approach to the regulation of marijuana that permits states to make their own decisions, more Republicans than Democrats supported regulation of the drug at the federal level. John Hudak & Christine Stenglen, "Public Opinion and America's Experimentation with Cannabis Reform," in *Marijuana Federalism: Uncle Sam* and *Mary Jane*, pp. 15, 25, 28. Jonathan Adler, ed. (Washington, D.C.: Brookings Institute Press, 2020).

118. Angela Dills, Sietse Goffard, & Jeffrey Miron, "The Effect of State Marijuana Legalizations: An Update," in *Marijuana Federalism*, p. 35.

119. Dills, Goffard, & Miron, *The Effect of State Marijuana Legalizations*; Florence Shu-Acquaye, "The Role of States in Shaping the Legal Debate on Medical Marijuana," *Mitchell Hamline Law Review*, vol. 42 (2016), p. 697. For a more general analysis of state legislative resistance to federal policies, see Austin Raynor, "The New State Sovereignty Movement," *Indiana Law Journal*, vol. 90 (2015), p. 613.

120. Ernest Young, "The Smoke Next Time: Nullification, Commandeering, and the Future of Marijuana Regulation," in *Marijuana Federalism*, pp. 85, 88.

121. Jonathan Adler, "Introduction: Our Federalism on Drugs," in *Marijuana Federalism*, pp. 1, 3.

122. Adler, *Introduction: Our Federalism on Drugs*, pp. 2–4. See also Robert Mikos, "The Evolving Federal Response to State Marijuana Reforms," *Widener Law Review*, vol. 26 (2020), p. 1.

123. S. 3032–115th Congress (2017–2018); Natalie Fertig, "How Elizabeth Warren Would Legalize Marijuana and Fight Big Tobacco," *Politico*, February 23, 2020; Catie Edmondson, "House Passes Landmark Bill to Decriminalize Marijuana," *New York Times*, December 5, 2020.

124. Patrick Flavin & Gregory Shufeldt, "The State of the Minimum Wage: Federalism, Economic Policy, and Workers' Well-Being," *The Forum*, vol. 15 (2016), p. 167, available at https://www.degruyter.com/view/journals/for/15/1/article-p167.xml.

125. "State Minimum Wages," National Conference of State Legislatures, January 8, 2021, https://www.ncsl.org/research/labor-and-employment/state-minimum-wage-chart.aspx.

126. Gillian Friedman, "Once a Fringe Idea, the $15 Minimum Wage is Making Big Gains," *New York Times*, December 31, 2020; "Raises From Coast to Coast in 2021," National Employment Law Project, December, 2020.

127. Washington v. Glucksburg, 521 U.S. 702 (1997); "Death with Dignity Acts," Death with Dignity, https://www.deathwithdignity.org/learn/death-with-dignity-acts/; Brian Bix, "Physician-Assisted Suicide and Federalism," *Notre Dame Journal of Law, Ethics, and Public Policy*, vol. 17 (2003), p. 53. The eight states are California, Colorado, Hawaii, Maine, New Jersey, Oregon, Vermont, and Washington. The state supreme court of a ninth state, Montana, has interpreted state law to not prohibit physician-assisted dying for individuals who are both terminally ill and mentally competent. Baxter v. Montana, 224 P.3d 1211 (Mt. 2009).

128. Gonzales v. Oregon, 546 U.S. 243, 274 (2006).

129. "Health Reform in Maine, Massachusetts, and Vermont: An Examination of State Strategies to Improve Access to Affordable, Quality Care," National Academy for State Health Policy, March 26, 2009, https://www.nashp.org/health-reform-maine-massachusetts-and-vermont-examination-state-strategies-improve/.

130. Pakinam Amer, "How Massachusetts Became a National Leader on Health Care—and How It Can Lead Again," *Boston Globe*, February 2, 2020. Between 2010 and 2020, legislators in twenty-one states introduced sixty-six bills that went beyond the ACA by proposing single-payer health-care systems. Erin Fuse Brown & Elizabeth McCuskey, "Federalism, ERISA, and State-Single Payer Health Care," *University of Pennsylvania Law Review*, vol. 168 (2020), p. 389.

Chapter 2

1. "Donald Trump Transcript: Our Country Needs a Truly Great Leader," *Wall Street Journal*, June 16, 2015.

2. Tara Golshan, "Donald Trump's Speech Showed 'Zero Tolerance' for Undocumented Immigrants," *Vox*, August 31, 2016; Brian Klaas, "A Short History of President Trump's Anti-Muslim Bigotry," *Washington Post*, March 15, 2019.

3. Edward-Isaac Dovere, "Democratic State Attorneys General Vow Action Against Refugee Order," *Politico*, January 29, 2017.

4. Christopher Lash et al., "Understanding Sanctuary Cities," *Boston College Law Review*, vol. 59 (2018), pp. 1703, 1719.

5. Michelle Alexander, *The New Jim Crow: Mass Incarceration in the Age of Color Blindness* (New York: New Press, 2010).

6. A 2018 review of the literature concluded that there is no link between increased immigration and increased crime. Graham Ousey & Charis Kubrin, "Immigration and Crime: Assessing a Contentious Issue," *Annual Review of Criminology*, vol. 1. (2018), pp. 63, 69–70. A 2019 study by researchers at the University of California, Davis, found that localities in which deportations increased did not experience a corresponding decrease in crimes. Annie Hines and Giovanni Peri, "Immigrants

Deportations, Local Crime, and Police Effectiveness," Institute of Labor Economics, Discussion Paper Series, June 2019, https://www.iza.org/publications/dp/12413/ immigrants-deportations-local-crime-and-police-effectiveness. See also Anna Flagg, "Deportations Reduce Crime? That's Not What the Evidence Shows," *New York Times*, September 24, 2019.

7. Lash et al., *Understanding Sanctuary Cities*, pp. 1720–1721.

8. Andrew Moore, "Introduction to the Symposium on Sanctuary Cities: A Brief Review of the Legal Landscape," *University of Detroit Mercy Law Review*, vol. 96 (2018), pp. 1, 3.

9. Illegal Immigration Reform and Immigrant Responsibility Act of 1996, Pub. L. No. 104–208 § 133, 110 Stat. 3009, codified as amended at 8 U.S.C. § 1357(g).

10. Lash et al., *Understanding Sanctuary Cities*, p. 1722.

11. Lash et al., *Understanding Sanctuary Cities*, p. 1773.

12. Lash et al., *Understanding Sanctuary Cities*, pp. 1726–1727.

13. Huyen Pham, "287(g) Agreements in the Trump Era," *Washington & Lee Law Review*, vol. 75 (2018), p. 1253.

14. Lash et al., *Understanding Sanctuary Cities*, p. 1730; Elina Treyger, Aaron Chalfin, & Charles Loeffler, "Immigration Enforcement, Policing, and Crime: Evidence from the Secure Communities Program," *Criminology & Public Policy*, vol. 13 (2014), pp. 285–322.

15. Moore, *Introduction to the Symposium on Sanctuary Cities*, p. 4.

16. Lash et al., *Understanding Sanctuary Cities*, p. 1733.

17. Galarza v. Szalczyk, 745 F.3d 634 (3d Cir. 2014).

18. Arizona v. United States, 567 U.S. 387, 407 (2012).

19. Lunn v. Commonwealth, 78 N.E.3d 1143, 1146 (Mass. 2017). The court in *Lunn* concluded that when Massachusetts law enforcement officials detain an individual solely on the basis of a federal immigration civil detainer order, they effectuate an illegal arrest because it is not authorized by either federal or state law.

20. Printz v. United States, 521 U.S. 898 (1997).

21. *Galarza*, 745 F.3d at 644. See also *Lunn*, 78 N.E.3d at 1152.

22. Prigg v. Pennsylvania, 41 U.S. 539 (1842).

23. This typology of sanctuary policies follows Lash et al., *Understanding Sanctuary Cities*, pp. 1738–1752.

24. Huyen Pham & Pham Hoang Van, "Subfederal Immigration Regulation and the Trump Effect," *New York University Law Review*, vol. 94 (2019), p. 125.

25. *Donald Trump Transcript: Our Country Needs a Truly Great Leader*; Golshan, *Donald Trump's Speech Showed "Zero Tolerance" for Undocumented Immigrants*.

26. "Donald Trump 2016 RNC Draft Speech Transcript," *Politico*, July 21, 2016.

27. Holly Yan & Dan Simon, "Undocumented Immigrant Acquitted in Kate Steinle Death," *CNN*, December 1, 2017.

28. Maggie Haberman & Liz Robbins, "Trump, on Long Island, Vows an End to Gang Violence," *New York Times*, July 28, 2017.

29. Eric Lach, "Trump's Dangerous Scapegoating of Immigrants at the State of the Union," *New Yorker*, February 5, 2019.

30. Noah Goldberg, "Immigrant Rights Group Says Trump's State of the Union Speech Sought to 'Exploit and Politicize' Assault and Slaying of 92-Year-Old Queens Woman," *New York Daily News*, February 5, 2020.

31. "Donald Trump Immigration Speech in Arizona," *Politico*, August 31, 2016.

32. Executive Order 13,768 (January 25, 2017).

33. County of Santa Clara v. Trump, 250 F.Supp.3d 497, 511 (N.D.Ca. 2017).

34. City of San Francisco Administrative Code § 12I.1.

35. *County of Santa Clara*, 250 F.Supp.3d at 512.

36. *County of Santa Clara*, 250 F.Supp.3d at 513.

37. City and County of San Francisco v. Trump, 897 F.3rd 1225 (9th Cir. 2018).

38. City of Chicago v. Sessions, 888 F.3d 272 (7th Cir. 2018); City of Philadelphia v. Attorney General of the U.S., 916 F.3d 276 (3rd Cir. 2018). See also City of Los Angeles v. Barr, 929 F.3d 1163 (9th Cir. 2019). But see City of Los Angeles v. Barr, 941 F.3d 931 (9th Cir. 2019).

39. In 2014, an appellate federal court concluded that when states abide by section 1373, they must, under the Tenth Amendment, be understood to do so voluntarily. Galarza v. Szalczyk, 745 F.3d 634 (3d Cir. 2014). Three federal district courts during the Trump years struck down §1373 as unconstitutional under the Tenth Amendment. New York v. U.S. Department of Justice, 343 F. Supp. 3d 213 (S.D.N.Y. 2018); City of Chicago v. Sessions, 321 F. Supp. 3d 855 (N.D. Ill. 2018); City of Philadelphia v. Sessions, 309 F. Supp. 3d 289 (E.D. Pa. 2018). The first ruling was overturned by a federal appellate court. State of New York v. Department of Justice, 951 F.3d 84 (2nd Cir. 2020). Federal appellate courts affirmed the second and third rulings, holding that the Trump administration had impermissibly withheld federal funds from the sanctuary cities because the withholdings were not authorized by Congress; the courts did not reach the Tenth Amendment issue. City of Chicago v. Barr, 961 F.3d 882 (7th Cir. 2020); City of Philadelphia v. Attorney General, 916 F.3d 276 (3rd Cir. 2019). For arguments that section 1373 is unconstitutional under the Tenth Amendment, see Vikram David Amar, "Federalism Friction in the First Year of the Trump Presidency," *Hastings Constitutional Law Quarterly*, vol. 45 (2018), p. 401; Bernard Bell, "Sanctuary Cities, Government Records, and the Anti-Commandeering Doctrine," *Rutgers Law Review*, vol. 69 (2017), p. 1553; Ilya Somin, "Making Federalism Great Again: How the Trump Administration's Attack on Sanctuary Cities Unintentionally Strengthened Judicial Protection for State Autonomy," *Texas Law Review*, vol. 97 (2019), p. 1247. For the argument that section 1373 is unconstitutional because it goes beyond Congress's delegated powers under Article I, see Josh Blackman, "Improper Commandeering," *University of Pennsylvania Journal of Constitutional Law*, vol. 21 (2019), p. 959.

40. Tim Arango, Thomas Fuller, & Jose Del Real, "Trump Inspires California Lawmakers to Go on Offense," *New York Times*, September 14, 2019.

41. Hearing on A.B. 450 Before the Assembly Committee on the Judiciary, 2017–2018 Session 1 (Cal. 2017).

42. California Government Code § 7282.5(a), § 7284.6(a). Also in 2017, the Illinois legislature passed, and the Republican governor signed, the Illinois Trust Act, which prohibited state and local law enforcement agencies from holding individuals solely on the

basis of an ICE detainer order and from stopping or arresting individuals solely on the basis of citizenship or immigration status. Illinois Public Act 100–10463 (2017). For its part, Vermont in 2014 enacted a statute prohibiting local law enforcement agencies from assisting in immigration enforcement. 2014 Vermont Laws No. 193, § 3 (S. 184).

43. California Government Code § 12532.

44. California Government Code § 7285.1(a), (e); California Labor Code § 90.2(a)(1). For an exploration of how some states provided immigrants with tax, education, and mortgage benefits while the national government was moving to deny them such benefits at the federal level, see Shayak Sarkar, "Financial Immigration Federalism," *Georgetown Law Journal*, vol. 107 (2019), p. 1561. For the argument that federalism offers a promising but "as-yet untapped reservoir of regulatory [state] authority to check federal outsourcing" of immigration detention tasks to private corporations, see David Rubenstein & Pratheepan Gulasekaram, "Privatized Detention & Immigration Federalism," *Stanford Law Review Online*, vol. 71 (2019), p. 224.

45. Texas Government Code § 752.053(a)–(b). Texas law also requires compliance with all ICE detainer orders and allows for the removal of officials who are found to be in violation of that requirement. Texas Code of Criminal Procedure § 2.251; Texas Government Code § 752.0565(c). A federal appellate court upheld the constitutionality of the Texas law. City of El Cenizo v. Texas, 890 F.3d 164 (5th Cir. 2018). Six other states—Alabama, Indiana, Iowa, Mississippi, North Carolina, and Tennessee—have enacted similar laws. For an analysis and critique of such laws, see Pratheepan Gulasekaram, Rick Su, & Rose Cuison-Villazor, "Anti-Sanctuary and Immigration Localism," *Columbia Law Review*, vol. 119 (2019), p. 837.

46. The only exception was that the court concluded that the provision requiring the California Attorney General to review the circumstances leading to the apprehension and transfer of immigration detainees was likely unconstitutional because it placed a unique burden on federal immigration detentions. United States v. California, 921 F.3rd 865, 885 (9th Cir. 2019).

47. United States v. California, 921 F.3rd at 887.

48. United States v. California, 921 F.3rd at 890.

49. United States v. California, 921 F.3rd at 890–891. In 2020, the Trump administration returned to federal court, challenging the laws of three jurisdictions that restricted the ability of local police to share information with federal authorities about residents' immigrations status. Katie Benner, "Justice Department Sues Over Sanctuary Laws in California, N.J., and Seattle," *New York Times*, February 10, 2020.

50. Jesse McKinley et al., "'Extortion': N.Y. Assails Trump Administration over Traveler Programs," *New York Times*, February 6, 2020; Complaint, New York v. Wolfe, 1:20-cv-01127 (S.D.N.Y 2020); "U.S. Judge Opens Probe into False Statements in New York 'Trusted Traveler' Suit," *New York Times*, July 29, 2020.

51. Miriam Jordan, "Judges Strike Several Blows to Trump Immigration Policies," *New York Times*, October 11, 2019.

52. Jordan, "Judges Strike Several Blows to Trump Immigration Policies."

53. Washington v. U.S. Department of Homeland Security, 408 F. Supp.3d 1191 (E.D. Wash. 2019).

54. New York v. USDHS, 408 F.Supp.3d 334, 349 (S.D. NY 2019), affirmed by 969 F.3d 42 (2nd Circ. 2020). See also Cook County v. Illinois, 962 F.3d 208 (7th Cir. 2020); City and County of San Francisco v. USCIS, 981 F.3d 742 (9th Cir. 2020).

55. Adam Liptak, "Supreme Court Allows Trump's Wealth Test for Green Cards," *New York Times*, January 27, 2020; Zolan Kanno-Youngs, "A Trump Immigration Policy Is Leaving Families Hungry," *New York Times*, December 4, 2020.

56. Connor O'Brien, "19 States Sue the Trump Administration Over Border Wall Money Shift," *Politico*, March 3, 2020.

57. Adam Liptak, "'There Is No Reason to Apologize' for Muslim Ban Remarks, Trump Says," *New York Times*, April 30, 2018.

58. Edward-Isaac Dovere, "Democratic State Attorneys General Vow Action Against Refugee Order," *Politico*, January 29, 2017.

59. Washington v. Trump, 2017 WL 462040 (W.D. Wash.).

60. Trump v. Hawaii, 138 S. Ct. 2392 (2018).

61. In encouraging progressives to embrace federalism, Ernest Young notes the important role that states can play in expressing dissent from federal policies. Ernest Young, "Welcome to the Dark Side: Liberals Rediscover Federalism in the Wake of the War on Terror," *Brooklyn Law Review*, vol. 69 (2004), pp. 1277, 1285.

62. Benjamin Weiser, "Judge to ICE: Don't Ambush Immigrants at New York Courthouses," *New York Times*, June 10, 2020.

63. New York v. U.S. Immigration and Customs Enforcement, 466 F.Supp.3d 439 (S.D.N.Y. 2020). See also Washington v. U.S. Department of Homeland Security, 2020 WL 1819837 (W.D. Wash. 2020). But see Ryan v. U.S. Immigration and Customs Enforcement, 974 F.3d 9 (1st Circ. 2020). States also joined universities in legally challenging efforts by the Trump administration to require foreign students to leave the country if they attended schools where most of the classes were to be held online as a result of the coronavirus. A day later, the administration reversed course and permitted the students to remain in the country. Anemona Hartocollis, "17 States Sue to Block Student Visa Rules," *New York Times*, July 13, 2020; Miriam Jordan & Anemona Hartocollis, "U.S. Rescinds Plan to Strip Visas From International Students in Online Classes," *New York Times*, July 14, 2020.

64. Arizona v. U.S., 567 U.S. 387 (2012).

65. Catalina Camia, "Texas Governor Hopeful Likes to Sue Obama," *USA Today*, July 15, 2013.

66. Erwin Chemerinsky, *Constitutional Law: Principles and Policies* (New York: Wolters Kluwer, 6th edition, 2019), pp. 271–280.

67. New York v. United States, 505 U.S. 167 (1992); South Dakota v. Dole, 483 U.S. 203 (1987); Adam Babich, "Our Federalism, Our Hazardous Waste, and Our Good Fortune," *Maryland Law Review*, vol. 54 (1995), pp. 1516, 1532.

68. For an overview of how cooperative federalism works in the field of environmental law, see Adam Babich, "The Supremacy Clause, Cooperative Federalism, and the Full Federal Regulatory Purpose," *Administrative Law Review*, vol. 64 (2012), p. 1. See also Philip Weiser, "Towards a Constitutional Architecture for Cooperative Federalism," *North Carolina Law Review*, vol. 79 (2001), p. 663.

69. California Air Resources Board, https://ww2.arb.ca.gov/about/history.

70. Section 209 of the Clean Air Act, codified at 42 U.S.C. § 7543(b)(1)(A)–(C).

71. 42 U.S.C. § 7542(b).

72. Section 177 of the Clean Air Act, codified at 42 U.S.C. § 7507.

73. "Vehicle Fuel Economy and Greenhouse Gas Standards: Frequently Asked Questions," GAO 45204, U.S. Government Accountability Office, May 24, 2018.

74. Massachusetts v. EPA, 549 U.S. 497 (2007).

75. "Endangerment and Cause or Contribute Findings for Greenhouse Gases under Section 202(a) of the Clean Air Act; Final Rule," Environmental Protection Agency, 74 Federal Register 66496, December 15, 2009.

76. 5 H.R. Rep. No. 294, 95th Cong., 1st Sess. 301–302 (1977).

77. Coral Davenport & Hiroko Tabuchi, "Trump's Rollback of Auto Pollution Rules Shows Signs of Disarray," New York Times, August 20, 2019.

78. Jeremy Schulman, "Every Insane Thing Donald Trump Has Said about Global Warming," Mother Jones, December 12, 2018. For a tally of Trump's lies on environmental issues, see "Trump Lies," National Resource Defense Council, https://www.nrdc.org/trump-lies.

79. "Mid-Term Evaluation of Greenhouse Gas Emissions Standards for Model Year 2022–2025 Light-Duty Vehicles: Notice; Withdrawal," Environmental Protection Agency, 83 Federal Register 16077, April 13, 2018.

80. "EPA Administrator Pruitt: GHG Emissions Standards for Cars and Light Trucks Should Be Revised" Press Release, Environmental Protection Agency, April 2, 2018; Evan Halper & Joseph Tanfani, "Trump Administration Moves on Two Fronts to Challenge California Environmental Protections," Los Angeles Times, April 2, 2018.

81. Hiroko Tabuchi, "The Oil Industry's Covert Campaign to Rewrite American Car Emissions Rules," New York Times, December 13, 2018. After the administration officially changed the federal fuel efficiency standards, nearly two dozen states, led by California, sued. Hiroko Tabuchi, "States Sue to Block Trump from Weakening Fuel Economy Rules," New York Times, May 27, 2020.

82. Trevor Houser et al., "The Biggest Climate Rollback Yet?," Rhodium Group, August 2, 2018, https://rhg.com/research/the-biggest-climate-rollback-yet.

83. Sean O'Kane, "California Leads 17 States in Suing the EPA for Attacking Vehicle Emissions Standards," The Verge, May 1, 2018.

84. Coral Davenport, "Automakers Plan for their Worst Nightmare: Regulatory Chaos After Trump's Emissions Rollback," New York Times, April 10, 2019.

85. Umair Irfan, "Trump's EPA is Fighting California Over a Fuel Economy Rule the Auto Industry Doesn't Even Want," Vox, April 6, 2019.

86. Coral Davenport & Hiroko Tabuchi, "Automakers, Rejecting Trump Pollution Rule, Strike a Deal with California," New York Times, July 25, 2019.

87. Davenport & Tabuchi, "Trump's Rollback of Auto Pollution Rules Shows Signs of Disarray."

88. Hiroko Tabuchi & Coral Davenport, "Justice Department Investigates California Emissions Pact That Embarrassed Trump," New York Times, September 6, 2019.

89. Editorial, "A Cruel Parody of Antitrust Enforcement," *New York Times*, September 6, 2019.

90. Cecilia Kang, "Sprint and T-Mobile Merger Approval, Said to be Near, Could Undercut Challenge by States," *New York Times*, June 14, 2019; Editorial, "Mr. Trump Casts a Shadow Over the AT&T–Time Warner Deal," *New York Times*, November 15, 2017.

91. Jim Rutenberg, "Trump's Attacks on the News Media Are Working," *New York Times*, October 28, 2018.

92. Coral Davenport, "Justice Department Drops Antitrust Probe Against Automakers That Sided with California on Emissions," *New York Times*, February 7, 2020.

93. Coral Davenport, "Trump to Revoke California's Authority to Set Stricter Auto Emissions Rules," *New York Times*, September 17, 2019.

94. Coral Davenport, "California and 23 States Sue U.S. in War on Auto Emissions," *New York Times*, September 21, 2019.

95. Nadja Popovich, Livia Albeck-Ripka, & Kendra Pierre-Louis, "The Trump Administration Is Reversing 100 Environmental Rules," *New York Times*, July 15, 2020.

96. Coral Davenport, "Trump Eliminates Major Methane Rule, Even as Leaks Are Worsening," *New York Times*, August 13, 2020; Lisa Friedman & Coral Davenport, "Curbs on Methane, Potent Greenhouse Gas, to Be Relaxed in U.S.," *New York Times*, August 29, 2019.

97. John Schwartz, "Major Climate Change Rules the Trump Administration Is Reversing," *New York Times*, August 29, 2019.

98. A report published at the end of 2019 found that state attorneys general had taken more than three hundred "significant regulatory and legal actions" to oppose the Trump administration's environmental regulation rollbacks. "300 and Counting: State Attorneys General Lead the Fight for Health and the Environment," State Energy and Environmental Impact Center, NYU School of Law, December 2019, https://www.law.nyu.edu/sites/default/files/300%20and%20Counting%20-%20State%20Impact%20Center.pdf.

99. National Resource Defense Council, *What Is the Clean Power Plan?*, September 29, 2017, https://www.nrdc.org/stories/how-clean-power-plan-works-and-why-it-matters.

100. Dena Adler, Jessica Wentz, & Romany Webb, "Four Important Points about EPA's Affordable Clean Energy Act," Climate Law Blog, Sabin Center for Climate Change Law, June 20, 2019, http://blogs.law.columbia.edu/climatechange/2019/06/20/four-important-points-about-epas-affordable-clean-energy-rule/.

101. Timothy Cama, "Two Dozen States Sue Obama Over Coal Plant Emissions Rule," *The Hill*, October 23, 2015.

102. Executive Order 13783 (March 28, 2017).

103. "EPA Takes Another Step to Advance President Trump's America First Strategy, Proposes Repeal of 'Clean Power Plan,'" Press Release, Environmental Protection Agency, October 10, 2017.

104. Lisa Friedman, "States Sue Trump Administration Over Rollback of Obama-Era Climate Rule," *New York Times*, August 13, 2019.

105. Friedman, "States Sue Trump Administration Over Rollback of Obama-Era Climate Rule"; American Lung Association v. EPA, 985 F.3d 914 (D.C. Circ. 2021).

106. Ariel Wittenberg, "Trump's WOTUS: Clear as Mud, Scientists Say," *E & E News*, February 18, 2019. The total number of wetland acreage that would have been left unprotected was approximately 42 million. In a state like Arizona, large parts of which have little rainfall, 83 percent of the streams and 99 percent of the lakes would have been left unprotected. Chris Wood, Collin O'Mara, & Dale Hall, "Trump Weakens the Nation's Clean Water Efforts," *New York Times*, February 10, 2020.

107. Lisa Friedman & Carol Davenport, "Trump Administration Rolls Back Clean Water Protections," *New York Times*, September 13, 2019.

108. Rebecca Beitsch, "14 States Sue EPA Over Rollback of Obama-Era Water Rule," *The Hill*, December 20, 2019.

109. Valerie Volkovici, "California, New York, Other States Sue U.S. Over Trump Clean-Water Rollback," *Reuters*, July 21, 2020.

110. Timothy Cama, "East Coast States Sue to Challenge Trump's Offshore Oil Move," *The Hill*, December 20, 2018; Chris Mills Rodrigo, "South Carolina Joins Lawsuit Against Trump Offshore Drilling Plan," *The Hill*, January 8, 2019.

111. New York v. EPA, 964 F.3d 1214 (D.C. Circ. 2020).

112. Massachusetts v. Environmental Protection Agency, 549 U.S. 497, 520 (2007).

113. Julie Hirschfeld Davis & Helene Cooper, "Trump Says Transgender People Will Not Be Allowed in the Military," *New York Times*, July 26, 2017; Samantha Allen, "National Guard in California, Nevada, Washington State, Oregon, and New Mexico Defy Trump's Trans Troops Ban," *The Daily Beast*, April 23, 2019.

114. Rebekah Barber, "Where the Movement to Expand Medicaid Stands," *Facing South*, June 21, 2019; Susan Milligan, "The States Tackle Health Care Reform," *U.S. News and World Report*, August 10, 2018.

115. Katie Jennings, "New Jersey Will Become Second State to Enact Individual Health Insurance Mandate," *Politico*, May 30, 2018.

116. "More States Protecting Residents Against Skimpy Short-Term Health Plans," Center On Budget and Policy Priorities, February 6, 2019, https://www.cbpp.org/blog/more-states-protecting-residents-against-skimpy-short-term-health-plans.

117. Milligan, "The States Tackle Health Care Reform." Law professor Craig Konnoth has detailed how the Trump administration used private corporations to preempt state efforts to provide their citizens with greater protections, benefits, and services than those available under federal law. Konnoth argues that "federalism can be used to check and balance privatization." Craig Konnoth, "Preemption Through Privatization," *Harvard Law Review*, vol. 134 (forthcoming, 2021).

118. New York v. U.S. Department of Health and Human Services, 414 F. Supp.3d 475 (S.D.N.Y 2019).

119. New York v. U.S. Department of Labor, 363 F.Supp.3d 109 (D.D.C. 2019).

120. Tim Pearce, "Trump Faces More Lawsuits from States Than Obama Administration Did in Eight Years," *Washington Examiner*, February 12, 2020.

121. Anthony Zurcher, "How Trump Turned Against Gun Control," *BBC News*, October 2, 2017.

122. Jill Colvin & Lisa Pane, "Trump Tells NRA He'll Fight for Gun Rights," *Chicago Tribune*, April 26, 2019.

123. Meg Anderson & Domenico Montanaro, "Donald Trump Teases That He Could Buck the NRA on One Aspect of Guns," *NPR*, June 15, 2017; Tara Golshan, "Trump's Madcap, Unscripted Gun Control Meeting with Lawmakers, Explained," *Vox*, February 28, 2018; John Cassidy, "Some Reasons to Be Skeptical About Trump's Embrace of Gun Control," *The New Yorker*, August 9, 2019.

124. Maggie Haberman, Annie Karni, & Danny Hakim, "N.R.A. Gets Results on Gun Laws in One Phone Call with Trump," *New York Times*, August 20, 2019; Annie Karni & Maggie Haberman, "After Lobbying by Gun Rights Advocates, Trump Sounds a Familiar Retreat," *New York Times*, August 19, 2019.

125. Maggie Astor & Karl Russell, "After Parkland, A New Surge in State Gun Control Laws," *New York Times*, December 14, 2018.

126. Steve Contorno, "Here Is Every New Gun Law in the U.S. Since the Parkland Shooting," *Tampa Bay Times*, February 13, 2019. See also Nick Corasaniti, "A Novel Gun Control Strategy: Pressure Banks and Retailers," *New York Times*, September 11, 2019.

127. Arthur Kellerman et al., "Gun Ownership as a Risk Factor for Homicide in the Home," *New England Journal of Medicine*, vol. 329(15), October 7, 1993, pp. 1084–1091.

128. Allen Rostron, "The Dickey Amendment on Federal Funding for Research on Gun Violence," *American Journal of Public Health*, vol. 108, July 2018, pp. 865–867.

129. Sheila Kaplan, "Congress Quashed Research into Gun Violence. Since Then, 600,000 People Have Been Shot," *New York Times*, March 8, 2018. Congress in 2019 restored some federal money for gun violence research.

130. Margo Sanger-Katz, "Gun Research Is Suddenly Hot," *New York Times*, April 17, 2019; Kate Washington, "Armed with Knowledge," *Sactown Magazine*, June/July, 2019; Patti Verbanas, "State of New Jersey and Rutgers University Announce New Gun Violence Research," *Rutgers Today*, September 9, 2019; Sara Green, "$1M in State Money to Fund Harborview Gun-Violence Research," *Seattle Times*, July 26, 2019.

131. Irwin Redlener, Jeffery Sachs, Sean Hansen, & Nathaniel Hupert, "130,000–210,000 COVID-19 Deaths—and Counting—in the U.S.," National Center for Disaster Preparedness, Columbia University, October 21, 2020.

132. Amy Feldman, "States Bidding against Each Other Pushing Up Prices of Ventilators Needed to Fight Coronavirus, NY Governor Cuomo Says," *Forbes*, March 28, 2020.

133. Jeanne Whalen et al., "Scramble for Medical Equipment Descends into Chaos as U.S. States and Hospitals Compete for Rare Supplies," *Washington Post*, March 24, 2020; Andrew Soergel, "States Competing in 'Global Jungle' for PPE," *U.S. News and World Report*, April 7, 2020; Nolan McCaskill & Alice Ollstein, "Trump Administration Tells States to Step Up as Governors Plead for Aid," *Politico*, April 5, 2020.

134. Linda Qiu, "Tracking Trump's Promises on Responding to the Virus," *New York Times*, April 16, 2020; Kate Bennett, "Maryland's First Lady Capitalizes on Her South Korean Heritage to Secure Test Kits," *CNN*, April 21, 2020; Andrew Beaton,

"A Million N95 Masks are Coming From China—on Board the New England Patriots' Plane," *Wall Street Journal*, April 2, 2020; Josh Wingrove, "Trump Oversells Breakthroughs in Boasts of U.S. Virus Response," *Bloomberg*, March 19, 2020.

135. Susan Rice, "Trump Is the Wartime President We Have (Not the One We Need)," *New York Times*, April 7, 2020; James Baker, "It's High Time We Fought This Virus the American Way," *New York Times*, April 3, 2020; Zolan Kanno-Youngs & Ana Swanson, "Wartime Production Law Has Been Used Routinely, but Not With Coronavirus," *New York Times*, March 31, 2020; Charlie Savage, "How the Defense Production Act Could Yield More Masks, Ventilators, and Tests," *New York Times*, March 20, 2020; Andrew Jacobs, "Despite Claims, Trump Rarely Uses Wartime Law in Battle Against Covid," *New York Times*, September 22, 2020.

136. Stephen Collinson, "Trump Seeks a Miracle as Virus Fears Mount," *CNN*, February 28, 2020.

137. Jane Timm, "Fact-Checking President Donald Trump's Claims about Coronavirus," *NBC News*, April 2, 2020.

138. Editorial, "Where Is Trump's Plan to Test Millions of Americans a Day?," *New York Times*, April 21, 2020. See also Margaret Bourdeaux, Beth Cameron, & Jonathan Zittrain, "Testing Is on the Brink of Paralysis. That's Very Bad News," *New York Times*, July 16, 2020.

139. Emma Tucker, "Trump to U.S. Governors: Get Your Own Ventilators," *Daily Beast*, March 16, 2020.

140. Peter Baker & Maggie Haberman, "Trump Leaps to Call Shots on Reopening Nation, Setting Standoff with Governors," *New York Times*, April 13, 2020.

141. John Yoo, "No, Trump Can't Force States to Reopen," *National Review*, April 13, 2020; Charlie Savage, "Trump's Claim of Total Authority in Crisis Is Rejected Across Ideological Lines," *New York Times*, April 14, 2020; Neal Katyal, "It's the Worst Possible Time for Trump to Make False Claims of Authority," *New York Times*, April 14, 2020.

142. Ross Baker, "Donald Trump's Laissez-Faire Federalism Is as Toxic as Covid-19," *USA Today*, July 14, 2020.

143. Nancy Knauer, "The COVID-19 Pandemic and Federalism: Who Decides?," *N.Y.U. Journal of Legislation and Public Policy*, vol. 23 (2021), p. 1.

144. Knauer, *The COVID-19 Pandemic and Federalism*.

145. Roni Rabin & Chris Cameron, "Trump Falsely Claims That '99 Percent' of Virus Cases Are Totally Harmless," *New York Times*, July 5, 2020.

146. Morgan Chalfant & Brett Samuels, "Trump's Support for Protests Threatens to Undermine Social Distancing Rules," *The Hill*, April 20, 2020.

147. Anna Edney, "Trump Touts Drug That FDA Says Isn't Yet Approved for Virus," *Bloomberg*, March 19, 2020; Linda Qiu, "Trump's Inaccurate Claims on Hydroxychloroquine," *New York Times*, May 21, 2020.

148. Katie Rogers et al., "Trump's Suggestion that Disinfectants Could Be Used to Treat Coronavirus Prompts Aggressive Pushback," *New York Times*, April 24, 2020.

149. Maeve Reston, "Governors on East and West Coasts Form Pacts to Decide When to Reopen Economies," *CNN*, April 13, 2020; Adam Uren, "Coronavirus: Minnesota

Joins Pact with 6 Midwest States on Reopening Economy," *Bring Me the News*, April 16, 2020. See also Richard Kreitner, "How Would You Like to Live in the Nation of New England?," *New York Times*, April 23, 2020.

150. Sarah Mervosh et al., "Mask Rules Expand Across the U.S. as Clashes Over the Mandates Intensify," *New York Times*, July 16, 2020.

151. Ilya Somin, "Federalism and the Coronavirus," *Reason*, March 31, 2020; Walter Olson, "Federalism and the Coronavirus Lockdown," *Wall Street Journal*, March 30, 2020.

152. Lazario Gamio, "How Coronavirus Cases Have Risen Since States Reopened," *New York Times*, July 9, 2020.

153. Sheryl Gay Stolberg et al., "The Surging Coronavirus Finds a Federal Leadership Vacuum," *New York Times*, November 11, 2020.

154. Rebecca Haffajee & Michelle Mello, "Thinking Globally, Acting Locally—The U.S. Response to Covid-19," *New England Journal of Medicine*, vol. 382, May 28, 2020, p. e75. For other early critical assessments of how the American federalist system of government responded to the coronavirus outbreak, see, for example, Sarah Gordon, Nicole Huberfeld, & David Jones, "What Federalism Means for the U.S. Response to Coronavirus Disease 2019," *JAMA Network*, May 8, 2020; Stephen Griffin, "American Federalism, the Coronavirus Pandemic, and the Legacy of Hurricane Katrina," *Constitutionnet*, April 22, 2020; Donald Kettl, "States Divided: The Implications of American Federalism for COVID-19," *Public Administration Review*, vol. 80, May 22, 2020; Richard Kreitner, "When Confronting the Coronavirus, Federalism is Part of the Problem," *The Nation*, April 1, 2020.

155. Jesse McKinley & Luis Ferré-Sadurní, "N.Y. Severely Undercounted Virus Deaths in Nursing Homes, Report Says," *New York Times*, January 28, 2021.

156. Erin Cox, "There's No National Strategy for Coronavirus. These States Banded Together to Create One," *Washington Post*, August 4, 2020.

157. Gary Gerstle, "The New Federalism," *The Atlantic*, May 6, 2020; Laurence Tribe, "Don't Let Coronavirus Failures Shake Your Faith in Federalism," *Boston Globe*, April 29, 2020.

158. Daniel Vock, "How Obama Changed the Relationship Between Washington, the States, and the Cities," *Governing*, June 2019.

159. National Federation of Independent Business v. Sebelius, 567 U.S. 519 (2012).

160. Erwin Chemerinsky, *We the People: A Progressive Reading of the Constitution for the Twenty-First Century* (New York: Picador, 2018), p. 123.

161. Erwin Chemerinsky, "The Values of Federalism," *Florida Law Review*, vol. 47 (1995), pp. 499, 504. Chemerinsky elaborates on this point in "Federalism Not as Limits, But as Empowerment," *University of Kansas Law Review*, vol. 45 (1996), pp. 1219, 1234–1239 and "Reconceptualizing Federalism," *New York Law School Law Review*, vol. 50 (2006), p. 729.

162. For exceptions to the Court's expansive understanding of Congress's authority to regulate interstate commerce, see United States v. Lopez, 514 U.S. 549 (1995); United States v. Morrison, 529 U.S. 598 (2000). For the Court's expansive understandings of Congress's taxing and spending authority, see South Dakota v. Dole, 483 U.S. 203 (1987); United States v. Butler, 297 U.S. 1 (1936).

163. For an institution-focused account of how federalism helps to insulate judicial, law enforcement, and election officials from the control of anti-democratic federal executive authority, see David Landau, Hannah Wiseman, & Samuel Wiseman, "Federalism for the Worst Case," *Iowa Law Review*, vol. 105 (2020), p. 1187.

164. See, for example, Printz v. United States, 521 U.S. 898 (1997); New York v. United States, 505 U.S. 144 (1992).

165. Jessica Bulman-Pozen, "Federalism as a Safeguard of the Separation of Powers," *Columbia Law Review*, vol. 112 (2012), p. 459.

166. I borrow the double helix metaphor from Laurence Tribe, who uses it to describe the joint work done by the equal protection and due process clauses in protecting individual rights. Laurence Tribe, "*Lawrence v. Texas*: The 'Fundamental Right' that Dare Not Speak its Name," *Harvard Law Review*, vol. 117 (2004), pp. 1893, 1989.

167. Sergio Olmos, Mike Baker, & Zolan Kanno-Youngs, "Federal Agents Unleash Militarized Crackdown on Portland," *New York Times*, July 17, 2020; Mike Baker, Thomas Fuller, & Sergio Olmos, "Federal Agents Push Into Portland Streets, Stretching Limits of Their Authority," *New York Times*, July 25, 2020.

168. Andrew Napolitano, "In Portland, Actions of Federal Agents are Unlawful, Unconstitutional, and Harmful," *Fox News*, July 23, 2020; Benjamin Haas, "Trump's Militarized Policing of Portland has No Place in the U.S.," *CNN*, August 7, 2020.

169. Mike Baker, "Federal Agents Envelop Portland Protests, and City's Mayor, in Tear Gas," *New York Times*, July 23, 2020; Mike Baker & Zolan Kanno-Youngs, "Federal Agencies Agree to Withdraw from Portland, with Conditions," *New York Times*, July 29, 2020.

170. Stephen Vladeck, "Elections Do Not Have to Be So Chaotic and Excruciating," *New York Times*, November 8, 2020; Charlotte Hill & Lee Drutman, "America Votes by 50 Sets of Rules. We Need a Federal Elections Agency," *New York Times*, November 6, 2020.

171. Michael Shear & Stephanie Saul, "Trump, in Taped Call, Pressured Georgia Official to 'Find' Votes to Overturn Election," *New York Times*, January 3, 2021; Richard Fausset & Danny Hakim, "In Georgia, Trump's Attacks on Election Still Haunts Republicans," *New York Times*, January 12, 2021.

172. Heather Gerken, "Federalism 3.0," *California Law Review*, vol. 105 (2017), pp. 1695, 1722. See also Andrew Karch, *Responsive States and American Public Policy* (New York: Cambridge University Press, 2019); Paul Nolette, *Federalism on Trial: State Attorneys General and National Policymaking in Contemporary America* (Lawrence: University of Kansas Press, 2015). See also Gillian Metzger, "Federalism Under Obama," *William & Mary Law Review*, vol. 53 (2011), pp. 567, 569.

173. The term "uncooperative federalism" comes from Jessica Bulman-Pozen & Heather Gerken, "Uncooperative Federalism," *Yale Law Journal*, vol. 118 (2009), p. 1256.

174. Donald Kettl, *The Divided States of America: Why Federalism Doesn't Work* (Princeton, NJ: Princeton University Press, 2020). See also Ezra Rosser, ed., *Holes in the Safety Net: Federalism and Poverty* (New York: Cambridge University Press, 2019).

175. Lisa Miller, "Amending Constitutional Myths," *Drake Law Review*, vol. 67 (2018), p. 947; Mark Graber, "Social Democracy and Constitutional Theory: An Institutional Perspective," *Fordham Law Review*, vol. 69 (2001), p. 1969.

176. The Tenth Amendment reads as follows: "The powers not delegated to the United States by the Constitution, *nor prohibited by it to the states*, are reserved to the states respectively, or to the people" (emphasis added).

Chapter 3

1. "Donald Trump's New York Times Interview: Full Transcript," *New York Times*, November 23, 2016; Michael Brice-Saddler, "While Bemoaning Mueller Probe, Trump Falsely Says the Constitution Gives Him the Right 'To Do Whatever I Want,'" *Washington Post*, July 23, 2019; Peter Baker & Maggie Haberman, "Trump Leaps to Call Shots on Reopening Nation, Setting Standoff with Governors," *New York Times*, April 13, 2020; "Excerpts from Trump's Interview with the Times," *New York Times*, December 28, 2017; James Naughton, "Nixon Says a President Can Order Illegal Actions Against Dissidents," *New York Times*, May 19, 1977.

2. James Pfiffner, *Power Play: The Bush Presidency and the Constitution* (Washington, D.C.: Brookings Institution Press, 2008), p. 59.

3. Michael Klarman, *The Framers' Coup: The Making of the United States Constitution* (New York: Oxford University Press, 2016), p. 213.

4. Forrest McDonald, *The American Presidency: An Intellectual History* (Lawrence: University Press of Kansas, 1994), ch. 6.

5. *The Federalist Papers*, n. 48 (James Madison), Lawrence Goldman, ed. (New York: Oxford University Press, 2008), p. 246.

6. *The Federalist Papers*, n. 47 (James Madison), p. 239.

7. *The Federalist Papers*, n. 51 (James Madison), p. 257.

8. INS v. Chadha, 462 U.S. 919 (1983).

9. *The Federalist Papers*, n. 51 (James Madison), p. 256.

10. Pfiffner, *Power Play*, p. 64.

11. McDonald, *The American Presidency*, p. 166.

12. Andrew Rudalevige, *The New Imperial Presidency: Renewing Power After Watergate* (Ann Arbor: University of Michigan Press, 2005), p. 22.

13. Rudalevige, *The New Imperial Presidency*, p. 22.

14. Akhil Reed Amar, "Actually, the Electoral College Was a Pro-Slavery Ploy," *New York Times*, April 6, 2019. But see Sean Wilentz, "The Electoral College Was Not a Pro-Slavery Ploy," *New York Times*, April 4, 2019.

15. Rudalevige, *The New Imperial Presidency*, p. 22.

16. Rudalevige, *The New Imperial Presidency*, p. 23.

17. Edward Corwin, *The President: Office and Powers, 1787–1984* (New York: New York University Press, 1984), pp. 3–4.

18. Alexander Hamilton, *Pacificus No. 1*, June 29, 1793; James Madison, *Helvidius No. 1*, August 24, 1793.

19. John Locke, *Two Treatises of Government* (1690), paragraph 160.

20. *Ex Parte* Merryman, 17 F. Cas. 144 (C.C.D. Md. 1861); Rudalevige, *The New Imperial Presidency*, p. 31.

21. *Ex Parte* Milligan, 71 U.S. 2 (1866).

22. Brenda Wineapple, *The Impeachers: The Trial of Andrew Johnson and the Dream of a Just Nation* (New York: Random House, 2019).

23. Myers v. United States, 272 U.S. 52 (1926).

24. Humphrey's Executor v. United States, 295 U.S. 602 (1935); Morrison v. Olson, 487 U.S. 654 (1988).

25. Rudalevige, *The New Imperial Presidency*, p. 36.

26. Rudalevige, *The New Imperial Presidency*, p. 37.

27. A.L.A. Schecter Poultry Corp. v. United States, 295 U.S. 495 (1935); Panama Refining Co. v. Ryan, 293 U.S. 388 (1935).

28. Gundy v. United States, 139 S. Ct. 2116, 2123 (2019).

29. Whitman v. American Trucking Association, Inc., 531 U.S. 457, 472 (2001); National Broadcasting Corp. v. United States, 319 U.S. 190, 216 (1943).

30. Chevron USA, Inc., v. National Resources Defense Council, 467 U.S. 837 (1984).

31. Neal Katyal, "Internal Separation of Powers: Checking Today's Most Dangerous Branch from Within," *Yale Law Journal*, vol. 115 (2006), pp. 2314, 2321. As a partial solution to the problem of presidential power accretion, Katyal in this article argues in favor of bureaucratic mechanisms that create friction within the executive branch. See also Gillian Metzger, "The Interdependent Relationship Between Internal and External Separation of Powers," *Emory Law Journal*, vol. 59 (2009), p. 423; Abner Greene, "Checks and Balances in an Era of Presidential Lawmaking," *University of Chicago Law Review*, vol. 61 (1994), p. 123.

32. Alfred McCoy, *In the Shadows of the American Century: The Rise and Decline of U.S. Global Power* (Chicago: Haymarket Books, 2017); Richard Van Alstyne, *The Rising American Empire* (New York: Norton, 1973).

33. Rudalevige, *The New Imperial Presidency*, p. 63, quoting "Statement on Signing the Military Appropriations Bill," November 17, 1971, *Public Papers of the Presidents*, 1971.

34. Gene Healy, *The Cult of the Presidency: America's Dangerous Devotion to Executive Power* (Washington, D.C.: Cato Institute, 2008), p. 109.

35. United States v. Curtiss-Wright, Corp., 299 U.S. 304, 320 (1936). See also Louis Fisher, *Supreme Court Expansion of Presidential Power: Unconstitutional Leanings* (Lawrence: University Press of Kansas, 2017).

36. David Rudenstine, *The Age of Deference: The Supreme Court, National Security, and the Constitutional Order* (New York: Oxford University Press, 2016), p. 7.

37. Korematsu v. United States, 323 U.S. 214 (1944).

38. Trump v. Hawaii, 138 S. Ct. 2392 (2018).

39. Rudalevige, *The New Imperial Presidency*, p. 45.

40. Healy, *The Cult of the Presidency*, p. 83.

41. Rudalevige, *The New Imperial Presidency*, p. 46.

42. Bruce Ackerman, *The Decline and Fall of the American Republic* (Cambridge, MA: Harvard University Press, 2010), p. 34.

43. Mitchel Sollenberger & Mark Rozell, *The President's Czars: Undermining Congress and the Constitution* (Lawrence: University Press of Kansas, 2012).

44. Rudalevige, *The New Imperial Presidency*, p. 60.

45. Rudalevige, *The New Imperial Presidency*, pp. 60–61.

46. Rudalevige, *The New Imperial Presidency*, pp. 44–45.

47. Rudalevige, *The New Imperial Presidency*, pp. 75–76.

48. United States v. Nixon, 418 U.S. 683 (1974).

49. Fisher, *Supreme Court Expansion*, pp. 5–11.

50. See, for example, Clinton Rossiter, *The American Presidency* (New York: Harcourt, 1956); Richard Neustadt, *Presidential Power and the Modern Presidents* (New York: John Wiley & Sons, 1960).

51. Arthur Schlesinger Jr., *The Imperial Presidency* (Boston: Houghton Mifflin Co., 1973), p. viii.

52. Rudalevige, *The New Imperial Presidency*, pp. 64–65.

53. Rudalevige, *The New Imperial Presidency*, p. 66.

54. Rudalevige, *The New Imperial Presidency*, pp. 51–52.

55. Stephen Knott, *The Lost Soul of the American Presidency: The Decline into Demagoguery and the Prospects for Renewal* (Lawrence: University Press of Kansas, 2019), p. 138.

56. Nardone v. U.S., 302 U.S. 379 (1937); Rudalevige, *The New Imperial Presidency*, p. 52.

57. Irvine v. California, 347 U.S. 128 (1954).

58. Jack Goldsmith, *In Hoffa's Shadow* (New York: Farrar, Straus and Giroux, 2019), p. 126.

59. Rudalevige, *The New Imperial Presidency*, p. 52.

60. Healy, *The Cult of the Presidency*, p. 107.

61. Healy, *The Cult of the Presidency*, p. 102.

62. Goldsmith, *In Hoffa's Shadow*, p. 129.

63. Goldsmith, *In Hoffa's Shadow*, p. 141.

64. Schlesinger, *The Imperial Presidency*, p. 248.

65. Schlesinger, *The Imperial Presidency*, p. 265.

66. Schlesinger, *The Imperial Presidency*, p. 275.

67. Schlesinger, *The Imperial Presidency*, p. 208.

68. Fisher, *Supreme Court Expansion*, p. 175, citing *Public Papers of the Presidents*, 1973, p. 62.

69. Fisher, *Supreme Court Expansion*, pp. 175–76. For a discussion of the limited impoundments under twentieth-century presidents before Nixon, see James Sundquist, *The Decline and Resurgence of Congress* (Washington, D.C.: Brookings Institution Press, 1981), pp. 202–203. See also Louis Fisher, "Funds Impounded by the President: The Constitutional Issue," *George Washington Law Review*, vol. 38 (1969), p. 124.

70. Sundquist, *The Decline and Resurgence of Congress*, p. 203.

71. Schlesinger, *The Imperial Presidency*, p. 238.

72. Schlesinger, *The Imperial Presidency*, p. 238.
73. Rudalevige, *The New Imperial Presidency*, p. 89.
74. *The Federalist Papers*, n. 58 (James Madison), p. 289.
75. Rudalevige, *The New Imperial Presidency*, p. 89.
76. Rudalevige, *The New Imperial Presidency*, p. 89.
77. Sundquist, *The Decline and Resurgence of Congress*, p. 212.
78. Louis Fisher, *Presidential Spending Power* (Princeton, NJ: Princeton University Press, 1975), pp. 175–201.
79. Local 2677 v. Phillips, 358 F. Supp. 60, 77 (D.D.C. 1973). See also State Highway Commission of Missouri v. Volpe, 479 F.2d 1099 (8th Cir. 1973).
80. Train v. City of New York, 420 U.S. 35 (1975).
81. Rudalevige, *The New Imperial Presidency*, p. 128.
82. Sundquist, *The Decline and Resurgence of Congress*, p. 214.
83. Rudalevige, *The New Imperial Presidency*, p. 114.
84. Rudalevige, *The New Imperial Presidency*, p. 114.
85. Catherine Padhi, "Emergencies without End: A Primer on Federal States of Emergency," *Lawfare*, December 8, 2017.
86. National Emergencies Act § 202(b), codified at 50 U.S.C. § 1622(d) (202).
87. Loch Johnson, *A Season of Inquiry Revisited: The Church Committee Confronts America's Spy Agencies* (Lawrence: University Press of Kansas, 2015).
88. Rudalevige, *The New Imperial Presidency*, p. 112.
89. Rudenstine, *The Age of Deference*, pp. 140–141. Rudenstine provides a detailed exploration of the limits and flaws of FISC judicial review in Chapters 8 and 9.
90. A 2019 report by the Department of Justice's inspector general criticized the sloppy work done by the FBI in petitioning for a FISA warrant to surveil a Trump campaign employee, leading to a rare public rebuke of the government by the FISC's chief judge. Charlie Savage, "Court Orders F.B.I. to Fix National Security Wiretaps After Damning Report," *New York Times*, December 17, 2019.
91. Morrison v. Olson, 487 U.S. 654 (1988).
92. Pub. L. 95–452, 1978, 92 Stat. 1101, codified at 5 U.S.C. App. §1 et seq. Congress amended the Inspector General Act in 2008 by strengthening the roles of and protections for IGs. Inspectors General Reform Act of 2008. Pub. L. 110–409, 2008, 122 Stat. 4302.
93. Rudalevige, *The New Imperial Presidency*, p. 148.
94. Clinton v. City of New York, 524 U.S. 417 (1998).
95. Charlie Savage, *Takeover: The Return of the Imperial Presidency and the Subversion of American Democracy* (Boston: Little Brown, 2007), p. 44.
96. Healy, *The Cult of the Presidency*, pp. 11–12.
97. Executive Order 12,291 (February 17, 1981).
98. Peter Shane, *Madison's Nightmare: How Executive Power Threatens America's Democracy* (Chicago: University of Chicago Press, 2009), p. 150.
99. Rudalevige, *The New Imperial Presidency*, p. 169.
100. Shane, *Madison's Nightmare*, p. 154.
101. Robert Percival, "Presidential Management of the Administrative State: The Not-So-Unitary Executive," *Duke Law Journal*, vol. 51 (2001), pp. 963, 996.

102. Ackerman, *The Decline and Fall of the American Republic*, p. 36.

103. Ackerman, *The Decline and Fall of the American Republic*, p. 36.

104. Stephen Skowronek, "The Conservative Insurgency and Presidential Power," *Harvard Law Review*, vol. 122 (2009), p. 2070.

105. Elena Kagan, "Presidential Administration," *Harvard Law Review*, vol. 114 (2001), p. 2245.

106. A 2017 study found that while Congress in recent years had enacted about fifty significant laws annually, executive agencies were issuing roughly four thousand substantive rules a year. Morton Rosenberg, *When Congress Comes Calling* (The Constitution Project, 2017), p. 8.

107. Shane, *Madison's Nightmare*, p. 158. See also Percival, *Presidential Management of the Administrative State*, p. 966; Robert Percival, "Who's in Charge? Does the President Have Directive Authority Over Agency Regulatory Decisions?," *Fordham Law Review*, vol. 79 (2011), p. 2487.

108. Steven Calabresi & Christopher Yoo, *The Unitary Executive: Presidential Power from Washington to Bush* (New Haven, CT: Yale University Press, 2008). See also Skrowronek, *The Conservative Insurgency and Presidential Power*.

109. Morrison v. Olson, 487 U.S. 654 (1988); Calabresi & Yoo, *The Unitary Executive*.

110. This is the position adopted by the Department of Justice's Office of Legal Counsel. Opinion, "A Sitting President's Amenability to Indictment and Criminal Prosecution," Office of Legal Counsel, Department of Justice, October 16, 2000; Memorandum, "Amenability of the President, Vice President and other Civil Officers to Federal Criminal Prosecution while in Office," Office of Legal Counsel, Department of Justice, September 24, 1973. Although the courts have not addressed the question of whether a sitting president can be criminally *charged*, the Supreme Court has rejected the notion that they are immune from criminal *investigation* for acts committed before their presidency. Trump v. Vance, 140 S. Ct. 2412 (2020).

111. For in-depth studies of presidential directives, see Phillip Cooper, *By Order of the President: The Use and Abuse of Executive Direct Action* (Lawrence: University Press of Kansas, 2014); Graham Dodds, *Take Up Your Pen: Unilateral Presidential Directives in American Politics* (Philadelphia: University of Pennsylvania Press, 2013).

112. Rudalevige, *The New Imperial Presidency*, p. 172.

113. Julie Turkewitz, "Trump Slashes Size of Bears Ears and Grand Staircase Monuments," *New York Times*, December 4, 2017; Coral Davenport, "Trump Opens National Monument Land to Energy Exploration," *New York Times*, February 6, 2020.

114. Both statements quoted in Dodds, *Take Up Your Pen*, p. 5.

115. Youngstown Sheet & Tube Co v. Sawyer, 343 U.S. 579 (1952). See also Maeva Marcus, *Truman and the Steel Seizure Case: The Limits of Presidential Power* (Durham, NC: Duke University Press, 1991).

116. Terry Moe & William Howell, "The Presidential Power of Unilateral Action," *Journal of Law, Economics, and Organization*, vol. 15 (1999), pp. 132–179.

117. Ackerman, *The Decline and Fall of the American Republic*, pp. 71–72.

118. For an exploration of how "presidential government by emergency" can lead to a "constitutional dictatorship," see Sanford Levinson & Jack Balkin, "Constitutional

Dictatorship: Its Dangers and Its Designs," *Minnesota Law Review*, vol. 94 (2010), pp. 1789.

119. Shane, *Madison's Nightmare*, p. 19.

120. Rudalevige, *The New Imperial Presidency*, pp. 156–157.

121. On the general ineffectiveness of the War Powers Resolution in circumscribing presidential war-making authority, see, for example, Louis Fisher & David Gray Adler, "The War Powers Resolution," *Political Science Quarterly*, vol. 113 (1998), p. 1; Peter Irons, *War Powers: How the Imperial Presidency Hijacked the Constitution* (New York: Henry Holt & Co. 2005), pp. 199–204; Rudalevige, *The New Imperial Presidency*, pp. 192–200.

122. Matthew Weed, "Presidential References to the 2001 Authorization for Use of Military Force in Publicly Available Executive Actions and Reports to Congress," Congressional Research Service, February 16, 2018.

123. Savage, *Takeover*, p. 124.

124. Bob Woodward, *Bush at War* (New York: Simon & Schuster, 2002), pp. 145–146.

125. Shane, *Madison's Nightmare*, ch. 4.

126. Mark Mazzetti & Michael Schmidt, "Ex-Worker at C.I.A. Says He Leaked Data on Surveillance," *New York Times*, June 9, 2013.

127. Savage, *Takeover*, pp. 134–139.

128. On the Geneva Conventions, see, for example, Matthew Evangelista & Nina Tannenwald, eds., *Do the Geneva Conventions Matter?* (New York: Oxford University Press, 2017).

129. 18 U.S.C. § 2441.

130. The Supreme Court in 2004 held that the administration could not hold American citizens as enemy combatants without affording them due process, including a meaningful hearing in which they "must receive notice [from the government] of the factual basis for [their] classification [as enemy combatants], and a fair opportunity to rebut the government's factual assertions before a neutral decision maker." Hamdi v. Rumsfeld, 542 U.S. 507, 533 (2004). Although the ruling was widely perceived as a significant loss for the administration, Charlie Savage argues that "it was generally pleased with the ruling.... [The Court] had not specified that the hearings had to be before a civilian court, so the Pentagon swiftly designed its own quickie hearings before a panel of military officers." Savage, *Takeover*, p. 194.

131. Article 3 of the Convention Against Torture specifies that no signatory nation "shall expel, return . . . or extradite a person to another State where there are substantial grounds for believing that he would be in danger of being subjected to torture." Article 3, Convention against Torture and other Cruel, Inhuman or Degrading Treatment or Punishment. The Convention also makes clear that "no exceptional circumstances whatsoever, whether a state of war or a threat of war, internal political instability or any other public emergency, may be invoked as a justification of torture." Article 2, §2.

132. Savage, *Takeover*, p. 149.

133. Healy, *The Cult of the Presidency*, p. 170.

134. Savage, *Takeover*, p. 203.

135. On the DTA, see Michael Garcia, "Interrogation of Detainees: Requirements of the Detainee Treatment Act," Congressional Research Services, August 26, 2009.

136. Hamdan v. Rumsfeld, 548 U.S. 557 (2006).

137. The Supreme Court in 2008 struck down the denial of habeas corpus as an unconstitutional suspension of the Great Writ. Boumedine v. Bush, 553 U.S. 723 (2008). On enemy combatants and habeas corpus, see Jennifer Elsea and Michael Garcia, "Enemy Combatant Detainees: Habeas Corpus Challenges in Federal Court," Congressional Research Services, February 3, 2010.

138. Pfiffner, *Power Play*, pp. 10–11. In 2015, Congress prohibited additional bulk collection of phone records but authorized the National Security Agency to require phone companies to maintain the records already gathered for possible future government use. Four years later, the agency shut down the program. A report later concluded that the massive data collections, which cost the government $100 million from 2015 to 2019, yielded only two leads and one significant investigation. Charlie Savage, "N.S.A. Phone Program Cost $100 Million, but Produced Only Two Unique Leads," *New York Times*, February 25, 2020.

139. Frustrated by Congress's lack of response to Bush's aggressive exercise of presidential authority, John Conyers Jr. (D-MI), the chairman of the House Judiciary Committee, issued an almost five-hundred-page report in 2009 itemizing and documenting Bush's power grabs. The report foreshadows many of the abuses of power that later took place during the Trump presidency. "Reining in the Imperial Presidency: Lessons and Recommendations Relating to the Presidency of George W. Bush," House Committee on the Judiciary Majority Staff Report to Chairman John Conyers Jr., January 13, 2009.

140. American Bar Association, *Task Force on Presidential Signing Statements and the Separation of Powers Doctrine* (2007).

141. Shane, *Madison's Nightmare*, p. 135.

142. Ackerman, *The Decline and Fall of the American Republic*, p. 90.

143. In 2006, Sanford Levinson estimated that presidents had vetoed 2,550 bills, of which only 106 (or 4 percent) had been overridden. Sanford Levinson, *Our Undemocratic Constitution: Where the Constitution Goes Wrong* (New York: Oxford University Press, 2006), p. 40.

144. Charlie Savage, "Bush Challenges Hundreds of Laws," *Boston Globe*, April 30, 2006.

145. Rudalevige, *The New Imperial Presidency*, p. 262.

146. For an argument that DACA was legal, see Shoba Sivaprasad Wadhia, *Banned: Immigration Enforcement in the Time of Trump* (New York: New York University Press, 2019), ch. 4. For an opposite argument, see Robert Delahunty & John Yoo, "Dream On: The Obama Administration's Nonenforcement of Immigration Laws, the DREAM Act, and the Take Care Clause," *Texas Law Review*, vol. 91 (2013), p. 781.

147. Charles Schumer & Lindsey Graham, "The Right Way to Mend Immigration," *Washington Post*, March 19, 2010.

148. Muzaffar Chishti, Sarah Pierce, & Jessica Bolter, "The Obama Record on Deportations: Deporter in Chief or Not?," Migration Policy Institute, January 26, 2017, https://www.migrationpolicy.org/article/obama-record-deportations-deporter-chief-or-not.

149. For a selection of Obama's statements on immigration in 2010, see Louis Fisher, *President Obama: Constitutional Aspirations and Executive Actions* (Lawrence: University of Kansas Press, 2018), pp. 125–127.

150. Obama statements quoted in Fisher, *President Obama*, p. 129.

151. Fisher, *President Obama*, p. 129.

152. Obama statements quoted in Josh Blackman, "The Constitutionality of DAPA Part II: Faithfully Executing the Law," *Texas Review of Law and Politics*, vol. 19 (2015), pp. 213, 270–273.

153. Fisher, *President Obama*, p. 130.

154. Memorandum from Janet Napolitano, Secretary of U.S. Department of Homeland Security, June 15, 2012.

155. Regents of the University of California v. U.S. Department of Homeland Security, 908 F.3d 476, 488–489 (9th Cir. 2019).

156. Texas v. United States, 809 F.3d 134, 148 (5th Cir. 2015). In addition to implementing the DAPA program, the Obama administration in 2014 expanded DACA "by removing the age cap, shifting the date-of-entry requirement from 2007 to 2010, and extending the deferred action and work authorization period [from two] to three years." Department of Homeland Security v. Regents of the University of California, 140 S. Ct. 1891, 1902 (2020).

157. Fisher, *President Obama*, pp. 135–136.

158. Texas v. United States, 809 F.3d 134 (5th Cir. 2015). The Supreme Court affirmed through an equally divided vote of 4-4. United States v. Texas, 136 S. Ct. 2271 (2016) (per curiam).

159. Michael Shear & Julie Hirschfeld Davis, "Trump Moves to End DACA and Calls on Congress to Act," *New York Times*, September 5, 2017. The Trump administration allowed individuals with DACA status to retain that status (unless revoked for particular reasons) and permitted renewal applications by those who applied before October 5, 2017. But the administration refused to accept new applications to the program. Wadhia, *Banned*, pp. 68–69.

160. Wadhia, *Banned*, pp. 66–67.

161. Department of Homeland Security v. Regents of the University of California, 140 S. Ct. 1891 (2020).

162. Claire Hansen, "Trump Says He'll Try Again to End DACA," *U.S. News & World Report*, June 19, 2020; Molly O'Toole, "Despite Supreme Court Ruling, Trump Administration Rejects New DACA Applicants," *Los Angeles Times*, July 16, 2020.

163. Corey Brettschneider, *The Oath and the Office: A Guide to the Constitution for Future Presidents* (New York: Norton, 2018), pp. 48–49.

164. "Joint Interim Rule on Asylum and Presidential Proclamation: What You Need to Know," Center for Immigrants Rights Clinic, Penn State Law School, November 23, 2018, https://pennstatelaw.psu.edu/sites/default/files/documents/pdfs/Immigrants/

Blocking_those_seeking_entry_policy_update_11.23.18.pdf; https://www.govinfo. gov/content/pkg/FR-2018-11-09/pdf/2018-24594.pdf.

165. Michael Shear, "Trump Claims New Power to Bar Asylum for Immigrants Who Arrive Illegally," *New York Times*, November 8, 2018.

166. East Bay Sanctuary Covenant v. Trump, 349 F. Supp.3d 838, 844 (N.D. Ca. 2018). See also Maria Sacchetti & Isaac Stanley-Becker, "In Blow to Trump's Immigration Agenda, Federal Judge Blocks Asylum Ban For Migrants Who Enter Illegally From Mexico," *Washington Post*, November 20, 2018.

167. East Bay Sanctuary Covenant v. Trump, 932 F.3d 742, 774 (9th Cir. 2018). The same court later upheld an injunction against the enforcement of the administration's new rule. East Bay Sanctuary Covenant v. Trump, 950 F.3d 1242 (9th Cir. 2020).

168. Michael Tackett, Caitlin Dickerson, & Azam Ahmed, "Migrants Seeking Asylum Must Wait in Mexico, Trump Administration Says," *New York Times*, December 20, 2018; Kirk Semple, "Migrants in Mexico Face Kidnappings and Violence While Awaiting Immigration Hearings in U.S.," *New York Times*, July 12, 2019; Jason Kao & Denise Lu, "How Trump's Policies Are Leaving Thousands of Asylum Seekers Waiting in Mexico," *New York Times*, August 18, 2019; Zolan Kanno-Youngs & Maya Averbuch, "Waiting for Asylum in the United States, Migrants Live in Fear in Mexico," *New York Times*, April 5, 2019.

169. Miriam Jordan, "'I'm Kidnapped:' A Father's Nightmare at the Border," *New York Times*, December 21, 2019.

170. Innovation Law Lab v. Wolf, 951 F.3d 1073 (9th Cir. 2020).

171. Gustavo Solis, "Remain in Mexico Has a 0.1 Percent Asylum Grant Rate," *San Diego Union Tribune*, December 15, 2019.

172. Michael Shear & Zolan Kanno-Youngs, "Most Migrants at Border with Mexico Would Be Denied Asylum Protections Under New Trump Rule," *New York Times*, July 15, 2019.

173. East Bay Sanctuary Covenant v. Barr, 964 F.3d 832 (9th Cir. 2020).

174. Zolan Kanno-Youngs & Maggie Haberman, "Trump Administration Moves to Solidify Restrictive Immigration Policies," *New York Times*, June 12, 2020.

175. Thomas McGarity, "Avoiding Gridlock Through Unilateral Executive Action: The Obama Administration's Clean Power Plan," *Wake Forest Journal of Law and Policy*, vol. 7 (2017), p. 141.

176. Fisher, *President Obama*, pp. 70–71.

Chapter 4

1. Michael Schmidt, Mark Mazzetti, & Matt Apuzzo, "Trump Campaign Aids Had Repeated Contacts with Russian Intelligence," *New York Times*, February 14, 2017.

2. Ashley Parker & David Sanger, "Donald Trump Calls on Russia to Find Hillary Clinton's Missing Emails," *New York Times*, July 27, 2016.

3. Adam Entous, Ellen Nakashima, & Greg Miller, "Sessions Met with Russian Envoy Twice Last Year, Encounters He Later Did Not Disclose," *Washington Post*, March 1, 2017.

4. Peter Baker & Katie Benner, "Trump Calls Sessions' Handling of Surveillance Abuse Allegations 'Disgraceful,'" *New York Times*, February 28, 2018. When Trump learned of Sessions's recusal, he rhetorically and angrily asked "where is my Roy Cohn?," referring to his former lawyer and fixer, who had been Senator Joseph McCarthy's top aide during the anti-communist witch hunts of the 1950s. Michael Schmidt, "Obstruction Inquiry Shows Trump's Struggle to Keep Grip on Russia Investigation," *New York Times*, January 4, 2018. Trump's anger at Sessions lasted for years. In 2020, after Sessions attempted to regain the Republican nomination for his old Senate seat representing Alabama, Trump enthusiastically supported his opponent. Sessions was trounced in the primary election. Elaina Plott & Jonathan Martin, "Sessions Pays the Price for Incurring Trump's Wrath, Losing Alabama Senate Race," *New York Times*, July 14, 2020.

5. Susan Hennessey & Benjamin Wittes, *Unmaking the Presidency: Donald Trump's War on the World's Most Powerful Office* (New York: Farrar, Straus and Giroux, 2020), p. 166.

6. Baker & Benner, "Trump Calls Sessions' Handling of Surveillance Abuse Allegations 'Disgraceful.'"

7. Peter Baker, Katie Benner, & Michael Stern, "Jeff Sessions Is Forced Out as Attorney General as Trump Installs Loyalist," *New York Times*, November 7, 2018; Peter Baker, "'Very Frustrated' Trump Becomes Critic of Law Enforcement," *New York Times*, November 3, 2017.

8. Veronica Stracqualursi & Jessica Schneider, "Trump to DOJ: Don't Let Debbie Wasserman Schultz, Aide, 'Off the Hook,'" *CNN*, June 7, 2018; David Sanger, "Taking Page from Authoritarians, Trump Turns Power of State Against Political Rivals," *New York Times*, October 10, 2020.

9. Michael Schmidt, "Comey Memo Says Trump Asked Him to End Flynn Investigation," *New York Times*, May 16, 2017.

10. Special Counsel Robert S. Mueller III, "Report on the Investigation into Russian Interference in the 2016 Presidential Election," Volume II, p. 4, March 2019 [hereinafter Mueller Report].

11. Mueller Report, Volume II, p. 4.

12. Michael Schmidt & Maggie Haberman, "Trump Ordered Mueller Fired, but Backed Off When White House Counsel Threatened to Quit," *New York Times*, January 25, 2018. See also Mueller Report, Volume II, p. 4.

13. Mueller Report, Volume II, pp. 3–6.

14. Opinion, "A Sitting President's Amenability to Indictment and Criminal Prosecution," Office of Legal Counsel, Department of Justice, October 16, 2000.

15. Mueller Report, Volume II, p. 2 (emphasis added). For a detailed account of the Mueller investigation that criticizes its ineffectiveness, see Jeffrey Toobin, *True Crimes and Misdemeanors: The Investigation of Donald Trump* (New York: Doubleday, 2020).

16. Michael Schmidt et al., "Trump's Lawyer Raised Prospect of Pardons for Flynn and Manafort," *New York Times*, March 28, 2018.

17. Mark Greenberg & Harry Litman, "Trump's Corrupt Use of the Pardon Power," *Lawfare*, June 19, 2018.

18. Mike Allen, "Trump Lawyer Claims 'President Cannot Obstruct Justice,'" *Axios*, December 4, 2017.

19. Benjamin Weiser & Azi Paybarah, "If Trump Shoots Someone on 5th Ave., Does He Have Immunity," His Lawyer Says Yes," *New York Times*, October 23, 2019; Michael Gold, "Trump Lawyers Argue He Cannot Be Criminally Investigated," *New York Times*, September 19, 2019.

20. Trump v. Mazars USA, 140 S. Ct. 2019, 2028 (2020).

21. Trump v. Vance, 140 S. Ct. 2412 (2020); United States v. Nixon, 418 U.S. 683 (1974).

22. *Mazars USA*, 140 S. Ct. at 2036.

23. I thank my colleague Carlos Gonzalez for raising this comparison in an e-mail exchange.

24. Trump v. Hawaii, 138 S. Ct. 2392 (2018).

25. Romer v. Evans, 517 U.S. 620 (1996); Cleburne v. Cleburne Living Center, 473 U.S. 432 (1985).

26. *Mazars USA*, 140 S. Ct. at 2034.

27. On the long and troubling history of the Supreme Court's expansion of presidential power at the expense of Congress, see Louis Fisher, *Supreme Court Expansion of Presidential Power: Unconstitutional Leanings* (Lawrence: University Press of Kansas, 2017).

28. Sanford Levinson, *Our Undemocratic Constitution: Where the Constitution Goes Wrong* (New York: Oxford University Press, 2006), p. 108.

29. Neal K. Katyal, "What Trump Is Hiding from the Impeachment Hearings," *New York Times*, November 12, 2019.

30. Bob Bauer, "Trump Is the Founders' Worst Nightmare," *New York Times*, December 2, 2019. See also Harold Koh, "The Arrogance of Trump's Enablers," *New York Times*, January 7, 2020.

31. Bauer, "Trump is the Founders' Worst Nightmare."

32. Bauer, "Trump is the Founders' Worst Nightmare."

33. Katie Benner, "Barr Suggests Impeachment Inquiry Undermines Voters' Intent," *New York Times*, November 15, 2019. See also Charlie Savage, "Trump Says He Alone Can Do It. His Attorney General Usually Agrees," *New York Times*, January 14, 2019.

34. Emily Chochrane, Eric Lipton, & Chris Cameron, "G.A.O. Report Says Trump Administration Broke Law in Withholding Ukraine Aid," *New York Times*, January 16, 2020.

35. Nicholas Fandos & Michael Shear, "Impeachment Hearings Open with Revelation on Trump's Ukraine Pressure," *New York Times*, November 13, 2019.

36. Noah Weiland, "Impeachment Briefing: What Happened Today," *New York Times*, November 15, 2019; Noah Weiland, "Impeachment Briefing: What Happened in Sondland's Hearing," *New York Times*, November 20, 2019; Michael Shear, "With a

Tweet, Trump Upends Republican Strategy for Dealing with Yovanovitch," *New York Times*, November 15, 2019.

37. Peter Baker, "Impeachment Trial Updates: Senate Acquits Trump, Ending Historic Trial," *New York Times*, February 6, 2020.

38. Levinson, *Our Undemocratic Constitution*, p. 66; Daryl Levinson & Richard Pildes, "Separation of Parties, Not Powers," *Harvard Law Review*, vol. 119 (2006), p. 2312.

39. Charlie Savage, *Takeover: The Return of the Imperial Presidency and the Subversion of American Democracy* (Boston: Little Brown, 2007), p. 311.

40. Mark Leibovich, "Romney, Defying the Party He Once Personified, Votes to Convict Trump," *New York Times*, February 5, 2020. Former Republican Representative Justin Amash from Michigan, who had suggested earlier in 2019 that the Mueller Report contained valid reasons for impeaching Trump, was hounded from the party, became an independent, and announced that he would not run for re-election before he voted for impeachment on both counts. Karen Zraick, "Justin Amash, a Trump Critic on the Right, Leaves the G.O.P.," *New York Times*, July 4, 2019; Billy Binion, "Justin Amash on Impeachment: Republicans Are Betraying the 'Principles and Values They Once Claimed to Cherish,'" *Reason*, December 18, 2019.

41. Peter Baker et al., "Trump Fires Impeachment Witnesses Gordon Sondland and Alexander Vindman in Post-Acquittal Purge," *New York Times*, February 7, 2020.

42. Maggie Haberman, Charlie Savage, & Nicholas Fandos, "Trump to Fire Intelligence Watchdog Who Had Key Role in Ukraine Complaint," *New York Times*, April 7, 2020; Charlie Savage, "Endorsing Trump's Firing of Inspector General, Barr Paints Distorted Picture," *New York Times*, April 10, 2020.

43. Benjamin Wittes, "Why Is Trump's Inspector General Purge Not a National Scandal?," *Lawfare*, April 8, 2020.

44. Melissa Quinn, "The Internal Watchdogs Trump Has Fired or Replaced," *CBS News*, May 19, 2020; Eric Schmitt, Charlie Savage, & Noah Weiland, "Longtime Pentagon Watchdog Stepping Down from Post," *New York Times*, May 26, 2020.

45. Catie Edmondson & Michael Shear, "Trump Ousted State Department Watchdog at Pompeo's Urging; Democrats Open Inquiry," *New York Times*, May 16, 2020; David Sanger & Charlie Savage, "Trump Takes Aim at a Watergate Reform: The Independent Inspector General," *New York Times*, May 22, 2020; Edward Wong, Michael LaForgia, & Lara Jakes, "Pompeo Aide Said to Have Pressured Watchdog," *New York Times*, June 10, 2020; Tucker Doherty & Tanya Snyder, "Chao's Team Helped McConnell's State Win Its Largest DOT Grant," *Politico*, December 17, 2019.

46. Scott Shane & Karen Weise, "Trump Says He May Intervene in Huge Pentagon Contract Sought by Amazon," *New York Times*, July 18, 2019.

47. Charlie Savage & Peter Baker, "Trump Ousts Pandemic Spending Watchdog Known for Independence," *New York Times*, April 7, 2020.

48. Editorial, "Senator Grassley, Don't Back Down," *New York Times*, June 10, 2020.

49. Adam Blake, "Trump's Government Full of Temps," *Washington Post*, February 21, 2020; Lisa Rein, "Trump Replaces HHS Watchdog Who Found 'Severe Shortages' at Hospitals Combating Coronavirus," *Washington Post*, May 2, 2020.

50. Margaret Taylor, "Is It Time to Reform the Federal Vacancies Reform Act?," *Lawfare*, March 10, 2020.

51. Brian Naylor, "An Acting Government for the Trump Administration," *NPR*, April 9, 2019.

52. Lisa Friedman, "Judges Tell Trump His Officials Are Serving Illegally. He Does Nothing," *New York Times*, October 5, 2020. See also Michael Shear, "Top Homeland Security Officials Are Serving Illegally, G.A.O. Says," *New York Times*, August 14, 2020.

53. Adam Goldman, Charlie Savage, & Michael Schmidt, "Barr Assigns U.S. Attorney in Connecticut to Review Origins of Russian Inquiry," *New York Times*, May 13, 2019.

54. Charlie Savage, Adam Goldman, & Katie Benner, "Report on F.B.I. Russian Inquiry Finds Serious Errors but Debunks Anti-Trump Plot," *New York Times*, December 9, 2019. The IG did find systemic problems with the FBI's process for seeking wiretaps.

55. Adam Goldman & Katie Brenner, "U.S. Drops Michael Flynn Case, in Move Backed by Trump," *New York Times*, May 7, 2020. Katie Benner & Charlie Savage, "Dropping of Flynn Case Heightens Fears of Justice Department Politicization," *New York Times*, May 8, 2020; Charlie Savage, "'Never Seen Anything Like This': Experts Question Dropping of Flynn Prosecution," *New York Times*, May 7, 2020; Editorial, "Don't Forget, Michael Flynn Pleaded Guilty. Twice." *New York Times*, May 7, 2020.

56. Katie Benner, "Judge Appoints Outsider to Take on Justice Department in Flynn Case," *New York Times*, May 13, 2020; Charlie Savage, "Court Denies Flynn's Bid to End Case and Renews Fight Over McGahn Subpoena," *New York Times*, August 31, 2020.

57. Charlie Savage, "Trump Pardons Michael Flynn, Ending Case His Justice Department Sought to Shut Down," *New York Times*, November 25, 2020.

58. Sharon LaFraniere & Zach Montague, "Roger Stone Is Convicted of Impeding Investigators in a Bid to Protect Trump," *New York Times*, November 15, 2019.

59. Katie Benner, Sharon LaFraniere, & Adam Goldman, "Prosecutors Quit Roger Stone Case After Justice Department Intervenes on Sentencing," *New York Times*, February 11, 2020.

60. Eileen Sullivan & Michael Shear, "Trump Praises Barr for Rejecting Punishment Recommended for Stone," *New York Times*, February 12, 2004.

61. Sharon LaFraniere, "Roger Stone Is Sentenced to Over 3 Years in Prison," *New York Times*, February 20, 2020.

62. LaFraniere, "Roger Stone is Sentenced to Over 3 Years in Prison."

63. Peter Baker, Maggie Haberman, & Sharon LaFraniere, "Trump Commutes Sentence of Roger Stone in Case He Longed Denounced," *New York Times*, July 10, 2020.

64. Maggie Haberman & Michael Schmidt, "Trump Gives Clemency to More Allies, including Manafort, Stone and Charles Kushner," *New York Times*, December 23, 2020; Maggie Haberman & Michael Schmidt, "Trump Pardons Two Russia Inquiry Figures and Blackwater Guards," *New York Times*, December 22, 2020; "Here are Some of the People Trump Pardoned," *New York Times*, January 20, 2021.

65. Jack Goldsmith & Matt Gluck, "Trump's Circumvention of the Justice Department Clemency Process," *Lawfare*, December 29, 2020; Haberman & Schmidt, "Trump Gives Clemency to More Allies."

66. Charlie Savage, "Can Trump Pre-emptively Pardon Allies or Himself?," *New York Times*, December 2, 2020; Maggie Haberman & Michael Schmidt, "Trump Has Discussed with Advisers Pardons for His 3 Eldest Children and Giuliani," *New York Times*, December 1, 2020; William Rashbaum & Benjamin Weiser, "If Trump Pardons Manafort, Can State Charges Stick?," *New York Times*, February 26, 2019.

67. Gamble v. United States, 139 S. Ct. 1960, 1964 (2019).

68. Katie Benner & Sharon LaFraniere, "Justice Department Moves to Drop Charges Against Russian Firms Filed by Mueller," *New York Times*, March 16, 2020.

69. Alan Feuer et al., "Trump Fires U.S. Attorney in New York Who Investigated His Inner Circle," *New York Times*, June 20, 2020.

70. William Rashbaum et al., "Michael Cohen Says He Arranged Payments to Women at Trump's Direction," *New York Times*, August 21, 2018.

71. Michael Schmidt et al., "Giuliani Is Said to Be Under Investigation for Ukraine Work," *New York Times*, October 11, 2019; Eric Lipton & Benjamin Weiser, "Turkish Bank Case Shows Erdogan's Influence with Trump," *New York Times*, October 29, 2020.

72. John Bolton, *The Room Where It Happened* (New York: Simon & Schuster, 2020), pp. 458, 301.

73. Ben Berwick, Jamila Benkato, & Cameron Kistler, "The President's Legal Shell Game to Avoid Accountability," *Lawfare*, March 20, 2020; Quinta Jurecic & Alan Rozenshtein, "The Authoritarian Arguments for Trump's Acquittal," *Lawfare*, January 31, 2020; Michael Schmidt, "First Up at Trump's Impeachment: Can a Former President Stand Trial?," *New York Times*, February 8, 2021; Michael Gold, "Trump Lawyers Argue He Cannot Be Criminally Investigated," *New York Times*, September 19, 2019; Weiser & Paybarach, "If Trump Shoots Someone on 5th Ave., Does He Have Immunity? His Lawyer Says Yes"; Claire Finkelstein, "This Question Is More Important Than Removing Trump," *New York Times*, January 27, 2020; "Excerpts from Trump's Interview with the Times," *New York Times*, December 28, 2017; Vivian Salama & Jess Bravin, "Trump Asserts 'Absolute Right' to Pardon Himself," *Wall Street Journal*, June 4, 2018; John Wagner, "Giuliani: Under Constitution Trump Could Shoot Comey and Not Be Indicted," *Washington Post*, June 4, 2018; Sumner Park, "Gingrich: A President 'Cannot Obstruct Justice," *The Hill*, June 16, 2017; John Yoo & Saikrishna Prakash, "Don't Prosecute Trump. Impeach Him," *New York Times*, December 4, 2017; Mike Alen, "Trump Lawyer Claims 'President Cannot Obstruct Justice," *Axios*, December 4, 2017; Michael Gold, "Trump Lawyers Argue He Cannot Be Criminally Investigated," *New York Times*, September 19, 2019.

74. Walter Shaub Jr., "Ransacking the Republic," *New York Review of Books*, July 2, 2020, p. 55.

75. Amy Brittain et al., "Jared Kushner Made at Least $82 Million in Outside Income Last Year while Serving in the White House," *Washington Post*, June 11, 2018; Russ Buettner, Susanne Craig, & Mike McIntire, "Trump's Taxes Show Chronic Losses and Years of Income Tax Avoidance," *New York Times*, September 28, 2020.

76. Shaub, "Ransacking the Republic."

77. Shaub, "Ransacking the Republic"; Anita Kumar, "How Trump Fused His Business Empire to the Presidency," *Politico*, January 1, 2020.

78. Nicholas Confessore et al., "The Swamp That Trump Built," *New York Times*, October 10, 2020. See also Dan Alexander, *White House, Inc.: How Donald Trump Turned the Presidency into a Business* (New York: Portfolio, 2020).

79. Sharon LaFraniere, "Federal Appeals Court Rules for Trump in Emoluments Case," *New York Times*, July 10, 2019.

80. City of Chicago v. Sessions, 888 F.3d 272, 277 (7th Cir. 2018). See also City of Los Angeles v. Barr, 941 F.3d 931 (9th Cir. 2019); City of Philadelphia v. Attorney Gen., 916 F.3d 276 (3d Cir. 2019); City and County of San Francisco v. Trump, 897 F.3d 1225 (9th Cir. 2018). But see State of New York v. Department of Justice, 951 F.3d 84 (2nd Cir. 2020) (holding that administration had authority to withhold law enforcement funds from jurisdictions that did not comply with three immigration-related conditions imposed by the Attorney General).

81. Mark Niquette, "Trump Said Mexico Would Pay for the Border Wall. Now What?," *Washington Post*, May 30, 2019; Linda Qiu, "The Many Ways Trump Has Said Mexico Will Pay for the Wall," *New York Times*, January 11, 2019.

82. Colby Itkowitz, "Republicans Spent Two Years Resisting Trump's Border Wall. What Changed?," *Washington Post*, January 15, 2019; Julie Hirschfeld Davis & Peter Baker, "How the Border Wall Is Boxing Trump In," *New York Times*, January 5, 2019.

83. Rebecca Shabad & Doha Madani, "House Passes Stopgap Funding Bill with $5 Billion for Trump's Border Wall, at Odds with Senate," *NBC News*, December 20, 2018.

84. Julie Hirschfeld Davis & Emily Cochrane, "Government Shuts Down as Talks Fail to Break Impasse," *New York Times*, December 21, 2018.

85. Peter Baker & Glenn Thrush, "Trump Is 'Not Happy' With Border Deal, but Doesn't Say if He Will Sign It," *New York Times*, February 12, 2019.

86. Charlie Savage, "National Emergency Powers and Trump's Border Wall, Explained," *New York Times*, January 7, 2019; Joe Ward & Anjali Singhvi, "Trump Claims There Is a Crisis at the Border: What's the Reality," *New York Times*, January 11, 2019.

87. Savage, "National Emergency Powers and Trump's Border Wall, Explained."

88. Peter Baker, "Trump Declares a National Emergency, and Provokes a Constitutional Clash," *New York Times*, February 15, 2019.

89. Charlie Savage & Robert Pear, "16 States Sue to Stop Trump's Use of Emergency Powers to Build Border Wall," *New York Times*, February 18, 2019. The original lawsuit was replaced by a new one filed in 2020 by nineteen states. Connor O'Brien, "19 States Sue the Trump Administration Over Border Wall Money Shift," *Politico*, March 3, 2020.

90. Emily Cochrane & Charlie Savage, "House Adds Lawsuit to Challenges Against Trump's Emergency Declaration," *New York Times*, April 4, 2019.

91. Catherine Padhi, "Emergencies Without End: A Primer on Federal States of Emergency," *Lawfare*, December 8, 2017.

92. Report of the Special Committee on the Termination of the National Emergency, U.S. Senate, November 19, 1973, p. iii.

93. In addition to Roosevelt's banking and Truman's Korea emergency declarations, there were two other states of emergencies in place in 1973, both declared by Nixon: one in 1970 following a postal strike and the other in 1971 due to a monetary crisis. As a result of the first, Nixon used the military to transport mail; as a result of the second, he unilaterally imposed stringent import controls. "National Emergency Powers," Congressional Research Service 98–505, August 5, 2019, https://crsreports.congress.gov/product/pdf/RL/98-505; *Report of the Special Committee on the Termination of the National Emergency*, p. iii.

94. *Report of the Special Committee on the Termination of the National Emergency*, p. iii. On the history of the NEA, see Padhi, *Emergencies Without End*.

95. Gerald Dickinson, "The National Emergencies Act Was Never Meant for Something Like Trump's Wall," *Washington Post*, January 31, 2019.

96. Padhi, *Emergencies Without End*.

97. National Emergencies Act § 202(b), 50 U.S.C. § 1622(d).

98. Bruce Ackerman, "The Emergency Constitution," *Yale Law Journal*, vol. 113 (2004), pp. 1029, 1078–1081.

99. Padhi, *Emergencies Without End*.

100. Bob Bauer & Jack Goldsmith, *After Trump: Reconstructing the Presidency* (Washington, D.C.: Lawfare Press, 2020), p. 341. The majority of existing states of emergency have been declared to impose sanctions on foreign countries under the International Emergency Economic Powers Act of 1977 (IEEPA), codified at 50 U.S.C. §§ 1701–1708. The IEEPA authorizes the president to impose sanctions and other trade restrictions on foreign nations after declaring a national emergency under the NEA. As Andrew Rudalevige notes, "sometimes these 'emergencies' simply [have] provided means for unilateral implementation of policy preferences, as when President Reagan applied IEEPA sanctions against Nicaragua in 1985 as a substitute for those Congress had refused to enact." Andrew Rudalevige, *The New Imperial Presidency: Renewing Power After Watergate* (Ann Arbor: University of Michigan Press, 2005), p. 172. On the irony that IEEPA was intended to restrain presidential authority in matters related to trade sanctions, but ended up significantly augmenting it in all sorts of ways, see Peter Harrell, "How to Reform IEEPA," *Lawfare*, August 28, 2019.

101. INS v. Chadha, 462 U.S. 919, 103 S. Ct. 2764 (1983).

102. Richard Pildes, "The Supreme Court's Contribution to the Confrontation Over Emergency Powers," *Lawfare*, February 19, 2019. See also Charlie Savage, "Presidents Have Declared Dozens of Emergencies, but None Like Trump's," *New York Times*, February 15, 2019.

103. Padhi, *Emergencies Without End*; Congressional Research Service, "National Emergency Powers," pp. 19–20; Emily Cochrane, "Trump Again Vetoes Measure to End National Emergency," *New York Times*, October 15, 2019.

104. Emily Cochrane, "Administration to Divert Billions from Pentagon to Fund Border Wall," *New York Times*, February 13, 2020. The Supreme Court in 2019 permitted the building of the wall to continue despite the pending lawsuits challenging the legality of the administration's diversion of funds. Adam Liptak, "Supreme Court Lets

Trump Proceed on Border Wall," *New York Times*, July 26, 2019. On the diversion of funds as further evidence of the erosion of Congress's power of the purse, see Emily Cochrane, "As Trump Seizes Wall Money, Congress's Spending Power Weakens," *New York Times*, February 21, 2020.

105. Sierra Club v. Trump, 963 F.3d 874, 887 (9th Cir. 2020). Unfortunately, the Supreme Court, without reaching the merits of the case, allowed the administration to continue funding the wall while it appealed the court of appeals' ruling. Adam Liptak, "Supreme Court Lets Trump Keep Building his Border Wall," *New York Times*, July 31, 2020.

106. Youngstown Sheet & Tube Co v. Sawyer, 343 U.S. 579 (1952).

107. Executive Order 13765, January 20, 2017; Julie Hirschfeld Davis & Robert Pear, "Trump Issues Executive Order Scaling Back Parts of Obamacare," *New York Times*, January 20, 2017.

108. Executive Order 13783, March 28, 2017; Executive Order 13778, February 28, 2017.

109. Jay Wexler, *The Odd Clauses: Understanding the Constitution through Ten of Its Most Curious Provisions* (Boston: Beacon Press, 2011), p. 16.

110. Bruce Ackerman, *The Decline and Fall of the American Republic* (Cambridge, MA: Harvard University Press, 2010), p. 9. Ackerman elaborates on the role of executive branch lawyers, especially those who work for the Department of Justice's Office of Legal Counsel and for the Office of White House Counsel, in expanding presidential powers in *The Decline and Fall of the American Republic*, pp., 87–88 and 95–116. See also Peter Shane, *Madison's Nightmare: How Executive Power Threatens America's Democracy* (Chicago: University of Chicago Press, 2009), pp. 97–111. As Jack Goldsmith, who served briefly as the head of the Office of Legal Counsel under George W. Bush and who pushed to have the administration end its warrantless surveillance of American citizens on the ground that it was illegal, explains, "even the finest executive branch lawyers, acting in good faith, have a tendency to interpret away constraints on actions deemed important by the president, especially when the actions take place outside of public scrutiny." Jack Goldsmith, *In Hoffa's Shadow* (New York: Farrar, Straus and Giroux, 2019), p. 126.

111. In 2019, the Senate Homeland Security Committee approved such a measure, called the Article One Act, by a vote of 12-2. Elizabeth Goitein, "The Power Trump Can Wield Like a Dictator," *New York Times*, February 12, 2020.

112. Gary Hart, "How Powerful Is the President?," *New York Times*, July 23, 2020.

113. Elizabeth Goitein, "The Alarming Scope of the President's Emergency Powers," *The Atlantic*, January/February, 2019.

114. Korematsu v. United States, 323 U.S. 214, 246 (1944) (Jackson, J., dissenting).

115. Hennessey & Wittes, *Unmaking the Presidency*, p. 174. The guidelines were promulgated by Attorney General Edward Levin in 1976. Their most recent version is titled "The Attorney General's Guidelines for Domestic FBI Operations."

116. Bruce Green & Rebecca Roiphe, "May Federal Prosecutors Take Direction from the President?," *Fordham Law Review*, vol. 87 (2019), p. 1817.

117. Green & Roiphe explain why federal prosecutors represent the nation's interests and not the president's in *May Federal Prosecutors Take Direction from the President?*

118. Green & Roiphe, *May Federal Prosecutors Take Direction from the President?*, pp. 1833–1834. In this article, Green and Roiphe argue that imbuing prosecutorial discretion with these types of illegitimate factors violates prosecutors' ethical obligations and may constitute constitutional violations of the rights of criminal defendants. In another article, they argue that Congress has *implicitly* granted the Attorney General and subordinate prosecutors sufficient prosecutorial discretion that delegates to them, rather than to the president, the power to make individualized decisions as to who should be prosecuted. Bruce Green & Rebecca Roiphe, "Can the President Control the Department of Justice?," *Alabama Law Review*, vol. 70 (2018), p. 1. My suggestion here is that Congress make that protection of prosecutorial independence, and thus that allocation of prosecutorial power, *explicit*. Going further than what I am proposing here, law professor Cass Sunstein, building on a proposal made by Senator Sam Ervin after Watergate, has suggested that Congress make the Department of Justice an independent agency that is "legally immunized from the president's day-to-day control." Cass R. Sunstein, "Imagine that Donald Trump Has Almost No Control Over Justice," *New York Times*, February 20, 2020.
119. Morrison v. Olson, 487 U.S. 654 (1988).
120. Humphrey's Executor v. United States, 295 U.S. 602 (1935).
121. Green & Roiphe, *Can the President Control the Department of Justice?*
122. Youngstown Sheet & Tube Co v. Sawyer, 343 U.S. 579, 637 (1952) (Jackson, J., concurring).
123. Barack Obama, "The President's Role in Advancing Criminal Justice Reform," *Harvard Law Review*, vol. 130 (2017), p. 811.
124. "Inspectors General: Independence Principles and Considerations for Reform," U.S. Government Accountability Office, June 8, 2020. This report contains several suggestions on how Congress can strengthen the oversight functions of IGs.
125. Seila Law LLC v. Consumer Financial Protection Bureau, 140 S. Ct. 2183 (2020). Jack Goldsmith, after noting that several of the IGs whom Trump removed had been appointed in an acting capacity, has suggested that Congress "limit the president's discretion to temporarily fill vacant inspectors general slots," a proposal that does not raise constitutional questions under *Seila Law*. Jack Goldsmith, "A Constitutional Response to Trump's Firings of Inspectors General," *Lawfare*, June 10, 2020.
126. Bauer & Goldsmith, *After Trump: Reconstructing the Presidency*.
127. H.R. 8363, 116th Congress (2020).
128. A.L.A. Schecter Poultry Corp. v. United States, 295 U.S. 495 (1935); Panama Refining Co. v. Ryan, 293 U.S. 388 (1935).
129. See, for example, Gundy v. United States, 139 S. Ct. 2116, 2123 (2019), and cases cited therein.
130. *Gundy*, 139 S. Ct. at 2135, 2142 (Gorsuch, J., dissenting). For representative arguments in favor of a more robust judicial enforcement of the nondelegation doctrine, see Ronald Cass, "Delegation Reconsidered: A Delegation Doctrine for the Modern Administrative State," *Harvard Journal of Law and Public Policy*, vol. 40 (2017), p. 147; David Schoenbrod, *Power Without Responsibility: How*

Congress Abuses the People Through Delegation (New Haven, CT: Yale University Press, 1993).

131. See, for example, Nicholas Bagley, "'Most of Government in Unconstitutional,'" *New York Times*, June 21, 2019. For a summary of progressive concerns about the consequences of implementing a more robust nondelegation doctrine, see William Araiza, "Toward a Non-Delegation Doctrine That (Even) Progressives Could Like," *American Constitution Society Supreme Court Review 2018–2019*, p. 211. See also Cass Sunstein, "Is the Clean Air Act Unconstitutional?," *Michigan Law Review*, vol. 98 (1999), p. 303.

132. Martin Redish proposes ways in which the nondelegation doctrine can be rendered judicially viable in "Pragmatic Formalism, Separation of Powers, and the Need to Revisit the NonDelegaton Doctrine," *Loyola University Chicago Law Journal*, vol. 51 (2019), p. 363. For thoughts on how the nondelegation doctrine can be applied in ways that account for at least some progressive concerns and priorities, see Araiza, *Toward a Non-Delegation Doctrine that (Even) Progressives Could Like*.

133. Redish, *Pragmatic Formalism*, p. 363.

134. Thomas Mann & Norman Ornstein, *It's Even Worse Than It Looks: How The American Constitutional System Collided with the New Politics of Extremism* (New York: Basic Books, 2012); Thomas Mann & Norman Ornstein, *The Broken Branch: How Congress Is Failing America and How to Get It Back on Track* (New York: Oxford University Press, 2006).

135. Burt Neuborne, *When at Times the Mob Is Swayed: A Citizen's Guide to Defending Our Republic* (New York: The New Press, 2019), p. 195.

136. Gene Healy, *The Cult of the Presidency: America's Dangerous Devotion to Executive Power* (Washington, D.C.: Cato Institute, 2008), p. 193.

137. Rudalevige, *The New Imperial Presidency*, p. 264.

138. Arthur Schlesinger Jr., *The Imperial Presidency* (Boston: Houghton Mifflin Co., 1973), pp. ix, x.

Chapter 5

1. For representative writings by progressive civil libertarians, see Floyd Abrams, *The Soul of the First Amendment* (New Haven, CT: Yale University Press, 2017); Nadine Strossen, *Hate: Why We Should Resist It with Free Speech, Not Censorship* (New York: Oxford University Press, 2018); and James Weinstein, *Hate Speech, Pornography, and the Radical Attack on Free Speech Doctrine* (New York: Routledge, 1999). The free speech philosophy of progressive civil libertarians is usually traced back to famous dissents and concurrences by Supreme Court justices Oliver Wendell Holmes Jr. and Louis Brandeis in cases involving the speech-based prosecutions of leftist radicals following World War I. Abrams v. United States, 250 U.S 616 (1919); Whitney v. California, 274 U.S. 357 (1927). See Thomas Healy, *The Great Dissent: How Oliver Wendell Holmes Changed His Mind—And Changed the History of Free Speech in America* (New York: Metropolitan Books, 2013).

2. See, for example, Richard Delgado & Jean Stefancic, *Must We Defend Nazis?* (New York: New York University Press, 1997); Catharine MacKinnon, *Only Words* (Cambridge, MA: Harvard University Press, 1994); and Jeremy Waldron, *The Harm in Hate Speech* (Cambridge, MA: Harvard University Press, 2012).

3. P.E. Moskowitz, *The Case Against Free Speech* (New York: Bold Type Books, 2019), pp. 9–10.

4. Moskowitz, *The Case Against Free Speech*, pp. 83–96; Aryeh Neier, *Defending My Enemy: American Nazis, The Skokie Case, and The Risks of Freedom* (New York: E.P. Dutton, 1979); Collin v. Smith, 578 F.2d 1197 (7th Cir. 1978); Skokie v. National Socialist Party of America, 373 N.E.2d 21 (Ill. 1978). For an account of how the ACLU, in effect, went from a progressive egalitarian organization before World War II to a civil libertarian one, see Laura Weintraub, *The Taming of Free Speech: America's Civil Liberties Compromise* (Cambridge, MA: Harvard University Press, 2016).

5. Alex Blasdel, "How the Resurgence of White Supremacy in the US Sparked a Debate Over Free Speech," *The Guardian*, May 31, 2018.

6. Moskowitz, *The Case Against Free Speech*, pp. 16–20; Sheryl Gay Stolberg & Brian Rosenthal, "Man Charged After White Nationalist Rally in Charlottesville Ends in Deadly Violence," *New York Times*, August 12, 2017.

7. Christopher Brennan, "KKK Leader Says He Is 'Glad' about Heather Heyer's Death," *New York Daily News*, August 15, 2017; Michael Shear & Maggie Haberman, "Trump Defends Initial Remarks on Charlottesville; Again Blames 'Both Sides,'" *New York Times*, August 15, 2017.

8. See, for example, K-Sue Park, "The ACLU Needs to Rethink Free Speech," *New York Times*, August 17, 2017.

9. Dara Lind, "Why the ACLU Is Adjusting Its Approach to Free Speech After Charlottesville," *Vox*, August 21, 2017.

10. David Cole, "Why We Must Still Defend Free Speech," *New York Review of Books*, August 24, 2017.

11. Erwin Chemerinsky & Howard Gillman, *Free Speech on Campus* (New Haven, CT: Yale University Press, 2017); Strossen, *Hate*; Keith Whittington, *Speak Freely: Why Universities Must Defend Free Speech* (Princeton, NJ: Princeton University Press, 2018).

12. Mary Anne Franks has noted that, as of 2014, there were 4,172 degree-granting institutions of higher education in the United States and that, according to a report by the Foundation for Individual Rights in Education (FIRE), there were forty-two attempted efforts to disinvite speakers on college campuses in 2016. About one-quarter of those efforts involved the same controversial speaker (Milo Yiannopoulos). Mary Anne Franks, *The Cult of the Constitution: Our Deadly Devotion to Guns and Free Speech* (Stanford, CA: Stanford University Press, 2019), p. 141.

13. Ulrich Baer, *What Snowflakes Get Right: Free Speech, Truth, and Equality on Campus* (New York: Oxford University Press, 2019); Franks, *The Cult of the Constitution*.

14. American Booksellers Association v. Hudnut, 771 F.2d 323, 328 (7th Cir. 1977).

15. See, for example, Amanda Shanor, "The New *Lochner*," *Wisconsin Law Review*, vol. 2016, p. 133; Jeremy Kessler & David Pozen, "The Search for an Egalitarian First Amendment," *Columbia Law Review*, vol. 118 (2018), p. 1953; Genevieve Lakier, "Imagining an Antisubordinating First Amendment," *Columbia Law Review*, vol. 118 (2018), p. 2156.

16. Catharine MacKinnon, "The First Amendment: An Equality Reading," in *The Free Speech Century*, p. 140. Lee Bollinger & Geoffrey Stone, eds. (New York: Oxford University Press, 2019).

17. Citizens United v. Federal Elections Commission, 558 U.S. 310 (2010); Amicus Curiae Brief of the American Civil Liberties Union in Support of Appellant on Supplemental Question, Citizens United v. Federal Election Commission, U.S. Supreme Court (2009).

18. Jeffrey Clements, *Corporations Are Not People: Reclaiming Democracy from Big Money and Global Corporations* (Oakland, CA: Berrett-Koehler, 2014); Derek Cressman, *When Money Talk$: The High Price of "Free" Speech and the Selling of Democracy* (Oakland, CA: Berrett-Koehler, 2016).

19. For an exploration of these issues, see Carlos A. Ball, *The First Amendment and LGBT Equality: A Contentious History* (Cambridge, MA: Harvard University Press, 2017).

20. See, for example, Morse v. Frederick, 551 U.S. 393 (2009); Garcetti v. Ceballos, 547 U.S. 410 (2006); United States v. Kokinda, 497 U.S. 720 (1990).

21. Ronald Krotoszynski Jr., *The Disappearing First Amendment* (New York: Cambridge University Press, 2019), p. 13. See also Gregory Magarian, *Managed Speech: The Roberts Court's First Amendment* (New York: Oxford University Press, 2017).

22. Lincoln Caplan, "The Embattled First Amendment," *The American Scholar*, March 4, 2015.

23. For a rigorous and thoughtful exploration of First Amendment issues raised during Trump's first two years in office, see Timothy Zick, *The First Amendment in the Trump Era* (New York: Oxford University Press, 2019).

24. Libby Cathey & Meghan Keneally, "A Look Back at Trump Comments Perceived as Encouraging Violence," *ABC News*, May 30, 2020; Veronica Stracqualursi, "How Donald Trump Handles Protestors and What He Thinks of Them," *ABC News*, March 10, 2016; Gabrielle Levy, "Nostalgic for 'Old Days,' Trump Wants to Punch Protester 'in the Face,'" *U.S. News & World Report*, February 23, 2016.

25. Michael Grynbaum, "Trump Renews Pledge to 'Take a Strong Look' at Libel Laws," *New York Times*, January 10, 2018.

26. Cathey & Keneally, "A Look Back at Trump Comments Perceived as Encouraging Violence."

27. Nwanguma v. Trump, 903 F.3d 604, 606 (6th Cir. 2018).

28. Sonja West, "Presidential Attacks on the Press," *Missouri Law Review*, vol. 83 (2018), pp. 915, 928. See also Michael Edison Hayden, "Critics Pounce on Trump After CNN Wrestling Tweet," *ABC News*, July 2, 2017.

29. Julia Carrie Wong & Sam Levin, "Republican Candidate Charged with Assault After 'Body-Slamming' Reporter," *The Guardian*, May 25, 2017; David Leonhardt, "The President Praises an Assault," *New York Times*, October 19, 2018.

30. Katie Robertson, "Trump Turns Attack on MSNBC Journalist into Rally Fodder," *New York Times*, September 23, 2020.

31. Michael Grynbaum, "Trump Calls the News Media the 'Enemy of the People,'" *New York Times*, February 17, 2017.

32. West, *Presidential Attacks on the Press*, p. 915; Zick, *The First Amendment in the Trump Era*, p. xiii.

33. Peter Baker, "Bolton Says Trump Impeachment Inquiry Missed Other Troubling Episodes," *New York Times*, June 17, 2020.

34. West, *Presidential Attacks on the Press*, p. 915. For the relationship between Trump and Fox News, see Brian Stelter, *Donald Trump, Fox News, and the Dangerous Distortion of Truth* (New York: One Signal, 2020).

35. Eli Rosenberg, "Trump Admitted He Attacks Press to Shield Himself from Negative Coverage, Leslie Stahl Says," *Washington Post*, May 22, 2018.

36. IPSOS, Americans' Views on the Media, August 7, 2018, https://www.ipsos.com/en-us/news-polls/americans-views-media-2018-08-07.

37. Amended Complaint for Injunctive and Declaratory Relief, PEN American Center, Inc. v. Trump, S.D.N.Y., February 6, 2019.

38. Amended Complaint, PEN American Center, Inc. v. Trump; Cathey & Keneally, "A Look Back at Trump Comments Perceived as Encouraging Violence."

39. Michael Grynbaum, "Another Year of Trump Attacks, 'Ominous Signs' for the American Press," *New York Times*, December 30, 2019.

40. West, *Presidential Attacks on the Press*, p. 920.

41. West, *Presidential Attacks on the Press*, p. 920.

42. Peter Baker, "Trump Bars CNN's Jim Acosta from the White House," *New York Times*, November 7, 2018; Michael Grynbaum & Emily Baumgaertner, "CNN's Jim Acosta Returns to the White House After Judge's Ruling," *New York Times*, November 16, 2018; Grynbaum, "Another Year of Trump Attacks"; Paul Farhi, "Judge Orders White House to Restore Press Pass of Reporter Involved in Confrontation," *Washington Post*, September 3, 2019; Karem v. Trump, 960 F.3d 656 (D.C. Circ. 2020).

43. Michael Levenson, "Pompeo Lashes Out at Reporter and Challenges Her to Find Ukraine on a Map," *New York Times*, January 24, 2020; Edward Wong, "Pompeo Denounces News Media, Undermining U.S. Message on Press Freedom," *New York Times*, January 25, 2020; Lara Jakes, "State Department Will Not Allow NPR Reporter on Pompeo's Plane Following Interview," *New York Times*, January 27, 2020.

44. Michael Grynbaum, "Trump Renews Pledge to 'Take a Strong Look at Libel Laws,'" *New York Times*, January 10, 2018.

45. Michael Wolff, *Fire and Fury: Inside the Trump White House* (New York: Henry Holt, 2018).

46. Charlie Savage, "Justice Department Escalates Legal Fight with Bolton Over Book," *New York Times*, June 17, 2020; John Bolton, *The Room Where It Happened* (New York: Simon & Schuster, 2020).

47. Katie Benner, "Justice Department Opens Inquiry into John Bolton's Book," *New York Times*, September 15, 2020.

48. Katie Benner & Charlie Savage, "Targeting Bolton, Justice Department Again in Alignment with Trump's Desires," *New York Times*, June 18, 2020.

49. Michael Schmidt & Charlie Savage, "White House Accused of Improperly Politicizing Review of John Bolton's Book," *New York Times*, September 23, 2020.

50. Hadas Gold, "Donald Trump: We're Going to 'Open Up' Libel Laws," *Politico*, February 26, 2016; Michael Grynbaum, "Trump Renews Pledge to 'Take a Strong Look' at Libel Laws," *New York Times*, January 10, 2018; Mark Stern, "Trump Is Now Openly Trying to Censor His Critics. He May Succeed," *Slate*, March 26, 2020; Mark Grynbaum & Marc Tracy, "Trump Campaign Sues New York Times Over 2019 Opinion Article," *New York Times*, February 26, 2020; Mark Tracy, "Trump Campaign Sues the Washington Post for Libel," *New York Times*, March 3, 2020; Michael Grynbaum & Maggie Haberman, "Trump Demands CNN Retract a Poll, as OANN Teases a Rosier View," *New York Times*, June 10, 2020; Jonathan Easley, "Trump Campaign Sues TV Station Over Democratic Super PAC Ad," *The Hill*, April 13, 2020.

51. Michael Shear, Nick Wingfield, & Cecilia Kang, "Trump Attacks Amazon, Saying It Does Not Pay Enough Taxes," *New York Times*, March 29, 2018; Jacqueline Thomsen, "Trump Accuses Washington Post of Being Lobbyist Weapon for Amazon," *The Hill*, July 24, 2017.

52. Damian Paletta & Josh Dawsey, "Trump Personally Pushed Postmaster General to Double Rates On Amazon, Other Firms," *Washington Post*, May 18, 2018.

53. Executive Order 13,829 (April 12, 2018); Michael Shear, "Trump, Having Denounced Amazon's Shipping Deal, Orders Review of Postal Service," *New York Times*, April 12, 2018.

54. Patricia Zengerle & David Morgan, "Trump Holds Up Coronavirus Aid to Block Funding for Mail-in Voting," *Reuters*, August 13, 2020; Michael Shear, Hailey Fuchs, & Kenneth Vogel, "Mail Delays Fuel Concern Trump Is Undercutting Postal System Ahead of Voting," *New York Times*, July 31, 2020.

55. Editorial, "Mr. Trump Casts a Shadow Over the AT&T-Time Warner Deal," *New York Times*, November 15, 2017.

56. West, *Presidential Attacks on the Press*, pp. 928–931; Brent Kendall & Drew FitzGerald, "AT&T Beats U.S. in Antitrust Fight Over Time Warner," *Wall Street Journal*, June 12, 2018.

57. David Nakamura, "Trump Escalates Threats Against Press, Calls News Coverage 'Frankly Disgusting,'" *Washington Post*, October 11, 2017; David Shepardson, "Trump Suggests Challenging TV Network Licenses Over 'Fake News,'" *Reuters*, October 11, 2017.

58. Editorial, "A Presidential Smear," *Wall Street Journal*, May 26, 2020; Peter Baker & Maggie Astor, "Trump Pushes a Conspiracy Theory That Falsely Accuses a TV Host of Murder," *New York Times*, May 27, 2020.

59. Zick, *The First Amendment in the Trump Era*, p. xiv.

60. Michael Shear, "With a Tweet, Trump Upends Republican Strategy for Dealing with Yovanovitch," *New York Times*, November 15, 2019.

61. Peter Baker et al., "Trump Fires Impeachment Witnesses Gordon Sondland and Alexander Vindman in Post-Acquittal Purge," *New York Times*, February 7, 2020.

62. Eric Schmitt & Helene Cooper, "Army Officer Who Clashed with Trump Over Impeachment Is Set to Retire," *New York Times*, July 8, 2020.

63. Michael Shear & Maggie Haberman, "Health Department Official Says Doubts on Hydroxychloroquine Led to His Ouster," *New York Times*, April 22, 2020; Sheryl Gay Stolberg, "Federal Watchdog Says Coronavirus Whistle-Blower Should Be Reinstated as It Investigates," *New York Times*, May 8, 2020.

64. Sheryl Gay Stolberg, "'Lives Were Lost as Warnings Went Unheeded,' Whistle-Blower Tells House," *New York Times*, May 14, 2020.

65. Stolberg, "Federal Watchdog Says Coronavirus Whistle-Blower Should be Reinstated as It Investigates."

66. Eric Schmitt, Charlie Savage, & Noah Weiland, "Longtime Pentagon Watchdog Stepping Down from Post," *New York Times*, May 26, 2020; Maggie Haberman, Charlie Savage, & Nicholas Fandos, "Trump to Fire Intelligence Watchdog Who Had Key Role in Ukraine Complaint," *New York Times*, April 7, 2020.

67. Catie Edmondson & Michael Shear, "Trump Ousted State Department Watchdog at Pompeo's Urging; Democrats Open Inquiry," *New York Times*, May 16, 2020; Edward Wong, "Inspector General's Firing Puts Pompeo's Use of Taxpayer Funds Under Scrutiny," *New York Times*, May 17, 2020.

68. Pranshu Verma & Edward Wong, "Another Inspector General Resigns Amid Questions About Pompeo," *New York Times*, August 5, 2020.

69. Ali Watkins, "'Kettling' of Peaceful Protestors Shows Aggressive Shift by N.Y. Police," *New York Times*, June 5, 2020.

70. Timothy Zick, "Protests in Peril," *U.S. News & World Report*, November 20, 2017.

71. Jacyln Peiser, "Journalist Charged with Rioting at Inauguration Goes Free," *New York Times*, December 21, 2017.

72. Moskowitz, *The Case Against Free Speech*, p. 151. Moskowitz provides a sobering account of the government's prosecutorial strategy and its chilling effect on dissent at pp. 143–153.

73. Julie Hirschfield Davis & Michael Shear, "Trump Revokes Ex-C.I.A. Director John Brennan's Security Clearance," *New York Times*, August 15, 2018; Press Briefing by Press Secretary Sarah Sanders, July 23, 2018; Adam Godman, "Andrew McCabe, Ex-F.B.I. Official, Will Not Be Charged in Lying Case," *New York Times*, February 14, 2020.

74. William McRaven, "Revoke My Security Clearance, Too, Mr. President," *Washington Post*, August 16, 2018.

75. Knight First Amendment Institute at Columbia University v. Trump, 928 F.3d 226, 232 (2nd Cir. 2019).

76. Benjamin Weiser & Alan Feuer, "Judge Orders Cohen Released, Citing 'Retaliation' Over Tell-All Book," *New York Times*, July 23, 2020; Michael Cohen, *Disloyal: A Memoir* (New York: Skyhorse, 2020).

77. Peter Baker, Katie Benner, & Michael Stern, "Jeff Sessions Is Forced Out as Attorney General as Trump Installs Loyalist," *New York Times*, November 7, 2018; Veronica Stracqualursi & Jessica Schneider, "Trump to DOJ: Don't Let Debbie Wasserman Schultz, Aide, 'Off the Hook,'" *CNN*, June 7, 2018; Michael Schmidt, "Mueller Report Reveals Trump's Fixation on Targeting Hillary Clinton," *New York Times*, April 24, 2019.

78. Maggie Haberman & Michael Crowley, "Trump Calls on Barr to 'Act' Against Biden Before the Election," *New York Times*, October 20, 2020.

79. Louis Nelson, "Trump Calls for Jailing, Revoking Citizenship of Flag Burners," *Politico*, November 29, 2016.

80. Cass Sunstein, "The President Who Would Bring Back the Sedition Act," *Denver Post*, August 29, 2018.

81. Anemona Hartocollis & Miriam Jordan, "As Universities Seek to Block Visa Rules, Trump Threatens Tax Status," *New York Times*, July 10, 2020.

82. Daniel Chaitin, "Trump Asks if FEC, FCC Should Investigate 'SNL' and Late-Night Shows," *Washington Examiner*, March 17, 2019.

83. Julie Hirschfeld Davis, "Trump Calls for Boycott if N.F.L. Doesn't Crack Down on Anthem Protests." *New York Times*, September 24, 2017; Ken Belson, "As Trump Rekindles N.F.L. Fight, Goodell Sides with Players," *New York Times*, June 5, 2020.

84. Ken Kirby, "Trump Wants Fewer Immigrants from 'Shithole Countries' and More from Places like Norway," *Vox*, January 11, 2018.

85. David Leonhardt & Ian Pasad Philbrick, "Donald Trump's Racism: The Definitive List, Updated," *New York Times*, January 15, 2018.

86. "Full Text: Donald Trump Announces a Presidential Bid," *Washington Post*, June 16, 2015; Jenna Johnson & Philip Rucker, "In San Diego, Trump Shames Local 'Mexican Judge' as Protestors Storm Streets," *Washington Post*, May 27, 2016.

87. Eric Lach, "The Corrupting Falsehoods of Trump's Oval Office Speech," *The New Yorker*, January 8, 2019.

88. Leonhardt & Philbrick, "Donald Trump's Racism: The Definitive List, Updated."

89. Peter Baker, "More Than Ever, Trump Casts Himself as the Defender of White America," *New York Times*, September 6, 2020.

90. David Smith et al., "Donald Trump Refuses to Condemn White Supremacists at Presidential Debate," *The Guardian*, September 29, 2020.

91. Katie Rogers & Nicholas Fando, "Trump Tells Congresswomen to 'Go Back' to the Countries They Came From," *New York Times*, July 14, 2019.

92. David Graham et al., "An Oral History of Trump's Bigotry," *The Atlantic*, June 2019.

93. Christina Caron, "Trump Mocks LeBron James's Intelligence and Calls Don Lemon 'Dumbest Man' on TV," *New York Times*, August 4, 2018; Paul Fahri, "What a Stupid Question: Trump Demeans Three Black Female Reporters in Three Days," *Washington Post*, November 9, 2018; Kara Alaimo, "Why Trump Keeps Calling Women 'Nasty,'" *CNN*, August 21, 2019; Katie Rogers, "Kamala Harris Crystallizes Trump's View of Women: They're 'Nasty' or Housewives," *New York Times*, August 12, 2020.

94. Jonathan Martin & Maggie Haberman, "Hand-Wringing in G.O.P. After Donald Trump's Remarks on Megyn Kelly," *New York Times*, August 8, 2015; Josh Dawsey & Felicia Sonmez, "Trump Mocks Kavanaugh Accuser Christine Blasey Ford," *Washington Post*, October 2, 2018; Jose Del Real, "Trump Denies He Mocked Journalist," *Washington Post*, November 27, 2015; Irin Carmon, "Donald Trump's Worst Offense? Mocking Disabled Reporter, Poll Finds," *NBC News*, August 11, 2016.

95. Abrams v. United States, 250 U.S. 616 (1919) (Holmes, J., dissenting).

96. Susan Hennessey & Benjamin Wittes, *Unmaking the Presidency: Donald Trump's War on the World's Most Powerful Office* (New York: Farrar, Straus and Giroux, 2020), pp. 109, 110, 113.

97. James Pfiffner, "The Lies of Donald Trump: A Taxonomy," in *Presidential Leadership and the Trump Presidency: Executive Power and Democratic Government*, pp. 15, 18. Charles Lamb & Jacob Neiheisel, eds. (New York: Palgrave, 2019).

98. Kate Conger & Davey Alba, "Twitter Refutes Inaccuracies in Trump's Tweets About Mail-In Voting," *New York Times*, May 26, 2020; Peter Baker & Daisuke Wakabayashi, "Trump's Order on Social Media Could Harm One Person in Particular: Donald Trump," *New York Times*, May 28, 2020.

99. Kim Barker & Matt Furber, "Bail Is at Least $1 Million for Ex-Officer Accused of Killing George Floyd," *New York Times*, June 8, 2020; Richard Fausset, "What We Know About the Shooting Death of Ahmaud Arbery," *New York Times*, June 24, 2020; Heather Murphy & Sarah Mervosh, "Louisville Police Move to Fire Officer in Death of Breonna Taylor," *New York Times*, June 19, 2020.

100. "Harper's Index," *Harper's Magazine*, December 2020 (citing data collected by the Armed Conflict Location and Data Project).

101. Michael Wines, "'Looting' Comment from Trump Dates Back to Racial Unrest of the 1960s," *New York Times*, May 29, 2020.

102. Kate Conger and Mark Isaac, "Twitter Permanently Bans Trump, Capping Online Revolt," *New York Times*, January 8, 2021.

103. Maggie Haberman & Liz Robbins, "Trump, on Long Island, Vows an End to Gun Violence," *New York Times*, July 28, 2017.

104. Caleb Ecarma, "Trump Supporters Are Staging Armed Protests to Stick It to Coronavirus," *Vanity Fair*, April 16, 2020.

105. Katie Rogers, Jonathan Martin, & Maggie Haberman, "As Trump Calls Protestors 'Terrorists,' Tear Gas Clears a Path for his Walk to a Church," *New York Times*, June 2, 2020.

106. Adam Goldman, "Trump Reverses Restrictions on Military Hardware for Police," *New York Times*, August 28, 2017; Julie Hirschfeld Davis & Michael Shear, "Obama Puts Focus on Police Success in Struggling City in New Jersey," *New York Times*, May 18, 2015.

107. "Harper's Index," *Harper's*, September, 2020.

108. Charlie Savage, "Incitement to Riot? What Trump Told Supporters Before Mob Stormed Capitol," *New York Times*, January 10, 2021.

109. Nicholas Fandos, "Trump Impeached for Inciting Insurrection," *New York Times*, January 13, 2021.

110. Maggie Haberman, "Trump Threatens White House Protestors with 'Vicious Dogs' and 'Ominous Weapons,'" *New York Times*, May 31, 2020; Christine Hauser, "What Is the Insurrection Act of 1807, the Law Behind Trump's Threat to the States?" *New York Times*, June 2, 2020.

111. K.K. Rebecca Lai, Bill Marsh, & Anjali Singhvi, "Here are the 99 U.S. Cities Where Protestors Were Tear-Gassed," *New York Times*, June 17, 2020.

112. Rogers et al., "As Trump Calls Protestors 'Terrorists.'"

113. Rogers et al., "As Trump Calls Protestors 'Terrorists'"; Peter Baker et al., "How Trump's Idea of a Photo Op Led to Havoc in a Park," *New York Times*, June 3, 2020.

114. Maggie Haberman, Nick Corasaniti, & Annie Karni, "As Trump Pushes into Portland, His Campaign Ads Turn Darker," *New York Times*, July 21, 2020; Marissa Lang, "'What Choice Do We Have?': Portland's 'Wall of Moms' Faces Off with Federal Officers at Tense Protests," *Washington Post*, July 22, 2020.

115. Sergio Olmos, Mike Baker, & Zolan Kanno-Youngs, "Federal Agents Unleash Militarized Crackdown on Portland," *New York Times*, July 17, 2020; Mike Baker, Thomas Fuller, & Sergio Olmos, "Federal Agents Push Into Portland Streets, Stretching Limits of Their Authority," *New York Times*, July 25, 2020.

116. Olmos et al., "Federal Agents Unleash Militarized Crackdown on Portland."

117. Index Newspaper LLC v. United States Marshals Service, 977 F.3d 817, 822–823 (9th Cir. 2020). See also Index Newspapers LLC v. City of Portland, 2020 WL 4220820 (D.C. Or.).

118. Mike Baker, "Federal Agents Envelop Portland Protests, and City's Mayor, in Tear Gas," *New York Times*, July 23, 2020; Mike Baker & Zolan Kanno-Youngs, "Federal Agencies Agree to Withdraw from Portland, with Conditions," *New York Times*, July 29, 2020.

119. Walker v. Texas Division, Sons of Confederate Veterans, Inc., 576 U.S. 200 (2015).

120. On government speech and constitutional protections, see Helen Norton, *The Government's Speech and the Constitution* (New York: Cambridge University Press, 2019). For the argument that government propaganda should be deemed to violate the Free Speech Clause, see Caroline Mala Corbin, "The Unconstitutionality of Government Propaganda," *Ohio State Law Journal,* vol. 81 (2020), p. 815.

121. Boos v. Barry, 485 U.S. 312, 322 (1988).

122. Snyder v. Phelps, 562 U.S. 447 (2011). Law professor Sonja West argues that Trump's verbal attacks on the press were constitutionally protected. West, *Presidential Attacks on the Press*, pp. 934–935.

123. Knight First Amendment Institute at Columbia University v. Trump, 928 F.3d 226 (2nd Cir. 2019).

124. Karem v. Trump, 960 F.3d 656 (D.C. Circ. 2020); Farhi, "Judge Orders White House to Restore Press Pass of Reporter Involved in Confrontation."

125. Charlie Savage, "Judge Rejects Trump Request for Order Blocking Bolton's Memoir," *New York Times*, June 20, 2020.

126. Benjamin Weiser, "U.S. Backs Down, Allowing Michael Cohen to Write Trump Tell-All Book," *New York Times*, July 30, 2020.

127. New York Times v. Sullivan, 376 U.S. 254 (1964).

128. Trump v. Hawaii, 138 S. Ct. 2392 (2018).

129. Tim Wu, "Trump's Response to Twitter Is Unconstitutional Harassment," *New York Times*, June 2, 2020.

130. Wu, "Trump's Response to Twitter is Unconstitutional Harassment."

131. Lozman v. City of Riviera Beach, 138 S. Ct. 1945, 1949 (2018). The Center for Democracy and Technology filed a lawsuit arguing that Trump's executive order was retaliatory and violated the social media companies' free speech rights. Kate Conger,

"Lawsuit Says Trump's Social Media Crackdown Violates Free Speech," *New York Times*, June 2, 2020.

132. Zick, *The First Amendment in the Trump Era*, p. xxiv.

133. Kristy Parker & Ben Berwick, "How White House Threats to Revoke Security Clearances Violate the First Amendment," *Lawfare*, July 27, 2018.

134. Robert Post, "Do Trump's NFL Attacks Violate the First Amendment?" *Politico*, September 27, 2017.

135. Garrison v. Louisiana, 379 U.S. 64, 74–75 (1964); First National Bank of Boston v. Bellotti, 435 U.S. 765, 777 (1978); Roth v. United States, 354 U.S. 476, 484 (1957).

136. New York Times v. Sullivan, 376 U.S. at 292.

137. Ms. L. v. U.S Immigration & Customs Enforcement, 310 F. Supp. 3d 1133, 1145–1146 (S.D. Cal. 2018). On the cruelty behind the family separation policy, see Jacob Soboroff, *Separated: Inside an American Tragedy* (New York: Custom House, 2020).

138. Jasmine Aguilera, "Here's What to Know About the Status of Family Separation at the U.S. Border, Which Isn't Nearly Over," *Time*, September 20, 2019. This article details how the administration continued to separate hundreds of children from their families even after it rescinded its "zero tolerance" policy. On the administration's chaotic efforts to return children to their families separated under the policy, see Julie Hirschfeld Davis & Michael Shear, *Border Wars: Inside Trump's Assault on Immigration* (New York: Simon & Schuster, 2019), ch. 25. On the hundreds of children who remained separated years later, see Caitlin Dickerson, "Parents of 545 Children Separated at the Border Cannot Be Found," *New York Times*, October 21, 2020.

139. Julianne Hing, "Shoved Aside Again, DACA Activists Keep Fighting," *The Nation*, February 9, 2018.

140. Larry Buchanan, Quoctrung Bui, & Jugal Patel, "Black Lives Matter May Be the Largest Movement in U.S. History," *New York Times*, July 3, 2020.

141. Nate Cohn & Kevin Quealy, "How Public Opinion Has Moved on Black Lives Matter," *New York Times*, June 10, 2020; Amy Harmon et al., "From Cosmetics to NASCAR, Calls for Racial Justice Are Spreading," *New York Times*, June 14, 2020.

142. Kim Parker, Juliana Menasce Horowitz, & Monica Anderson, "Amid Protests, Majorities Across Racial and Ethnic Groups Express Support for the Black Lives Matter Movement," Pew Research Center, June 12, 2020.

143. Packingham v. North Carolina, 137 S. Ct. 1730, 1737 (2017).

144. Megan Brennan, "Americans' Trust in Mass Media Edges Down to 41," *Gallup*, September 26, 2019.

145. "In 1,267 Days, President Trump Has Made 20,055 False or Misleading Claims," *Washington Post*, July 9, 2020.

146. Brian Stelter, "Trump's Relationship with Fox News Is Unprecedented," *CNN*, March 18, 2019; Paul Fahri, "Trump's Love-Hate Relationship with Fox News Just Turned to Hate Again," *Washington Post*, July 8, 2019.

147. Zick, *The First Amendment in the Trump Era*, pp. 22, 23.

148. Zick, *The First Amendment in the Trump Era*, p. 47.

149. Waldron, *The Harm in Hate Speech*, pp. 8–9.

150. Brandenburg v. Ohio, 395 U.S. 444 (1969); Black v. Virginia, 538 U.S. 343 (2003).

151. FBI, Hate Crimes Statistics, 2017, available at https://ucr.fbi.gov/hate-crime/2017.

152. Anti-Defamation League, 2017 Audit of Anti-Semitic Incidents, February 27, 2018.

153. Anti-Defamation League, 2019 Audit of Anti-Semitic Incidents, February 27, 2018. See also Liam Stack, "Most Visible Jews Fear Being Targets as Anti-Semitism Rises," *New York Times*, February 17, 2020.

154. Karsten Muller & Carlo Schwarz, "From Hashtag to Hate Crime: Twitter and Anti-Minority Sentiment," 2019, available at https://ssrn.com/abstract=3149103. Interestingly, Muller and Schwarz found that "the increase in hate crimes targeting Muslims predominantly originates in counties with high Twitter usage." But one study concluded that hate speech on Twitter did not increase during the 2016 presidential campaign and its aftermath. Alexandra Siegel et al., "Trumping Hate on Twitter, Online Hate in the 2016 Election and its Aftermath" (unpublished manuscript, 2020).

155. Ayal Feinberg, Regina Branton, & Valerie Martinez-Ebers, "Counties That Hosted a 2016 Trump Rally Saw a 226 Percent Increase in Hate Crimes," *Washington Post*, March 22, 2019.

156. Griffin Edwards & Stephen Rushin, "The Effect of President's Trump Election on Hate Crimes," available at https://ssrn.com/abstract=3102652. For media reporting on the increase in hate crimes during the Trump years, see, for example, Jaweed Kaleem, "Latinos and Transgender People See Big Increases in Hate Crimes, FBI Reports," *Los Angeles Times*, November 12, 2019; Michael Kunzelman & Astrid Galvan, "Trump Words Linked to More Hate Crime? Some Experts Think So," *Associated Press*, August 7, 2019; Sarah Ravani, "FBI: Hate Crimes in U.S., CA Surge in First Year of Trump's Presidency," *San Francisco Chronicle*, November 14, 2018; Maria Hinojosa, "Hate Crimes Against Latinos Increase in California," *NPR*, July 15, 2018; David Lohr, "Report Shows Massive Increase in Anti-LGBTQ Violence Since Trump Took Office," *Huffington Post*, January 22, 2018.

157. Tim Arango, "Hate Crimes in U.S. Rose to Highest Level in More Than a Decade in 2019," *New York Times*, November 16, 2020.

158. Jeannine Bell, "The Resistance and the Stubborn but Unsurprising Persistence of Hate and Extremism in the United States," *Indiana Journal of Global Legal Studies*, vol. 26 (2019), pp. 305, 306. See also Jamelle Bouie, "Trump's Embrace of Racial Bigotry Has Shifted What Is Acceptable in America," *Slate*, October 30, 2018; Tom Jacobs, "Trump's Election Made Bigotry More Acceptable," *Pacific Standard*, February 21, 2018.

159. Joseph Goldstein, "Alt-Right Gathering Exults in Trump Election with Nazi-Era Salute," *New York Times*, November 20, 2016.

160. Hillary Hanson, "Ex-KKK Leader David Duke Says White Supremacists Will 'Fulfill' Trump's Promises," *Huffington Post*, August 12, 2017.

161. See, for example, Timothy Garton Ash, *Free Speech: Ten Principles for a Connected World* (New Haven, CT: Yale University Press, 2016), pp. 219–220; Strossen, *Hate*, pp. 136–140.

162. Garton Ash, *Free Speech*, pp. 214–219; Strossen, *Hate*, pp. 122–128.

163. Miller v. California, 413 U.S. 15 (1973).
164. Gertz v. Robert Welch, Inc., 418 U.S. 323 (1974).
165. Holder v. Humanitarian Law Project, 561 U.S. 1 (2010).
166. Waldron, *The Harm in Hate Speech*.
167. "Full Text: Donald Trump Announces a Presidential Bid," *Washington Post*, June 16, 2015.
168. Rogers & Fando, "Trump Tells Congresswomen to 'Go Back' to the Countries They Came From."
169. Leonhardt and Philbrick, "Donald Trump's Racism: The Definitive List, Updated."
170. Brian Klaas, "A Short History of President Trump's Anti-Muslim Bigotry," *Washington Post*, March 15, 2019.
171. Philip Salzman, "Affirmative Action: The Systemic Racism No One Wants to Talk About," *PJ Media*, June 6, 2020.
172. Lisa Lerer, Giovanni Russonello, & Isabella Grullón Paz, "On LGBTQ Rights, a Gulf Between Trump and Many Republican Voters," *New York Times*, June 17, 2020. Following the violence that was part of the white supremacist rally in Charlottesville, the Massachusetts Republican Party considered issuing a condemnation of hate groups that, according to proponents, included Black Lives Matter. Frank Phillips, "State GOP Debates Condemning Hate Groups—and That Might Include Black Lives Matter," *Boston Globe*, August 27, 2017.
173. Erik Nelson, "If We Silence Hate Speech, Will We Silence Resistance?," *New York Times*, August 9, 2018.
174. Strossen, *Hate*, p. 89; Doe v. University of Michigan, 721 F. Supp. 852 (E.D. Mich. 1989).
175. Strossen, *Hate*, p. 89.
176. Glenn Greenwald, "In Europe, Hate Speech Laws Are Often Used to Suppress and Punish Left-Wing Viewpoints," *The Intercept*, August 29, 2017.
177. Strossen, *Hate*, pp. 28–29; Richard Seymour, "Azhar Ahmed—Charged with Treason Over Facebook Comments?," *The Guardian*, March 12, 2012.
178. Mary Frances O'Dowd, "Explainer: What Is Systemic Racism and Institutional Racism?," *The Conversation*, February 4, 2020.
179. Ralph Richard Banks & Richard Thompson Ford, "(How) Does Unconscious Bias Matter? Law, Politics, and Racial Inequality," *Emory Law Journal*, vol. 59 (2009), p. 1053.
180. Strossen makes a similar point in *Hate*, p. 15.
181. Vincent Blasi, "The Pathological Perspective and the First Amendment," *Columbia Law Review*, vol. 85 (1985), pp. 449, 449–450. My thanks to Tim Zick for reminding me of Blasi's theory in an e-mail exchange.
182. *The Federalist Papers*, n. 51 (James Madison), Lawrence Goldman, ed. (New York: Oxford University Press, 2008), p. 257.
183. Frederick Schauer, "The Second-Best First Amendment," *William & Mary Law Review*, vol. 31 (1989), p. 1.
184. For some of those arguments, see sources cited in note 15.

185. Louis Seidman, "Can Free Speech Be Progressive?," *Columbia Law Review*, vol. 118 (2018), p. 2219.
186. Ball, *The First Amendment and LGBT Equality*.
187. Seidman, *Can Free Speech be Progressive?*, pp. 2223, 2242.

Epilogue

1. Steven Calabresi, "Trump Might Try to Postpone the Election. That's Unconstitutional," *New York Times*, July 30, 2020; Sanya Mansoor, "President Trump Refuses to Say If He Will Accept the 2020 Election Results," *Time*, July 19, 2020.
2. Adam Liptak, "Trump Takes Aim at Appeals Court, Calling it a Disgrace," *New York Times*, November 20, 2018.
3. Trump v. Mazars USA, 140 S. Ct. 2019 (2020).
4. Bostock v. Clayton County, 140 S. Ct. 1731 (2020).
5. June Medical Services v. Russo, 140 S.Ct. 2103 (2020).
6. Susan Hennessey & Benjamin Wittes, *Unmaking the Presidency: Donald Trump's War on the World's Most Powerful Office* (New York: Farrar, Straus and Giroux, 2020), p. 290.
7. Eric Posner, "Why Joe Biden Must Not Shy Away From the Full Power of the Presidency," *New York Times*, January 21, 2021.

Index

Abbott, Greg, 67
Ackerman, Bruce, 127, 130, 172
ACLU, 2, 187–188, 190
Acosta, Jim, 195–196
acting appointments, 158
Adler, Jonathan, 49
administrative agencies, 110–111, 126–128, 170, 178–179
Administrative Procedure Act, 140, 142, 173
Affordable Care Act of 2010. *See* Obamacare
Ahmaud, Arbery, 206–207
Alabama, 42, 44
Alaska, 49
Amar, Akhil Reed, 18
Amazon. *See* Jeff Bezos
anti-commandeering doctrine
  and immigration enforcement, 57–58, 60–63
  and marijuana enforcement, 50
  and slavery, 27, 29, 31–33, 61
  and state cooperation, 92
  and Trump, 88, 234
  See also *Prigg v. Pennsylvania*; *Printz v. United States*
Anti-Defamation League, 223
Arkansas, 42
Articles of Confederation, 18–19, 34, 103, 104
Atkinson, Michael, 156–157
AT&T, 72, 198

Babich, Adam, 68
Baker, Charlie, 83
Baker, H. Robert, 30
Bannon, Steve, 161, 162
Barr, William, 154, 159–160, 162
Barrett, Amy Coney, 233
Bauer, Bob, 177
Becerra, Xavier, 71
Begala, Paul, 129
Bell, Jeannine, 224
Berman, Geoffrey, 162
Bezos, Jeff, 157–158, 197, 213
Biden, Hunter 154
Biden, Joe, 4, 85, 91, 181, 235
  and election certification, 207, 209
  and election polls, 197

and Trump pressure to investigate, 148, 202
  and Ukraine investigation, 99, 153–154
Bill of Rights, 19–20, 22, 38, 86
  and federalism, 94–95
Black Codes, 36, 37
Black Lives Matter
  Minneapolis protests, 194
  nationwide protests, 203, 206–207, 209, 211, 218–220, 222, 233
  Portland protests, 89, 210, 217
  Washington, D.C., protests, 207, 209–210, 217
Blasey Ford, Christine, 205
Blasi, Vincent, 229, 230, 231
Bolton, John, 163, 194, 196–197, 212
Booth, Sherman, 30
border wall, 65, 81, 122, 145, 165–170, 174
Bork, Robert, 124, 149
Brady Handgun Violence Prevention Act, 31–32, 33
Brandeis, Louis, 16
Brennan Center for Justice, 2
Brennan, John, 201
Brettschneider, Corey, 142
Bright, Rick, 200
Broidy, Elliott, 161
Brown v. Board of Education (1954), 42–43
Buchanan, James, 29
Bush, George H.W., 126, 130, 131, 140
Bush, George W., 129, 130, 141, 171, 173, 223
  and dignity-in-dying laws, 51
  and emergency declarations, 168
  and environmental policies, 69, 70
  and immigration enforcement, 56–57, 137
  and national security, 100, 128, 131–134
  and signing statements, 134–135
  and use of military force, 131
Byrd, Harry, 42

Calhoun, John, 31
California
  and clean air regulations, 68–69, 70–71
  and coronavirus, 83
  and gun safety, 79, 80
  and LGBTQ rights, 46, 76
  and mail-in ballots, 206
  and marijuana regulation, 48, 49

California (*cont.*)
  and opposition to Trump's environmental
    policies, 71–72, 73
  and opposition to Trump's immigration
    policies, 62–63, 65
California Air Resources Board, 68, 72
Capitol attack, 90, 207, 208–209
Caplan, Lincoln, 191–192
Carter v. Carter Coal Company (1936), 40–41
Carter, Jimmy, 115, 125, 168, 236
Centers for Disease Control and Prevention
    (CDC), 79
Central Intelligence Agency (CIA), 115, 116–117,
    118, 122, 130
Chao, Elaine, 157
Charlottesville (Virginia), 186–188, 207,
    223, 224
checks and balances. *See* veto points
Chemerinsky, Erwin, 40, 86–87
Church, Frank, 123
Citizens United v. Federal Elections Commission
    (2010), 190–191
Civil Rights Act of 1866, 35, 36
Civil Rights Act of 1875, 37
Civil Rights Act of 1957, 43
Civil Rights Act of 1964, 43–44, 48, 233
Civil Rights Cases (1883), 37
Clean Air Act, 68–70, 74–75
Clean Water Act, 68, 75–76
Cleveland, Grover, 109
Clinton, Bill, 6, 9, 10, 74, 129, 131
  and the Defense of Marriage Act, 46
  and emergency declarations by, 168
  and independent counsel investigation
    of, 124
  and presidential power, 126–127, 154, 173
  and signing statements, 134
Clinton, Hillary, 148, 202, 215
CNN, 72–73, 193, 194, 195–196, 197, 198
Cohen, Michael, 150, 162, 202, 212
Cole, David, 188
Colorado, 2, 49
Comey, James, 149, 201
Commerce Clause. *See* interstate commerce
Communications Decency Act of 1996, 214
Confederacy, 35, 37, 222
Congress
  and appropriation power, 120–122,
    165–166, 169
  and conditions on federal spending, 60–61, 165
  and constitutional powers of, 19–20, 88, 103,
    106, 108, 110–111, 113
  and cooperative federalism, 68

and presidential power, 124–125, 133–134,
    135, 143–144, 152–153, 156
  See also interstate commerce; nondelegation
    doctrine; U.S. Senate
Connecticut, 21, 28, 46, 83
conservatives
  and activist government, 6–7, 94
  and federalism, 4, 15, 18, 52, 67, 74, 77,
    85, 88, 95
  and free speech, 189, 194, 217
  and gerrymandering, 1–2
  and presidential power, 4, 125–126, 127, 178,
    180–181
  and racism, 226
  and religion, 227
  and Trump, 9–10, 155–156
Constitutional Convention, 104–105, 108
Controlled Substances Act of 1970, 48–49, 51
Convention against Torture Treaty, 133
Coolidge, Calvin, 112
coronavirus, 86
  and the firings of inspectors general, 156,
    157, 158
  and immigration restrictions, 144, 202,
    215, 220
  and impact on communities of color, 207
  Trump administration's response to, 53, 78,
    80–84, 99, 197–198, 199, 200, 208, 233
Corwin, Edward, 107
Cotton, Norris, 43
COVID-19. *See* coronavirus
Cox, Archibald, 124
Cummings, Elijah, 204
Cuomo, Andrew, 80, 83
Customs and Border Protection, 89, 210

Declaration of Independence, 18, 21, 22, 102
Defense of Marriage Act of 1996, 46, 47
Defense Production Act, 81
Deferred Action for Childhood Arrivals
    (DACA), 6, 67, 100, 136–142, 144–
    145, 218
Deferred Action for Parents of Americans and
    Lawful Permanent Residents (DAPA),
    140–141
Delaware, 79
Delbanco, Andrew, 28
delegation doctrine. *See* nondelegation doctrine
Democratic Party, 1–2, 37, 39, 160, 215
Democrats, 41, 46, 77, 166, 236
Department of Commerce, 110
Department of Defense, 115, 118, 132, 157
Department of Education, 110

Department of Health, Education, and
   Welfare, 110
Department of Health and Human Services, 77,
   110, 157, 200
Department of Homeland Security
   and acting Secretary, 158
   and asylum policies, 142
   and DACA, 64, 141
   and Secure Communities, 57
   and Trusted Traveler Program, 64
Department of Justice
   and its abuses of power, 72–73, 88, 148,
      159–161, 162, 164, 198–199
   and expansion of presidential power, 132,
      133, 277n110
   and immigration enforcement, 55
   and marijuana enforcement, 49–50
   and the Mueller investigation, 148–150
   reforms of, 174–176
   and voting rights, 44
Department of Labor, 77, 110
Department of State, 115, 130, 196
Department of Transportation, 157
Department of the Treasury, 202
Detainee Treatment Act of 2005, 133
detainer orders, 57–58, 60, 62, 63
Dickey Amendment, 79
dignity-in-dying laws, 51
District of Columbia, 51, 64, 65, 70, 77, 210, 219
Douglass, Frederick, 36
DREAM Act, 137, 141
Dreamers. See Deferred Action for Childhood
   Arrivals (DACA)
Dred Scott v. Sandford (1857), 29
Due Process Clause, 39, 94
Duke, David, 224
Duterte, Rodrigo, 11
Dworkin, Andrea, 189

Ehrlichman, John, 118
Eisenhower, Dwight, 43, 112, 114, 115, 117, 128
Electoral College, 11, 21, 90, 105, 126
emergency declarations, 166, 168–169,
   173–174, 177
   by Trump, 81, 122, 166–167, 168–170
   See also International Emergency Economic
      Powers Act of 1977; National Emergencies
      Act of 1976
Emmanuel, Rahm, 126
Emoluments Clauses, 165
Employee Retirement Income Security Act, 77
Endangered Species Act, 74, 75
Energy Policy and Conservation Act, 69

environmental policies, 67–76
Environmental Protection Agency (EPA), 68,
   69–70, 71–76, 110, 121, 145, 170
Equal Protection Clause, 38, 113
Erdoğan, Recep Tayyip, 11, 162
Ervin, Sam, 121
Establishment Clause, 65, 152
Ethics in Government Act of 1978, 123–124,
   130, 173, 236
executive orders
   by Bush (George W.), 128, 129
   by Clinton, 129
   and the courts, 129
   by Obama, 129
   pressure on Obama to issue, 138, 145
   by Reagan, 126, 128–129
   by Roosevelt, 113, 114
   by Trump, 59–60, 65, 74, 129, 170, 197, 206,
      213–214
executive privilege, 115, 128

Facebook, 206, 214, 220, 231
Fair Labor Standards Act of 1938, 42
Fauci, Anthony, 82
Federal Bureau of Investigation (FBI)
   and hate crimes, 223–224
   and investigation guidelines, 175
   and Nixon, 116–117, 118
   and Robert Kennedy, 117
   and Trump, 149, 159
Federal Communications Commission, 110,
   128, 197, 198, 203, 215
federalism
   and anti-authoritarianism, 7, 88, 89–90
   and the Bill of Rights, 94–95
   conservatives use of, 67, 74, 77, 85, 88, 95
   cooperative, 68, 71, 82, 92–93
   and coronavirus, 80–84
   on "defense," 54–77, 90
   and definition of, 17
   and deregulation, 6, 93–94
   and dignity-in-dying laws, 51
   and economic regulations, 39–41
   and environmental policies, 67–77
   and immigration policies, 54–67
   and LGBTQ equality, 46–48
   and marijuana legalization, 48–50
   and minimum wage laws, 39, 42, 51
   and neutrality, 6, 17, 21, 33, 77, 91–92,
      234–235
   and the Obama administration, 67, 77, 85
   on "offense," 45–52, 90
   and progressives, 2, 5, 6, 34, 85–95

federalism (*cont.*)
  and racism, 35–39, 42–43, 44, 53
  and reasons for, 16–17
  and separation of powers, 89
  and slavery, 20–31
  and state crime prosecutions, 162
  and the Supreme Court, 51, 67–68, 87, 88
  See also anti-commandeering doctrine; Tenth
    Amendment
Federal Trade Commission, 110, 175, 177
Federal Vacancies Act, 158
Fields, James, 188
Fifteenth Amendment, 35, 38
Fine, Glenn, 157–158
Finkelman, Paul, 24, 26, 29, 31
First Amendment. *See* Establishment Clause;
    freedom of the press; freedom of speech
Florida, 79, 83
Floyd, George, 200, 206, 207, 219
Flynn, Michael, 149, 150, 151, 159–160, 162
Foner, Eric, 35
Food and Drug Administration, 110
Ford, Gerald, 115, 122, 125, 131
Foreign Intelligence Surveillance Act of 1978,
    123, 132, 133, 143, 173
Foreign Intelligence Surveillance Court, 123
Fourteenth Amendment, 35, 36, 37–38, 94
Fourth Amendment, 117, 132
Fox News, 194, 195, 198, 221
Freedmen's Bureau, 35
freedom of the press
  attacks of by Trump, 193–199, 212, 213, 215,
    220, 221, 230
  importance of, 185, 220–222
  See also freedom of speech; hate speech
freedom of speech
  attacks of by Trump, 192–193, 199–211,
    212–217, 230
  and government speech, 211–212
  and libel law, 196, 213, 215, 225
  and progressive skepticism of, 10, 185,
    186–192, 217–218, 230
  and protection of during Trump era, 185,
    211–217
  and retaliation, 212, 214–216
  and separation of powers, 214
  and use against Trump, 217–222
  See also freedom of the press; hate speech
fugitive enslaved people, 45, 50, 58, 61
Fugitive Slave Act of 1793, 25–27, 28, 31, 33
Fugitive Slave Act of 1850, 29–30
Fugitive Slave Clause, 23, 26

Galarza v. Szalczyk (2014), 57–58
Geneva Conventions, 132–133, 134
George III, 104, 106, 107
Gerken, Heather, 47, 92
gerrymandering, 1–3, 8, 9
Gianforte, Greg, 193
Giuliani, Rudy, 154–155, 162
Glover, Joshua, 30
Gluck, Matt, 162
Goldsmith, Jack, 162, 177
Google, 202, 206, 214, 220, 231
Gorsuch, Neil, 178, 233
Government Accountability Office, 155
Graham, Lindsay, 137
Grant, Ulysses, 39
Great Society, 94, 171
Green, Bruce, 175
gun control. *See* gun safety
gun rights, 32, 52, 79. *See also* National Rifle
    Association; Second Amendment
gun safety, 31–33, 61, 78–80, 92, 234

Halderman, H.R., 118
Hamilton, Alexander, 19, 107–108
Hammer v. Dagenhart (1918), 40
Harris, Dre, 188
hate crimes, 223–224
hate speech
  in Charlottesville, 187–188
  civil libertarian opposition to its regulation,
    186–189, 224–225
  on college campuses, 189–190
  definition of, 223
  egalitarian progressive critique of, 186–190,
    223, 225
  and future regulation of, 222–229
  and problems with regulation of, 226–230
  in Skokie, 187
Hawaii, 46, 49, 65, 79
Hayes, Rurtherford, 37, 39
Healy, Gene, 125–126, 181
Hennessey, Susan, 205–206, 235
Henry, Patrick, 106
Heyer, Heather, 186, 188
Hogan, Larry, 83
Holder, Eric, 2
Holmes, Oliver Wendell, 205
Hoover, J. Edgar, 117

Illinois, 83
Immigration and Customs Enforcement (ICE),
    58, 60, 66, 89, 210. *See also* detainer orders

Immigration and Naturalization Act, 55, 63, 136, 143
immigration policies, 54–67, 77, 94, 142–145, 165–166, 203, 218. *See also* border wall; Deferred Action for Childhood Arrivals (DACA); Muslim Travel Ban
Immigration Reform and Control Act of 1986, 140
impeachment, 109, 116
 Trump's first, 153–156, 163, 172, 196, 199
 Trump's second, 90, 209, 235
Impoundment Control Act of 1974, 121–122, 155, 177
impoundments, 99, 119–122, 155
independent counsels, 123–124, 128, 130. *See also* Mueller, Robert; special counsels
INS v. Chada (1983), 168
Inslee, Jay, 83
inspectors general, 88, 124, 156–158, 176–177, 200
Inspector General Act of 1978, 124, 173, 176, 236
Insurrection Act of 1807, 209
International Emergency Economic Powers Act of 1977, 276n100
interstate commerce, 19, 20, 40–41, 87, 106
Interstate Commerce Commission, 110
Iowa, 46
Iran-Contra, 130–131

Jackson, Andrew, 105, 109
Jackson, Robert, 174, 176
Jacobs, Ben, 193
James, LeBron, 204
Jefferson, Thomas, 105, 109
Jim Crow era, 17, 35, 38–39
Johnson, Andrew, 36, 109
Johnson, Lyndon, 112, 121, 125, 130, 133, 167, 171

Kagan, Elena, 127
Karem, Brian, 196
Katyal, Neal, 111
Kavanaugh, Brett, 205, 233
Keating-Owen Act of 1916, 40
Kelly, Megyn, 205
Kennedy, John F., 112, 116
Kennedy, Robert, 117
Kettl, Donald, 93
Kissinger, Henry, 115
Klarman, Michael, 102
Kleindienst, Richard, 118
Knauer, Nancy, 17, 82

Knight First Amendment Institute, 201
Korean War, 81, 129, 132, 167
Korematsu v. United States (1944), 113–114, 174
Kovaleski, Serge, 205
Krotoszynski, Ronald, 188
Ku Klux Klan, 36, 188, 224
Ku Klux Klan Act of 1871, 36
Kushner, Jared, 164

Latimer, George, 28
Lemon, Don, 204–205
Levinson, Sanford, 5–6, 153
LGBTQ rights
 and the Civil Rights Act of 1964, 48, 233–234
 and the First Amendment, 10, 185, 191, 217, 227, 230, 231
 and marriage equality, 16, 46–47, 50, 52, 88
 and state anti-discrimination laws, 47–48
 and transgender military ban, 76
Lincoln, Abraham, 34, 109, 128
Line Item Veto Act of 1996, 124–125
Linick, Steven, 157
local governments, 55–57, 62, 242n2, 248n113
Locke, John, 108
Louisiana, 37, 38, 42, 233, 234
Louisiana Purchase, 109

MacKinnon, Catharine, 189–190
Madison, James
 and the Articles of Confederation, 19
 and federal government powers, 20, 229
 and legislative power, 102, 120
 as owner of enslaved people, 105
 and presidential power, 107–108
Maduro, Nicolás, 11
Maine, 24, 28, 47, 49, 82, 164
Manafort, Paul, 150–151, 161, 162
Manhattan District Attorney's Office, 151, 233. *See also Trump v. Vance*
Manigault Newman, Omarosa, 205
marijuana legalization, 16, 48–50, 52, 88, 92
Marijuana Tax Act of 1937, 48
Marine Mammal Protection Act, 75–76
marriage equality. *See* LGBTQ rights
Maryland, 24–25
 and coronavirus, 83, 84
 and environmental laws, 75
 and gerrymandering, 1
 and gun safety laws, 79
 and marriage equality, 47
Mason, George, 104

Massachusetts, 102
    and coronavirus, 83, 84
    and environmental laws, 75
    and health-care reforms, 52
    and immigration laws, 65, 66
    and marriage equality, 46
    and slavery, 21–22, 28
Massachusetts v. EPA (2007), 69–70, 74
McCabe, Andrew, 201
McCain, John, 137
McConnell, Mitch, 157
McGhan, Donald, 149–150
McKinley, William, 112
McRaven, William, 201
Medicaid, 59, 64, 68, 176, 179
    and Obamacare, 51–52, 76, 85
medical assistance in dying. *See* dignity-in-
    dying laws
Medicare, 59, 60, 140, 141, 179
Meese, Edwin, 125
Michigan, 2, 5–6, 208
Military Commissions Act, 134
Miller, Lisa, 6
minimum wage laws, 39, 42, 51
Minnesota, 47, 65
Mississippi, 22, 36, 37, 44, 49
Mitchell, John, 118
Modi, Narendra, 11
Monroe, James, 105
Morgan, Margaret, 24–25, 27–28
Morris, Gouverneur, 104, 105
Morrison v. Olson (1988), 124, 175
Moskowitz, P.E., 201
Mueller, Robert, 149–150, 154, 159, 160, 161,
    162, 175
Murphy, Philip, 2–3
Muslim Travel Ban
    Supreme Court assessment of, 65, 152, 213
    Trump promotion of, 54, 58, 101, 114, 142, 213

National Emergencies Act of 1976, 122,
    167–168, 169, 173. *See also* International
    Emergency Economic Powers Act of 1977
National Environmental Policy Act, 75
National Football League (NFL), 203, 212, 216
National Highway Traffic Safety
    Administration, 69, 70
National Labor Relations Board, 110
National Rifle Association, 78, 79
National Security Agency, 132
National Security Council, 114–115, 130,
    156, 199
NBC, 194, 198, 203

Neuborne, Burt, 180
Nevada, 76
New Deal, 41, 67, 94, 171
New Hampshire, 28, 46
New Jersey, 1–3, 9, 22, 24, 76, 79, 80
New Mexico, 76
Newsom, Gavin, 72
Newsweek, 117
New York City, 55, 59
New York State
    and coronavirus, 83, 84
    and environmental laws, 75, 76
    and immigration laws, 63–64, 65, 66
    and marriage equality, 46
    and Personal Liberty Laws, 24, 28
    and slavery 22
New York Times, 117, 194, 195, 197, 213
New York Times v. Sullivan (1964), 213, 217
Nixon, Richard, 99, 128, 131, 141, 154, 161, 173,
    180, 199, 236
    and domestic surveillance, 116–117, 123
    and executive privilege, 115
    and impoundments, 99, 119–122, 155
    and the Vietnam War, 112, 116, 133, 167
    and war on drugs, 55, 130
    and Watergate, 118–119, 124, 149, 157, 172
    and White House staff, 115
nondelegation doctrine, 110–111, 178–180
North Carolina, 1, 208
North, Oliver, 130
NPR, 196

Obama, Barack, 2, 4, 6, 9, 129, 223
    and acting officials, 158
    and declared emergencies by, 168
    and Deferred Action for Childhood Arrivals
        (DACA), 100, 136–142
    and environmental regulations, 70–71, 72,
        73–74, 145
    and federalism, 67, 74, 77, 85
    and gun safety, 78
    and immigration enforcement, 56–57
    and marijuana enforcement, 49–50
    and military surplus supplies, 208
    and presidential power, 137–142, 145–146
    and Trump pressure to investigate, 148, 202
    and use of military force, 131
    See also Obamacare
Obamacare, 51–52, 67, 76, 77, 85, 170
Ocasio-Cortez, Alexandria, 204
Office of Economic Opportunity, 121
Office on Government Ethics, 123–124
Office of Legal Counsel, 133, 150, 277n110

Office of Management and Budget, 115, 126
Office of Policy Development, 115
Office of the Special Counsel, 200
Ohio, 30, 49
Omar, Ilhan, 204
Orban, Viktor, 11
Oregon, 49, 89, 210, 217, 219, 233

pardon power, 106, 131, 150, 161–162, 163, 177
PEN America, 194
Pence, Mike, 209
Pennsylvania, 21, 23–28
Personal Liberty Laws, 23–30
Pfiffner, James, 206
Poindexter, John, 130
political question doctrine, 170
Polk, James, 105, 111
Pompeo, Mike, 157, 196, 200
Portland, Oregon, 89, 210–211, 217, 219, 233
Posner, Eric, 235
preemption, 20, 26–27, 63, 87, 92, 256n117
presidency. *See* presidential power
presidential power
    accumulation of, 90, 107–135
    and administration lawyers, 132, 133, 150,
        277n110
    and administrative agencies, 110–111, 126–128,
        170, 178–179
    and Congress, 124–125, 133–134, 135, 143–144,
        152–153, 156
    in the Constitution, 104–107
    and criminal prosecution, 128, 150, 265n110
    effectiveness of, 115–116, 181–182
    and the executive's prerogative, 108
    and executive privilege, 115, 128
    and impoundments, 99, 119–122
    and inspectors general, 176–177
    and line item vetoes, 125
    and military force, 111–112
    and national security, 131–134
    and pardons, 106, 131, 150, 161–162,
        163, 177
    and progressives, 171–182, 234–237
    and prosecutorial independence, 174–176,
        278n118
    reforms of, 100–101, 121–124, 171–182,
        235–237
    and removal power, 109–110, 128, 175, 176–177
    and rhetoric about, 129–130, 138
    and signing statements, 134–135
    and the Supreme Court, 109–110, 113, 115,
        121, 125, 129, 133, 151–153
    and the unitary theory, 125, 128, 175

    and the veto power, 109, 111, 121, 124–125,
        134–135, 168
    and White House staffing, 114–115
    See also emergency declarations; executive
        orders; impeachment; separation of powers
Pressly, Ayanna, 204
Price, John, 30
Prigg, Edward, 24–25, 27–28
Prigg v. Pennsylvania (1842), 25–31, 32–33, 58, 61
principled constitutionalism, 4–5, 7–9, 91, 141,
    146, 234
Printz v. United States (1997), 31–33, 57–58, 61
Privileges or Immunities Clause, 37–38
progressives
    civil libertarians vs. egalitarians, 186–190
    definition of, 11
    and federalism, 7, 15–18, 32–34, 44–52,
        53–95, 234
    and First Amendment skepticism, 10, 185,
        186–192, 217–218, 230
    and free speech, 185, 217–232
    and gerrymandering, 1–3
    and individual rights, 7
    and presidential power, 7–8, 100–101, 127,
        135–146, 147, 171–182, 234–237
    See also principled constitutionalism;
        situational constitutionalism
Protecting Our Democracy Act, 177
Pruitt, Scott, 71
Putin, Vladimir, 11

racism
    and coronavirus, 207
    and federalism, 34, 37, 39, 44, 52, 53
    and the New Deal, 41–42
    and opposition to Reconstruction, 35–38
    and police brutality, 203, 207, 209, 215, 219
    and school desegregation, 42–43
    stoked by GOP, 9
    systemic, 17, 207, 209, 219, 220, 222, 224, 228, 236
    and by Trump, 54, 202, 203–205, 207, 219, 225
    and unconscious biases, 228
    and voting rights, 38
    See also Black Lives Matter; hate crimes; hate
        speech; Jim Crow era
Randolph, Edmond, 104
Reagan, Ronald, 133, 140
    and Iran-Contra, 130
    and military force, 131
    and presidential power, 125–126, 128–129,
        173, 180
    and signing statements, 134
    and war on drugs, 55, 130

Reconstruction, 35–37, 109
Reconstruction Act of 1867, 36
Reid, Harry, 137
removal power, 109–110, 128, 175, 176–177
Republican Party, 1–2, 9–10
Republicans, 181, 219, 236
Rhode Island, 21, 79
Rice, Susan, 201
Richardson, Elliott, 118, 124
Riker, William, 44
Roberts, John, 151, 152–153
Rogers, William, 115
Roiphe, Rebecca, 175
Romney, Mitt, 156
Roosevelt, Franklin D., 120, 125, 135
    and declared emergencies by, 114, 167
    and the Great Depression, 40
    and the internment of Japanese Americans,
        113–114, 122, 128, 174
    and proposing legislation, 114
    and re-election, 106, 173
    and the Supreme Court, 41, 173
    and White House staff, 114
    and wiretapping, 117
    See also New Deal
Roosevelt, Theodore, 112
Rosenstein, Rod, 149
Ruckelhaus, William, 124
Rudalevige, Andrew, 110, 135, 181
Rudenstine, David, 113
Russian investigation, 88, 148–149, 150, 154,
    159–160, 161, 162, 167, 213. See also
    Mueller, Robert

same-sex marriage. See LGBTQ rights
sanctuary. See immigration policies
Sanders, Sarah Huckabee, 195
San Francisco, 55, 59, 60
Santa Clara county, 60
Sasse, Ben, 162
Savage, Charlie, 125, 135
Scalia, Antonin, 32, 74, 175
Scarborough, Joe, 198–199, 215
Schauer, Frederick, 229–230
Schlesinger, Arthur, 116, 118–119, 120, 182
Schumer, Charles, 80, 137
Second Amendment, 78, 79. See also gun rights
Securities and Exchange Commission, 110, 128
Seidman, Louis, 231–232
Seila Law LLC v. Consumer Financial Protection
    Bureau (2020), 177
senate. See U.S. Senate
separation of powers, 3–7, 9, 101, 143, 157, 234

and the border wall, 165–167, 169
and congressional appropriations, 119–122,
    165, 169
and DACA, 137–142
and federalism, 89
and free speech, 214
history of, 101–103
and impoundments, 119–122
and progressives, 2, 5, 6, 171–182
and sanctuary jurisdictions, 60–61, 66,
    73, 165
    See also nondelegation doctrine; presidential
    power; veto points
September 11, 2001, 6, 55, 94, 100, 131,
    171, 205
Sessions, Jeff, 59, 141, 148, 149–150, 208, 270n4
Shane, Peter, 126, 127, 130
Shaw, Lemuel, 28
Shelby County, Alabama v. Holder (2013), 38, 45
signing statements, 134–135
Sinclair Broadcast Group, 194, 195
situational constitutionalism, 4–5, 7–8, 54, 91,
    141, 146, 229
Slaughterhouse Cases (1872), 37
slavery, 16, 20–31, 33–35
Snowden, Edward, 132
Social Security Act of 1935, 41
Sondland, Gordon, 155, 156, 199
South Carolina, 34, 36, 37, 75, 83
Southern Manifesto, 43
special counsels, 110, 149–150, 159, 175, 200.
    See also Mueller, Robert
Spencer, Robert, 224
Stanton, Edwin, 109
Starr, Kenneth, 124
Steinle, Kathryn, 59
Stevens, Ted, 125
Stone, Roger, 150, 160–162
Story, Joseph, 26–28, 31
Strengthening the Tenth Amendment by
    Entrusting States Act, 50
Sullivan, Emmett, 159
Sumner, Charles, 35, 37
Sundquist, James, 120
Supremacy Clause, 19–20, 25–26, 62–63, 87, 92,
    151. See also preemption
Supreme Court
    and the 2019–2020 term, 233–234
    and the Affordable Care Act, 51, 85
    and the border wall, 276n104, 277n105
    and DACA, 142
    and dignity-in-dying laws, 51
    and double jeopardy, 162

and economic regulations, 39–41
and environmental policy, 69–70, 74
and executive privilege, 115
and federalism, 15, 16–17, 37, 38, 45, 51,
    67–68, 69, 87, 88
and free speech, 190, 191, 211–212, 213–214,
    216–217, 219, 223, 224–225, 232
and gerrymandering, 1
and gun safety, 31–32, 58
and immigration, 64–65, 141
and impoundments, 121
and independent counsels, 124
and Jim Crow, 38
and legislative vetoes, 168
and LGBTQ rights, 47, 48, 50, 233–234
and the Line Item Veto Act, 125
and military tribunals, 133–134
and the Muslim Travel Ban, 65, 152, 213
and the nondelegation doctrine, 110–111,
    177–178
and presidential power, 109–110, 113, 115,
    121, 125, 129, 133, 151–153
and the removal power, 124, 128, 175,
    176–177
and school desegregation, 42–43
and slavery, 25–29, 30, 31

Taft, William, 112
Take Care Clause, 106, 120, 176
Taylor, Bill, 155
Taylor, Breonna, 206–207
Taylor, Zachary, 105
Tennessee, 36
Tenth Amendment
    and Congress, 88
    and individual rights, 94
    and preemption, 63
    scope of, 15, 32, 40, 53, 60
    violations of, 32, 37, 64
Tenure in Office Act, 109
Texas, 62, 67, 83, 234
Thirteenth Amendment, 35
Time Warner, 72, 198
Tlaib, Rashida, 204
transgender rights. See LGBTQ rights
Truman, Harry, 112, 125, 128, 129, 167
Trump, Donald
    and acting appointments by, 158
    and anti-commandeering doctrine, 88, 234
    attacks on free speech by, 192–193, 199–211,
        212–217, 233
    attacks on the press by, 193–199, 212, 213,
        215, 220, 221, 230

and the border wall, 65, 81, 165–167, 168
and challenge to 2020 election, 89–90, 233
and coronavirus, 80–84, 144, 197–198,
    199, 200
and emergency declarations by, 81, 122,
    166–167, 168–170
and environmental policies of, 70–76
and executive orders of, 59–60, 65, 74, 129,
    170, 197, 206, 213–214
and financial self-dealing by, 164–165
and firing of inspectors general by, 88, 156–158,
    176, 200
and gun safety, 78–79
and healthcare, 76–77
and immigration policies of, 54, 56, 58–67,
    142–144, 165
impeachments of, 90, 153–156, 163, 172, 196,
    199, 209, 235
and instigation of violence by, 193–194,
    207–209
and investigations of opponents, 148, 159,
    170, 198, 202, 213, 216
and lies by, 58–59, 81, 90, 157, 198–199, 200,
    205–206, 208, 209, 220, 221
militarized response to protestors by, 89, 207,
    209–211, 217, 219, 233
and military force, 131
and Muslims, 54, 58, 65, 101, 114, 142,
    205, 213
and pardon power, 150, 161–162, 163
and presidential power, 59–60, 99, 151, 153,
    163, 214
and racism of, 54, 202, 203–205, 207,
    219, 225
and Russian investigation, 148–150, 162
and separating children from parents, 54, 66,
    204, 218, 288n138
and Ukraine affair, 99, 153–156, 163–164,
    172, 221
and using presidency to help allies by, 149,
    150, 159–162, 170
Trump v. Hawaii (2018), 65, 152, 213
Trump, Ivanka, 164
Trump v. Mazars USA (2020), 151–153, 233
Trump v. Vance (2020), 151
Trusted Traveler Program, 63–64
Twenty-Second Amendment, 106, 173
Twitter, 201, 206–207, 212, 213–214, 216, 222
Tyler, John, 105

Ukraine affair, 99, 153–156, 163–164, 172, 221
unitary theory of the presidency, 125, 128, 175
United States v. Nixon (1974), 115, 151

U.S. Senate
  and its confirmation power, 103, 105, 106,
    114, 124, 158
  and equal state representation in, 11, 20
  and filibusters, 44, 137, 145
Utah, 2, 48, 76

Vance, Cyrus, 151. *See also* Manhattan District
    Attorney's Office
Van Cleve, George, 19
Velshi, Ali, 194
Vermont, 22, 28, 76, 79
veto points, 5–7, 93, 103, 171
veto power, 109, 111, 121, 124–125, 134–135, 168
Vietnam War, 100, 112, 116, 131, 167, 171
Vindman, Alexander, 156, 199–200
Voting Rights Act of 1965, 38, 44–45

Wagner Act of 1935, 41
Waldron, Jeremy, 225
War Crimes Act of 1996, 133
war on drugs, 49, 50, 55, 130
War Powers Resolution, 100, 131, 171
Warren, Elizabeth, 50
Washington, D.C. *See* District of Columbia
Washington, George, 105, 106, 107, 108
Washington Post, 158, 194, 195, 197, 213
Washington State
  and coronavirus, 83, 84
  and gun safety, 79, 80
  and marijuana regulation, 49
  and marriage equality, 47

and opposition to Trump's immigration
    policies, 65, 66
Wasserman, Schultz, 202
Watergate, 115, 116, 118–119, 149, 172, 175
  congressional responses to, 121–124, 125,
    157, 167, 180, 236
Waters, Maxine, 205
Weinberger, Caspar, 120, 131
welfare work requirements, 52
Wexler, Jay, 171
Wheeler, Andrew, 73
Whistleblower Protection Act, 156, 200
whistleblowers, 132, 155, 156, 177, 200
WikiLeaks, 160
Wilson, James, 104
Wilson, Woodrow, 112
Wisconsin, 1, 30, 48
Wittes, Benjamin, 205–206, 235
Wolff, Michael, 196
Woodward, C. Vann, 38
World War I, 114
World War II, 4, 58, 122, 128, 132
Wu, Tim, 214

Xi, Jinping, 163

Youngstown Sheet & Tube Co. v. Sawyer (1952),
    129, 176
Yovanovitch, Marie, 155, 196, 199

Zelensky, Volodymyr, 154–155
Zick, Tim, 199, 214, 221